THE FOUNDATION CENTER'S

GUIDE TO

Winning Proposals

II

Judith B. Margolin, Editor
Gail T. Lubin, Assistant Editor

Acknowledgments

Along with the many grantmakers who submitted proposals and the nonprofits who permitted us to use them, I would like to thank the following individuals who made significant contributions to this guide. Stephen Seward, former librarian at the Foundation Center turned fundraiser, added immeasurably to its content by providing in the Foreword his own frank and unique perspective on the role the proposal plays in the process of seeking funding from foundations. Gail Lubin, Public Services Assistant, the Foundation Center, contributed in innumerable ways from the initial call for funded proposals to the final proofreading of the manuscript. Kief Schladweiler, Online Librarian, the Foundation Center, and David Holmes, Reference Librarian, the Foundation Center-Cleveland, demonstrated great patience, perspicacity and objectivity in helping select which proposals to include in the guide and provided creative input into the chapter introductions. Thanks also to Christine Innamorato for her skill in designing the book.

—Judith Margolin

Library of Congress Cataloging-in-Publication Data

The Foundation Center's guide to winning proposals II / Judith B. Margolin, editor ; Gail T. Lubin, assistant editor.

      p. cm.

  Includes bibliographical references and index.

  ISBN 1-59542-054-1 (pbk. : alk. paper)

 1. Endowments—United States. 2. Research grants—United States. 3. Proposal writing for grants—United States—Case studies. I. Title: Guide to winning proposals II. II. Margolin, Judith B. III. Lubin, Gail T. IV. Foundation Center.

  HV41.9.U5F673 2005

  658.15'224—dc22

                         2005025471

ISBN 1-59542-054-1

Table of Contents

Foreword

When the Foundation Center asked me to share my perspective on the importance of the proposal in the grantseeking process, I thought back to my earliest days as a fundraiser. I remember my own first forays into this process, and I remember asking myself back then—how critical is this piece of the process? So, it is a familiar issue that the Foundation Center asked me to write about. Since that time I've written many a proposal. Like all fundraisers I've had my share of successes and disappointments. Now, many years later, I can say with assurance that proposals *definitely do matter*, but not more than what you do before you send a proposal to a foundation and not more than what you do after you submit your request. To support this statement, I offer some perspective below and, more importantly, refer you to the comments from grantmakers contained in this volume.

Over the years I've encountered many first-time grantseekers who are extremely dedicated to their organizations' missions, but are starting out without a lot of knowledge about the process. Even more daunting, the groups and projects they represent are often unfamiliar to funders, and many have no track record of prior support. For these novice grantseekers, a guide like this one will be a tremendous help. But it's important to remember that their ultimate success—and I've seen a lot of that as well—is usually the result of a combination of creativity, persistence, and hard work.

In opening up a book entitled "Guide to Winning Proposals," you have probably asked yourself variations of at least three questions. The first is: "What are the crucial steps in raising money for my organization?" The second is: "How are funding decisions actually made by institutional grantmakers?" And the third is a very specific question: "How important is the proposal anyway?"

The first two questions have wide-ranging implications for fundraisers everywhere, and clear answers aren't easy to come by because the whole process is so subjective. Good grantmaking can't be done by a formula. What one foundation considers a stellar funding request could be judged by another to be vastly inadequate. But I am confident that if you read the proposals and the grantmakers' commentaries in *The Foundation Center's Guide to Winning Proposals II*—and especially if you read between the lines for insights into the funding process itself—some good answers to these questions will become apparent.

This guide offers 31 proposals in a wide range of styles and content, along with comments by grants decision makers about what specifically impressed them about the proposals they selected for inclusion in this collection. These proposals and the accompanying commentary offer unique insights into the criteria foundation staff members use to decide what to fund and what to reject. Through this collection, a number of valuable ideas emerge about the critical steps that will be important to you in the process of securing funding for your organization.

So what about the third question? How can we gauge the role of the proposal itself in the grantseeking process? I frequently hear two points of view on the importance of proposal writing, and I don't agree with either one. They both reflect pessimistic approaches to the task of writing grant proposals, although they come at the issue from opposite ends of the spectrum. The first is a kind of awed response upon reading proposals like the ones in this book: "How could I ever do that?" or "My program doesn't lend itself to that kind of presentation." The second attitude is more cynical: "Raising money is about whom you know, not what you put in your proposal or how you say it." What I would like to do right here is challenge both of these attitudes and, at the same time, offer some observations on how to use the proposals you will find in this book.

The novice grantseekers I mentioned earlier and many of the individuals whose successful proposals are included in this volume no doubt quickly discovered a critical fact: foundations have to be nurtured. Successfully engaging funders in a relationship that ultimately convinces them to support one's program takes persistence and hard work. The grantor/grantee relationship, when it works well, is one of mutual courtesy and fair play. And it can be accomplished, whether you start out with a track record or not. I mention the importance of developing a relationship here not to discourage you but because I believe that readers of this guide will learn that you, too, can raise money if you are willing to put in the time and effort and have the necessary creativity and determination to succeed. That's important because confidence is crucial in fundraising. After all, you can't very well convince others to invest in your work if your own doubts are all too noticeable.

The proposals in this volume cover many different situations and describe many varied programs. You may be tempted to find the ones that most closely fit your own situation. However, I suggest you go beyond the obvious connections you see—and seek to find something for you and your organization in each and every one, rather than just focusing on the "best" one for your needs. Look for a proposal with a great opening line, for example. Find another that offers a dramatic hook in the second or third paragraph, since a compelling analysis on pages four and five won't help if the reader doesn't get past page two. Seek out a budget that isn't just a group of line items, but that reflects clear thinking, solid planning and actually helps "sell" the program. And also find some wording that injects appropriate drama into the statement of need. Then try to do the same in your own proposal, because even if your program isn't inherently dramatic, your writing must reflect your own passion about moving it forward.

My point is that this guide is best used for the breadth of its examples of successful grantsmanship. When I was starting out in fundraising there was a book that was a lot like the one you are holding now. It was called *The Proposal Writer's Swipe File*. A catchy title I thought then, and I still do. But it was a very misleading title, too, since you weren't likely to find specific ideas that you could use in your own work. Nor could you actually "swipe" any of the proposals; and that isn't likely here, either. We have made progress, though, because with that earlier book you were completely on your own to take away whatever you could. Fortunately, in this volume, the commentary by grants decision makers gives you solid guidance on what they feel works for them, how their decisions are made and why they selected these proposals. I suggest that you recognize the proposals in this book as "winners" selected by various grantmakers. The accompanying comments are useful not just as introductions to the proposals themselves, but because they offer insights into the funders' preferences and the decision-making process that they adhere to.

In my experience as a fundraiser, I have seen many instances where the quality of the proposal was enormously important in securing funding. Today I am even more convinced than ever that a bad proposal can dim (or doom!) your chances. That doesn't mean you have to be E.B. White or Walt Whitman. It surely helps to be a gifted writer, but you can and should get whatever assistance you may need on that front. Please do admire the writing contained here. But don't do that at the expense of the thoughtful content and the thoroughness of the preparation that went into these program descriptions.

In my mind, a "good" proposal is only partly about the writing. It's even more about the program planning that goes into the write-up. So another temptation to avoid in using this book is to grab a good idea and set out to write your proposal. Ultimately, your results will improve dramatically if you take the time to think through your project in advance of sitting down to write your proposal. Try reading the proposals in this volume with that idea in mind. What you will find is a consistent demonstration of the critical role of thorough planning and thoughtful analysis *before* the writers of each of these proposals sat down to start typing.

I consider good project planning far more essential than good writing, and so do funders. Sure, a skillful writer can make a proposal "sing," and that can help. But you and your organization also must have very clear answers to crucial questions like "What's our reason for thinking we are the best ones to offer this program?" "How do we plan to begin our project—by phasing it in or by starting it all at once?" "How much, exactly, will this cost?" and "What do we plan to do if we only raise half of the money we need?" These questions are pretty obvious, and no doubt there's a lot more where they come from. But you need answers to all of them before you tackle the proposal itself. Otherwise, you aren't going to effectively address the issues that funders will want to know you have already considered and hopefully resolved.

A useful analytical tool many proposal writers employ is creating a list of the assets and liabilities that apply to their organization and its new project. It's not easy to play devil's advocate about your own work, but I suggest you take this step and try to be as objective as possible about your organization's strengths and weaknesses. That way, as you work on your proposal you can be sure to highlight the pluses and address perceived weaknesses before the grants decision maker does.

I recognize that this extra step may seem like a luxury to organizations desperately in need of funding. But I guarantee that the grantmakers you approach will tell you that your ultimate success depends on taking adequate time not only to plan, but also to critique your own planned outcomes and to anticipate their concerns. So before you "write it up" or revise your well-worn proposal to turn it into a winner, make sure the plan itself is clear and that you are ready for the scrutiny an effective proposal is designed to invite.

One final issue raises an important question of strategy for proposal writers. Should you customize a proposal to fit a foundation's interests? To me, the answer is obvious. Of course you should. Your job is to "sell" your program. You certainly should identify points of overlapping interest with each potential funder and point them out. If you are a skillful writer, don't hesitate to revise the proposal to emphasize aspects of your work that you think "fit" a specific foundation's guidelines. You can even change the title of your project if you think that will help you connect with a grantmaker's priorities.

But don't change what you plan to do because of some real or perceived idea of what a given funder wants. Remain confident instead that you know a lot more than the funder does about your own program and your field of work (and the chances are very good that you do!). Realize also that the foundations will catch on quickly if your overriding strategy is to change your plan to match their current interests as you understand them. That's a dangerous step to take. It's wrong, not only because it's likely to be transparent to the grantmakers you want to impress, but also because your proposal might actually be successful—and you'll end up with funding for a program that meets their priorities rather than your own and those of your clients.

This book is filled with solidly written, carefully constructed proposals and some fine examples of proposal budgets and cover letters as well. I hope that when you are done reading you will emerge thinking that there's nothing mysterious about what makes a good proposal. The idea here is not to leave you intimidated by others' proposals, but rather to provide "role models," since it is encouraging to see that these extremely varied proposals were all funded. And that should be cause for celebration and inspiration for us all.

Lurking behind many of the how-to questions I am asked about fundraising is an underlying one that can be bluntly stated: Is fundraising logical, or is it more like a lottery? There is indeed logic behind the grantmaking practices of many foundations. Certainly the comments made by grantmakers in this book support that view. That is not to say that the process itself is always logical. In fact, it often does not feel that way at all, and can seem downright irrational.

Grantmaking, at its best and its worst, is almost always subjective. An additional factor that makes grantseeking seem lottery-like is the sheer number of requests that pour into foundation offices across the country. So what can you do to improve your chances? More to the point, how do you even get a genuine hearing for your proposal? My comments earlier about the combination of creativity and persistence required to cultivate funders are instructive here. And clearly, the proposal is vitally important in order to "put your best foot forward." Whether you are about to start your first grant proposal or have been writing them for years, and whether you raise funds full-time or you only write proposals on an as-needed basis, I hope that you will find this book a useful resource for its "lead by example" approach, for the insights provided by the grantmakers' commentary, and for the inspiration that is implicit in reading about others' successful work.

Stephen Seward
New York State Director of
Philanthropy
The Nature Conservancy

Introduction

When we introduced the first volume of *The Foundation Center's Guide to Winning Proposals* in the fall of 2003, we were gratified but not surprised by the overwhelmingly positive response we received from members of our audience. For many years visitors to our Web site and libraries, attendees at our classes, participants in our Meet the Grantmaker events, and those posing questions to our online librarian via e-mail have asked us over and over again: "Where can I find sample proposals?" In issuing the second volume of *The Foundation Center's Guide to Winning Proposals* the Foundation Center is taking another step in building resources dedicated to assisting both novice and experienced grantseekers in their quest for funding.

As we stated in the introduction to Volume I of the guide, novice grantseekers often approach the assignment of crafting a grant proposal with trepidation, because most new fundraisers rarely have the chance to see an actual proposal that has been funded. This book provides many examples of various types of proposals for the novice. And not just beginners but all those who seek grants will appreciate the opportunity this guide affords to learn from the successful efforts of their colleagues.

While creating the "perfect" proposal may be an elusive goal, excellent requests for funding are crafted every day by seasoned development officers as well as by first-timers. The proposals included here were selected by grantmakers who also contributed commentary as to why these proposals succeeded. In some instances these decision makers also shared insights about how the proposals might have been further improved. *The Foundation Center's Guide to Winning Proposals II* does not supercede but rather serves as a companion to the first volume. Taken together the two volumes offer an impressive array of grant projects and an amazing breadth and depth of fundable ideas, along with a great variety of formats and fine examples of persuasive writing.

As with the inaugural volume, the grantmaking community responded graciously to our second call for funded proposals. We sought to collect a diverse selection of proposals ranging from seed money to requests for equipment, from relatively small grants for general operating support to multiyear special projects. We aimed to include proposals submitted to large national foundations as well as small, locally oriented ones and from as many sites around the country as possible. In this volume you will find 31 outstanding proposals, arranged under chapter headings by the type of project for which they seek funding. In addition we have included two letters of inquiry, five proposal budgets, and five cover letters in separate chapters.

Anyone reading this guide might ask: What does it take to write a successful proposal? The basic elements common to the proposals in this volume consist of thorough knowledge on the part of the proposal writer of her/his organization and its program, a concise writing style, appropriate attention to detail, empathy for the reader, and, perhaps most importantly, passion for the project to be funded. As is evident from the commentary supplied by the grants decision makers, the commitment and enthusiasm that are demonstrated in the proposals included here were significant factors in getting these projects funded.

Though grant proposals can take many forms, most have specific components presented in a fairly standardized way. The great variety of proposals in this volume demonstrates that different writers succeed by customizing their proposals once they've mastered the basic techniques. One way to think of the grant proposal is as a recipe: in order to achieve the desired result, all of the ingredients must be included. It may or may not make a difference in which sequence you add them to the mix. But if something is left out entirely, the final product won't come out quite right.

Along with a wonderful selection of proposals that serve as models and inspiration to those seeking to hone this particular skill, the hidden treasure among these pages resides in the quite candid commentary from the grantmakers who said "yes" to these requests. Anyone reading their comments cannot help but be impressed with the sincerity of these individuals and with their dedication to the practice of giving money away effectively. It is obvious, for example, that grantmakers like the ones whose commentary is included here are paying careful attention to the projected impact and outcomes of the projects they fund.

An apparent trend worth noting is the fact that a number of grantmakers who submitted proposals for this second volume accept common application forms designed by their regional associations. And quite a few of the grantmakers whose proposals are included in this volume have their own preferred form or application format, often available at their Web sites. Filling in a form judiciously where space may be tight is just one skill that proposal writers need to develop.

While in the first nine chapters of the guide the reader will find full proposals, including the cover letter and budget, it was not practical to include every single attachment. Notes at the end of the grantmaker's commentary in each chapter provide a list of attachments that were submitted with each proposal. When asked to do so by the nonprofit organization or by the funder, we have removed or masked confidential or personal information in the body of the proposal or in the budget. That deletion will most often be indicated by XXX.

For those unfamiliar with terminology used in the field, we have supplied a glossary of basic terms related to proposal writing in Appendix A.

Today's proposal writer is fortunate to have many resources to call upon. A number of print and Web-based resources will be found in the selected resources on proposal development provided in Appendix B. All resources listed are available for perusal at Foundation Center libraries.

Along with the two volumes of this guide, serious grantseekers would do well to refer to *The Foundation Center's Guide to Proposal Writing*, 4th edition, by Jane C. Geever, which lays out the basic elements foundations expect to find in a standard proposal as well as some very helpful do's and don'ts supplied by grantmakers surveyed by Ms. Geever. Those seeking additional instruction might also consider registering for the short free classes on the basics of proposal writing and proposal budgeting offered at any of the Foundation Center's five library/learning centers or the more intensive full-day Proposal Writing Seminar, Proposal Writing Seminar II: Tailoring Your Proposals to Maximize Success, and/or Proposal Budgeting Workshop given by the Foundation Center in various locations around the country. To learn more about dates and times and about additional educational offerings, refer to the Foundation Center's Web site at http://fdncenter.org.

Finally, new to this volume is a brief index, enabling those who want to examine just those proposals in particular subject fields, of benefit to certain population groups, or in a particular location, to do so.

The Foundation Center is deeply indebted to the grantmakers who submitted proposals for inclusion in this guide and who so generously gave of their time in supplying opinions and advice. We are also most grateful to the nonprofit organizations for their willingness to share these proposals in order to help their colleagues learn from their success.

Judith B. Margolin
Vice President for Public Services
The Foundation Center
September 2005

List of Contributors

The following grantmakers participated in the preparation of this book by generously contributing proposals that they admired. Some submitted multiple proposals for our consideration. In addition, they graciously took the time to provide thoughtful and perceptive commentary on the proposals. We are very grateful for their collaboration on this project.

Grantmakers

Joseph Dolan, Secretary and Executive Director
The Achelis and Bodman Foundations
New York, New York

Karen Topakian, Executive Director
Agape Foundation
San Francisco, California

Kate Liebman, Program Officer
Altman Foundation
New York, New York

Don A. Sultzbach, Executive Director
Austin-Bailey Health and Wellness Foundation
Canton, Ohio

Mary Quinn, Senior Manager of Operations
Avon Foundation
New York, New York

Melissa Warlow, Program Officer
Baltimore Community Foundation
Baltimore, Maryland

Mary Gregory, Program Officer
Bella Vista Foundation
San Francisco, California

Matthew Klein, Executive Director
Blue Ridge Foundation New York
Brooklyn, New York

Dianne Yamashiro-Omi, Program Officer
The California Endowment
Woodland Hills, California

Valerie Raines, Vice President of Administration and Philanthropic Services
Catholic Diocese of Cleveland Foundation
Cleveland, Ohio

Marci Lu, (former) Program Officer
The Cleveland Foundation
Cleveland, Ohio

Maggie Cretella, Community Research and Grants Management Officer
Emily Hunter Savors, Director of Community Research and Grants Management
The Columbus Foundation and Affiliated Organizations
Columbus, Ohio

Lita Ugarte, Program Officer
The Community Foundation for Greater
   Atlanta, Inc.
Atlanta, Georgia

Victoria Kovar, Grants Administrator
Cooper Foundation
Lincoln, Nebraska

Lara Galinsky, Vice President, Strategy
Echoing Green
New York, New York

Margaret Siegel, Program Director
Lois and Richard England Family Foundation
Washington, DC

Sara Salley, (former) Program Officer
Georgia Humanities Council
Atlanta, Georgia

Helen Alessi, Senior Program Officer
Edwin Gould Foundation for Children
New York, New York

Frances Phillips, Arts Program Officer
Walter and Elise Haas Fund
San Francisco, California

Ilene Mack, Senior Program Officer
The Hearst Foundation, Inc.
New York, New York

Barbara Valocore, President
The Lifebridge Foundation, Inc.
New York, New York

Cindy M. Patrick, Senior Program Officer
The Meadows Foundation
Dallas, Texas

Rayna Aylward, Executive Director
Mitsubishi Electric America Foundation
Arlington, Virginia

Cynthia Freeman, Program Officer
New York Foundation
New York, New York

Michele Pritchard, Grants Administrator
The Peyton Anderson Foundation
Macon, Georgia

Nancy Wiltsek, Executive Director
Pottruck Family Foundation
San Francisco, California

LaTida Smith, Program Officer
Saint Luke's Foundation of Cleveland
Cleveland, Ohio

Fred Plotkin, Secretary and Treasurer
Adolph & Ruth Schnurmacher Foundation, Inc.
New York, New York

David Ford, Executive Director
Richard and Susan Smith Family Foundation
Chestnut Hill, Massachusetts

We wish to thank the following nonprofit organizations whose representatives graciously allowed us to share their successful proposals:

Nonprofit Organizations

Clare Auwarter, Project Manager
Athens-Clarke County Library
Athens, Georgia

Deborah Goetz, Senior Director of
   Marketing and Communications
Baltimore Opera Company
Baltimore, Maryland

James L. Clark, President and
   Chief Executive Officer
Boys & Girls Clubs of Greater Milwaukee
Milwaukee, Wisconsin

Hans E. Hageman, Esq., Executive Director
David L. Hertz, Ed.D., Director of
   Institutional Advancement
Boys & Girls Harbor, Inc.
New York, New York

Elizabeth Hosler Voudouris, Acting
   President and Chief Executive Officer
Business Volunteers Unlimited
Cleveland, Ohio

Janet Knipe, Executive Director
California Youth Connection
San Francisco, California

Forrest Gok, Director of Resource
    Development
Chinatown Community Development Center
San Francisco, California

Maria Isabel Boss, President and Chief
    Executive Officer
Cleveland Scholarship Programs, Inc.
Cleveland, Ohio

Helen M. Dumski, Vice President, Programs
    and Services
Diabetes Association of Greater Cleveland
Cleveland, Ohio

Dorothy Truax, Executive Director
El Paso Area Foster Parent Association
El Paso, Texas

Amy Lemley, Executive Director
The First Place Fund for Youth
Oakland, California

Joshua Solomon, Interim Director
The Food Project, Inc.
Lincoln, Massachusetts

Tiffany L. Mullison, Executive Director
Fresh Start, Inc.
Lincoln, Nebraska

Jonathon Miller Weisberger, Director
Grupo Osanimi (Osa Foundation)
El Cerrito, California

Maureen Holla, Executive Director
Higher Achievement Program
Washington, DC

Diana Campoamor, President
Hispanics in Philanthropy
San Francisco, California

David A. Simpson, Chief Executive Officer
Hospice of the Western Reserve
Cleveland, Ohio

Ronald J. Scroggy, Chief Executive Officer
    and President
Inner Harbour for Children & Families
Douglasville, Georgia

Suzanne C. Helmick, Executive Director
Kids Voting Central Ohio
Columbus, Ohio

Mattie H. Eley, President
Angela Goggins, Director of Operations
Literacy Action, Inc.
Atlanta, Georgia

Robert M. Hayes, President
Joan Brown, Director of Development
Medicare Rights Center
New York, New York

Steve L. Rumford, A.C.S.W., President and
    Chief Executive Officer
The Methodist Home for Children and Youth
Macon, Georgia

Dr. Daniel A. Kane, Ph.D., President and
    Chief Executive Officer
Nassau Health Care Corporation/Nassau
    University Medical Center
East Meadow, New York

Adam Friedman, Executive Director
New York Industrial Retention Network
New York, New York

Paul Mertz, Executive Director
Holly Gauthier, Vice President of
    Development (and Director, Beth Health
    Care Foundation)
Newark Beth Israel Medical Center
Newark, New Jersey

Karen Berke, Program Director
North Street Community Resource Center
Pescadero, California

Beth Shapiro, Executive Director
Outdoor Explorations
Medford, Massachusetts

Gloria Gilbert Stoga, President and Founder
Puppies Behind Bars
New York, New York

Mark Toney, Executive Director
Reentry Solutions
Oakland, California

Bernard Neal, Chairman and President
Katie Anderson, Museum Director
Rome Area History Museum
Rome, Georgia

Michelle Raymond, Organizer and
    Counselor
San Diego Military Counseling Project
    (SDMCP)
San Diego, California

MarieLou Catalano, Director of
    Institutional Advancement
Elizabeth Seton Pediatric Center
New York, New York

Juhu Thukral, Director
The Sex Workers Project at the Urban
    Justice Center
New York, New York

Jack Huck, President
Southeast Community College
Lincoln, Nebraska

R. Flip Hagood, Senior Vice President
The Student Conservation Association
Arlington, Virginia

Eden Werring, Executive Director
Summer Search New York City
Brooklyn, New York

Linda J. Fanning, Executive Director
Tuscarawas County Health Department
Dover, Ohio

Sam Davis, Director
United Genders of the Universe!
San Francisco, California

Matt McCann, Director of Development
Year Up
Boston, Massachusetts

Rachel Alterman Wallack, Executive
    Director
Youth Communication: Metro Atlanta
Atlanta, Georgia

David Dower, Artistic Director and Founder
The Z Space Studio
San Francisco, California

Chapter 1

Special Project: Single Year

The ten proposals in this chapter are requests for funding for special projects. These grants support discrete projects within the organization. Special project support can cover a wide variety of grant projects from program enhancements, to short-term studies and educational initiatives. These projects can be for new programs or for aspects of ongoing programs that the organization needs funding to initiate, to continue, or to improve. The requests can come from organizations new to the funders or from those they have supported in the past. The proposals in this chapter all cover a one-year period.

Grantmakers may prefer to provide special project support for any number of reasons. Often the strategies presented are new (at least to the organization planning to implement them or to the audience that will benefit) and the ideas tend to be innovative. And since the projects typically are time delimited, with fixed start and end dates, it is relatively easy for the funder to disengage at a particular date in the future, a factor that many foundations find attractive.

The ten proposals in this chapter request special project funds ranging from $6,200 to $75,000 for a single year of funding. Each is for a discrete project that continues or builds upon existing program activities within the organization. In each case the proposal writer adopts effective methods to clearly delineate the parameters of the project, distinguishing it from the ongoing operations of the organization.

First is a proposal to the Cleveland Foundation from Business Volunteers Unlimited of Cleveland, Ohio, requesting $75,000 for its Services to Nonprofits program that supplies board development and management assistance services to nonprofit organizations. A repeat grantee of the Cleveland Foundation, this proposal from Business Volunteers Unlimited includes letters of support, case studies, user data, financial information on membership revenues, and a summary of studies conducted on the needs of nonprofit organizations, in response to the funder's request for materials to help back up the case for special project support.

Next is a proposal from Cleveland Scholarship Programs, also of Cleveland, Ohio, requesting a grant of $10,000 from the Catholic Community Fund of the Catholic Diocese of Cleveland Foundation for a project that provides information and counseling on postsecondary education for high school students. Funds are required to continue to provide advisory services in 13 parochial schools throughout greater Cleveland.

The Diabetes Association of Greater Cleveland in Ohio submitted the third proposal in this chapter to the Saint Luke's Foundation of Cleveland, requesting $22,500 to develop the *Guide for Successful Management of Diabetes* for distribution throughout the Cleveland Municipal School District. This special project will also create tracking forms for students with diabetes and provide in-service education for school personnel and parents about diabetes identification and treatment. Particular care is given in this proposal to demonstrating how this new project fits precisely with the missions of both the diabetes association and the foundation.

The next proposal was submitted to the Meadows Foundation of Dallas, Texas, by the El Paso Area Foster Parent Association, requesting one year of funding in the amount of $39,000 for its On My Own Program that provides housing, employment, and other services to youth who have "aged out" of the foster care system. Employing the Meadows Foundation's optional grant application form, the proposal writer makes excellent use of the space provided to explain the need for the project and the goals and objectives it seeks to accomplish in the 12-month period, while at the same time detailing rather complicated interactions with various agencies as the association seeks more permanent funding from government sources to ensure the project's future.

The next proposal presented here is for program development. It is a $20,000 request submitted by the First Place Fund for Youth of Oakland, California, to the Pottruck Family Foundation of San Francisco, California, for expansion of the First Place Fund for Youth's Supported Housing Program. This program helps youth who are transitioning out of foster care find safe and affordable housing. First Place Fund for Youth plans to use the special project grant funds to meet its goal of doubling its housing capacity. Though somewhat lengthy, this proposal gives a comprehensive description of the services provided by the program, as well as a clear vision of the plans for the future.

Next is a $42,500 request to the New York Foundation from the New York Industrial Retention Network (on behalf of the Zoning for Jobs Coalition). The request is for funds to support the Zoning for Jobs Coalition's ongoing project aimed at increasing public awareness of neighborhood zoning and land use strategies that minimize blue-collar job loss and promote job creation. Charts and maps are used to good effect in this proposal.

The North Street Community Resource Center proposal included here requests $42,724 from the Bella Vista Foundation of Pacific Foundation Services for the Parent Involvement Project (PIP). The Center itself is a project of the South Coast Collaborative of Pescadero, California, a small rural community outside of San Francisco. The PIP program provides parental support and education for families with children up to age six. Funds requested from the Bella Vista Foundation of San Francisco, California, will support one year's service to 25 families. The proposal writer does a fine job of tracing the growth of the PIP program and demonstrating how Bella Vista special project funds will enable the organization to support the level of service initially achieved through AmeriCorps funding.

Next is a request for $6,200 submitted by the Rome Area History Museum of Rome, Georgia, to the Georgia Humanities Council. The museum proposes to work with Rome City Schools to create a new exhibit and oral history project about life in Floyd County, Georgia, during World War II. The "Audience Development" section of this proposal succinctly demonstrates the commitment of museum staff to utilize special project funding to extend the reach of this cultural institution beyond its normal audience.

The next proposal is one that the Sex Workers Project at the Urban Justice Center of New York City submitted to the New York Foundation in the amount of $45,000. This program advocates for sex workers, former sex workers, and those at risk of engaging in such work. The unique needs of this audience and the unusual difficulties that arise in serving them are well delineated here. A significant amount of text in this proposal is devoted to past accomplishments, before proceeding to the new request, which is for a third year of special project funding.

The final proposal in this chapter is a $10,000 request to the Cooper Foundation of Lincoln, Nebraska, submitted by Southeast Community College also in Lincoln, Nebraska. The request is for a single year of funding for a Newcomers Educational Center, designed to help adult English language learners by providing a bridge from English as a second language classes to college-level vocational programs through faculty training, new classes, and enhanced student advising. The proposal writer uses the Lincoln/Lancaster County Grantmakers Common Application form, providing concise, detailed, and readable responses to the questions on the form. Tables inserted within the narrative, particularly in the evaluation section, make complex special project plans easy to understand.

A Proposal From

Business Volunteers Unlimited

Cleveland, Ohio

To

The Cleveland Foundation

Cleveland, Ohio

Requested amount: $75,000; **Amount received:** $75,000

Funder's comments:

"While we do not use a set application form at the Cleveland Foundation, we do require applicants to fill out a two-page cover sheet and budget form with each proposal submission. And we require applicants to include a project summary of no more than 150 words on our cover sheet to help expedite proposal assignment. Just by way of background, this proposal was submitted after a meeting with the Acting Chief Executive Officer and Project Director of Business Volunteers Unlimited (BVU). Additionally, the Cleveland Foundation had helped to establish BVU and has continued to provide support on an annual basis.

"The various components one would expect to find were all present and well balanced in this proposal. The project description section was detailed and well structured. For the most part the budget was presented clearly with the level of detail we need. The writing was also clear and well organized. For example, in the project description section, BVU included information on the program objectives, action steps and evaluation approach for each service that would be supported by the Cleveland Foundation grant.

"The organizational background section of this proposal was especially informative, particularly the part detailing BVU's various sources of revenue. We do require financial information with each submission, but it is always helpful when the applicant breaks down the percentage of each revenue stream for us. This gives us a quick overview of the diversification of the organization's funding base and how our potential support fits into that picture. As part of our decision-making process, we did have additional discussions with BVU about the status of other anticipated sources of project support.

"This was a very clear, well developed proposal with many specific attached documents that helped support the case for funding. For example, in the Appendix, BVU provided a description of studies it has conducted over the years to inform the development of specific services to nonprofit organizations. This was helpful. However, last year the Cleveland Foundation suggested the need for a more recent study and is working with BVU on a more current assessment of the impact of the organization's nonprofit services. Additionally, more information on the need for low-cost nonprofit capacity building services and BVU's role among the mix of existing service providers and consultants would further strengthen the proposal.

"One missing component was the organization's plans to sustain its nonprofit services on an ongoing basis. In this case, we know the organization's financial model relies upon continuing philanthropic support to subsidize its nonprofit services. Nevertheless, a discussion of future fundraising efforts and plans is a necessary part of the due diligence phase.

"BVU was very thorough about attachments. In fact, the organization provided extensive service data from the previous year, letters of support, staff biographies, etc. This year BVU also included three narratives illustrating the impact of its board development and management assistance services. These qualitative 'case studies' brought BVU's services to life and illustrated its impact on nonprofit organizations on many levels."

—Marci Lu, (former) Program Officer, The Cleveland Foundation

Notes:

The complete proposal included the following attachments: organizational budget, nonprofit services summary, nonprofit needs assessment, impact summary, activities summary, letters of support, population served summary, calendar of events, list of board members, biographies of key staff, IRS tax-exempt letter, equal opportunity policy, and audited financial statement.

The project description section referenced above by the funder has been deleted to ensure confidentiality.

Proposal written by Elizabeth Hosler Voudouris, Acting President and Chief Executive Officer. Contributions to the proposal made by Ann Kent, Director, Services to Nonprofits, and Alice Korngold.

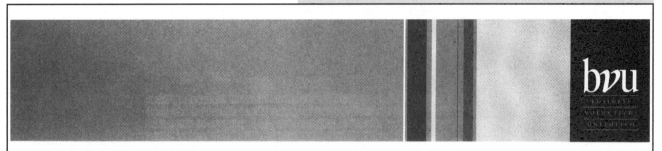

February 15, 2005

HELPING BUSINESSES HELP COMMUNITIES

Ms. Marci Bernstein Lu
Program Officer
The Cleveland Foundation
1422 Euclid Avenue, Suite 1300
Cleveland, OH 44115

Dear Marci:

Business Volunteers Unlimited appreciates the significant support from The Cleveland Foundation since its inception in 1993. Over the past twelve years, BVU has worked to develop and offer innovative services to further strengthen the governance and management of nonprofit organizations in Northeast Ohio. Funding from The Cleveland Foundation is vital to support BVU's services to nonprofits in our community.

Attached please find BVU's proposal to The Cleveland Foundation for $75,000 in 2005 to continue serving nonprofits seeking board development and management assistance services. The demand for services from nonprofits continues to be very strong, increasing each year. To meet this demand, there are four services that BVU provides to nonprofits that require full or partial funding support, including nonprofit needs assessments, customized board training and education services, board consulting services and management assistance services.

Marci, we greatly appreciate your time and guidance to strengthen BVU's proposal to The Cleveland Foundation. Per your suggestions, please note that we have included two support letters from local chief executives of nonprofits; three "stories" illustrating the impact at nonprofits that have utilized many of BVU's services over the past five years; data demonstrating nonprofit "repeat business"; financial information regarding our successful efforts to strengthen business membership revenues in 2004; and a summary of the studies that BVU has conducted in past years to assess the needs of nonprofit organizations.

Thank you again for your on-going support and consideration. The BVU board and staff are looking forward to another highly productive year in 2005.

Very Truly Yours,

Elizabeth Hosler Voudouris
Acting President & CEO

cc: Robert E. Eckardt

BUSINESS VOLUNTEERS UNLIMITED
Proposal to The Cleveland Foundation
February 2005

I.   PROPOSAL OVERVIEW

BVU seeks $75,000 from The Cleveland Foundation in 2005 to continue serving nonprofits seeking board development and management assistance services. The demand for services from nonprofits continues to be very strong, increasing each year. To meet this demand, there are four services that BVU provides to nonprofits that necessitate full or partial funding support. These include including nonprofit Needs Assessments, customized board training and education services, board consulting services and management assistance services. Funds will also be used to subsidize board consulting services for nonprofits with limited resources. Of the 680 nonprofits served by BVU in 2004, 59% had annual operating budgets under $1 million, so subsidized services are important to them.

II.   ORGANIZATIONAL BACKGROUND

Mission and origins:
BVU serves businesses and nonprofits by promoting effective volunteerism and strengthening leadership.

Business leaders, in collaboration with the Cleveland and Gund foundations and United Way Services, established BVU in 1993. BVU is governed by a board of directors that includes corporate and community leaders.

National recognition. BVU is recognized by a number of prominent national institutions as a model to other communities in the nation. BVU Maryland was established in Baltimore two years ago. BVU has been featured at national conferences of the Independent Sector, BoardSource, The Conference Board, the Public Affairs Council, the Council on Foundations, the Points of Light Foundation, and the U.S. Chamber of Commerce.

Sources of revenue:
BVU is funded by businesses (38%), United Way Services (12%), fees for services (15%), foundations (33%), and BVU board member contributions (2%). Revenues from businesses cover BVU's services to businesses; revenues from foundations, United Way Services, board member contributions, and fees for service cover BVU's services to nonprofits.

- **Business memberships** – Over 120 businesses pay annual fees to BVU in return for BVU's assistance in involving employees in productive and meaningful leadership and volunteer opportunities. Revenues from business memberships declined in recent years due to corporate mergers, corporate attrition in the region, and a slow economy. In response, BVU's board and staff reviewed the business membership plan and increased the fees at targeted membership levels to better align the plan with services provided. In addition, BVU staff (with board support) conducted proactive and targeted marketing to middle market companies to identify new business members. As a result, there were 30 new business members in 2004, for a total of $88,000 in new member revenues. Furthermore, several BVU board members increased their companies' membership levels. The bottom line was an increase of $53,520 (16% increase) in business revenues in 2004 compared to 2003 (2004 total was $390,020; 2003 total was $336,500).
- **United Way Services** provided $127,424 in 2004 to fund the community's volunteer clearinghouse (or "Volunteer Center").

1

Cleveland Foundation Proposal
February 15, 2005

- **Foundations** provided $339,134 in 2004 for BVU to conduct nonprofit Needs Assessments – as requested by the nonprofits themselves -- and to respond to requests from nonprofits that seek BVU's management assistance and board development services – including training and education and consulting.
- **Fees for service** from nonprofit organizations generated $150,898 in 2004. However, <u>BVU is committed to making all its services for nonprofits accessible to *all* nonprofits regardless of their ability to pay. This is only possible with support from foundations that understand the importance of capacity-building services.</u>

III.   BVU'S ROLE IN STRENGTHENING NONPROFIT ORGANIZATIONS:

The challenge. Strategic and financial challenges are driving nonprofit organizations to build organizational capacity by strengthening governance and management and being innovative in garnering financial resources to meet growing community needs. The success of a nonprofit depends on the CEO and the board developing a competitive and forward vision, leading the organization through change, and ensuring sufficient staffing and resources.

BVU as a vital service to strengthen nonprofits by improving their capacity. BVU provides a set of complementary services that are highly effective in helping nonprofits to strengthen governance and management. Nonprofits use a variety of BVU services that are customized to meet each organization's particular needs and circumstances. BVU services for nonprofits include the following:

- Training and placing business executives and professionals on nonprofit boards of directors, based on the needs of nonprofits for particular skills and expertise and the qualifications and interests of each candidate. BVU has trained and placed 1,003 executives on 277 boards; many of these candidates have risen to board leadership positions. BVU's focus on increasing board diversity is demonstrated with 41% of elections being women and 15% being racial minorities.
- Providing customized board consulting and training services to 40-60 nonprofits annually
- Providing management assistance on a variety of topics to over 350 nonprofits annually
- Conducting 20 workshops annually on board governance and management topics for over 1,000 board members and nonprofit executives from over 300 nonprofits. Topics include financial management, strategic alliances, the role of the board, effective board leadership, fund raising, developing and implementing a communications plan, and other highly relevant and timely issues.
- Engaging business professionals as volunteer consultants to assist nonprofits in areas of finance, law, human resources development, strategic planning, facility planning, information technology, marketing and communications, and other key issues.
- Involving thousands of volunteers from businesses and the community-at-large in volunteer opportunities at over 350 nonprofits. This includes school groups, youth organizations, and religious institutions.

Assessing nonprofit needs through research and analysis
BVU has conducted several studies since 1993 in order to develop services specific to the needs of nonprofit organizations. (See page 12 in the Appendix for descriptions of the studies that BVU conducted.)

2

Cleveland Foundation Proposal
February 15, 2005

IV.   PROJECT DESCRIPTION

(This section has been omitted)

V.   METHODS OF EVALUATION:

1. **On - going** - BVU creates a report for each and every nonprofit for which BVU provides services. The report tracks all services provided by BVU and the outcomes; these reports are provided to the nonprofit clients at the end of the year. The reports for all nonprofits are then summarized in statistics that are provided to the BVU Board and all funders. *(See summary statistics for 2004 on page 16 in the Appendix)*

2. **Community Feedback** - BVU's Committee on Nonprofit Services (a committee of the BVU Board) reviews BVU's progress in meeting the needs of nonprofits, and meets with nonprofit clients for their feedback regarding services and their input for future planning. BVU also receives frequent letters of support from community leaders. *(See two examples attached on pages 17 - 18 in the Appendix.)*

3. **Repeat business** – Hundreds of nonprofit organizations utilize BVU's services repeatedly (including seminars, board member referrals, board consulting, customize board trainings, management assistance and coaching.) For example:
   - Since 1999, 1,072 different nonprofit organizations have used BVU's services (not including the Volunteer Center). Of these 1,072 organizations, 773 have used at least a second BVU service.
   - Since 1997, 21 nonprofits have engaged BVU to conduct at least *two* board development consultations; and 12 have engaged BVU for *three* or more board development consultations.

4. **Evaluation of services to nonprofits** - BVU is currently working with John A. Yankey, Ph.D., to conduct an evaluation of services to nonprofits, funded by The Cleveland Foundation. This evaluation will include qualitative feedback from 10-15 Executive Directors. In addition, BVU staff is compiling and analyzing twelve years of seminar evaluation forms (collected after each seminar) to evaluate attendee satisfaction.

3

Cleveland Foundation Proposal
February 15, 2005

VI.   STAFF

Bios of the BVU staff members who are involved in conducting nonprofit Needs Assessments, board development consultations/training sessions, and management assistance and volunteer consultant referral services are attached (see pages 24 – 27 in the Appendix). Included are:
- Ann C. Kent, Director, Services to Nonprofits
- Elizabeth H. Voudouris, Acting President & CEO
- Kerianne Hearns, Director, Leadership Development
- Nicole Clayborne, Director, Board Referral Services

VII.   PROJECT BUDGET

Board development and management assistance services to nonprofits will comprise 51% of BVU's budget in 2005 ($561,508). A significant portion of this expense – 27% ($154,000) – will be covered by fees for services paid for by nonprofits (especially nonprofits with the means to pay). **BVU seeks 73% ($407,508) from foundations, businesses and other philanthropic sources (including board member contributions) to subsidize the costs of providing board development and management assistance services to nonprofits.**

The Cleveland Foundation Project Budget Request Form is on pages 8-9.

VIII.   ORGANIZATIONAL BUDGET

BVU's budget for 2005 is on page 10 of the Appendix. Included in the back of the Appendix is the 2003 Audit Report.

IX.   SUPPORTING DOCUMENTS – ATTACHED

The Appendix includes the following:
- BVU 2005 Budget – **Page 10**
- Grid showing BVU's services to nonprofits – **Page 11**
- BVU studies assessing nonprofit needs – **Page 12**
- Three narratives illustrating the impact of BVU's board development and management assistance services – **Pages 13 – 15**
- Summary of BVU activities in 2004 – **Page 16**
- Two support letters from nonprofit chief executives – **Pages 17 - 18**
- Budget size of organizations served by BVU; and focus areas of nonprofits served by BVU – **Pages 19 - 20**
- Calendar of forums fall 2004 and spring 2005 – **Pages 21 - 22**
- List of BVU Board members – **Page 23**
- Bios of key staff – Elizabeth Hosler Voudouris, Ann Kent, Kerianne Hearns, and Nicole Clayborne – **Pages 24 - 27**
- IRS letter – **Pages 28 - 30**
- BVU's equal opportunity policy – **Page 31**
- Nonprofits served by BVU in 2004 – **Pages 32 - 35**
- 2003 Audit Report - **attached**

4

THE CLEVELAND FOUNDATION
PROJECT BUDGET
(Must be accompanied by the Project Narrative)

Name of the organization: **Business Volunteers Unlimited**
Fiscal year end date: **12/31/2005**
Project title: **Services to Nonprofits**
Total amount requested from The Cleveland Foundation: $75,000
Project start and end date: **01/01/05 - 12/31/05**

PROJECT INCOME

	Anticipated	Committed	Total	Internal Use Only
Contributed Income				
Local Government			$0	
State Government			$0	
Federal Government			$0	
The Cleveland Foundation *(itemize below)*	$75,000		$75,000	
Other Foundations*	$210,000	$55,000	$265,000	
Corporations*	$42,508		$42,508	
Board/Individual Contributions	$25,000		$25,000	
Other*			$0	
Earned Income				
Client Fees	$71,000		$71,000	
Membership Dues (nonprofit)	$83,000		$83,000	
Contract Services*			$0	
Publications and Products			$0	
Ticket Sales			$0	
Organization Income			$0	
Other*			$0	
Total Project Income	**$506,508**	**$55,000**	**$561,508**	

PROJECT EXPENSES

	Cleveland Foundation Request	Other Funding	Total	Internal Use Only
Personnel Expenses	$75,000	$329,286	$404,286	
Salaries and Wages*			$0	
Fringe Benefits			$0	
Non-Personnel Expenses		$157,222	$157,222	
Contract Services/Professional Fees*			$0	
Office Space			$0	
Equipment/Supplies			$0	
Staff/Board Development			$0	
Travel/Related Expenses			$0	
Indirect Costs*			$0	
Other*			$0	
Total Project Expenses	**$75,000**	**$486,508**	**$561,508**	
Excess (Deficiency)*			$0	

* please list or explain in narrative

Contact person:
Phone number:
E-mail:

A Proposal From

Cleveland Scholarship Programs, Inc.
Cleveland, Ohio

To

Catholic Diocese of Cleveland Foundation
Cleveland, Ohio

———————————————————

Requested amount: $10,000; **Amount received:** $6,000

Funder's comments:
"This organization was invited to apply for funding. They were nominated based upon the criteria of the grant program.

"As to well-developed components, they provided well documented information on the benefits of their programs to those who are served by them. They also provided clear information on the services they offer and how funding would be used. And they gave us the option of 'buying their product' in portions we could afford.

"The various components of the proposal were well-balanced, and each section well-identified. It was well-written, easy to follow, easy to skim and to find relevant information, and very concise. Information that we did not request was provided in attachments rather than the body of the proposal, and that also was easy to read and concise. As to strongest features, the budget and layout are worth noting. This proposal is a good model of clear and concise answers to our questions, relevant information, and research-based need and benefits."

—Valerie Raines, Vice President of Administration and Philanthropic Services,
Catholic Diocese of Cleveland Foundation

Notes:
The proposal was written using the Catholic Community Fund grant application form. The complete proposal included the following attachments: college access barriers summary, Office of Catholic Education statistics, IRS tax-exempt letter, annual report, list of board members, audited financial statement, and letters of support.
Proposal written by Hope Latiak, Grants Writer.

Catholic Community Fund
Application Form

Cover Sheet
(Feel free to make copies of this form or generate this one-page cover sheet on your computer.)

Date of application: September 10, 2003

Name of organization to which grant would be paid. Please list exact legal name.
Cleveland Scholarship Programs, Inc.

Address of organization: BP Tower, Suite 3820
200 Public Square
Cleveland, OH 44114

Director/Principal/Pastor: Maria Isabel Boss, President and CEO

Contact person and title (if different): Hope Latiak, Grant Writer

Phone No: (216) 241-5587   **Fax:** (216) 241-6184   **E-mail:** mboss@cspohio.org

Purpose of the grant (one sentence): To increase the number of Cleveland-area parochial high school students pursuing and completing postsecondary education through counsel and financial aid, thus preparing the future workforce of our community.

Amount Requested: $10,000   **Total Project Budget:** $674,819 (includes advisory services in
47 Cleveland-area high schools

Total Operating Budget (for current year): $6,601,131

I. PROPOSAL SUMMARY

Cleveland Scholarship Programs, Inc. (CSP) requests $10,000 from the Catholic Community Fund to support 37 days (at $270 per day) of advisory services for deserving high school students attending 13 Cleveland-area parochial high schools. The mission of CSP is to provide educational opportunity and workforce development through a broad range of financial aid and advisory programs. Our philosophy shall be to encourage all individuals to meet their highest potential through education, thereby enhancing the quality of their lives and strengthening the regional economy.

The main objective of CSP's advisory services program is to break down the barriers that exist for students wishing to obtain postsecondary education. CSP advisors assist parochial school students in preparing and planning for, applying to and financing college. Such services are particularly helpful to low- to middle-income parochial school students who are the first generation in their families to attend college. Increasing access to postsecondary education for parochial high school students will improve their chances of obtaining a college degree. In the long term, those who reach this goal will raise their earning capability and become a part of Greater Cleveland's workforce, increasing the pool of college graduates needed to spur economic growth and development.

II. NARRATIVE

BACKGROUND
History and Mission
A local humanitarian established CSP in 1967 to lend a helping hand to Cleveland students. He recognized that hundreds of bright young people were not reaching their full potential because their families were financially unable to send them to college. CSP's mission remains essentially the same—*to provide educational opportunity and workforce development through counsel and financial aid.*

CSP is the largest and oldest college access program in the United States, and the CSP model has been replicated in many cities across the United States, including Miami, Baltimore and Boston. CSP was instrumental in forming the National College Access Network (NCAN), an organization that promotes college access across the country. CSP has also led the way in establishing the Ohio College Access Network (OCAN), which consists of 44 member organizations. Further, CSP is ranked the sixth most "consistently excellent" charity in the United States by Charity Navigator.

Population Served
This grant will provide 37 days (at $270 per day) of advisory services for the students of 13 parochial high schools including: Benedictine, Cleveland Central Catholic, Holy Name, Magnificat, Padua, Regina, Saint Augustine Academy, Saint Edward, Saint Ignatius, Saint Joseph Academy, Saint Peter Chanel, Trinity and Villa Angela/Saint Joseph. During 2002-2003, more than 3,000 parochial students and their families participated in 52 group meetings and advisors made over 1,500 contacts with individual students at these schools.

The Catholic Community Fund will support high school seniors with strong academic performance from low- to middle-income families. The parochial school students served by CSP in 2002-2003 have on average a SAT of 1120, an ACT score of 23 and a GPA of 3.34. In other words, this dedicated, bright student population is a solid investment.

When it comes to higher education, Ohio is one of the least affordable states in the country. Unfortunately this has a huge impact on low-income, and even middle-income, families. Many of the students that CSP helps are the first in their families to attend college and need extra assistance planning for, pursuing and financing a college degree.

The average family income of parochial high school students served by CSP during the 2002-2003 academic year was $34,681 and the average college cost for scholarship awardees was $22,927 or nearly 66 percent of family income. The unmet financial need is the amount that remains after students have subtracted grants, loans, work-study earnings and the expected family contribution from the total cost of attending college. On average, CSP parochial students borrowed $3,250 (2002-2003) in loans to help pay for college. Even after incurring this debt, the average amount of unmet need for CSP students during 2002-2003 was $4,272, up 28 percent from $3,329 the previous year. It is this gap that CSP's "last dollar" scholarships help to cover. During 2002-2003, the average scholarship amount given by CSP to parochial school students was $867.

Current Programs, Staff, Volunteers and Community Relationships

CSP is the only nonprofit organization providing college access services in Cuyahoga County. CSP's team of approximately 75 employees and over 100 volunteers served 31,000 individuals during academic year 2001-2002. College access services offered by CSP in the community included:

- **Advisory services:** early awareness services in ten Cleveland Municipal School District (CMSD) middle schools; high school advisory services extended to students attending 47 Greater Cleveland suburban inner-ring, parochial and CMSD high schools; adult learner advisory services
- **Financial aid:** $2.2M in scholarship awards to 2,117 high school and adult learner students and located $12 dollars in aid for every scholarship dollar awarded during academic year 2001-2002
- **Resource Center:** nationally recognized and emulated center provides *free* college access services to the northeastern Ohio community
- **Graduates Council:** CSP and the Greater Cleveland Growth Association's workforce development initiative, which connects business leaders with high-achieving college students

To ensure the success of its mission, CSP leverages its strong partnerships with Cleveland-area middle and high schools, colleges and universities. Further, advisors work with several community organizations to enhance the reach of CSP's services including: the City of Cleveland, the Cleveland Municipal School District, Cuyahoga Community College, Greater Cleveland Growth Association, National College Access Network, Ohio Board of Regents, Ohio College Access Network and Vocational Guidance Services.

STATEMENT OF NEED

Part of the Catholic Community Fund's vision is that "children will be able to... receive an education which will prepare them for a life of meaningful employment." The purpose of CSP's high school advisory services program is to enhance the number of Cleveland-area high school students pursuing and completing postsecondary education through counsel and financial aid, thus preparing the future workforce of our community.

The economic advantages of obtaining postsecondary education for students and their communities are clear. The average lifetime earnings of a worker with a high school education is about $1.2M, compared with $2.1M for a college graduate ("Census Report Says Education Pays, Even More So Now," *The Washington Post*, July 23, 2002). Yet many parents find the postsecondary education process and rising tuition costs so daunting that they discourage their children from attending college – despite the long-term advantages (The Condition of Education, 2001).

According to the Ohio Board of Regents, "a high school degree will never again provide a guarantee of a comfortable middle-class life for our citizens. The increased complexity of most occupations, the increasing reliance on technology in almost all businesses and jobs, and the rapid pace of change will require that more and more of our citizens obtain 2-year, 4-year, and even more advanced degrees." Strikingly, only 11 percent of Cuyahoga County residents, ages 25 and over, possess a bachelor's degree or higher.

Further, by all national statistics and comparisons available, Ohio has historically under-invested in higher education. Ohio ranks 40th among states in terms of public support per student for higher education and consequently has the 10th highest tuition in the nation. Collectively, these trends produce barriers to college access and success. For these very reasons, CSP was formed to break down the barriers between our citizens and postsecondary education attainment. See Attachment A for current statistics on the barriers to postsecondary education.

Yet, according to the Office of Catholic Education, 20 percent of students attending parochial schools served by CSP are "high need" students (or students whose family income is at or below the 50th percentile) and 13 percent of students are from families that are at or below poverty level (see Attachment B). Forty-five percent of students apply for some sort of financial aid to help cover the costs of pursuing a postsecondary education.

PROJECT DESCRIPTION
Goals and Objectives
The overarching goal of CSP's advisory services program is to increase the number of Cleveland-area high school students who complete postsecondary education. The goal of this project is to provide supplemental college access services to Cleveland-area parochial high school guidance departments. The objectives of the advisory services program are:

1. To provide information concerning academic preparation, career counseling, test tutoring and applying to and financing postsecondary education to parochial high school students and their families.

2. To identify qualifying seniors and recommend them for CSP "last dollar" scholarships.

Advisory Services Provided, Timeline, Staff and Number of Beneficiaries
Each parochial school requests CSP's advisory services for a specific number of days during the academic year based on its needs and space to accommodate a CSP advisor. Most parochial schools are able to cover the costs of a portion of the days needed by their students. However, students in these schools depend on additional funding from sources such as the Catholic Community Fund, to support the remaining advisory service days not covered. The advisor then works with guidance/counseling offices to schedule days of service typically from January through March when demand for service peaks.

The dedicated team of parochial school advisors include: Gary Croy, Rosemary Cunningham, Charles Dockery, Linda Frank, Barry Harbison, Edward Hoeningman, Christopher Mitchell, Linda Ross, Pamela Sandoval and John Skinner. These advisors will serve approximately 3,000 students during academic year 2003-2004. The following services are provided to parochial school seniors and their families:

Career counseling
Advisors work with students to assess their academic strengths as well as personal interests and discuss relevant career paths. Students then connect their overall career goals to degree attainment

and future courses of study. Finally, advisors educate students about long-term financial benefits of establishing a successful career.

Test tutoring

Tenth, eleventh and twelfth graders are encouraged to take the PSAT, SAT and ACT tests. Registration information is provided and advisors determine which students qualify for test fee waivers. Students receive information on how to prepare for the tests by using books and/or software, as well as exam requirements in terms of identification, transportation, etc.

College admissions

When high school students near graduation, CSP helps them to complete their financial aid forms, college admissions paperwork and test registrations. Students who qualify secure fee payments for SAT, ACT, Profile, TOEFL, college orientation, enrollment and housing and tuition deposits. They may also obtain waivers for college application fees, as well as apply for CSP administered grants.

Scholarships and Financial Aid

Even after all financial aid options are fully explored, many low- and middle-income students are still unable to afford college. Families work together with CSP's expertly trained advisors to fill out the Free Application for Federal Student Aid (FAFSA) and thus apply for all applicable financial assistance. When students receive award letters from colleges, advisors help interpret financial aid packages. If all financial needs are not met then advisors inform students and parents of the various options available to cover gaps, including CSP "last dollar" scholarships that are renewable for up to four years.

Students are also encouraged to visit CSP's free, public Resource Center where they can research national, regional and local scholarship listings through one of Ohio's largest scholarship databases. Advisors also connect low-income and special need students to funding sources of which they may be unaware.

College Transition

Once scholarship recipients are admitted to college, they are encouraged to remain in contact with advisors for advice and information relative to postsecondary issues through a toll free college access hotline. Scholarship recipients are also required to meet with an advisor annually during CSP's summer interviews.

Community Impact

Thousands of aspiring parochial high school students across Greater Cleveland face a variety of obstacles as they prepare to enroll in postsecondary education including sharply rising college costs, lack of information on how to prepare and apply for college admission and financial aid and growing reliance on loans – rather than grants – to cover their education expenses.

By breaking down preparation, affordability and retention barriers, CSP advisory services and scholarships provide access to postsecondary education for many Greater Cleveland parochial students who would not otherwise seek higher education. CSP's programs in turn help minority and economically disadvantaged parochial high school students increase their earning capabilities through education, enhancing our community's talent pool, economic development and future. Further, more than 70% of CSP students remain in the Greater Cleveland area to live and work after college graduation. This is a remarkable return on investment for our community, resulting in a 'brain gain' rather than drain.

PARTNERSHIP WITH THOSE SERVED

Due to the one-on-one counseling nature of CSP's advisory services, parochial high school students are involved in every aspect of the college planning, application and financial aid process. Advisors then share and incorporate knowledge based on their experiences with individual students into program policy and procedures.

CSP's advisors serve as guides to provide students with the knowledge and resources needed to pursue and complete postsecondary education. Further, overworked guidance counselors receive much needed assistance during the time when their services are in the greatest demand.

BUDGET NARRATIVE

Advisory services funds are allocated on a per-day basis. Funds provided by the Catholic Community Fund would cover the salary and benefits of advisors, as well as related costs (see Attachment C). The funding will provide advisors with adequate training and technological resources needed to efficiently deliver current college access information. CSP continually seeks new funding sources for parochial school advisory services and scholarship dollars.

EVALUATION

Our success will be measured through program evaluation and students' persistence to graduation. Currently, each CSP advisor is equipped with a laptop computer to track the number of students served and services provided. All advisors have access to CSP's main database where demographic, financial aid and service data are logged for each student. Over the last year, CSP's Information Systems department has developed a tracking system to monitor specific financial aid awards and services provided to students at each school. Thus, CSP may tailor analyses to more specific populations and assess the need for particular services.

CSP has hired a dedicated analyst to refine outcome measures and program evaluation. In collaboration with the Ohio College Access Network (OCAN) and the Ohio Board of Regents, CSP is working to develop an online college access data system that will be part of the larger Higher Education Information System of Ohio and serve as a model for other college access programs.

PROPOSAL ATTACHMENTS

Attachment A: College Access Barriers
Attachment B: Office of Catholic Education Statistics
Attachment C: Parochial Advisory Services Budget
CSP 501 (c) 3 Letter
2001-2002 CSP Annual Report
CSP Board of Directors Roster
2001-2002 CSP Audited Financial Statement
Letters of Support

Cleveland Scholarship Programs, Inc, (CSP)   Attachment C

Catholic Community Fund Proposal Budget
September 2003

EXPENSE	COST PER DAY	ADVISORY DAYS SUPPORTED BY CCF	CCF TOTAL
Advisor Salary	XXXXX	XXXXX	$4,662
Advisor Benefits	XXXXX	XXXXX	$1,073
Administrative Salaries (includes Advisory Supervisor, accounting, information systems, clerical support)	XXXXX	XXXXX	$925
Training and Development	$15	37	$555
Equipment (includes lap tops, computer toner, computer maintenance, college access software)	$18	37	$666
Printing (includes in-house photocopying of hand-outs and other support documents	$10	37	$370
Postage and Supplies	$7	37	$259
Student Fee Payments	$40	37	$1,480
TOTAL ADVISORY COSTS	$270	37	$9,990

INCOME	ADVISORY SERVICE DAYS	COST PER DAY	TOTAL
CATHOLIC COMMUNITY FUND	37	$270	$9,990
FUNDING FROM OTHER SOURCES	208	$270	$56,160
2003-2004 ADVISORY DAYS REQUESTED	245	$270	$66,150

A Proposal From
Diabetes Association of Greater Cleveland
Cleveland, Ohio

To
Saint Luke's Foundation of Cleveland
Cleveland, Ohio

Requested amount: $22,500; **Amount received:** $22,500

Funder's comments:

"Saint Luke's Foundation requires an initial letter of inquiry, after which applicants are asked to submit a full proposal following our required format. We also require a logic model, which is an aid for applicants in finding the connection between the proposed activities and the proposed outcomes—it is essential that a proposal reflect alignment between the two.

"This proposal had several strong components. The cover letter was effective because it demonstrated the organization's commitment to the project at the board and executive levels. The proposal's need statement was well prepared. There was a clear link between the need and the project. The statistics used weren't too broad; instead, they were specific and local, and they substantiated the relevance of this approach. The writing was clear and succinct.

"The budget was standard and sufficient for the project. The budget in conjunction with the rest of the proposal was compelling because it demonstrated a project with great impact that would require no ongoing costs. "

—LaTida Smith, Program Officer, Saint Luke's Foundation of Cleveland

Notes:

The proposal was written using Saint Luke's Foundation of Cleveland's required format, proposal budget form, and proposal logic model.

Proposal written by Tracy Cordes.

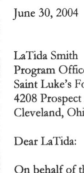

DIABETES ASSOCIATION OF GREATER CLEVELAND
fighting the diabetes epidemic right here at home.

June 30, 2004

LaTida Smith
Program Officer
Saint Luke's Foundation
4208 Prospect Avenue
Cleveland, Ohio 44103

Dear LaTida:

On behalf of the board and staff of the Diabetes Association of Greater Cleveland (DAGC), we are pleased to submit the enclosed proposal for consideration by the Saint Luke's Foundation. This proposal requests funding in the amount of $22,500 to support the development of the Guide for Successful Management of Diabetes and Related Programming in the Cleveland Municipal School District.

DAGC's health educators, including 2 registered dietitians and a registered nurse who holds a certification in diabetes education, will implement this program. The Cleveland Municipal School District has requested DAGC's assistance in developing a district-wide diabetes care guide, creating standardized forms and letters, and providing diabetes in-services for District nurses. The need for such initiatives is great: Cleveland school nurses perform 1,800 insulin injections and 3,200 blood glucose tests each school year. No standard of diabetes care currently exists, and more and more school-aged children are being diagnosed with diabetes.

Meeting these identified needs in the Cleveland Municipal School District is a priority for DAGC in 2004. DAGC hopes to eventually expand the Guide for Successful Management of Diabetes beyond the Cleveland Municipal School District to standardize diabetes care in other area school districts. Therefore, the potential impact of this project is great. We feel that this project furthers DAGC's mission to serve the northeast Ohio community as an advocate in the management, prevention, and cure of diabetes. The development and adoption of a district-wide diabetes care guide for the Cleveland Municipal School District will enable school personnel to be an advocate and provider of care for children with diabetes.

We appreciate your consideration of this proposal. Please do not hesitate to contact us if you have any questions.

Sincerely,

Harriet L. Fader, CAE
President & CEO

Kevin C. Keene
Chairman of the Board

3601 S. Green Road • #100 • Cleveland, OH 44122-5719 • Phone: (216) 591-0800
Fax: 591-0320 • E-mail: information@dagc.org • www.dagc.org

A United Way Agency

ASSOCIATIONS ADVANCE AMERICA

MISSION FIT

The Diabetes Association of Greater Cleveland (DAGC) shares Saint Luke's Foundation vision of a healthier Greater Cleveland. Diabetes is a serious health issue in northeast Ohio, with one in 16 people affected by the disease. With type 2 diabetes increasing at epidemic proportions as a result of poor nutrition and inactivity, diabetes is rapidly becoming a disease of paramount concern, especially among our community's youth. As a local, independent (not nationally affiliated) nonprofit organization, DAGC is able to invest all of its resources to meet the needs of those with diabetes and those at risk for diabetes in northeast Ohio.

DAGC's proposed project to the Saint Luke's Foundation – Guide for Successful Management of Diabetes and Related Programming in the Cleveland Municipal School District – fits both the mission of DAGC and the Foundation. The proposed project, which involves creating a diabetes manual, standardized forms and letters, and providing diabetes in-services to District school professionals, will enable DAGC to improve access to appropriate, comprehensive, affordable, high-quality healthcare for those students in the Cleveland Municipal School District who have type 1 or type 2 diabetes.

PROGRAM DESIGN

Community Need:

The Cleveland Municipal School District has 125 students with type 1 diabetes (juvenile diabetes) and 35 known students with type 2 diabetes. However, initial data from a DAGC study in the Cleveland Municipal School District indicates that 18% of students are overweight and 15% are in a high-risk category for type 2 diabetes. 13 of the 55 full-time District nurses are in particular schools because of a high percentage of students with diabetes in those schools. In 2003, elementary and middle school nurses saw 172,000 students. 1,800 of these visits were for insulin injections and 3,200 were for blood glucose testing. To put this in context of a 180-day school year,

Diabetes Association of Greater Cleveland
Guide for Successful Management of Diabetes in Cleveland Municipal School District

1

District nurses perform an average of 10 insulin injections a day and 18 blood glucose tests a day in elementary and middle schools (high school students are allowed to inject insulin and test blood glucose themselves, so this number is not tracked).

Although diabetes is obviously a health issue that affects many school-aged children (and the number of newly diagnosed cases of type 2 diabetes rapidly increasing), no district-wide policy or procedure manual exists that addresses diabetes in school-aged children in the Cleveland Municipal School District. And so, David Harrison, Director of Health and Social Services, and Debbie Aloshen, Nursing Manager, have specifically requested DAGC's assistance in developing a district-wide diabetes guide, creating standardized forms and letters, and providing diabetes in-services for Cleveland Municipal School District staff, including nurses, teachers, and administrators.

For most children, having diabetes does not mean that they are different from other children, but they do have health concerns that require reasonable accommodation at school. For children with diabetes, it is important that school personnel encourage and enable effective diabetes self-management during the school day. To do so, school professionals must understand the needs of children with diabetes and have the tools to assist them in daily care and in the event of emergencies. The proposed project will enable DAGC to further educate District staff on diabetes so that all students receive proper care and will increase knowledge of diabetes among teachers, parents, nurses, administrators, and students in the Cleveland Municipal School District.

Project Description:

The Diabetes Association of Greater Cleveland (DAGC) respectfully requests consideration of funding in the amount of $22,500 from the Saint Luke's Foundation of Cleveland to support the development of the Guide for Successful Management of Diabetes and Related Programming in the Cleveland Municipal School District. The program has three components:

I.   Guide for Successful Management of Diabetes

Diabetes Association of Greater Cleveland   2
Guide for Successful Management of Diabetes in Cleveland Municipal School District

II.   Standardized Forms and Letters

III.   In-Service Education Program for staff, teachers, and parents

DAGC educators, including 2 registered dietitians and a registered nurse who is a certified diabetes educator, will facilitate and implement this program, in conjunction with the Cleveland Municipal School District.

The following is a detailed description of each of the three components that will be implemented as part of the Guide for Successful Management of Diabetes and Related Programming in the Cleveland Municipal School District. The concepts for all components were jointly developed by DAGC and the Department of Health and Social Services of the Cleveland Municipal School District.

I. Guide for Successful Management of Diabetes

DAGC will work with the Cleveland Municipal School District in the design, development, printing, and distribution of a guide that will be adopted as the standard of care for children in the schools with both type 1 and type 2 diabetes. Currently, no such guide exists and each teacher, school nurse, administrator, P.E. teacher, and lunchroom supervisor has the responsibility of developing his or her own standards for dealing with a child with diabetes. This guide will alleviate that burden and standardize the policies, procedures, and care that children currently receive district-wide.

II. Standardized Forms and Letters

DAGC will create standardized forms to record information about each student with diabetes. School nurses must carefully record the treatments of and communications about a student with diabetes, although no standardized form exists. Forms that DAGC will create include:

- Blood glucose test log;

- Insulin dose log;

Diabetes Association of Greater Cleveland   3
Guide for Successful Management of Diabetes in Cleveland Municipal School District

- Medication log;

- Hypoglycemia/Hyperglycemia emergency plan; and

- Diabetes medical management plan.

DAGC will also create standardized form letters to send to parents if a diabetes problem occurs in school and to send to personal physicians to create a management plan for each student with diabetes.

III. In Service Education Program

Teachers, school nurses, administrators, and parents are in need of education surrounding diabetes. In both 2002 and 2003, DAGC provided in-services about diabetes to all District nurses. DAGC will continue this in-service educational programming to complement the district-wide policy and standardized forms and letters that will be developed.

The in-service education session topics may include but will not be limited to:

- Identifying children at risk for type 2 diabetes;

- Signs and symptoms of elevated blood sugar levels;

- Assisting children in properly managing their diabetes;

- Obesity in children; and

- How to use a blood glucose monitor.

ORGANIZATIONAL CAPACITY AND SUPPORT

DAGC is in its 50th year of serving the northeast Ohio community as an advocate in the management, prevention, and cure of diabetes. DAGC is a local, independent 501 (c)(3) organization, not affiliated with any national organization. DAGC's President & CEO and Vice-President and COO have each been with the organization for over twenty years.

Unique from other diabetes organizations in northeast Ohio, DAGC has 4 health educators (2 registered dietitians, 1 registered nurse/certified diabetes educator, and 1 dietetic technician) on

Diabetes Association of Greater Cleveland   4
Guide for Successful Management of Diabetes in Cleveland Municipal School District

staff to perform diabetes risk assessments in the community, provide diabetes self-management education, facilitate community and professional education programs, and answer diabetes-related questions. DAGC's health educators are active in professional associations (DAGC's Nutrition Educator, for example, is the President of the Cleveland Dietetic Association) and community health initiatives. In 2002, DAGC's health educators began working in the Cleveland Municipal School District to respond to the need for diabetes education for teachers, school nurses, administrators, and parents identified by District administrators. In both 2002 and 2003, DAGC provided diabetes in-services to all District nurses. The District nurses identified a lack of blood glucose monitoring equipment as a barrier to providing minimal diabetes care during the school days. In 2003, DAGC facilitated the donation of 100 needed blood glucose meters to the District nurses, valued at $7,000 total.

Continued involvement with the Cleveland Municipal School District is a priority of DAGC's Board of Directors and staff. In its most recent strategic plan (2001), DAGC identified reaching more people with diabetes through collaborations with non-medical professionals, institutions, and organizations as an agenda item to achieve the outcome of improved understanding of self-management issues and increased self-care skills for people with diabetes in northeast Ohio. Certainly a collaboration with the Cleveland Municipal School District to provide standardized diabetes care will result in improved diabetes self-management. Moreover, the project will educate school professionals about the disease.

Since the Health and Social Services Department requested DAGC's assistance to develop a diabetes guide, standardized forms and letters, and provide in-services for school professionals, the Cleveland Municipal School District enthusiastically supports this project. The enclosed letter of support from District CEO Barbara Byrd-Bennett reaffirms this commitment.

Diabetes Association of Greater Cleveland   5
Guide for Successful Management of Diabetes in Cleveland Municipal School District

OUTCOMES

Project Goals:

The general goals of the Guide for Successful Diabetes Management and Related Programming in the Cleveland Municipal School District include:

1. To provide optimal care for children with diabetes in the Cleveland Municipal School District.

2. To decrease the incidence of diabetes-related adverse events during the school day.

3. To educate school personnel about the multi-faceted nature of diabetes so they are comfortable and knowledgeable about the disease.

Evaluation Plan:

The ultimate determination of success of the Guide for Successful Diabetes Management and Related Programming in the Cleveland Municipal School District will be measured by the following:

1. The adoption and implementation of a district-wide diabetes care manual and standardized forms and letters in print and CD format.

2. Increased communication between the school and parents of children with diabetes and the physicians who care for these children. This will be assessed through parent and staff surveys.

3. The number of school professionals who participate in the in-service education sessions. Evaluation of in-service programs will be evaluated on a per program basis, utilizing pre and post tests and/or written evaluations as is appropriate to the format.

4. Decreased incidence of hypoglycemia and other diabetes related adverse events during the school day.

5. The adoption of the Guide for Successful Management of Diabetes in other school districts

Diabetes Association of Greater Cleveland 6
Guide for Successful Management of Diabetes in Cleveland Municipal School District

in Greater Cleveland.

LONG-TERM VIABILITY

The manual, forms, and letters will be available in both print and CD format, and will serve as the basis for similar publications that DAGC hopes to provide to other area school districts in the future. Ultimately, DAGC would like to be in a position to devote a full-time diabetes educator to the Cleveland Municipal School District. The educator will implement a comprehensive diabetes education program for students, parents, teachers, and school nurses covering such topics as nutrition, exercise, and the risk factors for type 2 diabetes. Because of the increase of type 2 diabetes among our community's youth as a result of poor nutrition and inactivity, more and more children in the District will be diagnosed with type 2 diabetes in the coming years. The Guide for Successful Management of Diabetes will serve as the foundation for all future programming that DAGC provides to the Cleveland Municipal School District, as well as other school districts in Greater Cleveland that DAGC collaborates with in the future.

Beyond this specific project, DAGC's leadership is very interested in taking the lead in a coalition of organizations interested in the broader program of obesity in youth. The experience with the Cleveland Municipal School District that will result from this project will educate DAGC about successful strategies in working with the schools and will build the trust of school personnel in the agency. Obesity in the school age children is an increasing burden both the community and health care costs. The schools seem an ideal place to attack that problem as part of a larger group.

SAINT LUKE'S FOUNDATION OF CLEVELAND, OHIO
PROPOSAL BUDGET FORM
(To be submitted with proposal and electronically - include budget narrative)

Name of organization: Diabetes Association of Greater Cleveland
Project title: Guide for Successful Management of Diabetes and Related Programming in the Cleveland Municipal School District
Amount requested from Saint Luke's Foundation: $22,500 Year: 1

Person completing budget (name, phone, e-mail): Helen Dumski, RD, LD; (216) 591-0800 x 30; hdumski@dagc.org

For multi-year projects, separate budgets must be submitted for each year (indicate year 1, 2, etc.)				
Budget Expense Item	Saint Luke's Request	Agency Contribution	Contributions From Other Funders"	Total Project Budget
Personnel:				
Salary and wages (list each position)				
Program Director	XXXXX			XXXXX
Nurse Educator	XXXXX			XXXXX
Nutrition Educator	XXXXX			XXXXX
Clerical and Administrative Support		XXXXX		XXXXX
Total Fringe (Benefits and Payroll Taxes)	XXXXX			XXXXX
SUBTOTAL PERSONNEL	$13,450.00	$1,000.00		$14,450.00
Nonpersonnel Expenses: (list)				
Supplies	$500.00			$500.00
Literature	$500.00			$500.00
Design of Manual	$400.00			$400.00
Printing of Manual	$7,450.00			$7,450.00
Telephone		$50.00		$50.00
Occupancy		$500.00		$500.00
Local Transportation	$200.00			$200.00
Unrestricted Program Grant from RPM (Received):			$2,500.00	$2,500.00
SUBTOTAL NONPERSONNEL	$9,050.00	$550.00	$2,500.00	$12,100.00
TOTAL	$22,500.00	$1,550.00	$2,500.00	$26,550.00

*CONTRIBUTIONS FROM OTHER FUNDERS FOR THIS PROJECT (in the narrative, list funder, dollar amount, and indicate if proposal is pending or awarded/received)
SALARY AND WAGES (in narrative, list each position to be funded by Saint Luke's including percentage of effort)

SAINT LUKE'S FOUNDATION OF CLEVELAND, OHIO
PROPOSAL BUDGET NARRATIVE
(submit with proposal and electronically)

AGENCY NAME: Diabetes Association of Greater Cleveland

PROJECT TITLE: Guide for Successful Management of Diabetes and Related Programming in the Cleveland Municipal School District

The budget and budget narrative should clearly outline all expenses the applicant agency will incur to successfully implement the proposed project.

PERSONNEL DIRECT COSTS

Provide the title and amount requested from Saint Luke's in the first column. In the second column, list percent of effort and primary responsibilities and tasks for all key project personnel.

OTHER DIRECT COSTS

Itemize all office space, office operations (printing, postage, etc.), equipment, supplies, travel, training, and professional services needed to directly support the implementation of the project.

INDIRECT COSTS

This includes overhead costs required for the applicant's operation, but not directly associated with a specific project; and can also include executive oversight, accounting, utilities and facility maintenance. Up to **9%** of the project's total personnel and direct costs may be requested for overhead expenses.

BUDGET ITEM	EXPLANATION
PERSONNEL:	
Program Director - XXXXX requested	3% of Program Director's time allocated for project supervision.
Nurse Educator -XXXXXrequested	15% of Nurse Educator's time allocated to be responsible for the development of all components of the manual, forms and letters, and in-service programming, with the exception of the nutrition components.
Nutrition Educator - XXXXX requested	5% of Nutrition Educator's time allocated to be responsible for nutrition components of the manual and in-service programming.
Clerical and Administrative Support -DAGC In-Kind	Includes data entry, mailings to school personnel and parents, and other administrative duties as needed.
Employee Benefits and Payroll Taxes -XXXXXrequested	Represents DAGC's standard 25% fringe benefit rate.
NONPERSONNEL:	
Supplies - $500 requested	Includes office supplies, materials for in-services, etc.
Literature - $500 requested	Includes printing and distribution of DAGC's diabetes literature.
Design of Manual - $400 requested	Design by Premier Printing Corporation.
Printing of Manual - $7,450 requested	250 manuals ($30/each) estimated to be printed.
Telephone - $50 DAGC In-Kind	Associated telephone costs.
Occupancy - $500 DAGC In-Kind	Associated rent costs.
Local Transportation - $200 requested.	645 miles x $0.31/mile = $200 for local mileage for DAGC's health educators.

SAINT LUKE'S FOUNDATION OF CLEVELAND, OHIO
PROPOSAL LOGIC MODEL

Please complete the form by answering the questions below in the space provided. Return a printed copy of the logic model with your completed proposal and send an electronic copy as noted in the guidelines.

AGENCY NAME: Diabetes Association of Greater Cleveland

PROJECT TITLE: Guide for Successful Management of Diabetes and Related Programming in the Cleveland Municipal School District (CMSD)

MISSION/VISION	GENERAL GOALS	SPECIFIC ACTIVITIES	INPUTS AND RESOURCES	OUTCOMES Short term	IMPACTS Long term
HOW DOES THIS GRANT SUPPORT THE MISSION AND VISION OF YOUR AGENCY?	*WHAT ARE THE GENERAL GOALS OF THE GRANT? WHAT ISSUES WILL BE ADDRESSED?*	*WHAT SPECIFIC ACTIVITIES OF THE GRANT WILL ADDRESS THESE ISSUES?*	*WHAT SPECIFIC RESOURCES WILL BE ASSOCIATED TO THESE ACTIVITIES?*	*WHAT SHORT TERM CHANGES WILL OCCUR AS A RESULT OF THIS GRANT?*	*WHAT WILL LONG TERM SUCCESS BEYOND THE LIFE OF THE GRANT LOOK LIKE?*
The mission of the Diabetes Association of Greater Cleveland is to serve the community as an advocate in the management, prevention, and cure of diabetes. The development and adoption of the Guide for Successful Management of Diabetes in the CMSD will enable school personnel to be an advocate and provider of care for children with diabetes.	1. To provide optimal care for children with diabetes in the CMSD. 2. To decrease the incidence of diabetes-related adverse events during the school day. 3. To educate school personnel about the multi-faceted nature of diabetes so they are comfortable and knowledgeable about the disease.	1. To develop a district-wide diabetes care manual that includes educational materials and standardized forms and letters in print and CD format. 2. To increase communication between the school and parents of children with diabetes and the physicians who care for these children. 3. To conduct in-service diabetes educational programming for school professionals so they understand the special needs of children with diabetes.	1. DAGC education staff, including Program Director, Nurse Educator, and Nutrition Educator 2. Design and printing of manual and standardized forms and letters. 3. Diabetes education materials for training programs.	1. CMSD will adopt and implement a district-wide plan of care for children with diabetes. 2. CMSD personnel will have the necessary education and tools to provide diabetes care during the school day. 3. CMSD personnel will have increased knowledge of diabetes and feel comfortable managing children with diabetes in the schools.	1. A decrease in diabetes related adverse events during the school day in the CMSD. 2. Standards for communication between CMSD personnel and the child's primary care physician will improve. 3. Manual can be utilized by other area school districts.

A Proposal From
El Paso Area Foster Parent Association
El Paso, Texas

To
The Meadows Foundation
Dallas, Texas

Requested amount: $39,000; **Amount received:** $39,000

Funder's comments:

"The Meadows Foundation had originally provided two years of funding to the El Paso Area Foster Parent Association to pilot the On My Own Program, a housing and support program designed to help former foster care youth transition to independent living. According to a recent national study, within 18 months of leaving foster care, 50 percent of these youth will be unemployed, 33 percent will be on public assistance, and almost a third of the males will become incarcerated.

"During the first two years, the organization exceeded its original goals and expanded its services as it learned how to better serve this population of youth. Six youth left Section 8 housing because the assistance they received enabled them to get jobs with incomes that exceeded HUD guidelines. The agency arranged for additional housing for former foster youth who are parents. By utilizing the comprehensive services of another nonprofit, the youth had access to a transportation network, legal assistance, medical clinic, mental health services, substance abuse program, job counselor, educational help, and meal program.

"The project was included in a federal grant proposal that would be funded toward the end of its third year of operation, and at the time the proposal was submitted, the agency needed bridge funding to continue its program efforts until the federal grant became available.

"Based on its past success and honesty in detailing the challenges encountered while serving youth in transition, the Meadows Foundation approved a $39,000 grant in 2004 to continue the program for a third year. The proposal was successful because it capitalized on the lessons learned during its first two years to improve and expand its services to youth. Specific and measurable goals were set for its third year and described in detail in the proposal. This program serves a population that is 'invisible' to the public and with a little support, will have a great positive impact on the lives of foster youth venturing into adulthood on their own."

—*Cindy M. Patrick, Senior Program Officer, The Meadows Foundation*

Notes:

The proposal was written using the Meadows Foundation grant application form.

The complete proposal included the following attachments: list of board members, organizational budget, audited financial statement, IRS tax-exempt letter, and annual report.

Proposal written by Dave Gillooly.

EL PASO FOSTER
PARENT ASSOCIATION, INC.

June 28, 2004

Mr. Michael K. McCoy, Senior Program Officer
The Meadows Foundation
Wilson Historic District
3003 Swiss Avenue
Dallas, Texas 75204-6090

Dear Mr. McCoy,

The attached proposal is being submitted for consideration by the Meadows Foundation following my conversation with Gayle Stoumbaugh. As you may recall, the El Paso Area Foster Parents Association recently submitted the program report for the On My Own Program. It was from the issuance of the report and our cover letter to Ms. Cindy Patrick that Ms. Stoumbaugh suggested a more formal application.

For the past two years the Association has been working with aged out foster youth in the greater El Paso community who have become homeless and in need of specialized care and services. This program has been quite successful in the placement of these youth in scattered site housing via the Section 8 Certificate program operated by the Housing Authority of the City of El Paso. Supportive services for these youth have included extensive case management, educational assistance, and placement within specialized training programs, transportation assistance and extensive crisis intervention.

It was and continues to be the intention of the Association to develop the program in such a manner as to assure its long-term operations through a more stabilized funding mechanism. Our initial request to The Meadows Foundation was for a two year funding cycle while long term funding was secured. As explained in our application, the Association was denied our first attempt at HUD funding and will be approaching the effort in a different manner in the current SuperNOFA process.

It is our desire to secure one additional year of funding in the amount of $39,000.00 as a means of continuing the current level of services from the Meadows Foundation. The Association has also submitted a similar request to the Hogg Foundation for Mental Health and is awaiting a final determination. From every indication all current funding will terminate during the month of August, thus placing the program in serious jeopardy of continuing.

1208 Myrtle Ave
El Paso, TX 79901

Phone: (915) 577-0069 ext. 241
Fax: (915) 544-2459
dmtruax@yahoo.com

The Association has been actively pursuing funds for the programs continuation throughout the past 16 months. This pursuit included applications to the El Paso Community Foundation, Moor-Moleen Charitable Trust, and Kenneth P. Gifford Foundation, Hervey Foundation as well as our recent submission to the Swalm Foundation. Unfortunately, many of our requests were denied or only provided a maximum of $2,000.00 to $2,500.00.

Now more than ever, before our community is in need of continuing this program and services to aged out foster youth. The continued cutbacks in state and federal funding for foster youth will ultimately have a domino effect on the local agencies efforts to help these youth. We have already seen and experienced major cutbacks in state funding for youth currently under the supervision of DFPS. I can only anticipate the effects these cutbacks will have on those youth preparing to enter society without any form of support.

I urge you and the members of The Meadows Foundation to look with favor on our request for one year of transitional funding for the On My Own program. Should you need additional information, please contact my office directly at (915) 577-0069, ext. 241 or via cellular at (915) 274-2598.

Thank you again for your past support of our project. I look forward to speaking with you in the near future to discuss this proposal and to address any issues you may have concerning the On My Own program.

Sincerely,

Dorothy Truax
Project Coordinator

APPLICATION TO

The Meadows Foundation
3003 Swiss Avenue
Dallas, Texas 75204

For the Continued Operation of the

ON MY OWN PROGRAM
For Homeless Foster Youth

Submitted by:

El Paso Area Foster Parent Association

July 5, 2004

El Paso Area Foster Parent Association
1208 Myrtle Avenue
El Paso, Texas 79901

THE MEADOWS FOUNDATION

GRANT APPLICATION

While there is no required application form for applying for a grant from The Meadows Foundation, for your convenience, this *optional* form includes all the information requested in the Grant Guidelines. You may download this form, fill in the appropriate information using your own word processing software, print the document, and submit is through U.S. Mail to the address given at the end of this document.

Name:	**On My Own Program for Aged Out Foster Youth**
Organization:	**El Paso Area Foster Parent Association**
Address:	**1208 Myrtle Avenue**
City:	**El Paso,**
State:	**Texas**
Zip Code:	**79901**
Phone:	**(915) 577-0069 ext 242 Cellular (915) 274-2598**
Fax:	**(915) 544-2459**
E-mail address:	dmtruax@yahoo.com or daveg@htg.net
Website address:	**NOT AVAILABLE AT THIS TIME**

Brief History of the Organization and Description of Existing Services:
(Please include mission, current programs and accomplishments, current number of staff, and volunteers, and current population served, e.g., number served per year, geographic location, socio-economic status, ethnicity, gender, or age.)

The Mission Statement of the El Paso Area Foster Parent's Association is "to increase the public awareness of the community's responsibility toward children in foster care, improve services to foster children, and enhance the public image of foster/adoptive parents and foster children. Through groups, foster parents gain encouragement and support from one another in fulfilling their role as foster/adoptive parents and are more able to meet the needs of the children in their care. The Association will also strive to provide a comprehensive approach to assist youth who have aged out of the state system and are facing life on their own."

To this end, the El Paso Area Foster Parent Association will seek to provide training; establish a mutual support system among members thus developing a foster parent retention program; provide recreational activities for foster youth and parents; provide and support a recruitment program for the Association; develop a mechanism whereby the community is apprised of issues related to abuse and neglect of children; and finally to support the special needs of current and former foster children in the greater El Paso community.

Since its inception in 1976 the Association has been viewed as the leader in addressing the placement and support of foster youth in the greater El Paso community. For many years the

1

Association simply served as a support mechanism for the recruitment, training and provision of support programs for foster parents in our community. Realizing the growing number of foster youth who aged out of the state run system and in need of continued support, the Association established the "On My Own" program. This program provides long term housing placement and supportive services for aged out foster youth between the ages of 18 and 24. To the dismay of the Association members many of the youth were falling through the cracks of a state system that was not geared to the thinking of what happens after discharge. A large percentage of the youth were found to be living on the streets, staying in area homeless shelters, placing themselves in precarious living situation and having no mechanism in place to assure their self-sufficiency. Through negotiations with the Housing Authority of the City of El Paso, the local Department of Family and Protective Services division of the state and by participation in the El Paso Coalition for the Homeless, the Association received an initial 50 Section 8 Housing Certificates specifically for aged out foster youth. Funding to provide extensive case management, supportive services and general assistance to the youth was secured through a collaborative grant between the Meadows Foundation, the Hogg Foundation for Mental Health and the Association. During the initial two years of this pilot project, the Association has secured an additional 30 housing certificates and has 20 more certificates available as needed.

Volunteers have played a key role in the services offered to the foster children in general and those participating in the On My Own Program. Through the current mentoring program over 100 hours per month is provided by the mentors through direct contact and interaction with the youth. Foster parents and others provide an additional 200 hours of service to the Association in a variety of ways that includes fundraising efforts, planning social events for the foster children, attending meetings, trainings and being available for other foster parents for support and counseling.

The Annual Report of Services previously submitted (copy attached) provides a clear indication of the number of persons served through the On My Own program as well as information related to demographics, ethnicity and other pertinent data. The Association is proud of its success with the On My Own program and as such sees the continuation of this program a benefit to not only the program participants, but the community in general.

Funding for this project terminates on August 31, 2004 with the Meadows Foundation and on July 31, 2004 with the Hogg Foundation for Mental Health. In an effort to maintain long term funding, the Association submitted a request for inclusion in the El Paso Coalition for the Homeless-Continuum of Care application submitted in July 2003 to the U.S. Department of Housing and Urban Development. It was our desire to secure a three year renewable long term funding source. Unfortunately, the program was not funded by HUD due to the nature of the clients served. It is the determination of HUD that aged out foster youth is the sole responsibility of their respective state of residency. Not wanting to forego the program, the Association participated in a review of the HUD process and was encouraged to resubmit the application to HUD in the 2004 COC under the auspices of a dedicated homeless service provider. Following several meetings with the member agencies of the local Coalition it was determined that the Opportunity Center for the Homeless would serve as the lead agency for the new HUD-COC and the program would expand to include all homeless youth regardless of their status as "aged out foster youth". This new Homeless Youth Initiative will be submitted to HUD as part of this year's Continuum of Care application. Announcement of awards is expected to be received in December of 2004 and programs will become operational by July 1, 2005.

2

Downloadable Grant Application
August 2001

Description of the Proposed Program:

Every year approximately 25 teens "age out" of foster care in the local region (El Paso County, Texas) in addition to these twenty teens, the local CPS (Child Protective Services) staff estimate that another thirty to forty former foster youth under the age of 24 become homeless and are living on the streets, in abandoned buildings and other uninhabitable living areas. A significant portion of these youth are in fact parents themselves and are therefore adding to an already overburdened homeless population in our community. Based on data maintained by the Association and CPS we estimate that 98% of the foster youth have a history of receiving mental health therapy while in foster care under the conservatorship of CPS. The vast majority of these teens continue to need long-term mental health services.

Current social work theory indicates that foster children, to include those aging out of the system, face a higher risk of developing social and economic problems. These problems include depression, internalizing and externalizing problems, low levels of socio-ability and initiative, drug and alcohol abuse and problematic peer relationships. These problems eventually manifest themselves into limiting the foster child's ability to function normally in society and thus limiting their ability to function successfully in independent living.

The Association begins to address these issues and the issue of assuring housing for aged out foster youth through the On My Own program. Currently, through a collaborative effort with the Housing Authority of the City of El Paso, the Opportunity Center for the Homeless and the Association, we have secured Section 8 housing vouchers assuring the youth, to include foster youth up to the age of 24, are provided safe housing through a scattered site housing program. The program participant works directly with the On My Own staff in developing a plan of self-sufficiency that includes goals of successful housing, money management, job placement, continuing educational studies and addressing mental health issues as needed.

This project has been funded since 2002 by a joint venture of the Hogg and Meadows Foundations. The two year pilot project is facing termination in July 2004 unless a more secure means of funding is established. The Association, as a member of the El Paso Coalition for the Homeless, submitted a formal request to HUD as part of the communities Continuum of Care submission in 2003. We anticipated a favorable response to our request this past December, however, the project was not funded by HUD. This denial by HUD has forced the Association to look elsewhere for one year of gap funding until the project is able to be reconsidered by HUD in the next round of COC applications under the sponsorship of the Opportunity Center for the Homeless and will include homeless youth as well as aged out foster youth.

While the scope of services to be offered to the aged out foster youth will not see a dramatic change over the current program emphasis will be placed in this next year on further establishing a firm foundation for the program participants to build upon. In the short time frame that we have operated the On My Own program, the Association has seen a dramatic increase in the mindset of many of the youth who wish to overcome the stigma of foster program participation and move forward in their lives. As previously indicated in our report to the Foundation (issued June 2004) the On My Own program has served 99 former foster youth (persons who aged out of the state system), and an additional 16 significant others and 40 children of the program participants. It is this last number that is so startling to the staff and has called upon us to review the program in a manner that will assure the stability of these young families and young single women that are now parents in an extremely fragile and unstable time of their lives. Many (25) of the children of the program participants are under the age of two and are under the direct care of what some view as potentially volatile and unprepared parents. A second and equally startling finding was the number of youth who were in fact homeless, living

3

on the streets, in abandoned buildings, doubling up with friends or moving from place to place seeking shelter. 68 youth were directly referred into the program via the Emergency Night Shelter operated by the Opportunity Center for the Homeless and the El Paso Rescue Mission.

Specific Dollar Amount Requested from the Foundation and Date Payment is needed:

The Association is respectfully requesting continued level funding in the amount of $39,000.00 for the next 12 month period in order to continue providing the current level of services to homeless foster youth.

List All Entities asked to give Financial Support to the Proposed Project:
(Please include their responses to date and dollar amount committed.)

Hogg Foundation for Mental Health: Requested continuation funding of one year in the amount of $40,000.00. Determination is to be made at July meeting of the Board as per indications from staff members.

Swalm Foundation: Requested funding of $60,000.00 for one year operations (support staff and client expenses). Submitted letter of intent in June 2004, no response to date. *denied 8/9*

Project Budget: *(Please include income and expenses.)*

SEE ATTACHMENT #1-Project Budget

Plans to support the Project after the Grant Period: *(Please include projected income sources.)*

The Association sought long term funding through the submission of the HUD-Continuum of Care SuperNOFA application in 2003. The request would have provided a three year renewable funding commitment from HUD that would have assured the longevity of the project. Unfortunately, it was determined that a project of this nature, especially one specifically addressing aged out foster youth, was not in line with the HUD guidelines for funding. This denial was reviewed with HUD and the Association was specifically instructed to partner with a local social service agency that addresses homelessness and to consider expanding the program to include all homeless youth regardless of their status as a former foster child.

Following this request, the Association entered into discussions with member agencies of the El Paso Coalition for the Homeless. It was determined that a formal partnership with the Opportunity Center for the Homeless, a local 501-c-3 agency with over 10 years of service to the homeless and a regular recipient of HUD funds would be our best approach. At this time, the Opportunity Center for the Homeless is submitting a formal application entitled "Homeless Youth Initiative" that will target all homeless youth between the ages of 18 and 24 to HUD as part of the local Coalitions 2004 HUD COC Application. The final documents will be submitted on July 23, 2004 and a determination of funding is expected in December 2004. When approved, the funding will become available in July/August 2005. This project will require a matching 20% of funds (all HUD SHP projects require 20% matching funds) of which the Center and the Association will seek to generate.

A formal MOU is being developed between the partnering agencies that will assure the continuation of providing services to aged out foster youth, placement of foster youth within the Section 8 Housing Program operated by the Housing Authority of the City of El Paso and access of services offered by the Opportunity Center for the Homeless for our clients.

Plan to evaluate the Project:
(Please include measurable, time-specific goals, a description of information to be collected to measure progress and how that information will be collected. Evaluation guidelines, sample

4

Downloadable Grant Application
August 2001

goals and sample measures for different types of programs are available for your reference <u>evaluation tools</u>.

The Association will continue to maintain client data in a manner that will enable us to readily prepare reports and maintain statistical data that can be shared with funding sources. One such instrument that will be beneficial to the On My Own program staff is our participation in the HMIS (Homeless Management Information System) an integrated networking of local service providers to share data on homeless persons in an effort to maintain accurate counts of homeless and the services provided. Through this system the Association will be able to provide a wider array of data related to our clients and the actual services they receive from the program and other providers.

Realizing this funding request would be for a transitional year in an effort to maintain the program until a more permanent means of funds are attained, the On My Own program will seek to achieve the following goals and objectives:

Goal: <u>**Facilitate positive forms of interaction between program participants and staff in an effort to develop a stronger base of support.**</u>

Objective: The Association will host 10 program based workshops and group discussions through out the year as a means of developing program participants life skills, communication skills, employment and educational opportunities, financial management, and others as deemed appropriate. 80% of all program participants (to include significant others and children) will be involved in the monthly meetings. 100 % of all program participants will be actively involved with outside mental health services and will receive additional counseling from appropriate staff.

Objective: The Association will provide a three part series of discussions and presentations for program participants in the area of developing positive parenting skills; 90% of all program participants who are parents or who are expecting at the time of the series will be required to participate in the workshops.

Objective: No less than 4 contacts per month will be made by program staff with each program participant. These contacts will include 1 home visit monthly, and 3 face to face or phone contacts to assure participants are compliant with housing standards, addressing plans of self-sufficiency and maintaining a positive living environment.

Goal: <u>**Facilitate placement of aged out foster youth into scattered site or other supportive service type housing program.**</u>

Objective: The Association will place an additional 15 eligible youth within housing provided through the Section 8 Housing Certificates as issued by the Housing Authority of the City of El Paso. An additional 10 youth will be screened for placement in other housing arrangements that are not eligible for Section 8 Certificates.

Objective: The Association will work with the local Housing Authority of the City of El Paso and apartment managers and housing program providers in an effort to assure compliance on the part of youth placed within the housing complexes. Staff will conduct routine visits with each apartment/housing complex quarterly to review client's compliance with the rules and guidelines.

Objective: Secure alternative housing sites for non-eligible foster youth throughout the greater El Paso area. Alternative sites may include placement within Supportive Housing Programs (SRO/TLC), shared living environments or placement with family member if permissible.

5

Goal: <u>Develop educational and employment skills and programs that will enable program participants to achieve advancement from current situation.</u>

Objective: Work with member agencies of the El Paso Coalition for the Homeless to include program participants in targeting specific programs such as GED, Self-Investment Programs, employment training programs, job placement programs and others as deemed appropriate and necessary for the advancement of program participants.

Objective: Provide one-on-one tutoring for program participants who are still in high school and those seeking to acquire their GED. 7 program participants will be enrolled in some form of advanced educational program as a means of developing their educational levels.

Objective: 25% of program participants how have not completed their high school education will be enrolled in a developmental educational enrichment program that will include GED classes. 25% of all current and future program participants will secure employment (part time/full time) in an effort to become self-sufficient. Work with the TACE program in the development of specialized skills training and education of program participants for potential employment opportunities.

A List of Trustees or Directors and Corporate Officers:

See Attachment #2-Board of Directors

Names and Qualifications of Staff involved with the Proposed Project:

Dorothy Truax-Project Coordinator: Ms. Truax holds a Masters Degree in Social Work from New Mexico State University and has been working with foster youth as a state employee for over 27 years. Ms. Truax has been actively involved with the Association since 1983 and has served as the Project Coordinator for the On My Own program since its inception.

Mr. Christino Heredia is a case manager who is in the process of completing his degree in Social Work. Mr. Heredia brings to the program over 8 years of working with the homeless through the Opportunity Center for the Homeless-Emergency Night Shelter where he was a supervisory staff member. Mr. Heredia's experience in working with hard to serve populations, as well as interaction skills with the program participants, has been quite beneficial to the success of the program.

Mr. Derek Goff holds a Masters Degree in Social Work from New Mexico Highlands. As a former staff member with the local mental health program, Mr. Goff is specially trained in assessing and addressing specialized needs of the clients. While his emphasis is to work with youth in the PAL (Preparation for Adult Living) program and is funded through a grant from DFPS, Mr. Goff works with the other program staff in a manner that enhances the services to the program participants.

The Organization's Current Operating Budget and Year-To-Date Financial Statements:

See Attachment #3-Agency Budget

See Attachment #4-Year to Date Financial Statements as of June 23, 2004

The Last Certified Audit

See Attachment # 5-Agency Audit for the year ending December 31, 2003

A Copy of the Latest Verification of Tax-Exempt Status from the Internal Revenue Service under Section 170 of the IRS Code

See Attachment # 6—IRS Certification

6

El Paso Foster Parent Association
Attachment #1
Project Budget
On My Own Program

BUDGET FORM
Program 1-A

EL PASO FOSTER PARENT ASSOCIATION
ON MY OWN PROGRAM
OPERATIONAL BUDGET
July 1, 2004 to June 30, 2005

GENERAL AGENCY FINANCIAL INFORMATION

Cost Component	Current Agency Budget (2003-2004)	Estimated Agency Budget (2004-2005)
Salaries (2.0 FTE)	69,675.00	70,000.00
Fringe Benefits (2.0FTE)	4,544.00	4,500.00
Office Expense (copies, software, supplies, postage, printing, etc.)	2,496.00	2,500.00
Operations Admin Expense	2,374.00	2,500.00
Communication (Telephone/internet)	3,237.00	3,300.00
Youth Activities	14,309.00	14,500.00
Youth Assistance	10,152.00	15,000.00
Travel	6,017.00	7,000.00
Rent and Utilities	4,300.00	4,500.00
Miscellaneous	4.00	50.00
TOTAL	117,108.00	123,850.00

BUDGET FORM
Program 1-B

EL PASO FOSTER PARENT ASSOCIATION
ON MY OWN PROGRAM
July 1, 2004 to June 30, 2005
SOURCES OF SPECIFIC PROGRAM SUPPORT

Funding Component	Current 2003-2004	Estimated 2004-2005
Private Foundations		
Meadows Foundation	39,000.00	39,000.00
Hogg Foundation	50,000.00	40,000.00
Moor Moleen Charitable Trust	2,000.00	2,000.00
El Paso Community Foundation	6,765.00	6,800.00
Stern Foundation	5,000.00	10,000.00
Cardwell Foundation	5,000.00	5,000.00
Trull Foundation	0.00	5,000.00
Special Activities (shirt sales, fundraisers)	2,879.00	3,000.00
Interest Income	395.00	250.00
Donations (Business/Individual)	2,360.00	2,500.00
El Paso County Child Welfare Board	11,342.00	12,000.00
Totals	124,741.00	125,550.00

A Proposal From
The First Place Fund for Youth
Oakland, California

To
Pottruck Family Foundation
San Francisco, California

Requested amount: $20,000; **Amount received:** $20,000

Funder's comments:

"The Pottruck Family Foundation began funding in a new program area, foster care, in 2004, with the goal to improve the ability of foster youth to thrive and successfully transition out of the foster care system. Supportive (or 'Supported') Housing is a model that has been shown to safely and successfully move former foster youth from the child welfare/foster care system to independent living. The First Place Fund for Youth is one of the preeminent organizations providing supportive housing to former foster youth in the San Francisco Bay Area.

"Applicants must download a proposal submission form from our Web site to be sent in with their proposal and they can view a proposal checklist so they know exactly what is expected. First Place Fund for Youth submitted a complete proposal. The short cover letter clearly and succinctly communicates the amount requested, what the funds will be used for, and why the grant is important. The proposal begins with an executive summary that, in one paragraph, clearly states the who, what, when, where, and how of the organization, as well as the baseline services provided and the precise goal it seeks to achieve (doubling the housing capacity, and thus the number of youth served, by a specific date).

"The next section relates to the organization, its mission, history, and capacity to effectively and efficiently carry out its work. It cites national awards the organization has received and offers specific examples of the results of their work. I also like the way the management principles and practices are described and that all stake-holders—board, staff, and participants—contributed to the process. It gives the impression that they are results-driven while at the same time committed to their mission and values. And their shared values inform both what they do (programs/services) and how they do it.

"The Program Description section is comprehensive and well written; it backs up the need statement with research, demonstrates deep knowledge of the population served, and clearly describes the resources and services to be provided, often addressing why they are important to client success. I also like that they included a description of the program staff. It's the people who make the program(s) happen, as well as being the largest budget line item. This format is preferable in that it communicates the qualities of the staff in a short amount of space. If I need more information, I can always ask for résumés and/or ask to meet with specific staff during the site visit.

"The proposal then discusses program goals and objectives and how they will be measured, showing success to date and how success will be assessed in the coming year. My board, like so many others, is very interested in outcomes. First Place is asking (and answering) the basic question that my board would ask: Are their clients significantly better off than former foster care youth who do not participate in the program?

"Regarding revenue, most proposals we receive show sources of support in list form with the source's name and amount, either pending or received. First Place provided this in an attachment, as well as a narrative describing their fundraising strategies and challenges. This, as so much of First Place's proposal, truly enables the reader to understand how they are addressing these issues and how the organization fits into the larger context. Finally, the management challenge they wrote about—whether to replicate their model regionally or work in other cities nationally—is an interesting one, and offers a glimpse into the thinking that is going on at all levels of the organization to plan and prepare for its future.

"The financial information is clear and easy to read, and they've provided exactly what we've asked for: the budgets for the organization and the program, for the current year and the year in which the grant will be used (if different); the revenue sheet shows sources, amounts, and a subtotal for each category.

"The board roster provides names and affiliations, which is sufficient; some lists give more information, e.g. address and contact information, but I find it's not necessary. Other attachments—the newsletter, newspaper articles, and audited financial statements—are not required but round out the proposal.

"Areas for improvement: Quite frankly, I found no substantive weaknesses with the proposal. They could have included the revenue sources for fiscal year 2004 so that I had the same information for both fiscal year 2004 and fiscal year 2005, and I would have liked to know if any proposals were declined, and if so, why. It would have been useful if they could show revenue for the organization and the program so that the revenue sources report matched the budget report. However, unless their accounting software could do this easily, I would not insist on it."

—Nancy Wiltsek, Executive Director, Pottruck Family Foundation

Notes:
The complete proposal included the following attachments: list of board members, evaluation summary, audited financial statement, organizational newsletter, and newspaper clippings. Proposal written by Deanne Pearn, Co-founder and Director of Donor and Corporate Relations.

The **First Place** Fund for Youth

ASSISTING FOSTER YOUTH IN THEIR TRANSITION TO INDEPENDENT LIVING

May 12, 2004

Nancy Wiltsek
Executive Director
Pottruck Family Foundation
1016 Lincoln Blvd. #221
San Francisco, CA 94129

Dear Ms. Wiltsek,

On behalf of The First Place Fund for Youth, I am pleased to submit the enclosed proposal to the Pottruck Family Foundation.

First Place is requesting $20,000 from the Pottruck Family Foundation over one year to help support the expansion of our Supported Housing Program and to simultaneously leverage a permanent source of funding for these services, the state Transitional Housing for Foster Youth Fund. As the proposal describes, the Supported Housing Program is dedicated to providing emancipated foster youth with access to safe, affordable housing, where they have the opportunity to develop and practice life skills to achieve long-term self-sufficiency.

Through its support of First Place, the Pottruck Family Foundation will help bridge the considerable gap in services that currently exists for youth who are making the precarious transition from foster care to independent living and will support the replicability of a model that has a proven track record for helping youth achieve long term self sufficiency after exiting care.

Thank you for your time and concern, and please contact me at
(510) 272-0979 ext. 23 if you have any questions regarding the proposal.

Sincerely,

Deanne Pearn
Associate Director

Tel: 510.272.0979 • **Fax:** 510.272.9303 • **www.firstplacefund.org**
Administration: 1755 Broadway, Suite 304 • Oakland, CA 94612
Emancipation Training Center: 1759 Broadway • Oakland, CA 94612

I.   Executive Summary

The First Place Fund for Youth is an innovative, grassroots organization founded to prevent poverty and homelessness among a growing, yet largely overlooked population: youth who "age out" or "emancipate" from foster care. Since its inception in 1998, First Place has aggressively pursued this mission by developing services that address the fundamental needs of emancipated foster youth in the areas of education, housing, and employment. First Place is requesting $20,000 from the Pottruck Family Foundation for one year to support the expansion of its Supported Housing Program. Currently, the Supported Housing Program provides affordable housing and support services to 40-45 at-risk youth making the difficult transition from foster care to independent living. First Place's most recent strategic plan calls for doubling its housing capacity by the end of fiscal year 2006.

II.   Organizational Overview

A.   Organizational Mission and History

The First Place Fund for Youth is an Oakland-based nonprofit organization founded to remedy the lack of services available to youth who are making the difficult transition from foster care to independent living. In the current system, youth are discharged from foster care at age 18, or at age 19 if they remain in high school. After discharge, county-funded foster care services are discontinued for the vast majority of these young adults. Similarly, there are limited community-based services available. Instead of receiving support and guidance during this critical transition, emancipated foster youth are without housing, a source of income, adult encouragement, or community support. Given this lack of resources, a disproportionate number of emancipated foster youth experience homelessness, low educational attainment, unemployment, poverty, and poor health in adulthood.

It is the mission of First Place to promote long-term self-sufficiency among emancipated foster youth by providing them with the skills, resources, and support to make a healthy transition to adulthood. First Place pursues this goal through two programs: the Supported Housing Program and the Emancipation Training Center.

- **Supported Housing Program (SHP)**: The objective of SHP is to provide emancipated foster youth with access to permanent, affordable housing, where they have the opportunity to **develop** life skills and address their emotional and psychological needs to achieve long-term self-sufficiency. SHP participants are either single or parenting young adults. Single youth live in shared two-bedroom apartments in the East Bay whereas parenting youth live in studio or one-bedroom apartments with their child. All SHP participants receive a wide range of services and support. These include financial assistance to pay housing start-up costs, monthly rental subsidies, weekly in-home case management, mental health supports, weekly life skills training, economic literacy training, transportation assistance, monthly food vouchers, community building peer events, and health advocacy. Last year, First Place served 45 youth and 15 children in SHP.

- **Emancipation Training Center (ETC)**: In addition to the Supported Housing Program, First Place provides training and assistance through its Emancipation Training Center. The mission of the Emancipation Training Center is to **prepare** youth for emancipation and **support** youth after discharge from foster care. The Emancipation Training Center is staffed by two Emancipation

Specialists who provide intensive case management to 40 at-risk youth who are within two years of "aging out" of foster care. Together, the Emancipation Specialist and youth develop goals and identify community resources in the critical areas of education, housing and employment. In addition, the ETC is staffed by a full-time Youth Advocate and a 60 percent time Peer Educator, who is a former foster youth. These two staff members provide additional services through the Emancipation Training Center, such as crisis case management, referrals, regular housing search assistance workshops, emergency food vouchers, emergency utility assistance, free credit checks for housing search, access to housing listings, computers, and educational resources. Last year, First Place served over 425 youth through the Emancipation Training Center.

B.   Organizational Capacity

In little more than 5 years, First Place has grown from a grassroots project into a thriving community-based organization, with 15 full-time employees and an annual budget of $1.3 million. For the last three years, First Place has served as the lead agency and fiscal sponsor of the Alameda County Foster Youth Alliance, a 14-member collaborative working to improve and expand services available to youth aging out of care. As the fiscal sponsor for the Alliance, First Place has successfully managed over $1.2 million dollars in collaborative funds from the Oakland Fund for Children and Youth that is distributed among four subcontractors. Through its programs, First Place has directly helped over 1,000 foster youth throughout the Bay Area make a safe, supported transition to independent living.

In addition to making a difference in over 1,000 individual lives, First Place has helped shape state and local policy to ensure that these critical housing resources and supportive services are available to all former foster youth that need them. As a direct result of our advocacy, California recently passed two key pieces of legislation that will greatly improve the lives of former foster youth. The first, California Assembly Bill 427 is a landmark piece of legislation that is the state's first-ever commitment of resources to young adults who have exited care. First Place is working in partnership with San Francisco and Alameda Counties to pave the way for statewide implementation of this law. The second, California Assembly Bill 2972, allows organizations to target housing programs to youth without running afoul of state and federal fair housing laws.

First Place's approach and leadership in stemming the negative outcomes among former foster youth has been recognized as innovative and results-oriented. In addition to providing technical assistance to programs all over California seeking to set up similar programs, First Place has received several prestigious national awards. For example, the Supported Housing Program was nominated for a National Best Practices Award from the US Department of Housing & Urban Development in January 2001. In addition, in five years, First Place has received six national awards honoring its social entrepreneurship, including the University of California at Berkeley Peter Haas Public Service Award, the prestigious Brick Award, the Manhattan Institute Social Entrepreneurship Award, a three-year echoing green fellowship, and a three-year Ashoka Fellowship.

C. Management principles and practices

As a community-based organization, community residents, parents, former foster youth, and participating youth heavily influence the governance and decision-making of First Place. The Board of Directors of First Place is a diverse group of nine community members who provide responsible fiduciary and legal oversight. First Place also relies on the active participation of the Youth Advisory Board, which consists of current and former foster youth. In addition to these community boards, First Place collaborates closely with community providers to increase awareness about the needs of emancipated foster youth and to ensure that services are provided in a comprehensive, coordinated manner.

The work of First Place is guided by seven principles, jointly developed by the Board of Directors, participants and all team members. These principles include: respect, honesty, responsibility, accountability, justice, community and empowerment. First Place has identified concrete ways that these principles are to be implemented in our daily work with youth, community members and each other.

First Place is committed to creating a human work environment where staff has manageable workloads, ample support and quality professional development opportunities. As an agency, we make a strong effort to maintain high-level communication across and within all departments to ensure that our strategic goals are being met and to ensure that all team members have a clear understanding of how their work supports the goals and direction of the organization. First Place has implemented a number of practices to make us better advocates for youth and employees. These include:

- Annual team meetings and agency-wide planning retreat: Prior to the beginning of each fiscal year, each team meets to identify and prioritize issues that need to be resolved in order to make their work flow better. Each team presents its goals and work plan for the year at an annual staff retreat, and all of the work plans are captured in an agency strategy document that is shared with all staff.

- Professional development trainings: First Place promotes the professional development of all of its staff members. For non-direct service staff members, First Place will pay for up to 24 hours of individualized professional development each year. The staff member and their supervisor agree upon topics. In addition, First Place has teamed up with several other community partners to sponsor a 10-part professional development series each year for direct service staff members. Each training is at least three hours long and covers topics ranging from how to work with youth exhibiting overly-sexualized behavior, how to support youth in domestic violence situations, how to understand and work with varying mental health diagnoses, etc.

- Annual reviews and regular raises: First Place is committed to providing all employees with an annual review and regular raises. All staff receives a 90-day review, a 6-month review, a one-year review and then annual reviews from that point forward. The review is an opportunity for the staff member and their supervisor to discuss what is going well, identify areas for growth, and discuss what sorts of professional development opportunities the employee would like to seek in the future. All staff members receive an annual cost-of-living raise as well as a merit raise each year.

- Clinical supervision: First Place provides individual and/or group clinical supervision to all First Place staff members who are master's level counselors and seeking licensure.

- Weekly staff meetings: Each week, First Place conducts a one-hour agency-wide staff meeting in which each department has an opportunity to make key announcements, share successes and challenges, and ask for help if needed.

- Individual meetings with supervisors: All First Place staff meet once a week with their supervisor to review priorities, receive support, and discuss the staff member's professional development and training needs.

- Regular team meetings: Each team also meets at least twice a month as a unit to coordinate work, set priorities, and seek assistance from colleagues if needed. We have the following team meetings on a regular basis: the Supported Housing Program team, the Emancipation Training Center team, and the Management Team.

III. Program Description

A. Statement of Need

Each year in the Bay Area, an estimated 500 youth are discharged from foster care when they turn 18 years old. These "emancipated" foster youth were originally removed from their homes due to parental abuse, neglect, or absence, and have often lived the majority of their lives with a foster family or in a group home. Upon turning 18, youth are discharged from their foster care placement, regardless of their resources or preparation for independent living. Once discharged, foster care services are terminated for all but a small fraction of these young adults. Moreover, there are limited community-based services available. Instead of receiving support and guidance during this critical transition, emancipated foster youth are suddenly without housing, a source of income, adult encouragement, or community support.

The number of youth facing these daunting circumstances has increased significantly, according to data from the Child Welfare Research Center at UC Berkeley. A recent study conducted by the Department of Human Services in San Francisco found that the number of youth emancipating from foster care has increased 600 percent since 1989. Parallel demographic trends and caseload growth indicate that a similar increase is occurring in Alameda County. This substantial increase in the number of emancipating foster youth is alarming, given the serious difficulties they face after discharge from foster care, such as:

- **Housing Instability & Homelessness**: Once discharged from foster care, many youth attempt to return to the families from which they were removed, only to find that abuse, overcrowding, poverty and drug involvement continue. Other youth live temporarily with friends, extended family, in homeless shelters, in vacated cars, or directly on the streets. Studies of emancipated foster youth have found that these trends are widespread. In 2002, the California Department of Social Services found that over 65 percent of emancipated foster youth in the state of California face imminent homelessness upon discharge from foster care.

- **Unemployment**: Given their disproportionate lack of education, experience, and job search assistance, emancipated foster youth do not fare well in the job market. According to a 2003 study by the University of Chicago Chapin Hall Center for Children, 22 percent of California former foster youth remain unemployed for the two years after discharge from foster care. Additionally, former foster youth make slower wage progress in the labor market than non-foster youth.

- **Low Educational Achievement**: Foster youth are often educationally delayed due to numerous transfers within the foster care system. This factor leads to low rates of educational attainment: emancipated foster youth are 44 percent less likely to have graduated from high school than the general population of 18 to 24 year olds, according to a study conducted by the Department of Health and Human Services.

- **Poverty & Early Childbirth**: Emancipated foster youth are over *six times* more likely than non-foster youth to give birth to a child before age 21. According to an analysis conducted by the San Francisco Department of Human Services, this early childbearing leads former foster youth to access public assistance at rates three times greater than non-foster youth.

- **Health & Safety**: Emancipated foster youth also experience poor health and a lack of personal safety. Approximately 26 percent of emancipated males and 15 percent of females will be seriously beaten within a year after discharge, according to a recent study from the University of Wisconsin. An additional 10 percent of female foster youth will be victims of rape.

B.   Program Purpose

In March of 2003, First Place completed a three-year strategic planning process, drawing insight from our participants, staff, and funders, and backed by the financial and programmatic expertise of our Board of Directors. The cornerstone of the plan calls for the significant expansion of the Supported Housing Program, making permanent, safe affordable housing available to 90 youth and 30 children by the end of the fiscal year 2006, up from 45 youth and 15 children last fiscal year. First Place will begin increasing its capacity in fiscal year 2005 when we provide housing and support services to 60 youth and 20 children in FY 2005.

The Supported Housing Program incorporates a continuum of services that reflect the unique experiences of foster youth and meets their needs in a caring and practical manner. Through our services, First Place strives to achieve the following goals:

Supported housing: Provide youth with access to safe, affordable, permanent housing, where they will have the opportunity to develop and practice their independent living skills.

Economic empowerment: Promote long-term self-sufficiency among emancipated foster youth by providing them with access to traditionally unattainable sources of capital and by cultivating their ability to successfully manage those resources.

Life skills development: Provide foster youth with the skills and support required to make a lifetime of good decisions in the areas of housing, education and employment.

Community building: Develop a long-term support system of adults and peers to guide youth in their transition to adulthood and promote a sense of responsibility and connection to the community at large.

First Place approaches these goals grounded in two core principles:

- **Sustainability**: First Place is dedicated to providing long-term housing solutions- not temporary housing. To accomplish this, First Place provides a two-year rental subsidy to help youth pay their rent. Over time, the portion paid by First Place gradually decreases and the portion paid by the youth increases. Once the rental subsidy has terminated, tenancy of the apartment officially transfers over to the youth and they may remain living in the unit as long as they wish.

- **Community Integration**: First Place master leases individual rental units throughout the East Bay and subleases them to its participants. This "scattered-site" model is effective because it integrates youth into the community, provides an opportunity to develop and practice independent living skills in a real-world setting and removes the stigma of foster care.

First Place provides a comprehensive network of resources and supportive services to ensure their first experience in independent living is successful. These average 4 to 6 hours of individual services each week per youth. These resources and supportive services include:

1. **Economic Literacy:** Prior to moving into an apartment, all Supported Housing Program participants must attend an 8-part economic literacy course. In addition to learning about mainstream financial systems, youth master concepts such as budgeting, searching for housing, bill paying, and credit and lending. As important as mastering these concepts is the fact that, during economic literacy, participants begin to form the basis of an interdependent community of peers who will sustain them long after the program has ended. To promote this interdependence, all members of the class must pass an individual and group exam prior to being eligible to move into their First Place apartments.

2. **Housing micro-loan:** Upon graduating from the economic literacy class, participants apply for a micro-loan to cover their security deposit. First Place employs a peer-based lending strategy, modeled after the Grameen Bank micro-lending process, in which members of the class approve, monitor and mutually support one another's efforts to repay their loans. The micro-loan is used as a vehicle for social engagement and youth empowerment. It promotes interdependence among class members, creates a sense of ownership and accountability among youth when they are moved into their apartments, and provides youth the satisfying opportunity to see themselves taking responsibility for their own needs.

3. **Access to a First Place Apartment:** Once youth have passed economic literacy and qualified for a housing micro-loan, they are eligible to live in a studio, one- or two-bedroom apartment, predominately located in Oakland. First Place staff secures apartments with both private property owners and nonprofit developers. All rental units are selected based on their accessibility to public transportation and community amenities, including commercial areas, county service centers, community-based organizations, and educational services, such as GED classes, community colleges or vocational training.

4. **Monthly Rental Subsidy:** Each month, First Place assists participants in the payment of their rent. When youth enter the program, they pay 30 percent of their income towards rent and First Place pays the remainder. As their participation in the program continues, participants pay an increasingly greater percentage of the market-rate rent. By the end of the two-year program period, the participant pays the full market-rate rent, and the First Place subsidy is removed entirely. To make this possible, the rental units selected by First Place for participants are based on their *ultimate affordability* to youth. For this reason, First Place works closely with nonprofit developers in the East Bay, such as the Affordable Housing Associates and the East Bay Asian Local Development Corporation (EBALDC) to secure permanently affordable rental units in their developments. Once the First Place subsidy has expired, the apartment is fully transferred to the youth, and he or she may continue to live in it indefinitely.

5. **Weekly Youth Advocacy:** Youth meet weekly with their Youth Advocate to discuss the specific steps that they are taking to meet their individual goals in the areas of employment,

health, education, financial management, and personal relationships. These meeting are designed to provide a wide variety of individualized services to participants, including assistance in securing child care, enrolling in school, locating employment and addressing health issues. The Youth Advocate also meets with youth participants to address practical questions about their apartment, such as bill payment, cooking, shopping and cleaning. To ensure that a strong, trusting relationship is established, the Youth Advocate works with no more than 15 youth.

6. **Specialized Parenting Assistance**: First Place's Supported Housing Program addresses the needs of pregnant and parenting youth by first realizing that the need for stability is far greater for a parent and young child. Parenting youth receive a one-bedroom apartment. They also participate in a support group with other parenting youth to share their experiences as parents and together learn how to best care for their child. Parents are able to form a support network among each other, share experiences, and work through feelings of isolation.

   First Place realizes that pregnant or parenting youth face an even greater challenge to becoming self-sufficient adults than the general foster youth population. First Place Youth Advocates are trained to address these needs, including how to access a broad range of child-related community resources such as day care, public nurses, parenting classes and child nutrition education.

7. **Weekly Transition Support Groups:** Youth exit foster care with few of the practical and emotional skills required to face the challenges of young adulthood. SHP addresses this by providing a weekly two-hour transition support group, where youth learn these critically needed skills. Training topics include stress reduction, conflict resolution, domestic violence issues, identifying unhealthy influences, nutrition, setting boundaries with family members, beginning the process of forgiveness and addressing past abuse and neglect.

8. **Monthly Community Building Events:** All youth greatly benefit from community-building events that help to decrease the level of isolation youth experience during the transition from foster care to independence. Events provide youth with the opportunity to feel connected with other people, allowing them to experience healthier relationships. These types of experiential connections lead to a sense of belonging to a community, which contributes to better mental health.

9. **Move-In Assistance:** Participants receive a great deal of assistance when they move into their apartment. First Place pays for the cost of a rental truck, up to $75. In addition to having access to a rental truck, participants benefit from the assistance of members of the loan class, First Place staff, and the Youth Advisory Board on move-in day. We also encourage participants to involve their family and friends in the process.

10. **Move-In Stipend:** First Place awards a $200 move-in stipend to all participants who successfully complete Economic Literacy and move into a First Place apartment. The stipend may be used for necessities in the apartment, and will be paid directly to the store where the home supplies are purchased. Top priority necessities include a bed and bedding, kitchen utensils such as plates, glasses, flatware and pots and pans, and bathroom supplies, such as bath mat, shower curtain and towels.

11. **Monthly Food Stipend**: Many emancipated foster youth barely have enough money to pay their rent, let alone buy healthy food. Through the Supported Housing Program, youth participants receive a $50 grocery voucher to Albertson's or Safeway.

C. Population Served

First Place assists youth, ages 16 to 22, who are preparing to or have "aged out" from the foster care system and are either homeless or at-risk of homelessness. The constituency of First Place reflects the general foster care population in the Bay Area. Seventy-one percent of the youth served are African American, 15 percent Caucasian, 10 percent Hispanic and 4 percent other; youth served are equally split between girls and boys. One hundred percent of the youth served are very low income, with annual earnings less than 80 percent of the federal poverty level.

D. Program staff

First Place's Supported Housing program is composed of a five-member team led by SHP Manager Jennifer Leland. Ms. Leland holds a Masters in Family Therapy and has eight years experience working with at-risk youth, as well as extensive program management experience. Prior to joining the staff at First Place, Ms. Leland served as the Program Manager and Mental Health Specialist for DreamCatcher Youth Project for five years. Prior to working with DreamCatcher, Ms. Leland served as a Mental Health Resource Specialist for LaCheim, Inc. for two years. Ms. Leland has logged over 2,400 clinical hours and will receive her license in June 2005.

Other team members include three Youth Advocates and one Housing Specialist. All team members have, at a minimum, earned their bachelors degree in Psychology, Social Work or some other counseling field and have a minimum of four, and as much as ten years' prior experience working directly with at-risk youth. The demographic composition of the staff mirrors that of First Place's client population, and is: 60 percent African American, 20 percent Latino (bi-lingual), 20 percent Caucasian, 20 percent Lesbian, Gay, Bi-Sexual, Transgender or Questioning (LGBTQ), 60 percent female, and 40 percent male.

E. Program goals/objectives and how measured

The goals of the Supported Housing Program are to prevent homelessness and promote long-term self-sufficiency among former foster youth. First Place has had tremendous success in helping our youth achieve these outcomes. To date, First Place has provided safe, affordable housing to 132 youth through its Supported Housing Program. The following measures compare First Place youth with the general population of former foster youth 12 to 18 months after discharge from foster care:

- **Incarceration**: First Place youth are 6 times less likely to be arrested or incarcerated. (3% for First Place participants vs. 18% for general population of former foster youth)

- **Homelessness**: First Place youth are 6 times less likely to be homeless. (4% for First Place participants vs. 65% for general population of former foster youth)

- **Early Child Bearing**: First Place youth are 3 times less likely to give birth within 18 months after discharge from foster care. (10% for First Place participants vs. 30% for general population of former foster youth)

The First Place Fund For Youth proposal to the Pottruck Family Foundation
May 12, 2004

p. 8

- **Public Assistance Utilization**: First Place youth are 3 times less likely to receive GA or TANF. (10% for First Place participants vs. 32% for general population of former foster youth)

- **Employment**: First Place youth are 50 percent more likely to be employed. (90% for First Place participants vs. 49% for general population of former foster youth)

First Place anticipates that future youth will enjoy the same level of success that previous participants have experienced and will continue to track their outcomes through our comprehensive Program Information System. With the support of the Evelyn and Walter Haas Jr. Fund, First Place has recently developed and implemented an integrated Program Information System (PIS). Development of the Program Information System began in October 2002 and included input from youth participants, board members, staff members and our evaluation consultants, the Center for Applied Local Research.

The system is divided into 5 major areas. These include:

1. **Initial intake form**: This captures information about youth before they have received any program services. Information collected includes basic demographic data as well as "status" data such as employment, educational, and housing status.

2. **Supplemental intake form**: This form collects additional intake information that is sensitive in nature, such as sexual orientation. This information is collected within the first month of receiving program services.

3. **Weekly service report form**: This form is filled out each time a staff member provides a service to a youth participant. The services are measured in increments of 15 minutes and are divided into 23 main service areas. Forms are submitted for data input twice a week.

4. **Monthly Status Update Forms**: This form is generated by the Program Information System monthly and distributed to staff members based on the youth they assist in the programs, Staff members review the information on the form and update any changes in a youth's status. The purpose of this form is to ensure that First Place has the most current data on each participant and to note changes in employment, education, housing and health.

5. **Monthly Event Update Form**: This form provides a comprehensive list of events that a youth may experience in a given month, such as enrolling in school, obtaining a job, successfully applying for SSI, and graduating from high school.

The Program Information System provides a tremendous amount of information. On the most fundamental level, it informs First Place of exactly how many services each program is providing to youth, both by service units as well as by the total number of hours of service provided. It is also useful as a staff management tool. Program managers have set expectations with direct service staff as to how many hours of service they are to provide to youth weekly.

First Place is also working with CAL Research to conduct an outcome evaluation study to determine the long-term impact of the Supported Housing Program. The question we are trying to answer is: do First Place participants fare better in the long term than foster youth who did not participate in the program? To answer this important question, First Place is preparing to implement the second phase of the Program Information System. First Place will again contract with the Center for Applied Local

Research (CAL Research) to conduct an outcome evaluation study. Preliminary results of the study will be available in late summer, 2004.

F.   Organizational and Program Budget (current year and next)
   See pages 12 and 13

G.   Sources of support and fundraising plan for the Supported Housing Program

First Place's committed and pending sources of support are summarized in the subsequent sheet titled "First Place Fund for Youth: Proposed Revenue Sources FY 2005" found on page 14. To support our Supported Housing Program expansion campaign, First Place is pursuing three broad fundraising strategies, including increasing our individual donor contributions, leveraging the State Transitional Housing for Foster Youth Fund, and convening funding partners to apply for a Robert Wood Johnson Foundation (RWJF) Local Initiative Fund matching grant. Each of these three strategies is described in greater detail below.

- Increase our individual donor base

First Place's strategic plan calls for us to strengthen our funding position by increasing the total proportion of funds that are raised through individual donors, from 7 percent in FY 2004 to 12 percent in FY 2006. First Place is taking several steps to achieve this goal, including: adding six house-parties to our fundraising calendar, building on our annual fundraising event, and adding staff resource to focus on developing and executing a major donor strategy.

- Leverage the State Transitional Housing for Foster Youth Fund

First Place was instrumental in helping pass legislation in 2001 to set up the State Transitional Housing for Foster Youth Fund. Established by Assembly Bill 427, the legislation was the first-ever public commitment of resources in California for emancipated foster youth and set up a fund that could be used by counties to contract with agencies to provide housing and supportive services to foster youth up to the age of 21. Unfortunately, the structure of the legislation required counties to put forward a 60 percent match in order to leverage 40 percent from the state fund. Given the decline in the economy, no county was able to opt into the program. First Place worked closely with both San Francisco and Alameda counties to encourage the counties to implement the program. In Alameda County, created a unique partnership with the County and private foundations in which First Place privately fund-raised the county share of cost and signed it over to the County to draw down the additional state funds. In October 2003, Alameda County became the first in the state to access these resources. San Francisco County quickly followed in November of 2004 and to date, these are the only two counties statewide that have implemented the program. Nine other counties are currently developing plans to access these funds, and many are looking at the creative public-private partnership forged in Alameda County as a model.

While County officials are committed to trying to allocate General Fund dollars over time to serve as the match to the state fund, it will be several years before they are able to identify those resources in their budget. In the meantime, First Place is continuing to seek Foundation partners to support the housing program so that we may draw down additional funds through the State Transitional Housing for Foster Youth Fund.

The First Place Fund For Youth proposal to the Pottruck Family Foundation   p. 10
May 12, 2004

- <u>Convene foundation partners to apply for a Robert Wood Johnson Foundation (RWJF) Local Initiative Fund matching grant</u>

In addition to utilizing foundation dollars to leverage additional state resources, First Place is in the process of convening a group of foundation partners to support our application to the RWJF Local Initiative Fund. The RWJF Local Initiative Fund will provide up to a $500,000 dollar-for-dollar matching grant over several years to leverage local foundation dollars raised by an organization such as First Place. The Walter S. Johnson Foundation has agreed to act as the sponsoring local foundation for our application, and we are currently in conversation with several funders about supporting our application to the Local Initiative Fund. First Place will submit a letter of intent to the RWJF in July 2004 and would plan to use the funds to support the expansion of our Supported Housing Program over the next several years. We would be delighted if the Pottruck Family Foundation would consider signing on as a collaborating foundation.

H.   Management challenge

First Place's Supported Housing Program is gaining increasing recognition as a national model for supporting foster youth in making a healthy transition to independent adulthood. In the last six months, First Place has hosted interested parties from Boston, Seattle, Nevada and several counties around the state who are interested in replicating the work that First Place is doing.

While our current strategic plan calls for us to double our housing capacity locally, we are beginning to grapple with the question about what should come next for the agency, and how do we best replicate our model to have the greatest positive impact on former foster youth. Essentially, we are beginning to see two possible strategies emerge: replicate regionally, with aggressive expansion in the Bay Area, or respond to the requests of providers from other parts of the country and begin helping them build the infrastructure there. At this point, it doesn't seem feasible to do both at once. First Place will need to explore various replication models, from serving as a technical assistance agent, to "licensing" our model to opening satellite offices in other areas. First Place will look at this question closely as we begin to develop our next strategic plan, to take effect after June 2006. We will conduct a literature review of the different types of replication strategies, bring in experts to educate our Board, staff, youth and community partners about the trade-offs, and have high level discussions with all of these groups to discern how best to move forward to meet our goal of ending homelessness among all emancipated foster youth. The results of this work will be incorporated in our next strategic plan.

The First Place Fund for Youth
Organization and Supported Housing Program Budget
FY 2005

Expenses	Total FY 2005 Budget	SHP Program Budget FY 05
Operating Expenses	162,162	37,210
Program Expenses		
Community Building Events	10,100	4,600
Economic Literacy Wrkshp Materi	4,800	4,800
Credit Checks & Application Fees	1,280	1,080
Grocery Vouchers	32,880	29,880
Move-In Stipends	3,150	3,150
Moving Transportation	1,975	1,975
Repair, Maintenance, Security	10,000	10,000
Rental Payments for Youth	367,200	367,200
Homefinders/Rent Tech Subs	400	-
Youth Telephone	1,300	-
Youth Computer Maintnenance	3,000	-
Subscriptions - ETC	200	-
Emergency Utility Assistance	2,550	750
Peer Educator Stipends	2,520	720
Outreach Postage, Printing	1,400	500
Life Skills Workshop Materials	5,720	5,720
Healthy Snacks	1,200	-
Unrefunded Security Deposit Payments	2,500	2,500
Transportation (Youth)	4,800	2,400
Staff Mileage & Parking	17,700	7,200
Consultants	26,263	21,263
Childcare Stipends	6,460	6,460
Emancipation Spec Incentives	30,000	-
Program Evaluation	10,000	4,300
Misc Program Expense	-	-
Total Program Expenses	**547,398**	**474,498**
Personnel		
SHP Personnel	244,257	244,257
ETC Personnel	109,004	-
Admin Personnel	296,868	-
PR Taxes and Benefits	134,055	55,518
Total Personnel	**784,184**	**333,107**
Foster Youth Alliance Reimbursements		
ILSP Auxiliary	37,477	-
AC Foster Parents Association	1,000	-
Community Colleges Foundation	6,600	-
Total FYA Reimbursements	45,077	-
Total Expenses	**1,538,821**	**844,815**

The First Place Fund for Youth Proposal to the Pottruck Family Foundation

p. 13

The First Place Fund for Youth
Proposed Revenue Sources
FY 2005

Revenue Source FY 2005	Amount
Individual Contributions Committed	
Mail Solicitations	48,773
Sub-Total	48,773
Foundation Grants Committed	
United Way Foster Youth Initaitive	40,000
Evelyn & Walter Haas, Jr. Fund	12,469
Walter S. Johnson Foundation	50,000
David B. Gold Foundation	37,500
Ashoka Foundation	55,000
Morrison & Forester Foundation	100,000
Friend Family Foundation	4,000
Firedoll Foundation	15,000
West Davis & Bergard Foundation	4,000
Callison Foundation	4,000
Manhattan Institute Award	10,000
Stulsaft Foundation	23,630
Vodafone-US Foundation	10,000
EBCF	5,000
Sub-Total	355,599
Government Grants Committed	
City of Oakland CDBG	69,000
Oakland Fund for Children & Youth	240,000
Alameda County Office of Education	0
AC Social Services Agency THP+	0
SF DHS THP+ Grant	237,600
Sub-Total	552,600
Total Committed Funding	956,972
Foundation Grants Pending	
Pottruck Family Foundation	**20,000**
Bernard Osher Foundation	20,000
The California Wellness Foundation	75,000
East Bay Community Foundation	15,000
Richard & Rhoda Goldman Fund	100,000
Hearst Foundation	37,500
Stuart Foundation	75,000
Sub-Total	342,500
Government Grants Pending	
Alameda County Office of Education	100,000
Alameda County THP+	180,000
Sub-Total	280,000
Total Pending Grants	622,500
Total committed + pending	**1,579,472**

The First Place Fund for Youth Proposal to the Pottruck Family Foundation   p. 14

A Proposal From
New York Industrial Retention Network
on behalf of Zoning for Jobs Coalition
New York, New York

To
New York Foundation
New York, New York

Requested amount: $42,500; **Amount received:** $45,000

Funder's comments:

"Although New York Foundation does not require a specific format, we do accept the New York/New Jersey Area Common Application Form and recommend its use. This grantee had submitted their original proposal using the common application form, and this proposal for renewed funding is very similar.

"The summary portion of the proposal is extremely effective—this is important for our first 'read' of the proposal, which is really a skim. The bullets, pictures, and other formatting aids all help in breaking up the text. Images are always useful if they add something to the proposal.

"The budget was good because there were no indecipherable categories and no abbreviations; it is fully self-explanatory and well-organized. There were also some other helpful attachments, including a sheet with one-paragraph bios of the major players and a prioritized list of past achievements. The description of how the coalition is set up and the mentions of familiar groups were also useful. If you have connections it's good to say so—research the foundation's grantees, and note those that you know in the proposal.

"The need statement is strong, creating a sense of urgency without being strident. The proposal tells a story, but also includes hard facts—a nice mix of qualitative and quantitative data. The proposal's strongest feature is its internal logic, linking the problem directly to the strategy and the outcomes."

—Cynthia Freeman, Program Officer, New York Foundation

Notes:
The proposal was written using the New York/New Jersey Area Common Application Form. The complete proposal included the following attachments: operating budget, income summary, list of endorsing organizations, and biographies of key staff.
Proposal written by Adam Friedman and Jenifer Roth.

New York Foundation
New York/New Jersey Area
Common Application Form
Cover Sheet

Date: November 4, 2004

Name: Zoning for Jobs Coalition c/o New York Industrial Retention Network

Purpose of grant: Renewal of funding for a grassroots advocacy campaign to increase awareness of the continuing importance of blue-collar jobs and to create new zoning tools that promote job creation and reduce the risk of job losses threatened by recent City proposals to rezone some of the highest density job concentrations in New York City.

Address of Organization: 11 Park Place, N.Y. N.Y. 10007

Telephone: (212) 404-6990 ext. 11   Fax: (212) 404-6999 E-mail: afriedman@nyirn.org

Executive Director: Adam Friedman

Contact Person: Same

Is your organization an IRS 501[c](3) not-for-profit? Yes

Grant request: $42,500 (for one year)

Check one: General support _____

              Project support   __X__

Total organizational budget (for current year): $764,000

Dates covered by this budget: 7/1/04 - 6/31/05

Total project budget (if requesting project support) $189,000 (of which $15,000 would be passed through to community development organizations.)

Dates covered by project budget   7/1/04 – 6/31/05

Project name: Zoning for Jobs Initiative

1

I   PROPOSAL SUMMARY

The Zoning for Jobs coalition is a grassroots advocacy campaign to implement new
types of zoning and other land use strategies. These new land use tools would allow
development of new housing and offices but minimize displacement and job loss. They
would also encourage job creation by stabilizing the remaining industrial areas, thereby
encouraging reinvestment and improving the competitiveness of those companies.

The campaign was sparked by recent proposals by the Department of City Planning to
change the zoning in some of the densest industrial areas of New York City, threatening
thousands of well-paying blue-collar jobs and the stability of many moderate income
mixed residential/industrial neighborhoods. If enacted in their present form, these zoning
changes would represent a massive shift in economic resources away from working
people and communities, and to residents of luxury waterfront housing.

In addition, many communities have developed community-based plans that represent a
consensus for the future of their neighborhoods. These plans frequently call for the
development of both affordable housing and the retention of businesses that provide
jobs for residents. Implementation of these plans has been frustrated, in part, by the
absence of specific zoning tools that could be used to translate those plans into reality.

After its first year, the coalition includes more then 45 groups including city-wide
research, policy and advocacy organizations, local development and environmental
justice groups, and labor organizations, all of whom share an interest in preserving jobs
for local residents. (A list of the participants is attached.)

The campaign is coordinated by a steering group of representative organizations staffed
by the New York Industrial Retention Network (NYIRN). NYIRN is a city-wide
organization dedicated to promoting a diverse economy that provides employment and
entrepreneurial opportunities for all New Yorkers based on principles of economic and
environmental justice and sustainability. NYIRN is uniquely positioned to build alliances
between the diverse groups of stakeholders and has the technical expertise and
credibility to support both local organizing efforts and the City-wide campaign. Additional
technical assistance in mapping and the development of specific zoning proposals is
being provided by the Pratt Institute Center for Community and Environmental
Development (PICCED) and the Municipal Art Society (MAS).

NYIRN is subcontracting with the local development organizations in Sunset Park, East
Williamsburg and Greenpoint; communities which have a significant number of blue-
collar jobs. The local groups have expressed strong interest in using these new zoning
tools and are collaborating to galvanize resident and business support and to help define
their application.

2

II   NARRATIVE

A.   Background

1.   History and Mission: The members of the ZFJ Coalition share an interest in
retaining and creating blue-collar jobs. Their interest may have different origins such as
the Labor community's concern for job retention and job quality, the environmental
justice and community development communities' concern for resident employment and
health, and the economic development community's concern with stimulating business
growth and increasing business revenues, expanding the tax base and creating jobs.
However, the groups are united in their insight that the City's land use policies are
antiquated and undermine local economies, and in their desire to create new 21st
century land use tools.

The extraordinary volume of recent zoning changes that the City has proposed has
dramatically increased the threat of job losses and the gentrification of many
communities. These zoning changes represent a tremendous reallocation of land away
from low- and moderate-income workers and communities. The government's decision
to rezone and reallocate land should be reviewed and open to public debate at least as
much as are government programs and tax expenditures. Unfortunately, the zoning
process is often less public because it is cloaked in technical jargon and overshadowed
by budget decisions with more immediate, obvious impacts.

The threats posed by the re-zonings, however, have galvanized the organizations in the
Coalition to increase their advocacy efforts and launch this campaign. The campaign
seeks to increase awareness of the role that industrial sectors play in providing decent
jobs for less-skilled workers and in sustaining both local economies and moderate-
income neighborhoods, and to implement new zoning and financing tools to preserve
and create industrial jobs.

These new zoning tools and programs that have been developed over the past four
years and are included in a series of reports:
1. The Little Manufacturing That Could (NYIRN, 1999) assessed the economic impact
    and needs of the manufacturing sector based on a survey of 250 companies and
    recommended a variety of policy and programmatic changes to encourage the
    preservation and new development of industrial space;
2. Making It In New York (Municipal Art Society and Pratt Institute Center for
    Community and Environmental Development, 2001) contained a comprehensive set
    of recommendations for maintaining a healthy manufacturing sector, encouraging
    residential development in abandoned manufacturing areas, stabilizing mixed-use
    neighborhoods and promoting sustainable development; [1]
3. The Big Squeeze (Center for an Urban Future, 2000) documented the growing
    shortage of industrial space and included zoning and financing recommendations to
    preserve and expand the supply; and
4. Red Hook and Gowanus Reborn (SBLDC, 2002) told the story of the business
    owners in that area detailing their economic and other contributions to the community
    and the risks that various proposed land use changes would mean to their continued
    operations.

---

[1] PICCED, MAS and NYIRN have received funding from the Alfred P. Sloan Foundation to update and
provide additional details on the recommendations contained in the Making It report. This additional
analysis would support the proposed campaign seeking implementation of the recommendations.

3

2.   The Problem: For decades, City policies favored a narrow range of sectors that provide high-paying jobs to the most highly skilled and low paying jobs for everyone else. The City's over-dependence on too few industries has led to a drop in real wages during the 1990s for most New Yorkers and the growth in income disparity, which is greater in New York than any other city in the country. (See Chart 1.)

Chart 1: Growth In Wage Disparity

*Wages Have Dropped Or Been Stagnant
For Most New Yorkers Since 1989*

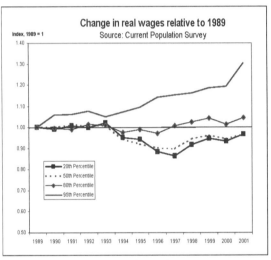

Source: Fiscal Policy Institute

A consensus has emerged that the City's economy must diversify and that City Hall has not provided adequate support for the industrial sector which generally provides the type of moderate- and middle-income wage jobs that the City has lost. Groups as diverse as the Real Estate Board, the trade association representing major properties owners in Manhattan, and the Center for an Urban Future, a progressive think tank, have both recently released reports that called for greater support for manufacturing.[2]

The City has begun to reassess its industrial policy. In a recent economic development speech to the Association for a Better New York, the Mayor made diversifying the City's economy one of three major economic objectives. The City has engaged a consulting firm to report on the status and needs of the manufacturing sector as a first step in developing a new City policy. Though the report has not yet officially been released, it confirmed that the shortage of affordable space and the instability of the real estate market were two of the biggest challenges threatening blue-collar jobs.

While the City appears open to revising its economic development programs, it continues to pursue land use strategies that place blue-collar jobs at risk. These ill-conceived policies are the result of the City's misunderstanding about the role of

---

[2] Zoning & Manufacturing: A Balanced Approach to New York City's Growth, July 2003, Real Estate Board of New York; Engine Failure, September 2003, Center for an Urban Future.

4

industrial jobs in neighborhood economies, reluctance to implement new land use tools necessary to address the problem and the lack of access to decision-makers on behalf of the workers, small business owners and residents.

City policy is based on the experience of industrial job losses that occurred between 1960 through the early 1990s and was due to competition from low-wage areas around the world. Furthermore, current public policy is built on the misperception that most manufacturing areas are underutilized and even abandoned, and that redevelopment does not pose any risks of job losses.

Today's remaining manufacturers, however, are viable and have developed strategies that allow them to compete despite New York's high costs. For example, they produce smaller runs that are uneconomical to produce abroad (such as theatrical lighting) or high quality design-oriented products that require the customers, designers and manufacturers to meet and check the goods while being produced (such as printing and high-end fashion). These manufacturers typically want to stay in New York near their customers, suppliers and workforce, but are being pushed out by City land use policy.

In addition, NYIRN has identified several sectors as presenting growth opportunities:
1. NYIRN launched Food From New York to help small ethnic food companies capitalize on growing national demand for specialty foods by crossing over from local to regional markets. Food manufacturing added 1,600 jobs between August 2002 and August 2003 and now employs approximately 14,400 people;
2. Green manufacturing is likely to expand as New York adopts high performance building standards which emphasize local sourcing; and
3. Entertainment related production, which includes wood and metal working, lighting and apparel, is likely to expand as large film studio projects begun years ago, such as Steiner Studios in the Brooklyn Navy Yard, now reach completion.

In fact, the City's study concluded that the number of industrial jobs is likely to increase. The industrial sector includes not only manufacturing but all sorts of warehousing, transportation and other blue-collar jobs that involve the movement or alteration of physical goods and generally must be located in Manufacturing Zones. Reducing the amount of Manufacturing Zoned land increases pressures on these sectors as well.

Maintaining high-quality industrial jobs is critical to the long-term health of the City's economy and stabilizing many neighborhood economies. More then 245,000 people hold blue-collar jobs in New York City. Census data reports that 84% of the production workforce is minority and 63% is immigrant. (See Chart 2.) The jobs tend to be heavily unionized, pay better and are more likely to provide health coverage then jobs in retailing or restaurants, other sectors frequently pointed to as alternative sources of employment for less-skilled workers.

Chart 2: Wage and Benefits Comparisons

Manufacturing Provides Decent JobsFor Less-Skilled Workers

Sectors	Avg. Wages	% w/ health Coverage
Manufacturing	$28,250	63%
Restaurants	$18,000	18%
Retailing	$17,965	38%

5

The City is now pursuing zoning changes in or adjacent to some of the densest concentrations of industrial jobs in New York City. These areas include the Garment Center in Manhattan, Greenpoint and Williamsburg in Brooklyn, and Jamaica in Queens and along Bruckner Boulevard in the Bronx. Even in industrial areas where re-zonings are not currently proposed -- such as Red Hook, Sunset Park, the East Williamsburg Industrial Park, and Chinatown -- industrial jobs are threatened by City policies that are encouraging real estate speculation which causes dis-investment and displacement. (See Map 1.)

The impact of these zoning changes and real estate pressures would be dramatic at both the city-wide and neighborhood levels. For example, in Sunset Park, Red Hook and North Brooklyn, areas now targeted for zoning or other land use changes, there are many census tracks where more than 25% of the residents are employed in industrial jobs. A major rezoning would not only cause a drop in the number of industrial jobs but would ripple through the local economy. (See Maps 2 and 3.)

Map 1: Density of Unionized Manufacturing And Pending or Proposed Zoning Changes

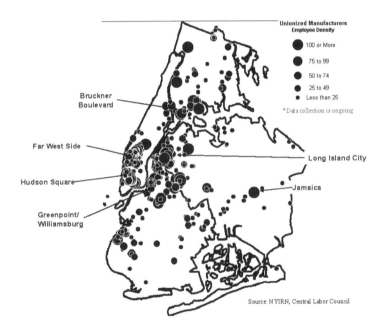

Source: NYIRN, Central Labor Council

6

**Maps 2 and 3: Location of Blue-Collar Jobs
And Resident Employment**

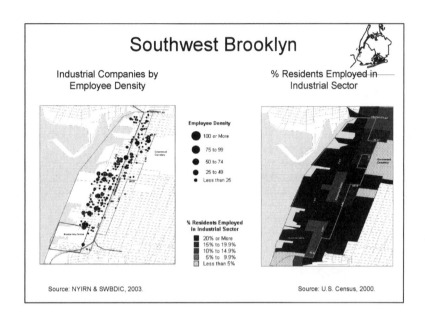

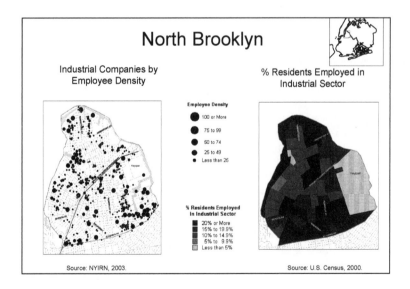

7

3.   Organizational Relationships

The Campaign is being organized by a growing coalition of citywide research and policy advocates, local development and environmental justice groups, and labor unions, all of whom share an interest in preserving jobs for local residents. The Executive Directors and/or key staff of these organizations meet regularly to discuss the program agenda, research needs and strategy for advocating the proposed changes. NYIRN provides staff support and is the fiscal conduit for funding for this coalition. NYIRN has subcontracted with some of the local groups on an as needed basis to provide local organizing in support of the Campaign. The steering committee includes:

◆   New York Industrial Retention Network
◆   Pratt Institute Center for Community and Economic Development
◆   Municipal Art Society
◆   Center for an Urban Future
◆   Brooklyn Economic Development Corporation
◆   Neighbors Against Garbage
◆   Southwest Brooklyn Local Development Corporation
◆   East Williamsburg Valley Industrial Development Corporation

A list of all the participants is attached.

4.   Organizational Background and Accomplishments

During its first year, ZFJ laid much of the foundation for a city-wide campaign while also working with community groups in areas that were particularly at risk. To date:
- More then 45 groups have endorsed the ZFJ agenda. ZFJ is increasingly focusing on strategic partnerships with groups that have city-wide leverage, such as Working Families Party and the Central Labor Council, as well as groups that have leverage in key districts such as UPROSE in Sunset Park and the East Williamsburg Valley Industrial Development Corp.;
- Two ZFJ proposals have been introduced as legislation into the City Council and a third is likely to be introduced in the near future;
- A core group of New York City Council supporters are organizing an "internal working" group to help push the ZFJ agenda;
- The Chair of the Land Use Committee has agreed to work with us on ZFJ legislation and have met repeatedly with land use staff to refine the legislation, and discuss various logistical and strategic issues;
- We have successfully positioned NYIRN as the "go to" organization for the media to learn about the issues and have generated significant favorable press. We have also trained more then 40 local groups and small business owners to prepare them as spokespeople;
- ZFJ organized a "lobby day" which included meetings with a dozen council members;
- ZFJ researched and published a study on the illegal conversion of 500,000 sq. ft. of manufacturing space inside an industrial park. The study opened the door at the relevant City agency and has led to discussions to improve enforcement;
- The Office of the Deputy Mayor has agreed to convene a working group to explore financing mechanisms to support more not-for-profit real estate development in the Garment Center. This work can be used as a model for other neighborhoods threatened by gentrification;
- We have developed high-quality promotional materials illustrating each of the ZFJ proposals;

8

- In Long Island City (Queens) we surveyed and mapped the companies and jobs, organized a campaign including postcards and testimony from the workers and owners, drafted guest editorials, organized tours for elected officials and the press, and successfully convinced the Community Board to adopt the ZFJ position on a proposed rezoning. This led to commitments from several council members on the ZFJ agenda;
- In Greenpoint and Williamsburg (Brooklyn), we provided very extensive support to the Community Board to analyze impact of the City proposals: We surveyed and mapped the companies, organized the owners, participated on the Community Board Task Force, and researched and drafted alternative zoning proposals. We continue to serve on this Task Force. The City's specific proposal has just been released and is beginning the approval process. This will require a very extensive amount of attention through the end of 2004 and first 6 months of 2005; and
- These successes were made possible as a result of more then $175,000 in foundation support. Supporters include; Independence Community Foundation, Bernard F. and Alva B. Gimbel Foundation, Mertz Gilmore Foundation, New York Community Trust, New York Foundation, and the Robert Sterling Clark Foundation.

B. Funding Request - Project and Scope of Services for 2004-2005:

The Coalition is seeking renewed funding for the ZFJ Campaign. As you can see from the above list of achievements, some of the ZFJ proposals and strategies have won the support of the Administration (such as proposals around non-profit development and better zoning enforcement) while others have gained more support from the City Council (such as the proposals for new zoning and conversion fees). ZFJ must therefore pursue carefully balanced strategies of working with the Administration on some proposals and continuing to push and advocate on others.

Some of the key elements include:
1. Collaborating with the City Council Working Group to advance the new zoning tools. This would include organizing hearings, surveying companies, drafting and revising text, mapping the location of companies and jobs and revising proposals based on those findings, and reaching out to additional council members to expand the coalition;
2. Demonstrating how city-wide tools will impact specific communities:
   - Identify projects and non-profit groups throughout the City that would benefit from funding under the ZFJ Conversion Fee proposal. We will then work with these constituencies to reach out to their elected representatives to encourage support.
   - Build consensus for a model for new industrial zoning in Brooklyn. The Borough President, the Brooklyn Economic Development Corporation and other major business and institutional leaders, several of whom are participants in the ZFJ Campaign, are collaborating on a comprehensive planning effort that includes the Initiative for a Competitive Inner City, a Harvard-based consulting practice. The collaboration has agreed to a planning process that will examine how to balance redevelopment and job retention issues, and to consider the ZFJ land use proposals in Brooklyn.
3. Maintaining public awareness and building support for the issue:
   - Enlist 1,000 small businesses to endorse the ZFJ campaign. We will use these endorsements for a press event and to keep elected officials focused on the issue;
   - Organize an event in collaboration with Working Families Party for elected officials to discuss ways to better link land use and job creation;

9

4. Collaborating with the Administration to research and draft the program to support more non-profit development. This includes participating in a working group to refine proposals for the Garment Center and the creation of the non-profit Fashion Space project;
5. Collaborating with the Administration to improve enforcement.
6. Organizing media tours and meeting with editorial boards;
7. Providing technical support to the Community Boards to analyze the impact of City proposals and help them develop their own alternative proposals. ZFJ has already spent considerable amount of resources in this effort. In the coming year, a significant amount of time will be spent on the proposed rezoning in Greenpoint/Williamsburg; and
8. Expanding support amongst the stakeholders for the policy agenda and develop a leadership council: While the list of organizations that has endorsed the ZFJ campaign has grown considerable over the past year, outreach should be ongoing. More community based groups, immigrants' rights organizations and labor unions need to be brought into the network.

C.   Evaluation:

This initiative can be evaluated based on its success in achieving both its substantive agenda and its process agenda. The substantive agenda includes the following policy initiatives:

1.   Creation of an industrial development fund to encourage the building of new industrial space. Revenue for this fund might be generated through a conversion fee on space that is converted from manufacturing or a special assessment on property in an area that is re-zoned from manufacturing to other uses;
2.   New zoning tools to both preserve existing manufacturing space by limiting its conversion to other uses as well as to stabilize mixed use neighborhoods;
3.   Technology and financing assistance to dramatically reduce energy consumption and raise environmental standards. This would both make manufacturing companies more cost competitive and better community partners by improving environmental conditions and reducing the need for new power plants in manufacturing areas which also tend to be environmental justice communities;
4.   Reform of the Board of Standards and Appeals which has become a vehicle to end-run zoning and community participation, and has contributed to the gentrification of industrial neighborhoods; and
5.   Changes made to City-initiated zoning proposals in response to community opposition where the City's plans do not adequately protect existing industrial jobs.

The process agenda against which this initiative might also be evaluated is the extent to which it unites community, labor and business organizations. This might be measured by:

1.   Number of groups endorsing the substantive initiatives;
2.   Number of groups actively engaged in advocacy activities, such as testifying and meeting with elected officials;
3.   Media coverage of substantive positions and issues; and
4.   Number of groups participating in ongoing leadership, strategy and committee discussions.

10

Expense Budget for Zoning For Jobs Initiative

Expense	2003-2004	Campaign	General Operating
Pers. Serv:			
Exec. Dir.	XXXXX	XXXXX	XXXXX
Dir. Research	XXXXX	XXXXX	XXXXX
Dep. Dir. Land Use	XXXXX	XXXXX	XXXXX
Director Operations	XXXXX	XXXXX	XXXXX
Dir. Communic: Made In NYC	XXXXX	XXXXX	XXXXX
Client Manager: RE	XXXXX	XXXXX	XXXXX
Client Manager: Food Industry	XXXXX	XXXXX	XXXXX
Office Mgr	XXXXX	XXXXX	XXXXX
PT Staff	XXXXX	XXXXX	XXXXX
Frng 19%	XXXXX	XXXXX	XXXXX
TOTAL PS	**$481,115**	**$136,393**	**$343,772**
		24%	
OTPS:			
Supplies	$8,000	$2,500	$5,500
Travel/Meeting	$3,000	$750	$2,250
Telephone	$10,000	$2,500	$7,500
Printing/Copy	$8,000	$2,000	$6,000
Postage	$6,000	$1,500	$4,500
Rent	$40,000	$10,000	$30,000
Internet	$2,040	$510	$1,530
Hosting	$1,860	$465	$1,395
Misc.	$7,000	$1,750	$5,250
Insurance	$5,500	$1,375	$4,125
Marketing Materials	$2,000	$0	$2,000
Computer Consultant	$12,000	$3,000	$9,000
Finance Charges	$6,000	$1,500	$4,500
Research & Reference Materials	$1,000	$375	$625
Payroll	$3,000	$750	$2,250
Computers	$5,000	$1,250	$3,750
Accounting/Bookkeeping	$13,000	$3,250	$9,750
Moving Costs	$15,000	$0	$15,000
Contingency	$15,000	$0	$15,000
Legal	$24,000	$0	$24,000
Indirect Sub Total OTPS	**$187,400**	**$33,475**	**$153,925**
Consultant	$2,000	$0	$2,000
Consultant Campaign	$20,000	$20,000	$0
Consultant LDCs	$40,000	$40,000	$0
Direct Sub Total OTPS	**$62,000**	**$60,000**	**$2,000**
Total	**$730,515**	**$229,868**	**$499,697**

A Proposal From
North Street Community Resource Center
Pescadero, California

To
Bella Vista Foundation
San Francisco, California

Requested amount: $42,724; **Amount received:** $25,000

Funder's comments:

"North Street Community Resource Center (NSCRC) did a good job of going from the general history of the project to the specifics in which Bella Vista Foundation is interested, thereby providing the context for the project. They also effectively described a very complicated set of collaborative relationships. Collaboration is a strength of a family resource center. While it's easy to confuse the reader by detailing all the relationships, NSCRC avoided that confusion.

"I was impressed that they covered all the information that Bella Vista requests—and we do request a lot of specific types of information in our guidelines—and still made the proposal logical, readable, and just over five pages. I was especially interested to learn that they are specifically focused on the attachment of the *toddlers* to their parents, because the attachment of the infants to parents in their client group is strong. This told me that not only are they well informed about child development, but that they are monitoring their clients very carefully, which is one sign of a high-quality program.

"I am always grateful when an organization provides all the information requested in and with the proposal. It saves me so much time, not having to follow up and request the missing pieces. The headings for each section make it easy to reread just the information I'm looking for as I prepare a one-page summary for my board members. It is also helpful that NSCRC provided easily accessible contact information: letterhead for the cover letter, and then an e-mail address *and* phone number right with the signature—it makes it a snap to call or e-mail to set up a site visit.

"What did they *not* do? They sent a budget for 2003–2004 instead of actual financial figures for that fiscal year, but the budget was easily readable and complete. NSCRC was not awarded the full amount requested only because it was their first request to the Bella Vista Foundation. The organization is eligible to reapply for funding next year."

—*Mary Gregory, Program Officer, Bella Vista Foundation*

Notes:
Proposal written by Jill Anderson, Consultant. Contributions to the proposal made by Karen Berke, Program Director, and Roxana Fine, Parent Involvement Project Coordinator.

North Street Community Resource Center
P.O Box 815 620 North Street   Pescadero, CA 94060
Phone 650-879-1691   FAX 650-879-0973

◆Family Literacy ◆ Family Support ◆ Health Services◆
◆ Community/Parent Participation and Leadership Development◆

January 11, 2005

Ms. Mary Gregory
Program Officer
Bella Vista Foundation
Presidio Building 1016; Suite 300
PO Box 29906
San Francisco, CA 94129

Dear Mary,

On behalf of the North Street Community Resource Center I am pleased to submit this proposal
to you for continuing funding for our Parent Involvement Project.

In this package you will find:
- Proposal to the Bella Vista Foundation with three Appendices
- North Street's Financial Statements for 2003-2004
- Project Budget
- Copy of Tax Exception Letter from School District

Please let me know if you need any further information or clarification of the materials sent to
you. We look forward to hearing back from you soon.

Sincerely,

Karen Berke
Executive Director
North Street Community Resource Center
karenb@southcoast.net

PROPOSAL TO THE BELLA VISTA FOUNDATION

The North Street Community Resource Center requests $42,724 in operating support for the Parent Involvement Project.

<u>**Organization Description:**</u>

The North Street Community Resource Center is a program of the South Coast Collaborative in Pescadero. The Center is housed on the campus of Pescadero Elementary School and serves as the hub of service delivery for families with children prenatal to eighteen years of age, as well as for other community members.

Pescadero is a small, rural community located in predominantly urban San Mateo County. Although just an hour in distance from the cities of San Francisco and San Jose, Pescadero seems a world away from these metropolitan areas. Isolated, insular and surrounded by large farms and ranches, Pescadero is the largest of the four communities collectively referred to as the "south coast". It has a population of 2500 people, including 300 children under the age of five. Most Pescadero residents are low-income, monolingual Spanish speaking families and single men, who work in the agricultural, floricultural, and service industries. More than sixty-four percent (64%) of the residents responding to a local 1999 survey, *Tu Voz Cuenta-Your Voice Counts*, reported incomes less than the national median family income and thirty-nine percent (39%) were below $15,000 per year.

In 1997, residents, organizations and human service providers came together to form the South Coast Collaborative (SCC). The mission of SCC is to build lasting, local services for the health, well-being, and life-long learning of the community. Between 1999 and 2003, SCC raised over 1.5 million dollars for the planning, development and delivery of local services to families and the community at large. This included one planning grant and two operational grants from the California State Department of Education's Healthy Start program, to serve students at both the elementary/middle school and the high school. This funding enabled the Collaborative to begin building the first local health, human, and educational support services for children and families in Pescadero. Today, SCC continues to be a model of effective collaboration between community members, civic leaders and service providers: a place where everyone can come together on behalf of the community and long-term sustainability of local services. The SCC Executive Committee meets monthly and currently consists of 13 members representing many segments of the community.

The North Street Community Resource Center was established in May of 2003, and was initially housed in a one-room office on the elementary school campus. At that time, the Center was staffed by two community workers, one funded by San Mateo County Human Services and one by the school district's Migrant Education Program. Services provided included Healthy Kids and MediCal registration, basic computer classes, information about county programs and services, translation and interpretation, and coordination of the monthly Second Harvest food distribution program. All other SCC staff members

1

were housed on the opposite side of campus. This included the SCC Manager, a secretary, an EL-Civics instructor, the Parent Involvement Project coordinator, two Healthy Start staff members, and a San Mateo County Human Services Agency Mental Health Counselor. While it was common for a family to be receiving services from several different SCC/Resource Center programs, it was a constant challenge for staff to coordinate and deliver services in a seamless, integrated manner.

In the summer of 2003, the South Coast Collaborative was awarded two significant grants: First Five of San Mateo County and Even Start California. Both of these funding streams enabled SCC to initiate or expand needed services. At this time, SCC was able to lease a second empty building from the School District, adjacent to the SCC office. This building became the new site for the Resource Center. In the late summer and fall of 2003, SCC, Resource Center and Healthy Start personnel came together to staff one organization, the North Street Community Resource Center.

With a current staff of fourteen, (ten who are bilingual), Resource Center programs and services now focus on four areas: 1) Family Literacy, 2) Health Services for Children and Adults, 3) Parent-Community Involvement and Leadership Development, and 4) Family Support Services. The specific programs of each focus area are listed below.

> 1) Family Literacy: Adult EL-Civics, Pescadero Even Start, North Street Tutoring and Mentoring Services, and Pescadero Preschool and Summer Kinder Transition Program.
>
> 2) Health Services for Children and Adults: School-based Mental Health, Care-Team, El Sol de Pescadero Medical Clinic/Sonrisas Dental Clinic, and San Mateo County Child Welfare Reform Initiative.
>
> 3) Parent-Community Involvement and Leadership Development: Lideres Communitarios de Pescadero, Quarterly "Family Events".
>
> 4) Family Support Services: Parent Involvement Project, Services Day, and Community Drop-In Center services (health benefits registration, classes, translation services, basic needs (food, clothing, etc.)

The Parent Involvement Project:

The Parent Involvement Project (PIP) began in January 2002 with one half-time staff member, through initial funding from the Lucile Packard Foundation for Children's Health. The primary purpose of PIP is to provide parent support and education for south coast families with children prenatal to age six. This is accomplished through home visiting, parenting classes, and parent-child play groups. While PIP services are available to all parents, the home visiting component of the program has focused primarily on low-income, monolingual Spanish-speaking parents in Pescadero.

2

One of the initial goals of PIP was to develop trust with local families with children prenatal to six, in order to build the foundation for future parent education services. Because of the nature of our rural area, many families live on remote ranches. To provide outreach in Pescadero often meant literally going out to locate mothers and their young children. Along with identifying these families who were interested in services, much of PIP's early work focused on helping families meet their basic survival needs. Families were assisted with diapers, baby wipes, food, clothing, and transportation to medical appointments.

For the parent education component of PIP, the Parents As Teachers model was chosen. Parents As Teachers (PAT) is a video-based home visiting curriculum which includes handouts on developmental issues and suggests play activities and books to share with children during visits. By June 2003, PIP had nine families enrolled who were receiving regular home visits and continued support with their resource needs. In addition, there was a waiting list of families needing services.

In July of 2003, PIP received two-year funding from First 5 San Mateo County for the continuation and expansion of the program. In the fall, a full-time community worker was added, allowing additional families to be served. In January of 2004, PIP received a one-year placement of an AmeriCorps member, again facilitating the expansion of services.

Currently, all three members of the PIP team are bilingual and bicultural. The program has 34 families enrolled, serving 59 adults and 50 children. Seventy-one percent (71%) of families include children under the age of three.

Services include monthly home visits using the PAT curriculum, parenting classes, a weekly parent and child group using the "Touchpoints" model, and "Las Platicas", an informal forum for sharing information and offering support, and ongoing assistance with medical appointments and basic needs. The "Touchponts" play group, co-facilitated with staff from the Half Moon Bay Library, is based on Dr. T. Barry Brazelton's work in helping parents appreciate and anticipate their child's developmental stages. "Las Platicas" topics have included Dental Hygiene, Discipline, and Home Financial Management, the latter facilitated by the Bank of America and attended by thirty parents.

PIP also participates in the Raising A Reader program,, providing the "Infant and Toddler" book bags to families. Another partner in PIP services has been the San Mateo County Sheriff's Department. Deputies provide car seat inspections every other month during the Second Harvest food distribution/Services Day. It is not unusual for families to be using very inadequate car seats. In these cases, the Sheriff's Department has been able to offer a new car seat to families at very low or no cost. Parents are also encouraged to enjoy the Quarterly Family Events, a no-cost, close-to-home way to join other parents and have fun with their children.

Mental health services and crisis intervention are available to PIP families through one of the school-based mental health clinicians housed at the Resource Center. This therapist

3

has specialized training in working with very young children and their families, and is available to make home visits, see families on campus, or see children in their preschool setting. PIP has initiated the above partnerships in order to bring more resources to the families served by the program. In this way, PIP is able to address each family's unique need for parent education, support, social services, and when needed, counseling.

Hypothesis:

If our program gives parents information about how their child learns, how they can support their child's development, and positive parenting practices, parents will use this information to support their child's healthy emotional development.

PIP believes that to be truly useful to parents, information must be shared within the context of a relationship with parents based on trust and respect and one which focuses on each family's strengths.

Measurable Objectives:

Home visiting services and parenting classes will be the two components of the program which will be used to evaluate progress toward the goal of improving parents' ability to support their children's emotional development.

1. Twenty-five (25) families with children age prenatal to three will receive monthly home visits by a PIP community worker who is trained as a Parents As Teachers parent educator. These visits will increase parents' understanding of child development, as measured by the PAT Parent's Knowledge Assessment. (See Appendix A) Families will complete the Knowledge Assessment at their second home visit. In October and November of 2005, families who have received at least six home visits will complete the Assessment again. 70% of families completing both assessments will show an increase on the score of the Knowledge Assessment.

2. Two 4 – 6 week parenting classes serving a total of 20 families will be offered. The curriculum to be used is Active Parents Today "1,2,3,4". This curriculum is designed for parents of children age four and younger. 70% of parents who complete the class will demonstrate an increased understanding of engaging cooperation, limit-setting and positive discipline strategies. To measure effectiveness of the class, parents will receive the pre-and post-test provided by Active Parents Today. (See Appendix B).

Risk Factors:

One-hundred percent (100%) of Pescadero families served by PIP are dealing with the core risk factors of low socioeconomic status, immigrant status, and minority status. Among the second tier risk factors, low maternal education is present in 97% of the families. Problematic maternal relationship history, child care by someone other than the

4

mother, and family composition issues are also common. In the third tier, low birth weight and psychophysiological problems have been present in a smaller percentage of families. Poor parenting practices, due to lack of information, is noted to some degree in nearly all PIP families prior to receiving services.

In spite of this constellation of concerns, PIP has not yet served a family in Pescadero where staff had reason to worry about the quality of attachment between mother and baby. Even when dealing with an array of economic and psychosocial hardships, the mothers served by PIP somehow manage to be responsive to their babies, reading their cues and meeting their emotional as well as their physical needs. During their child's infancy, parents enrolled in PIP have been very interested to learn about infant brain development and other relevant topics via the PAT videos, handouts, and play activities modeled by their home visitor.

Parents rely on home visits for support and a welcome break from the isolation of long days alone with their baby. However, it is in the second and third year of life, when children's normative drive for independence and mastery surface and make themselves known in virtually every interaction, that parents are challenged and often baffled by their child's behavior. At a recent Focus Group conducted by North Street and sponsored by the San Mateo County Childcare Coordinating Council, parents overwhelmingly responded that they would like to see more home visits, more parenting education and additional information about their children as they grow older. (See Appendix C for Focus Group Comments). By offering developmental information, PIP home visitors help parents make sense of each new phase of their child's development. But more than this, the PIP worker is always attuned to the relationship between parent and child and actively looks for ways to strengthen the bond that can become frayed during the toddler years.

Parenting classes are also a powerful way to support parents during these earliest years of their child's life. Parents not only have an opportunity to learn and practice skills to manage their child's behavior, but gain insight regarding how to manage their own *reactions* to their child's behavior in a way that honors parental authority while strengthening the parent-child relationship. For the vast majority of these parents, this is the first time they have been helped to consider alternatives to corporeal punishment. The most recent parenting class taught in Spanish, held during the lunch hour, was attended by fourteen parents, including four fathers.

5

Budget Request

We are requesting $42,724 from the Bella Vista Foundation for the continuation of PIP Services to 25 families, with children ages 0-3. Requested funding will be budgeted as follows from July 2005 – June 2006.

PIP Family Advocate Salary	XXXXX
PIP Family Advocate Estimated Benefits XXXXX	XXXXX
Travel/Mileage and Conferences	$ 2,500
Materials and Supplies for Program	$ 2,000
Communications	$ 500
Indirect/Administration Costs (8%)	$ 3,164
TOTAL BUDGET	**$42,724**

Conclusion

A grant from the Bella Vista Foundation for operating support would allow PIP services to continue at the current level. AmeriCorps funding created an opportunity to add a third PIP worker and serve additional families. The need is clearly present to retain this position. It is anticipated that the individual who has been with the program via AmeriCorps will remain with PIP, thus ensuring continuity for families and children. We welcome the opportunity to talk further with the Bella Vista Foundation about the Parent Involvement Project and the possibility of working together on behalf of Pescadero families.

Sincerely,

Karen Berke
Executive Director
North Street Community Resource Center
Pescadero, CA 94060
650-879-1691 X205
karenb@southcoast.net

6

PARENT INVOLVEMENT PROJECT
BUDGET FOR 2005-2006
July 2005 – June 2006

Revenue:

Lucile Packard Foundation for Children's Health	$55,000 (confirmed)
Bella Vista Foundation	$42,724 (pending)
First 5 San Mateo County	$18,000 (carryover confirmed)
Other Funding TBD	$60,000
Americorp Member	In kind Contribution
TOTAL	**$175,724**

Expenses:

Salary and Benefits	$137,000
Materials and Supplies	$ 10,000
Training and Conferences	$ 8,724
Travel Costs	$ 5,000
Rent	$ 2,000
Administrative/Indirect Cost	$ 13,000
TOTAL	**$175,724**

A Proposal From
Rome Area History Museum
Rome, Georgia

To
Georgia Humanities Council
Atlanta, Georgia

Requested amount: $6,200; **Amount received:** $6,200

Funder's comments:

"The mission of the Georgia Humanities Council (GHC) is to build community, character, and citizenship through humanities education. In our competitive grantmaking program, the GHC provides support for educational programs that are developed and carried out in local communities. Our goal is to support projects that bring Georgians together in learning and discussion, creating a portfolio of GHC-funded programs and projects that promote awareness of diverse values, experiences, traditions and cultures, particularly of Georgia's people, past and present. We grant funds to nonprofit organizations, and their programs must serve the people of Georgia.

"The Rome Area History Museum requested funds for 'World War II: The Home Front,' to conduct an oral history project and curate a temporary exhibit about home life in Floyd County during World War II. Transcriptions of the interviews were to be placed in the museum's archives and be available on the museum's Web site. A public program including a lecture and discussion was planned to coincide with the opening of the exhibit.

"As a whole, this proposal has everything that the GHC looks for in a grant application. The narrative is well-written and to the point, and the budget is very reasonable. They followed our grant guidelines to a 'T'. This local history museum has a solid staff and a strong partnership with the community. The proposal possessed many attributes the GHC looks for in humanities programming. We like the fact that this project has multiple levels. It consists of conducting an oral history project, creating an exhibit, conducting a public program, moving the exhibit to other organizations, and creating an archive of the oral history interviews. This project will have a long life after the grant period is over.

"Various aspects of the program appealed to us in particular: Rome Area History Museum will work within the community to implement all facets of the program. Gifted students from Rome City Schools will work with the local Marine Corps League to interview World War II veterans and other elderly residents to find out what life was like at home during this time. Libraries, schools, and other organizations will be contacted to house the traveling museum once the installation leaves the Rome Area History Museum. The museum is providing an excellent opportunity for young people to work with the elderly population of this community. By providing so may different types of programming, citizens of all ages from the city of Rome and from Floyd County will be served through this project."

—Sara Salley, (former) Program Officer, Georgia Humanities Council

Notes:
The proposal was written using the Georgia Humanities Council grant application cover sheet and guidelines.
Proposal written by Katie Anderson, Museum Director.

GEORGIA
HUMANITIES
COUNCIL

Grant Application Cover Sheet

1. Title of Project World War II: The Home Front Exhibit and Oral History Collection Project	

2. Name and Address of Applicant Organization Rome Area History Museum	3. GHC Grant Request $ 6,200

4. Project Director

a. Name and Mailing Address	b. Title/Position
Last: Anderson First: Katie Middle Inital	Museum Director
Street Address: 305 Broad St.	c. Telephone Number (include Area Code and Ext.)
City: Rome State: GA Zip Code: 30161	706-235-8051

5. Fiscal Agent*

Katie Anderson	Museum Director	706-235-8051
Name	Title/Position	Telephone

6. Project Dates

Begin: April 1 2004 Month Day Year	End: June 1 2005 Month Day Year

7. Proposed Grant Period*

Begin: April 1 2004 Month Day Year	End: April 1 2005 Month Day Year

8. U.S. Congressional District Where Organization is Located 011	9. Georgia Senate District 052
10. Georgia House District 013	11. County Floyd

Type of Grant (circle one)   Special Program   (Public Program)   Teacher Enrichment   Planning/Consultant

* The fiscal agent is the member of your organization responsible for handling the payments and receivables for your organization, ie. an accountant, finance officer, grants and contracts officer, or treasurer.

*The grant period is the time in which you will spend money for the grant and generate cost-share. Grant periods may be no longer than a twelve month period of time.

Mail or deliver completed applications to:
Georgia Humanities Council
50 Hurt Plaza, SE, Suite 595
Atlanta, Georgia 30303-2915
Call the Council at 404/523-6220 if you need assistance.

Certifications

The applicant certifies that the conduct of this program will be in compliance with the provisions set forth by the National Foundation on the Arts and Humanities Act of 1965 (as amended) and the policies of the Georgia Humanities Council.

1. Certification Regarding the Nondiscrimination Statutes. The applicant certifies that it will comply with the following nondiscrimination statutes and their implementing regulations:

(a) Title VI of the Civil Rights Act of 1964 (42 U. S. C. 200d et. seq.), which provides that no person in the United States shall, on the ground of race, color, or national origin, be excluded from participation in, be denied the benefits of, or be otherwise subjected to discrimination under any program or activity for which the applicant received federal financial assistance

(b) Section 504 of the Rehabilitation Act of 1973, as amended (29 U. S.C. 794), which prohibits discrimination on the basis of handicap in programs and activities receiving federal financial assistance;

(c) Title IX of the Educational Amendments of 1972, as amended (20 U. S. C. 1681et seq.), which prohibits discrimination on the basis of sex in education programs and activities receiving federal financial assistance; and

(d) the Age Discrimination Act of 1975, as amended (42 U. S. C. 6101 et seq.), which prohibits discrimination on the basis of age in programs and activities receiving federal financial assistance, except that actions which reasonably take age into account as a factor necessary for the normal operation or achievement of any statutory objective of the project or activity shall not violate this statute.

2. Certification Regarding Debarment, Suspension, Ineligibility and Voluntary Exclusion—Lower Tier Covered Transactions (45 CFR 1169)

(a) The prospective lower tier participant (applicant) certifies, by submission of this application for a grant, that neither it nor its principals is presently debarred, suspended, proposed for debarment, declared ineligible, or voluntarily excluded from participation in this transaction by any federal department or agency.

(b) Where the prospective lower tier participant (applicant) is unable to certify to any of the statements in the certification, such prospective participant will attach an explanation to this application for a grant.

Signed: _Bernard N. Neal_   Date: _3-31-04_
(Signature of Authorizing Official)*

Name (Please Print): Bernard Neal

Title: Chairman and President

Telephone Number: 706-291-4488

Street Address: 338 West 3rd St.

City, State, Zip: Rome, GA 30165

* The Authorizing Official is the person within an organization that has the authority to bind the organization to a contract. Some examples are the Chair of the Board, the President, an Executive Director, a Vice President or Principal.

Mail or deliver completed applications to:
Georgia Humanities Council
50 Hurt Plaza, SE, Suite 595
Atlanta, Georgia 30303-2915
Call the Council at 404/523-6220 if you need assistance.

World War II: The Home Front
A public program grant proposal by the ROME AREA HISTORY MUSEUM

Proposed project and its impact

The generation coming of age during World War II has been called the "Greatest Generation." They certainly dealt with much adversity during this transformational time in our Nation's history. While the general public may be most familiar with war stories and the bravery of servicemen abroad, there are many stories from home that also need to be told. We are requesting funds to conduct an oral history project and develop a temporary exhibit about life in Floyd County during World War II. The sad fact is that we are losing these individuals and their stories at a rapid rate.

The people of Floyd County have a long and proud tradition of supporting their country in times of need. In February 2003, the ROME AREA HISTORY MUSEUM hosted a reunion of local Iwo Jima veterans. Eleven men came to the event with their families. There are also several veteran survivors of Pearl Harbor in this community. We need to record the experiences of these and other war heroes. Just as importantly, we need to record the experiences of the people at home picking cotton, working in the mills, rolling bandages, and taking care of the homes and businesses while so many men went off to war. Once we have these recordings they can be made available to the general public through our archive and online.

The Rome City Schools system has requested our assistance in developing an oral history program with their gifted students. The goal is to help the students learn history but also make a lasting connection with history by talking to the people who lived through it. The local Marine Corps League will work with the students to help prompt further discussion with the interviewees. The League will also help us contact veterans and civilians to interview. This provides a growth opportunity for all involved, not just the students. Information from the interviews will guide us in the development of the exhibit.

This project consists of the following five components:

1. Temporary exhibit - *World War II: The Home Front*
    We will produce an exhibit of ten panels and several cases of artifacts. We will create lightweight, portable Sentra panels that can be reused, and sent out as a traveling exhibit. The design work will be done in-house. The panel fabrication will be outsourced. Panel topics will include:

    - Eight local textile mills produced canvas, gauze, rayon, tire cord, and broadcloth used for uniforms, tents, bandages, parachutes, belts, and tires. All these products furthered the war effort and many of the mills received Army-Navy E-Awards for their production.

    - Women's roles: from volunteering with the Red Cross rolling bandages to working the "men's jobs" at the mills.

    - Battey Hospital, named after a renowned Civil War surgeon, was built by the Army for wounded soldiers. It also housed German prisoners of war.

- Forms of communication with the troops. Young men created elaborate codes before going to war to let their families know where they were.

- Rationing: food, gas, shoes, metal, etc. Local scout troops collected aluminum and other metals to be used by the military.

- From a child's eye. What was it like to grow up in these times? One local man remembers being an "observer" and watching for enemy planes with his toy binoculars.

- A helping hand. Sears had a program allowing workers to spend a day helping local farmers pick cotton because they didn't have enough family members left at home during the war. What other programs offered assistance?

Artifacts and images will come from our permanent collection as well as loans from local individuals and other institutions. The exhibit will be housed in the ROME AREA HISTORY MUSEUM from December 3, 2004 through June 1, 2005. (We expect to serve approximately 3,000 people in this six month period.)

2. Exhibit opening program.
On opening night of *World War II: The Home Front*, we will have a special guest speaker to be determined. This speaker will talk about changes in American society brought on by World War II. This will put the locally-focused exhibit into a broader context. (We expect to serve approximately 75 people at this event.)

3. Oral histories and documentation of the lives of these men and women.
We plan to conduct at least 25 interviews using gifted students from Rome City Schools and Marine Corps League volunteers. These interviews will be conducted simultaneously at a special event. We can add more dates as needed depending on the responsiveness of the senior citizens in the community. We will team one student with one Marine. The student will ask predetermined questions but the Marine can step in to help flesh out a story. We will then have the tapes transcribed.

The transcriptions will be made available on our website as well as in our archives. The tapes will be stored in the ROME AREA HISTORY MUSEUM archives and will be available to the public. These tapes, transcripts, and documents will also be submitted to the Veterans History Project at the Library of Congress. (We expect to serve approximately 75 people at this event. However the tapes and transcriptions will be available for innumerable people to access for years to come.)

4. Series of discussions on World War II home life at various community groups.
We will visit 10 or more churches, senior centers, and other community groups to discuss the exhibit topics. We will ask attendees to share their experiences. Attendees will also be invited to loan or donate relevant artifacts or documents. (We expect to serve 200 people in these groups.)

5.   <u>Traveling exhibit</u>.
     After the run of the temporary exhibit in the MUSEUM, the exhibit panels will be loaned to local libraries, schools (focusing on the schools that have low attendance at the museum), and other institutions for a month at a time free of charge. We will reach a wider audience by sending the exhibit out to these varied institutions. (The number of people served will depend entirely on the location, traffic and length of stay at each venue.)

Audience development

We typically use a variety of strategies to promote our exhibits and programs. We will conduct a two pronged promotional campaign. One prong will target the general public. The other will target special audiences: senior citizens (age 70 and higher to be old enough to remember the war), military families, churches and school groups.

<u>To market to the general public we will:</u>

- Issue press releases to media outlets (radio, newspaper, and special publications in Rome, northwest Georgia, the Centre, Alabama area, Marietta, Atlanta, and Chattanooga) and local organizations (senior centers, schools, colleges, Chamber of Commerce, and visitor centers).
- Post information on our website and on the websites of local organizations and travel information sites.
- Distribute flyers about the exhibit and events at area libraries, hotels, visitor centers, and other local cultural institutions.
- Work with local radio talk show hosts and cable television show hosts to produce extended public service announcements featuring interviews with oral history participants (+12,000 listeners/viewers).
- Include information about the exhibit and programs in our quarterly newsletter *The Window* which goes out to over 900 museum supporters.

<u>To market to special audiences we will:</u>

- Work closely with activity directors at senior centers, with representatives from various military support groups, and with curriculum directors at the local school systems.
- Hang posters at the local American Legion posts, VFW posts, recruiting stations, and senior centers throughout the greater Rome area.
- Work with the Director of Gifted Education at Rome City Schools to involve students with the oral history program and to get the word out to other classes about the exhibit at the museum.
- Work with local church leaders to promote the exhibit and programs through their bulletins. The talks we conduct with church groups and other community organizations will help us gather information but will also be an opportunity to promote the exhibit and programs.
- Send special invitations for the exhibit opening to the students, Marines, and interviewees who participate in the oral history project.

Evaluation

Several types of informal evaluation will be used. During the exhibit a comment book will be available for visitors to give feedback. A simple survey will be handed out at the opening night program and at the discussion groups. Groups that use our traveling exhibit will be asked to share feedback they received at their institution with us. These evaluations will help us fine tune the discussion groups. They will also help us be more effective in creating future programs and exhibits.

Schedule

April 2004	Begin development of exhibit; create storyline; begin selection of artifacts and images from our collection; spread the word in the community that we are looking for artifacts, images, and interview subjects from WWII; locate speaker for opening night of exhibit.
July 2004	Begin promotional campaign for exhibit and programs; begin conducting discussion groups
August 2004	Continue research; continue promotional efforts; locate and arrange for locals over age of 70 to participate in the oral history project; continue discussion groups
September 2004	Host the oral history event; transcribe tapes; continue promotional efforts; continue discussion groups
October 2004	Incorporate information from oral histories into exhibit text; finalize text; finalize selection of graphics; begin design work on panels; continue promotional efforts.
November 2004	Finalize selection of artifacts; have 10 panels designed and produced; continue promotional efforts
December 1-3, 2004	Install exhibit; opening night event
June 1, 2005	Exhibit closes at ROME AREA HISTORY MUSEUM
June 2005	Exhibit panels loaned out to various institutions

Follow-up activities

After the exhibit closes, all of the images, oral histories, and research materials will be available to the public through the MUSEUM'S archives. The oral history transcripts and some images will also be available on our website. The exhibit panels will be available as a traveling exhibit well after the MUSEUM exhibit closes. We also plan to develop a World War II traveling trunk based on the research for this exhibit. It would contain photos, ration books, letters, ads, news clippings, and artifacts as well as activities and lesson plans for grades 5 and 8 complying with current Georgia State

Quality Core Curriculum guidelines. We would like to make this trunk available to local schools beginning in the fall of 2005.

Biographical sketches

RAHM currently has only one paid staff person, the Museum Director. RAHM will work closely with several community members to coordinate and implement this exhibit and programs.

Katie Anderson, the project director, is the Museum Director at the ROME AREA HISTORY MUSEUM. She has developed and installed two temporary and five permanent exhibits since becoming the Director in January 2003. Last year she coordinated 16 oral history interviews in one day with the help of local college students and volunteers. The subjects were former players from the Northwest Georgia Textile League from the 1930s and 40s. Thus began the ROME AREA HISTORY MUSEUM'S commitment to preserving the stories of this region's people through oral history interviews. She holds a B.A. in anthropology from Georgia State University and a M.A. in museum science from Texas Tech University.

Donna Hibbets has been teaching for 30 years. Currently she works with gifted students in the Rome City Schools system as the Director of Title I and Gifted Education. Donna has been excited about the opportunity for students to learn history first hand from veterans and their families.

Johnny Davis is a retired banker and former Marine from Rome. He is active in the Marine Corps League and has been a steadfast volunteer at the ROME AREA HISTORY MUSEUM. He will help us contact veterans to conduct interviews and to be interviewed.

Jessica Roy is currently an undergraduate history student at Berry College. She plans to pursue a graduate degree in public history. She will intern with the MUSEUM during the fall of 2004. The internship will focus on conducting research for the *World War II: The Home Front* exhibit.

Tammy Bryant, Special Populations Coordinator for Rome-Floyd Parks and Recreation Department will be our contact for the senior centers in Floyd County.

Al Castillo, local World War II historian, will coordinate discussion groups and promotional efforts with the various local veterans groups.

Rev. Warren Jones, retired minister and local historian, will assist with the coordination of discussion groups and promotional efforts at the local churches.

Dennis Abney, Curriculum Director Floyd County BOE, will assist with promotional efforts in the Floyd County Schools system.

Glen Kyle, Curator of Military History at the Atlanta History Center, will serve as a content advisor. He has a lifelong appreciation for our men and women who have served in uniform. A native of Georgia, Glen has spent the last two years developing a World War II exhibit and developing the AHC's participation with the Veterans History Project.

World War II: The Home Front
Exhibit and Oral History Public Program
Proposal submitted by the ROME AREA HISTORY MUSEUM

Budget

	GHC Funds	RAHM cost-share	Total
Staff			
Katie Anderson, project director		$ 7,000	
Jessica Roy, part-time intern fall 2004	$1,200		
Exhibit fabrication	$ 3,500		
Transcription of interview tapes (25 - 90 minute tapes @ $30/tape)	$ 750		
Honorarium for speaker at exhibit opening night program	$ 100		
Marketing and promotion			
Posters and flyers for exhibit and opening night program	$ 500		
Marketing of traveling exhibit to community groups (including postage)	$ 150		
Printing and postage for *The Window* newsletter promoting the exhibit and programs		$ 600	
Office space and equipment use: (computers, tape recorders, telephone, copier, office supplies, tapes, storage boxes) for 1year		$ 4,250	
TOTALS	$ 6,200	$ 11,850	$ 18,050

Exhibit design will be performed in-house by project director. Exhibit fabrication includes $500 for easels to hold the panels when the exhibit travels to other institutions. Not included in this budget are the dozens of volunteer hours that will go into this project.

The Sex Workers Project at the Urban Justice Center

New York, New York

To

New York Foundation

New York, New York

Requested amount: $45,000; **Amount received:** $47,500

Funder's comments:

"Since this proposal is for a small program, the Sex Workers Project, operating within a large organization, the project description becomes very important because the project is, in a sense, in competition with the larger organization in terms of funding. Here the project description is quite strong, first laying out the issues and then giving specifics for each one.

"The proposal is most effective, however, when it begins picking apart the different threads of need inherent to this population. A level of complication is unearthed, and the reader is educated about the problem.

"Although New York Foundation does not require a specific format, we do accept the New York/New Jersey Area Common Application Form and recommend its use. The proposal's format is reader-friendly, using bolding and underlining to distinguish sub-headings. In the budget, the footnotes explain line items, and all acronyms are fully explained."

—*Cynthia Freeman, Program Officer, New York Foundation*

Notes:

The proposal was written using the New York/New Jersey Area Common Application Form. The complete proposal included the following attachments: current operating budget and list of foundation supporters.

Proposal written by Juhu Thukral, Director, and Matt Isaac, Fundraising Consultant.

COVER SHEET

Please feel free to make copies
of this form or generate this
one-page cover sheet on your
computer.

Date of application: _July 28, 2003_

Name of organization to which grant would be paid.
Please list exact legal name.

URBAN JUSTICE CENTER

Purpose of grant (one sentence): _Renewal funding for the Sex_
Workers Project, which advocates on behalf of sex workers
in a context of human rights and harm reduction.

Address of organization: _666 Broadway, 10th Fl._
New York, NY 10012

Telephone number: _646/602.5690_

Executive director: _Douglas Lasdon_

Contact person and title (if not executive director):

Juhu Thukral, Director, Sex Workers Project

Is your organization an IRS 501(c)(3) not-for-profit? ☒ yes   ☐ no

If no, please explain: _____

Grant request: $ _45,000_

Check one: ☐ General support   ☒ Project support

Total organizational budget (for current year): $ _4,543,872_

Dates covered by this budget (mo/day/year): _July 1, 2003 - June 30, 2004_

Total project budget (if requesting project support): $ _95,000_

Dates covered by project budget (mo/day/year): _November 1, 2003 - October 31, 2004_

Project name (if applicable): _Sex Workers Project_

2

PROPOSAL SUMMARY: Sex Workers Project at the Urban Justice Center

This proposal seeks renewal funding ($45,000) for the third year of the **Sex Workers Project (SWP)** at the Urban Justice Center (UJC) in New York City. UJC is a not-for-profit agency which currently maintains nine distinct projects that work toward eradication of different social challenges that face the urban poor. UJC has been described as "an incubator for progressive ideas and projects."

The overarching mission of the SWP is to advocate for sex workers, former sex workers, and those who are profiled or at risk for engaging in sex work, including victims of trafficking, within a context of harm reduction and human rights. The SWP advocates for these sex workers within a context of worker's rights and economic justice, seeking to improve working conditions by minimizing the violence and harassment women may encounter. The SWP's goals also include normalizing the immigration status of undocumented trafficking victims. In pursuit of its mission, the SWP provides individual and systemic advocacy to sex workers in a variety of areas that present core problems presented below, and conducts research that will better inform such advocacy.

Sex workers experience identifiable problems in the following areas: criminal justice system; child welfare system; immigration and other problems associated with having been illegally trafficked into the country; and violence committed against them.

In order to meet the community's special needs, SWP staff engage in legal advocacy and outreach through collaboration with agencies that provide social services to sex workers. Because legal advocacy for sex workers in New York City is uncharted, the SWP conducts research in areas that affect sex workers, including criminal justice, immigration and legal needs. The SWP also trains community-based organizations on legal issues for sex workers and trafficking victims, and engages in policy advocacy.

Outcomes that the SWP hopes to achieve are: establishing outreach, training, and legal referral relationships with community-based organizations; conducting research on sex workers in New York City; and using knowledge gained from individual advocacy and research to affect policies relating to sex workers and victims of trafficking.

IIA. Background: Urban Justice Center and the Sex Workers Project: This proposal seeks renewed funding in the amount of $45,000 from the New York Foundation for the **Sex Workers Project (SWP)** at the **Urban Justice Center (UJC)** in New York City. UJC is a not-for-profit agency founded in 1984 with a mission to work toward eradication of a variety of social challenges encountered by the urban poor by providing legal aid to disadvantaged New Yorkers. UJC has grown from one project with a staff of one serving homeless adults in 1984 to an organization that currently has nine distinct programs with 66 full-time and 5 part-time staff members helping thousands of poor and disenfranchised people with an array of legal problems. Each year, UJC provides free assistance to nearly 20,000 needy New Yorkers.

UJC has been described as "an incubator for progressive ideas and projects"[1] and has received funding for and produced important results through innovative programs that serve traditionally underrepresented populations in New York City, both through one-on-one direct representation and through systematic advocacy and impact litigation that grows from our direct legal services. Specifically, UJC's projects engage in advocacy for the following populations: sex workers; homeless adults and families; victims of domestic violence; gay, lesbian, and transgender youth; persons affected by mentally illness; street vendors; and substance abusers.

UJC's recent accomplishments include representing a class of welfare recipients in a lawsuit seeking to preserve access to education and training necessary to enable them to transition from welfare to economic security; releasing the report, *Revolving Door*, which documents the conditions of street-based sex workers in New York City; settled *Brad H. v. City of New York*, winning a major victory requiring New York City jails to plan ongoing treatment for thousands of mentally ill inmates prior to release; and assisting over 100 youth through our Foster Care to Independence Program, which helps young adults with housing, education and employment, and provides individual and group counseling.

IIB. Funding Request

Primary Purpose and Need Addressed: This proposal is requesting a renewal grant from the New York Foundation in the amount of $45,000 to support the third year of activities for the SWP.

The overarching mission of the SWP is to advocate for sex workers, former sex workers, and those who are profiled or at risk for engaging in sex work, including victims of human trafficking, within a context of harm reduction and human rights. Harm reduction is a pragmatic and humanistic approach to diminishing the individual and social harms associated with sex work, placing an emphasis on human rights, common sense, and public health. We provide assistance to those that want to leave "the life," but also acknowledge that not every person is ready to leave. For those who are not ready to leave, the SWP's goals are to reduce the harm and danger associated with sex work. The SWP advocates for these sex workers within a context of worker's rights and economic justice, seeking to improve working conditions by minimizing the violence and harassment women may encounter. The SWP's goals also include normalizing the immigration status of undocumented trafficking victims. In pursuit of its mission, the SWP provides individual and systemic advocacy to sex workers in areas that present core problems presented below, and conducts research that informs our advocacy.

Sex workers constitute a population with special needs: they often encounter violence and harassment from customers, pimps and the police; those who want help to leave "the life" do not encounter much public assistance; and women who have been illegally trafficked and forced to become sex workers are fearful and unaware of how to leave their situation. Because their circumstances often makes them particularly vulnerable with few places to turn for assistance, and because they engage in illegal activity, sex workers' rights are often violated. However, engaging in illegal activity should not deprive people of their civil rights. Harsh stigmatizing

---

[1] Joyce Wadler, *Ferreting Out the Legal Rights of the Poor*, N.Y. TIMES, Oct. 31, 2000

and criminalization marginalizes sex workers, and prevents this population from seeking and receiving help. Prior to the founding of the SWP in 2001, there were no agencies in New York or elsewhere that focused solely on the provision of legal services and advocacy to this vulnerable population.

Sex workers experience identifiable problems in the following areas: criminal justice system; child welfare system; immigration and other problems associated with having been illegally trafficked into the country; and violence committed against them. These problems are described in detail in the paragraphs below.

Problems with the Criminal Justice System: Sex workers experience a variety of problems with police and the criminal justice system. There were 6,207 arrests for prostitution in New York City in 2000.[2] Beyond arrests and ticketing, the criminal justice system provides few alternatives for sex workers. Prostitutes who work on the street are particularly vulnerable since they play the most visible role in the industry.

In addition to being arrested, sex workers are often harassed by police. SWP clients and people whom the staff meet on outreach complain that police harassment of street prostitutes is pervasive. Prostitutes have been forced to strip on the street for "searches" or have been promised protection from arrest if they continue to provide the officer with free sexual services. Although prostitution is prohibited by law, its illegal status does not confer on police the right to harass and abuse prostitutes.

Finally, many prostitutes who are arrested find that their court-appointed defense attorneys do not engage in a vigorous defense. Many defense attorneys generally urge their clients to accept a plea, even where the client has a good chance of succeeding at trial, or where a conviction could have negative consequences for a client's immigration status, with a case with child welfare authorities, employment opportunities, or on eligibility for public housing.

Problems with the Child Welfare System: There exists a great need for sex workers to have assistance with child removal cases with Administration for Children's Services (ACS), New York City's child welfare agency. ACS routinely takes children from women who use drugs and get arrested. Family reunification is predicated on getting out of a life that involves prostitution and drug use. This problem appears to be worse for women who work on the street, because they tend to be poorer and involved in substance abuse. Women who are attempting to get their lives together are in need of advocates who can help prevent ACS from taking their children away permanently and help negotiate an appropriate level of contact with their children, such as visitation rights. Some level of contact with children is often an impetus for parents to seek treatment and get the help they need. Additionally, mothers who lose contact with their children entirely are more likely to have further problems with substance abuse and are at greater risk for engaging in sex work.

Special Problems for Immigrant and Undocumented Sex Workers: Many sex workers are immigrant and undocumented women and girls, and a large number of them come into the United States as a result of global trafficking. The traffickers may threaten victims, take their passports, and limit their contact with the outside world. The United States Department of State estimates that 18,000-20,000 people are trafficked into the United States every year;[3] many of the them are from Eastern Europe, China and Southeast Asia, and Mexico. With its large immigrant population, New York City is a major destination and hub for trafficking victims. Trafficked persons need a variety of services, particularly housing, mental health, and legal services. The Trafficking Victims Protection Act (TVPA) created the T visa, which offers work authorization and the possibility of adjustment to permanent resident status to "victim[s] of a severe form of trafficking," most often to victims

---

[2] Data obtained from State of New York, Division of Criminal Justice Services via e-mail correspondence on January 16, 2003.
[3] U.S. Department of State, *Trafficking in Persons Report* (2003) at 7.

2

who assist with prosecutions. Many women who have been trafficked are unaware of their legal rights and are afraid to seek help and assistance for fear they will be harmed, or deported to their country of origin.

While the TVPA is not a perfect law, it has allowed for more recognition of the problem of human trafficking, and it creates an avenue for victims of trafficking to seek both immigration benefits and public assistance, and it has helped many victims. Furthermore, the SWP and other advocates document problems with the implementation of the TVPA, and use this information to fight for changes that will better serve victims.

Violence Against Prostitutes: Prostitutes experience a great deal of violence, both from customers and the police. The SWP released a report in June 2003, *Revolving Door: An Analysis of Street-Based Prostitution in New York City*, which documents that 80% of street-based prostitutes interviewed had experienced or been threatened with violence while working. Sixty percent of the subjects had actually experienced violence that included sexual assault, mugging, and torture. When asked about police response, they reported that police did not take their complaints seriously and often told them that they should expect violence. "Carol" told researchers: "If I call them, they don't come. If I have a situation in the street, forget it. 'Nobody told you to be in the street.' After a girl was gang raped, they said 'Forget it, she works in the street.'" As mentioned above, prostitutes also experience at the hands of police themselves, which often goes unaddressed.

Lack of Data and Information on the Population. Because of the illegal and underground nature of most sex work, and that sex workers are often marginalized, there has been little research and data conducted on the population that could be used to respond to their needs and evaluate and re-examine current public policy. Lack of demographic information on sex workers' living and working conditions hinders public discussion and the consideration of alternative policies within a context of harm reduction and human rights.

Barriers to Improving Conditions. Efforts to assist sex workers and to organize around sex workers' rights received a setback in New York City when the city passed a zoning law in 1995 that affected video parlors, peep shows, strip clubs, and other sex-related businesses (due to legal challenges, the law was not enforced until 1998.) Rather than reducing or eliminating sex work, sex workers have been driven further into the shadows and underground, thereby increasing the dangers and possibilities for exploitation and other risks.

Target Population: The SWP serves sex workers, former sex workers, and those who are profiled or at risk for engaging in sex work, including victims of human trafficking, in New York City. Sex work is practiced in a variety of settings—on the street, in massage parlors and brothels, via escort services, and through the internet. Because of the lack of research and accurate data on the population, it is difficult to determine how many sex workers are currently working in New York City, and there is little definitive data regarding their living and working conditions.[4] In fact, the lack of recent empirical research into the needs of sex workers makes research such as the *Revolving Door* study one of the goals of this project.

Since December 2001, the SWP has worked in partnership with community-based organizations in Brooklyn and Manhattan to provide legal advocacy and outreach. Of the women served to date, some 40% are African American, 30% Latina, and 10% Asian; they include former and current sex workers and those at risk engaging in sex work. The target population is low-income, immigrant, or transgender—the most vulnerable groups who engage in sex work.

---

[4] There exists in general a need for more ethnographic and empirical information on sex workers. *See* Elizabeth Bernstein, *What's Wrong with Prostitution? What's Right with Sex Work? Comparing Markets in Female Sexual Labor*, 10 HASTINGS WOMEN'S L.J. 91 (1999) ("[T]here has been surprisingly little empirical research done to investigate the lived conditions of contemporary prostitution.")

3

Strategies and Accomplishments: In our second year of activities, with the support of the New York Foundation, the SWP has made significant progress in developing and implementing its programs. Since July 2002, the SWP has:

- Established ongoing, working relationships with community-based organizations, collaborating with them to conduct outreach and legal clinics in Manhattan and Brooklyn;
- Served more than 55 clients by providing legal assistance, advice, technical assistance, and referrals;
- Conducted 14 night outreach sessions with sex workers and brothels;
- Conducted 19 trainings for community-based agencies or other groups who serve sex workers on legal matters of their clients that could be referred to SWP and the rights available to trafficking victims;
- Released *Revolving Door: An Analysis of Street-Based Prostitution in New York City*, which documents the problems that street-based sex workers face with police and quality of life initiatives; and
- Advocated with federal law enforcement agencies to improve implementation of the TVPA.

The following SWP activities are designed to meet the needs described above.

Legal Advocacy and Outreach: SWP staff engage in legal advocacy and outreach through collaborations with agencies that provide social services to sex workers. The SWP collaborates with service providers who serve sex workers to offer legal advocacy and outreach. These agencies include *Amethyst Women's Project*, an organization in Coney Island, Brooklyn that offers referrals to detox, peer support, and harm reduction outreach to sex workers and substance-dependent persons; *Asian Pacific Islander Coalition on HIV/AIDS (APICHA)*, which is based in Chinatown and conducts an HIV testing project for high-risk Asian populations, including sex workers and their clients; *Positive Health Project*, which offers peer support, case management, and harm reduction outreach to transgender women and sex workers; and *From Our Streets With Dignity (FROSTD)*, which offers case management, shelter, and harm reduction outreach to sex workers.

Legal advocacy includes giving legal advice or technical assistance, conducting legal research, giving referrals, or engaging in legal advocacy with appropriate agencies on the client's behalf, on a variety of issues, including: Criminal Justice; Immigration; Child Welfare; Domestic Violence; and Family Law.

Additionally, the SWP directly represents clients in immigration cases that have the potential to make broader legal impact. The SWP represents two adolescent girls who were trafficked into the country and forced to work in a brothel against their will. It also represents a young Albanian adolescent who was kidnapped, sexually assaulted, and almost sold into prostitution, in a political asylum case. Finally, the SWP represents a transgender woman who was falsely arrested for loitering for prostitution, in a political asylum case.

The SWP also conducts legal outreach, most often with APICHA staff. Outreach serves the dual purposes of providing critical legal information to sex workers, and direct needs assessment. Outreach workers go out at night to either known sex worker strolls or sex work clubs and inform sex workers of legal and health services and conduct needs assessments on these issues, or go to massage parlors/brothels to discuss HIV testing and condom use. The SWP plans to continue to outreach to the parlors, and once we have built up a connection, we will try to talk to the women alone and discuss legal issues that they have. Through these outreach sessions, the SWP has advised clients on important legal issues, including criminal justice and housing problems. The SWP also trains APICHA and outreach staff on the legal issues relevant to sex workers and victims of trafficking so that they can recognize and assess when sex workers have legal problems that need to be addressed by the SWP.

4

In our third program year, we plan on continuing our collaborations with community-based organizations to conduct legal advocacy and outreach.

Training: The SWP also conducts legal trainings for community-based agencies and other organizations that provide services to sex workers, on legal matters of their clients that could be referred to SWP; how to recognize victims of trafficking; and the rights available to them. The trainings also allow the SWP to make connections for legal referrals with the collaborating organization's staff, without being as time-consuming as a weekly clinic. This is especially important because the SWP has a small staff. In addition to training Amethyst, APICHA, and Positive Health Project staff, the SWP has trained the staff at other community-based organizations on criminal justice, ACS, immigration, and trafficking issues. Finally, the trainings are critical because they create awareness of the rights and needs of sex workers and trafficking victims in the minds and agendas of groups who are critical partners in the fight to create community concern for this population.

In our third program year, the SWP will continue to conduct legal training for staff of collaborating and other agencies that serve sex workers and those at risk for engaging in sex work, and trafficking victims.

Research and Policy: Because legal advocacy for sex workers in New York City is uncharted, the SWP conducts research in areas that affect sex workers, including criminal justice, immigration, and legal needs. The SWP works with qualified research consultants to produce reports that document the conditions and needs of sex workers in New York City, and which provide a sound basis for policy advocacy. The SWP's first report, *Revolving Door: An Analysis of Street-Based Prostitution in New York City*, documents the effects of quality of life initiatives on street-based sex workers and paints a picture of life on the street.

The SWP also works with coalitions that work on local issues that affect sex workers, including the New York City Task Force on Sexually Exploited Youth , the New York City Anti-Trafficking Network, and the national Freedom Network, which advocates on behalf of trafficking victims. With the Freedom Network, the SWP documents problems with the implementation of the TVPA, and uses this information to fight for changes that will better serve victims. Recent advocacy has centered on resources offered to victims, and requirements for cooperation with law enforcement.

In our third program year, the SWP will advocate, with coalition partners, for implementation of the *Revolving Door* recommendations. We plan to target the New York Police Department, which has already expressed interest in the report and its findings, the Mayor's Office of the Criminal Justice Coordinator, and members of City Council. The SWP will also research and write its second report, which will document the needs and conditions of indoor sex workers in New York City. We will also continue our documentation and advocacy around the TVPA and its impact on victims of trafficking. The SWP provides a critical and unique voice in the public discussion of issues relating to sex workers and trafficked persons.

Project Staff: The SWP has a full-time Director/Attorney, Juhu Thukral, JD, (*See* Attached Bio), and three volunteer outreach workers. The SWP also hires research consultants on an as-needed basis.

C.   Evaluation

The SWP evaluates its effectiveness by engaging in a process evaluation that assesses how services were utilized, and what caused services to be effective in assisting clients. The project achieves this by interviewing clients and staff from collaborating agencies. The evaluations also focus on our ability produce sound research and to affect the public perceptions of sex workers and trafficking victims. This process allows the SWP to assess effectiveness, and point to new strategies for the project. The Advisory Board reviews evaluation.

SEX WORKERS PROJECT at the URBAN JUSTICE CENTER

<u>PROJECTED OPERATING BUDGET</u>
NOVEMBER 1, 2003 - OCTOBER 31, 2004

EXPENDITURES/INCOME

ITEM	TOTAL	FUNDING SOURCE	
PERSONNEL		New York Foundation	Other**
SWP Director/Staff Attorney XXXXX	XXXXX	XXXXX	XXXXX
Research Consultants	XXXXX	XXXXX	XXXXX
Fringe @ 28%	XXXXX	XXXXX	XXXXX
TOTAL PERSONNEL	74,400	35,000	39,400
OTPS			
Overhead Fee*	18,000	10,000	8,000
Travel	2,600	--	2,600
TOTAL OTPS	20,600	10,000	10,600
GRAND TOTAL	95,000	45,000	50,000

*The Sex Workers Project pays its OTPS in the form of a monthly payment to the Urban Justice Center ($18,000 per project employee). This covers all expenses, including rent and utilities, telephone, supplies, postage, computer equipment, insurance, administration, and miscellaneous costs.

**The Sex Workers Project has raised $25,000 from the New York Women's Foundation, and is currently seeking funding for the other $25,000 from other sources, including the New York Community Trust, Daphne Foundation, Sister Fund, Tides Foundation, Abelard Foundation, and Blue Ridge Foundation.

A Proposal From
Southeast Community College
Lincoln, Nebraska

To
Cooper Foundation
Lincoln, Nebraska

Requested amount: $10,000; **Amount received:** $10,000

Funder's comments:

"This proposal was submitted using the Lincoln/Lancaster County Grantmakers Common Application Form, which we require. At the time of the request, we were not accepting requests for multiyear funding. This was a three-year project, and the applicant was very clear in presenting the one-year request in context of their three-year plan.

"The first page summary was especially good, concisely noting major points of the project, the plan for funding and the importance of sustainability. The main text of the application expanded on these issues with a minimum of jargon. They made their case by stating the specific needs of the population served, summarizing the results of a pilot effort, and listing clear objectives to achieve their goals. They did not rely on anecdotes and used only statistics that applied directly to their project. This is significant because we often receive requests that include many local and national statistics (such as the total number of refugees resettled in our city or nationwide). While interesting, that information does not always relate to the specific population served by the program under consideration for funding and in fact can make a request less clear-cut.

"This was a large, multifaceted project with a very detailed work plan and evaluation plan. Both were organized in a way that made them easy to read and understand. Our guidelines state, 'It is essential that a convincing case is presented for the proposed project, why it is needed, and how it will meet the needs identified. Brevity and clarity are important.' This application is an exemplary model of that objective."

—*Victoria Kovar, Grants Administrator, Cooper Foundation*

Notes:
The proposal was written using the Lincoln/Lancaster County Grantmakers Common Application Form.
Proposal written by Judy Shonerd, Resource Development Specialist. Contributions to the proposal made by Jack Huck, President; Dennis Headrick, Vice President of Instruction; Mona Callies, Continuing Education Dean; and Susan Kash-Brown, ESL Assistant Director.

Lincoln/Lancaster County Grantmakers
Common Application Form (6/10/02)
Follow this format, and number and restate the headings.

Foundation Applied To: Cooper Foundation
Application Date: April 15, 2003
Federal Tax I.D. Number   47-054-9567

I. ORGANIZATIONAL INFORMATION

A. Organization Name   Southeast Community College
B. Address/9-digit Zip Code   8800 O Street, Lincoln, NE 68520-1299
C. Telephone Number   402-437-2722
D. Fax Number   402-437-2404
E. E-Mail Address   skashbro@southeast.edu
F. Website   www.southeast.edu
G. Chief Executive Officer   Jack J. Huck, President
H. Contact Person & Title   Susan Kash Brown, Assistant Director, ESL

I. Purpose of Request: (one paragraph, amount, purpose)

SCC is proposing a project to develop a Newcomers Educational Center (NEC) to serve adult English language learners. The purpose of the NEC will be to increase educational access and improve educational outcomes, ultimately leading to quality employment and increased self-sufficiency. The Newcomers Educational Center will provide a bridge from ESL classes to college-level vocational programs by

- Providing additional career and academic advising to ESL students.
- Developing new curriculum for nine additional preview courses over three years.
- Offering free preview classes (Nursing Assistant, Truck Driver Training, Welding Technology) for 80 students in year one and reduced tuition in years two and three for another 220 students (3-year total - 300 students). The ESL-focused previews provide a thorough and comprehensible college orientation, an introduction to specialized vocabulary used in the vocational area of interest, field experience that offers a hands-on preview of equipment and safety procedures, and an ESL explanation of workplace expectations for particular careers.
- Developing training modules for college faculty to increase their ability to teach students with language barriers.

For year one of the three-year project, the grant funding needed is $46,866. SCC will commit a match in year one of $10,170 to the project, both in-kind and cash. **SCC is requesting a one-year commitment of $10,000 from the Cooper Foundation.** A request for the remaining amount has been sent to the Woods Charitable Fund (in March) and will soon be forwarded to their board for consideration. Sustainable elements for the project include curriculum, tuition-producing courses, and teacher education modules. Sustainability of program personnel is an important issue that the College will address as the project progresses. The College has a history of sustaining projects and staffing initiated through grant models.

Southeast Community College   Newcomers Educational Center Project

J. Budget Summary for This Proposal

	(Year One)
1. Applicant's Contribution from Operating Funds, if any	$ 10,170
--from students' book purchases	$ 1,200
2. Applicant's Contribution from Reserve Funds, if any	$ 0
3. Amount of This Request	$ 10,000
4. Amount of Other Pending Requests, if any	$ 36,866
5. Amount of Other Confirmed Requests, if any	$ 0
6. Total Proposal Income (1+2+3+4+5=6)	$ 58,236
7. Total Proposal Expense	$ 58,236
8. Balance (6-7=8)	$ 0

(Explain positive, negative balances under II.B.3 referenced on the following page.)

K. Income & Expense Summaries for the Organization

	Actual	**Budget**	**Budget**
	Last Fiscal Year Ending: 6/30/02	Current Fiscal Year Ending: 6/30/03	Next Fiscal Year Ending: 6/30/04
Income	$62,199,640	$68,321,000	**Not set until**
Expense	57,913,482	68,321,000	**June-Sept**
Net	4,286,158	0	.
Net Assets	$83,570,775	$83,570,775	

_____   _____
(Signature of Chairperson of the Board)   (Signature of the Chief ExecutiveOfficer)

Cooper Foundation   Date Due: April 15, 2003   2

Southeast Community College   <u>Newcomers Educational Center Project</u>

Lincoln/Lancaster County Grantmakers
Common Application Form (6/10/02)

II. **PROPOSAL NARRATIVE:** (10 pages maximum. Clarity and brevity are encouraged.)

A. FUNDING REQUEST
1. The amount requested
Of the total $46,866 grant funds needed in year one, $10,000 is requested from Cooper Foundation.

2. The purpose of your request (the need, problem or opportunity)

Succeeding in a college-level classroom is not an easy task for English language learners for several reasons. Adequate language acquisition is difficult. Students can acquire rudimentary English through ESL courses, but even by persisting through several ESL levels, they do not acquire specialized vocabularies common to vocational college courses. Moreover, ESL students do not typically seek out academic or career advising services and may have trouble understanding college requirements and expectations, not to mention understanding related workplace expectations. Consequently, they may enroll in college programs inappropriate for their preparation and career goals. Failure of college courses is quite common for English language learners, resulting in frequent course repetition, or worse--dropping out. In addition, faculty face problems; most college teachers have little or no preparation for students with significant language barriers.

To help students bridge the gap more successfully from ESL classes to college classes, SCC designed and offered two pilot preview courses with funding from a Targeted Assistance to Refugees (TAG) grant: "ESL for Nursing Assistant" and "ESL for Truck Driver Training." The courses not only presented specialized vocabulary that would be needed if the student later enrolled in the vocational courses, but also included helpful modules on college orientation, safety, and workplace expectations.

Approximately 63 refugees completed these 10-week pilot courses. Follow-up is far from complete, but college records indicate that nine (14%) have already continued their education at SCC. Considering that this group had been in the U.S. less than five years (as required by the TAG grant) and had very limited English skills, these outcomes were very hopeful. With additional funding, SCC would be able to extend free preview classes to <u>mid-level English language learners</u>, many of whom wanted to take the TAG classes but didn't fit the criteria.

We believe the pilot project suggests a viable approach for improving the rate of transition from ESL classes to specific vocational education programs and then to employment opportunities. Thus SCC is proposing a project to develop a <u>Newcomers Educational Center (NEC)</u>. The goal of the NEC is to <u>increase educational access and improve educational outcomes of adult English language learners</u>, ultimately leading to

Cooper Foundation   Date Due: April 15, 2003   3

quality employment and increased self-sufficiency. Steps to achieve this goal include the following objectives:

(1) increasing academic and career advising to ESL students through preview courses and individual advising sessions with the project staff and vocational instructors.

(2) developing new materials, at least three new 10-week vocational preview courses per year, each including orientation, vocabulary, equipment usage, field experiences, and safety modules; most likely targeting the following SCC programs: Welding, Automotive Technology, Microcomputer, Business, additional Health Occupations, Electronic Technology, and Machine Tool.

(3) offering free preview vocational ESL courses to approximately 80 adult English language learners in year one, using grant funds to pay instructional costs. (In the next two years, student tuition will incrementally pick up more of the cost of preview courses, which is expected to be approximately $125-$150/student for a 10-week course.)

(4) developing and implementing supportive teacher training: (a) training at least 20 faculty per year to better prepare them for teaching ESL students; (b) broadening the impact by offering the teacher preparation modules to other educators through the SCC Continuing Education Division.

3. The population you plan to serve including numbers, location, socio-economic status, race, ethnicity, gender, sexual orientation, age, physical ability and language

The Newcomers Educational Center project will serve the Lincoln area and be located on Lincoln Campus (8800 O Street), where approximately 700 ESL students are regularly served per year. (See #D-4). In year one, the Project services will target 80 adult English language learners. The Project is planned to be ongoing and serve approximately 100 to 120 students per year. The target group will be composed of refugees, immigrants and other aliens who have settled in the Lincoln area, have English language literacy needs, and wish to acquire education and training in order to gain or improve employment status. As usual, the College will adhere to its policy of nondiscrimination for this project.[1] A secondary target group is composed of college faculty who will receive special support/training to prepare them for teaching individuals with language barriers. The project expects to serve at least 20 faculty per year.

4. The effect your action will have on need, problem or opportunity

The Newcomers Educational Center will provide ESL-focused educational advising and support services that do not now exist for vulnerable populations in the community. It will increase the target population's awareness of educational opportunities; increase their preparation for postsecondary education; and ultimately increase their ability to

---

[1] It is the policy of Southeast Community College to provide equal opportunity and nondiscrimination in all admission, attendance, and employment matters to all persons without regard to race, color, religion, sex, age, marital status, national origin, ancestry, veteran status, sexual orientation, disability, or other factors prohibited by law or College policy.

secure a viable career. The project will also increase teacher preparation for students with language barriers and thus improve the rate of retention and college course completion of the target population.

5. **Strategies you will employ to implement the project, including, if applicable, collaborations with other agencies. (include a workplan with key dates and actions)**

The primary strategy will be to establish a Newcomers Educational Center for initiating new services and expanding current services to English language learners. To implement the project, the College will utilize its relationships with agencies and organizations (including the Asian Community and Culture Center, Hispanic Community Center, African Multicultural Center, Lincoln Action Program, Catholic Social Services, Heartland Refugee Resettlement, Lincoln Housing Authority, New Americans Taskforce, and Lincoln Literacy Council) that serve the target population on a regular basis. These agencies will make referrals to help individuals desiring to further their education. Actions will include academic and career advising; development of new materials, primarily Preview Courses that will prepare students for entry into vocational programs or employment; development of teacher preparation modules in collaboration with SCC's Staff Development program and Continuing Education Division, to be offered to SCC faculty as well as other institutions.

Three-Year Workplan

Workplan – Key Actions	Jl	Ag	Se	Oc	No	De	Ja	Fe	Mr	Ap	My	Ju
YEAR ONE			2003						2004			
Organize Newcomers Center (hire staff, establish office, develop systems)	X	X	X	-	-	-	-					
Plan with Advisory Group		X	X			X				X		
Collaborate with ethnic centers and agencies (ongoing)		X	X	-	-	-	-	-	-	-	-	-
Establish advising function (ongoing)			X	-	-	-	-	-	-	-	-	-
Enroll ESL students in existing preview courses. (ongoing)				X			X	X				
Develop curriculum for ESL-Welding				X	-	-	-					
Enroll students in ESL-Welding. (ongoing)							X	X				
Develop curriculum for ESL for Automotive Technology							X	-	-	-	-	
Develop faculty training components.				X	-	-	-					
SCC faculty receive training (ongoing)							X					
YEAR TWO			2004						2005			
Offer teacher preparation modules to SCC and other institutions	X						X					
Continue development of new preview courses.	X		X				X			X		
Continue student advising.	-	-	-	-	-	-	-	-	-	-	-	-
Continue student enrollments in preview courses based on interest.	X		X				X			X		

Southeast Community College   Newcomers Educational Center Project

YEAR THREE*			2005				2006					
Workplan – Key Actions	Jl	Ag	Se	Oc	No	De	Ja	Fe	Mr	Ap	My	Ju
Offer teacher preparation modules to SCC and other institutions	X						X					
Continue development of new preview courses.	X			X			X			X		
Continue student advising.	-	-	-	-	-	-	-	-	-	-	-	-
Continue student enrollments in preview courses based on interest.	X			X			X			X		

6. The names and qualifications of those who will direct the project

Susan Kash-Brown, B.A, 1980; M.E. in International Education, School for International Training 1989, will direct the project. Ms. Kash-Brown has been involved in the Adult Basic Education and English as a Second Language Programs for a total of 10 years. After teaching in ABE and ESL classrooms for two years, she served as the ESL Coordinator for the ESL Program and later as Assistant Director of the SCC ESL Program. Earlier experience included teaching ESL in Japan and serving as International Student Advisor at Midwest Institute for International Studies, Doane College-Crete, and the University of Vermont. Kash-Brown is well known among local and state agencies serving the target population. She has served extensively on committees related to refugee resettlement and made presentations on the topic of ESL. For the new project described in this application, she will provide overall direction for and supervision of a Project Coordinator who will implement the objectives of the project. The Project Coordinator selected will have appropriate education, training, and experience in English as a Second Language teaching, testing, curriculum development, advising, social services, and/or administration. A proposed job description has been developed and is attached.

7. The impact of your project on diversity, if applicable

The project directly addresses the needs of refugees and immigrants for an educational system that effectively helps them make critical transitions in their educational process. Too many English language learners fail in the current educational environment. This project will strengthen Southeast Community College's support system, curricular offerings, and teacher preparation for students from diverse cultures and thus create an increasingly positive image of multicultural students. The project also has the potential of attracting a more diverse enrollment to the institution, where 91 percent of the students are white, non-Hispanic. For the community, the project will impact the readiness of immigrants and refugees to assume full responsibility for their economic support.

Cooper Foundation   Date Due: April 15, 2003   6

Southeast Community College   Newcomers Educational Center Project

B. FINANCIAL PLAN

1. The proposal budget. List the sources and amounts of all income, including this request, and their status: confirmed, pending, or not yet applied for

Year One, 2003-2004	Grant Funds	SCC Funds	Student Funds	Total
Salaries				
Project Coordinator (.725 FTE)	XXXXX			
Curriculum writers (3 x 120 hrs)	XXXXX			
Faculty for Preview Courses (7 x 1000)	XXXXX			
ESL Director (100 hours)		XXXXX		
Benefits				
FICA (Salaries x .0765)	3,256			
Educational Materials				
For Faculty (7 x $150)	1,050			
Student materials (80 x $15)			$1,200	
Facility Rental				
For Preview courses (70 sessions @ $100)		7,000		
Marketing				
Brochure design, production (1,000 @ .50)		500		
Mailing (1,000 @ .37)		370		
TOTALS	$46,866	$10,170	$1,200	$58,236

With this application, a request for support is being made to Cooper Foundation. A proposal for the remaining grant funds was also submitted the Woods Charitable Fund on March 15. The requests are pending.

2. When funding would be needed, and if multiple annual payments would be appropriate

Funding may be provided on a reimbursement basis either once a year or in multiple payments as preferred by the grantor.

3. Explanation of positive or negative balances if shown under I.J.8. on the cover sheet

None.

4. Outline of your development plan for securing funding for this proposal now and, if applicable, in the future

The start-up development plan includes a commitment from the College's ESL budget of $10,170 in year one, and requests totaling $46,866 to two foundations with an interest in initiating promising social support systems to foreign-born populations who have settled in Lincoln. SCC plans to continue the project indefinitely and will again request grant assistance in years two and three. In the future, several aspects of the project will be self-sustaining. For example, the newly developed curriculum will continue to be offered on an affordable tuition basis. The new teacher preparation modules will be provided on an ongoing basis by the Staff Development office and marketed to other institutions through Continuing Education on a cost-effective tuition basis. The part-time project coordinator position will be considered for College or grant support as the project progresses, a common operating procedure for SCC when new programs are introduced.

Cooper Foundation   Date Due: April 15, 2003   7

5. Evidence of financial ability, stability, and planning with reference to the project budget, operating budget, and the organization's long-range development plan

SCC's source of funding includes state appropriations, property taxes, tuition, and miscellaneous income, such as that generated through the campus bookstores. A copy of the most current financial audit is attached and previous years' audits are available for review. Long-range planning is an integral part of the College's process. A copy of the current five-year plan is available for review upon request. The mission specifically includes providing services to English language learners.

C. EVALUATION

1. The criteria and plan for measuring the proposed objectives during the grant period.

The project will be evaluated by both subjective and objective means, using the objectives as the measure of success.

Criteria	Evaluation Process	Timeline	Staff Responsible
1. By the end of year one, at least 80 English language learners will receive academic and career advising Through the Newcomers Educational Center.	**Objective Evaluation:** 1. Project records will track number of students served and the type of services provided. 2. Evaluation instrument: Students will complete an exit survey indicating strengths and weaknesses of the program. **Subjective Evaluation:** 3. Advisory Committee meetings will be held to discuss program management and improvements. 4. Reporting: An annual report will be made to the administration, funders, and other stakeholders outlining the lessons learned and project accomplishments.	Quarterly Quarterly Annually	Project Coordinator and Project Director PC and PD; Advisory Committee PC and PD
2. Three new vocational preview courses for English language learners will be developed in year one.	**Objective Evaluation:** 1. Course descriptions will be listed in the quarterly program brochure. **Subjective Evaluation:** 2. Courses will be reviewed to determine if they include all of the components necessary	Ongoing Prior to offering	PC, PD, Faculty, Community Centers/Agencies PC, PD, and Faculty in content areas

Southeast Community College   Newcomers Educational Center Project

Criteria	Evaluation Process	Timeline	Staff Responsible
	to prepare students for further college level study.		
3. 80 adult English language learners will enroll in preview vocational ESL classes in year one.	**Objective Evaluation:** 1. Class enrollment 2. Class completion 3. Pre and Post test results on specialized vocabulary 4. Enrollment in further education (credit, noncredit) 5. Completion of an additional class (ESL, Preview, or College level) 6. Enrollment in a program 7. Employment as a result of the project	Quarterly	PC, PD, Faculty in content areas
4. (a) 20 college instructors will receive training to assist them in teaching students with language barriers b) training will be offered to other institutions through Continuing Education	**Objective Evaluation:** 1. Teacher preparation modules were completed on schedule. 2. Records show that at least 20 faculty attended training in year one. 3. Number of external institutions and faculty enrolling in the teacher preparation classes. 4. Faculty pre- and post-surveys indicated increased understanding of ESL students. 5. As a condition of training, faculty will administer an evaluation to students to ascertain information about their performance. This data will become part of the final report.	Annual Report, July 2004 Jan. 2004, July, 2004 End of quarter	PC, PD, Staff Development Coordinator PC, Faculty Faculty, Students, PC, PD

2. **Names of those who will be involved in evaluation**
   ii. Project Director, Susan Kash-Brown
   iii. Project Coodinator, to be hired
   iv. Faculty: Mike Burdic, Welding instructor; other instructors involved in curriculum development and training
   v. Advisory Committee: Involved personnel from agencies and community centers

Cooper Foundation   Date Due: April 15, 2003   9

D. BACKGROUND OF THE ORGANIZATION
1. A brief description of your agency's history and mission
Southeast Community College (SCC) is a public, two-year postsecondary educational institution, one of six community college areas created in 1973 by Nebraska legislative statute. SCC has been continuously accredited since 1977 by the Higher Learning Commission of North Central Association for Colleges and Schools. The mission of the College is to provide high quality technical and occupational education, general academic transfer education, continuing education, developmental or remedial education, and education for those desiring to improve their English language proficiency. SCC provides 49 technical/vocational programs and Academic Transfer programs. It operates on three campuses (Lincoln, Milford, and Beatrice) and utilizes approximately 29 continuing education sites in the 15-county area.

2. The needs, problems or opportunities your organization addresses if different than A.2. above
Addressed in mission statement in D-1.

3. Current programs and accomplishments emphasizing achievements of the past year.
Southeast Community College has served English language learners for more than 30 years through its ESL and ABE programs as well as its vocational, academic and other Continuing Education programs. In the past year, SCC has sought to improve its outreach to multicultural students through establishment of the Student Leadership Symposium, which has a strong multicultural emphasis. This symposium reached out to 75 high school and college youth with its theme of inclusiveness and honoring diversity. The College also increased its commitment to global education, through formation of a Global Education team, which is developing a vision and action plan for the future. Last year, the College made a significant contribution to the state's future by educating a record number of students (8,912), graduating 1,571 students, and maintaining a placement/transfer rate of 95 percent. In 2002, SCC underwent a comprehensive evaluation by the Higher Learning Commission of North Central Association of Colleges and Schools, receiving continued accreditation through 2012, the longest period possible.

4. The population your agency serves if different from A.3. above

	Male	Female	White	Black	Hispanic	Asian	Nat. Am	Other	Total
Credit Students	4,222	4,690	8,063	211	173	287	36	142	8,912

The College also serves the following populations:
- Non-credit students: 21,757
- ESL non-credit students: 673
- ESL credit students – 57
- ABE students – 450
- Middle East grant students – 151
- Targeted Assistance to Refugees grant students – 135

- Newcomer grant students – 60

5. Number and composition (racial-ethnic-gender) of full and part-time staff, board and volunteers

	Male	Female	White	Black	Hispanic	Asian	Nat. Am	Other	Total
FT Staff	267	279	511	7	9	8	11	0	546
PT Staff	14	36	47	1	1	1	0	0	50
Adjunct Faculty - Credit	86	130	206	2	3	3	2	0	216
Adjunct Faculty - ESL	1	19	12	0	2	1	1	5*[2]	20
Board	7	4	10	1	0	0	0		11
Volunteers									44

[2] Two from Pakistan, two from Iraq, one from former USSR.

Chapter 2

Special Project: Multiyear

As in the previous chapter, the proposals included here are devoted to special projects, as opposed to general support for the organizations. The proposals in this chapter are for multiyear special projects. Because of the extended time frame, devising a multiyear proposal demands careful program planning, since the proposal writer is required to look into the future for her/his grantseeking organization in order to describe the project and its outcomes. This planning may depend on several variables and can be subject to change as the initiative progresses. Despite the number of variables and potential unknowns, becoming more pronounced with each year as the project continues, funders still expect the multiyear proposal to demonstrate clarity of objectives and methods and to be highly specific as to projected outcomes. The inclusion of a timeline in multiyear proposals, as demonstrated in the proposal from the Beth Health Care Foundation, helps both nonprofit and funder visualize the intended progress of the grant.

The budgets accompanying these multiyear special project proposals demonstrate that establishing and presenting financial details—anticipated expenses and revenues for several years—can be accomplished in various ways. The four proposals that follow are for two- and three-year special projects that range in size from $150,000 to $495,000.

The first proposal is a request for $425,410 over three years from the Beth Health Care Foundation (on behalf of Newark Beth Israel Medical Center) under the Avon Foundation's Supporting the Safety Net Program. The bulk of the grant would pay for two bilingual positions—a nurse practitioner and an administrative assistant—with the ultimate aim of delivering targeted education on breast health and cancer prevention to low-income African American and Latina women over age 40 in underserved communities.

The second proposal was submitted by the Boys & Girls Clubs of Greater Milwaukee, Wisconsin, to the Hearst Foundation, Inc., of New York, New York. The request is for $150,000 over three years in support of the expansion of the Clubs' ongoing Literacy Program and implementation of its new Reading First Program. The proposal makes effective use of a variety of formatting techniques, and it includes photographs of children doing their homework, using computers and other resources, and meeting with tutors. It also contains a wealth of relevant statistics and quotations. Included also are details on the ways in which the Hearst Foundation's support of this special project will be acknowledged in the community.

The third proposal in this chapter is from the Chinatown Community Development Center of San Francisco, California, and requests $495,000 over three years from The California Endowment's CommunitiesFirst Program to support a new Language Access and Multicultural Health project. The project will assist Chinese, Russian, and Tagalog-speaking seniors in San Francisco by increasing their ability to communicate about their health needs and by helping them to become health advocates and community leaders. This proposal sets forth specific measurable objectives for each year of the three-year grant period.

The final proposal in this chapter is a $160,000 request to the Altman Foundation of New York, New York from the Medicare Rights Center also of New York, that requests two years of funding to pilot Health Buddies, an Internet-based healthcare counseling program for New York City residents. The new project builds on the Medicare Rights Center's previous education and counseling work, and proposes to expand the numbers of volunteer counselors and of individuals served by counselors. Descriptions of the problems of typical clients and the attributes of counselors ("Angela" and "Mike") make the text come alive.

A Proposal from

Beth Health Care Foundation on behalf of Newark Beth Israel Medical Center

Newark, New Jersey

To

Avon Foundation

New York, New York

Requested amount: $425,410; **Amount received:** $425,410 over three years

Funder's comments:

"Beth Health Care used the Avon application form, after first approaching us by means of the RFP process for 'safety net' gifts. In this case the cover sheet contains, for all intents and purposes, an executive summary of the program, which is clear and effective. Reviewers from our foundation appreciated the level of specificity present in the text, the detailed nurse practitioner job position, and overall, the clear and well-written nature of this proposal.

"The length of the proposal, at approximately 15 pages, is appropriate. It is well balanced, with each component weighted equally. There is a good level of detail in each section, without being overly specific. The need statement, in particular, displays a depth of knowledge about the pressing need for early breast cancer detection in Essex County, New Jersey, especially among the African-American population, where the incidence of early detection is low, health and screening services are few and far between, and many patients present with late-stage cancers. This section does a good job of illustrating the problem and proposing ways to address it.

"The writing is clear and not overly reliant on statistics and medical terminology, although both are employed effectively. While a sound proposal, it is also very understandable, even to those who might not have a deep background in breast cancer health care. The budget is also well-written and presented clearly. All necessary budget elements are represented, making analysis easy. One strong feature of the budget was the inclusion of a clear timeline, demonstrating the grantseeker's assumptions about what will happen when, the amount of funds to be contributed by Avon Foundation and other sources, and in-kind contributions from the agency itself. Overall, the quality of the writing, with its clarity and detail, is a real plus for this proposal. Beth Health Care included all necessary attachments, and all were helpful."

—*Mary Quinn, Senior Manager of Operations, Avon Foundation*

Notes:

The proposal was written using the Avon Foundation grant request cover sheet and
guidelines.

Proposal written by Amy G. Engel, Director of Development, Beth Health Care Foundation,
and Stacey Abate, Grants Consultant.

APPLICATION COVER SHEET
THE AVON FOUNDATION "Supporting the Safety Net"

Organization Name: Beth Health Care Foundation on behalf of Newark Beth Israel Medical Center

Street Address: 201 Lyons Avenue at Osborne Terrace

City/State/Zip: Newark, NJ 07112

Primary Contact Name/Title: Amy G. Engel, Director of Development

Telephone: 973-926-4398   Fax: 973-923-1206   E-mail (required): aengel@sbhcs.com

Proposed use of funds description (one sentence only): Newark Beth Israel Medical Center, a safety net hospital, is requesting funding for a Nurse Practitioner and an Administrative Assistant (both bilingual) to strengthen patient care and follow up for breast cancer patients; ensure that women in our outpatient centers are receiving timely mammograms; and provide targeted education on breast health and prevention throughout our community.

Population to be served (age, ethnicity, income level):

This program will primarily benefit low-income African American and Hispanic/Latino women age 40 and over in the city of Newark and surrounding communities.

Geographic area to be served: Greater Newark metropolitan area

Exact amount of funding requested: $ 425,410   Timeline for use of funds: Oct, 2004- Sept. 2007

What is the annual operating budget of your hospital? $378,067,000 (2004)

Have you previously received funding from the Avon Foundation or Avon Foundation Breast Care Fund?
_____ Yes __x__ No

If yes, provide date(s) of funding: _____

Statement of Applicant

By signing in the space below, the representative of the gift applicant (a) affirms that he or she is an authorized representative of the applicant; (b) affirms that the information in this application is complete and accurate; (c) agrees to provide additional information to Avon and to be available for site visits by Avon, if requested; (d) understands and agrees that funding decisions are made by Avon at its sole discretion and are final, and that Avon shall have no responsibility to any applicant not selected for receipt of a gift; and (e) if selected for funding, agrees to provide semi-annual reports in the format to be specified, to sign a gift agreement stipulating certain terms and conditions of funding and to cooperate with Avon Foundation in local and national publicity about the "Supporting the Safety Net" initiative and the gift received from this initiative.

Unless this sentence is crossed out by the applicant, applicant gives Avon permission to share the applicant's contact information and program objective, solely for information exchange purposes among Avon Foundation beneficiaries.

Beth Health Care Foundation   ~ By _____
Name of Organization   Signature of authorized representative

Name: Amy G. Engel   Title: Director of Development   Date: 3/31/04

2. NARRATIVE

A. Assessment
i)   Geographic area
The primary constituency of the Flo Okin Oncology and Blood Disorders Center at Newark Beth Israel Medical Center is the low income and minority women of Essex County, New Jersey. Approximately 80% of all of Newark Beth Israel's patients come from Newark and the adjacent communities of Irvington and East Orange. The majority of women in the immediate service area are African American. There are significant numbers of Caribbean women in Irvington, Hispanics in north Newark and Elizabeth, and Russian immigrants in west Newark. The city of Newark has some of the highest concentrations of poverty in New Jersey (2000 census). As a "safety net" hospital, NBIMC provides health care to the entire community; no patient is turned away based on their inability to pay for services.

ii)   Patient population(s)
Newark Beth Israel Medical Center (NBIMC) is located in Newark's South Ward, where 42,961 (92.5%) of the residents are African American. Data from the 2000 census indicates that there are 201,000 minorities in Newark, representing 73% of the total population. Newark, Irvington, and East Orange combined are home to 258,278 African Americans, 140,069 who are women.

The second greatest minority presence is individuals of Hispanic/Latino origin, any race. In 1990 Essex County had 97,777 residents fitting this classification; in 2000 the number rose to 122,347, accounting for 15.4% of the total county population. In Newark alone, there are now 80,622 individuals characterized as Hispanic or Latino (of any race) (2000 census). Even those areas of Newark that were predominately Hispanic in 1990 saw an additional 10% increase in the numbers of Hispanic individuals by 2000.

NBIMC has the highest number of low income (Medicaid, charity care and self pay) patients in the state and treats more low-income cancer patients than any other hospital in New Jersey. Thirteen percent (13%) of NBIMC patients are either charity care or self pay; 26% are Medicaid patients; 26% have Medicare; the balance have private, managed care or employer sponsored insurance. In 2003, between 12-13% of all inpatient admissions were uninsured, forcing NBIMC to write off nearly 25 million dollars in health care costs provided to these uninsured patients.

iii)   Needs
Cancer is a pressing health concern in the Newark community. In 2002, there were 11,000 cancer-related visits at NBIMC; that number increased to 12,500 in 2003 and is expected to swell to 14,000 by the end of 2004. Breast Cancer is consistently the highest incidence cancer seen at NBIMC, representing 17% of all cancers and 35% of cancer in women. There are approximately 750 active cases of breast cancer patients receiving care at NBIMC; each year oncologists see about 100 women who are newly diagnosed with breast cancer.

The *Community Needs Assessment,* a report recently published by the Susan G. Komen Foundation, North Jersey Affiliate, identifies a substantial need for early detection of breast cancer in Essex County, "where the largest population of African American women reside." It also states that "Early detection has not yet reaped its full benefit for women of this race." The

1

Newark Beth Israel Medical Center

minority and low income women of NBIMC's service area have limited access to health care due to socio-cultural barriers, a scarcity of screening services, and a lack of health insurance. Shockingly, approximately 48% of the cancer patients seen at NBIMC already are in the late stages of cancer (stage III or IV). Sixty-one percent of the late stage cancer patients are already in stage IV. Most of those coming in with later stage cancers are African-American women who have delayed seeing a health care provider for a variety of reasons. The reasons for this lack of early care vary, from failing to recognize the early signs of the disease to being unaware of how to treat it and where to go for financial and medical assistance.

NBIMC must make improvements on two fronts: 1.) The Cancer Center must provide more dedicated care to women with breast cancer– oncologists and nurses currently provide care for all cancer patients, and cannot devote as much time as is needed to breast cancer patients. 2.) NBIMC must improve minority women's awareness of available screening services and treatment options in order to improve outcomes among this underserved group. Research has indicated that, in general, African Americans are comfortable and familiar with their churches, while skeptical about and distrustful of hospitals. Avon funds will provide a Nurse Practitioner (NP) who can provide care to breast cancer patients in the hospital and serve as a nurse educator/community liaison in the community, breaking down these barriers to care so women will feel more at ease in accessing preventative care measures and early detection services.

B. Program Description
Current services
NBIMC, a 671-bed regional care, teaching hospital, is Newark's busiest hospital. NBIMC is well known and respected throughout Newark and Essex County for providing high quality health care in a customer friendly environment regardless of a patient's income or insurance.

The Flo Okin Oncology and Blood Disorders Center at NBIMC, recognized as the leading center for cancer care in the greater Newark region, offers comprehensive, quality cancer care and facilities for the diagnosis and treatment of all types of cancer. Treatment options include surgery, radiation, immunotherapy, chemotherapy, and reinfusion. An inpatient unit and extensive outpatient ambulatory care services are available. The Center's treatment capabilities are complemented by a full range of diagnostic imaging services, including CT Scan, MRI, digital subtraction angiography, mammography, ultrasound, and nuclear medicine. Support services include individual and family counseling, educational programs and support groups.

Since its inception more than 30 years ago, the cancer program's mission has been to meet the needs of the whole patient, physically, and emotionally. To achieve this goal, NBIMC has assembled a team of professionals representing a broad range of disciplines that are highly experienced in and specifically dedicated to cancer care.

Relationships
NBIMC is a major teaching affiliate of the Mount Sinai School of Medicine, New York. NBIMC hosts junior clerkships in the core curriculum and senior electives for Mount Sinai as well as for students from New York College of Osteopathic Medicine, and St. George's University School of Medicine, Grenada. Fellowship programs are offered in Cardiology, Hematology/Oncology, and Nephrology. Residency programs are offered in Cardiovascular Diseases, Internal Medicine,

2

General Surgery, Obstetrics-Gynecology, Med/Peds, Pediatrics, Diagnostic Radiology, Pathology, and Emergency Medicine.

An existing partnership, the School Based Youth Services Program, will provide a point of entry for this Avon initiative into Newark's public schools. Five clinics provide extensive health care services, including medical, dental, mental health and social services to seven Newark schools. In year 1 the project will offer educational programs at these schools while project staff establishes a schedule for the rest of the district. The second main community access point will be the minority serving churches throughout Newark. This project proposes to establish new partnerships with area churches to reach a wider audience of Newark's African Americans and Hispanics. Potential church partners for year 1 are Bethany Baptist Church, Berean Baptist Church, Jehova-Jirch Praise and Worship Church Center and Mount Pleasant Baptist Church.

Hospital departments partnering in this project are the Family Health Center, (which houses the Adult Health Center and the Women's Health Center), and the Center for Geriatric Health Care, all of which serve low-income women. The Adult Health Center provides comprehensive medical services for the entire family while the Women's Health Center provides prenatal care, family planning, pregnancy testing, gynecological services, nutritional consultations, social work services, health education, and adolescent services. The Center for Geriatric Health Care services the local senior population with three board-certified geriatricians, specialty services, house calls for the home bound, a geriatric inpatient unit, and extensive community outreach.

The final route into the community will be through a Center for Geriatric Health Care program, "SWAT" – Senior Wellness Action Team. The Team goes to senior housing sites in the Newark area to offer education and screening programs on a variety of topics such as depression, fall prevention, stress management, tobacco cessation, dementia/memory loss, and many others. Many of these educational programs are accompanied by screenings or risk assessments; the NP will use these established sites to conduct educational seminars and to schedule mammograms.

Research

The Cancer team is a member of the National Surgical Adjuvant Breast and Bowel Project (NSABP), a clinical trials cooperative group supported by the National Cancer Institute. The senior physician in charge of these trials, and Project Director for this initiative, is Dr. Alice Cohen, Medical Director of the Flo Okin Oncology and Blood Disorders Center (CV attached). NBIMC participates in trials on both treatment and prevention of breast cancer. In regard to prevention, NBIMC participates in the Study of Tamoxifen and Raloxifene (STAR), one of the largest breast cancer prevention studies ever. NBIMC also participates in the following treatment trials -

- Protocol B-30: A Three-Arm Randomized Trial To Compare Adjuvant Adriamycin and Cyclophosphamide followed by Taxotere (AC6T); Adriamycin and Taxotere (AT); and Adriamycin, Taxotere, and Cyclophosphamide (ATC) in Breast Cancer Patients with Positive Axillary Lymph Nodes,
- Protocol B-31: A Randomized Trial to Compare the Safety and Efficacy of Adriamycin and Cyclophosphamide followed by Taxol Plus Herceptin in Node-Positive Breast Cancer Patients who have Tumors that Overexpress HER2,

3

Newark Beth Israel Medical Center

- B-34: A Clinical Trial Comparing Adjuvant Clodronate Therapy vs. Placebo in Early-Stage Breast Cancer Patients Receiving Systemic Chemotherapy and/or Tamoxifen or No Therapy, and
- B-35: A Clinical Trial Comparing Anastrozole with Tamoxifen in Postmenopausal Patients with Ductal Carcinoma In Situ Undergoing Lumpectomy with Radiation Therapy.

C. Use of Funds
i)   Personnel

Cancer Center staff consists of six physicians, five nurses, one Breast Cancer Counselor (funded by the Susan G. Komen Foundation), one social worker and one nursing assistant. The staff sees patients with all types of cancers; none of the medical staff is devoted to breast cancer, even though it is the most common cancer at NBIMC. Also, none of the physicians or nurses are bilingual, so the nursing assistant, capable of translating Spanish and Portuguese, is called upon daily. A Nurse Practitioner devoted to breast cancer, preferably bilingual, will be incorporated into the team under this initiative and will report to Dr. Cohen, Medical Director and to the Administrative Director who will oversee the integration of the NP into the patient care team.

The full-time Nurse Practitioner will have responsibilities on three fronts. S/he will spend 50% of time in the Cancer Center providing direct clinical services to breast cancer patients. S/he will spend 30% of time in the community, providing educational programs on the importance of mammography and Self Breast Exam. S/he will devote 20% of time to coordinating with staff at the Women's Health Center, the Center for Geriatric Health, and the Adult Health Center to ensure that all women seen in any center for any reason are informed about their risk factors and screened for breast cancer. A part-time Administrative Assistant, preferably bilingual, will assist the Nurse Practitioner in these duties. Combined, these two new staff positions will provide a dedicated focus for the largest cancer incidence in Newark, resulting in a coordinated breast cancer service that will improve the quality of care of all breast cancer patients seen at NBIMC.

The NP will become a member of the multidisciplinary care team, providing anticipatory guidance, patient and family education, psychosocial and emotional support and dedicated patient follow-up. While current nurses either administer chemotherapy or assist physicians, the NP will use advanced skills in the evaluation, diagnosis and treatment of breast cancer patients and manage therapeutic regimens for acute and chronic problems associated with the disease.

The Administrative Assistant will work two full days. S/he will provide general administrative support, schedule community outreach events, and provide follow-up with patients seen in the Health Centers (Geriatric, Adult, or Women's). The Administrative Assistant will call to confirm appointments and reschedule missed appointments, thus reducing the number of patients lost to follow up by 50%. This position will require extensive phone work, corresponding with clients and partners, and coordinating with clinics, schools, and community agencies. Because s/he will regularly communicate with patients, a bilingual Administrative Assistant is preferred.

ii)   Increase in services

Avon funds will create a coordinated breast cancer service for underserved individuals throughout the greater Newark area. The bilingual NP's role will be as follows:

4

50% of time
a) Provide direct clinical services to Breast Cancer Patients and reduce the number of women lost to follow-up. The NP will act as the clinical link to the hospital for those women s/he meets in the community. S/he will also provide care and support to existing breast cancer patients, thereby addressing the increasing needs presented by a growing patient population.

30% of time
b) Each year, the NP will reach out to 20 local churches to discuss breast cancer issues; s/he will hold breast educational seminars in at least 10 of them. During year 1, the NP will work with the churches that already have a relationship with NBIMC; in years 2 and 3, the NP will forge new relationships.
c) The seven schools that receive services from the school-based clinics will each host one parent workshop each year and provide an entrée into the other 75 Newark public schools/Parent Teacher Associations. Project Director Dr. Alice Cohen is frequently asked to speak at Newark PTA meetings; each meeting is typically attended by about 10 women. The NP to be hired will expand this outreach with the goal of providing an educational program in each school at least once during the grant period.
d) The NP will attend the 16 health fairs sponsored annually by NBIMC in order to raise her/his visibility in the community and provide information to those in attendance.
e) The NP will coordinate with the Senior Wellness Action Team. SWAT gives more than 2,400 seniors at 14 different senior buildings the opportunity to take part in a variety of interactive programs that promote better health care. Under the auspices of SWAT, the NP will offer Breast health seminars and schedule mammograms.
f) Finally, the NP will act as Liaison with the American Cancer Society Community Education Program to ensure that NBIMC is reaching the greatest number of Newark's underserved minority women and providing them with the most up-to-date information about other resources in the community.

20% of time
g) The NP will work with NBIMC's Center for Geriatric Health Care, Women's Health Center, and Adult Health Center to determine an appropriate referral mechanism in each clinic to ensure that all women over the age of 40 who present at any clinic for any reason receive a breast cancer screening and appropriate follow-up. In 2003, there were 4,096 female patients seen at the Center for Geriatric Health Care. Additionally, more than 5,000 women age 40 or over were seen at the Adult Health Center with another 2,217 women over 40 receiving services at the Women's Health Center. Currently, approximately 20% of the women seen in these clinics are screened. The goal is to increase the number of women screened for breast cancer by 15% in each clinic, each year, so that by the end of year 3, 65% of all women over the age of 40 are screened. Whether a woman presents with high blood pressure, diabetes, or any other ailment, she will be offered breast cancer screening services at NBIMC.

iii)   Improvement in the quality of care
A bilingual Nurse Practitioner will provide clinical services, conduct community outreach, and ensure coordination among departments. The Administrative Assistant will assist with follow through and referrals while relieving some of the pressure on existing Flo Okin administrative staff, who deal with all cancer patients. By providing targeted breast cancer screening and

5

Newark Beth Israel Medical Center

treatment services to low-income minority women, these two new positions will improve quality of care for all women. There will be a true continuum of care as there will be one NP devoted to breast cancer that women can meet in their own community, speak with in their own language, and then be seen by that same health care provider in the hospital setting. Working with the three outpatient centers that treat low-income individuals will allow for an overall coordination of services that is unprecedented in Newark. Every woman over the age of 40 that presents in any of the three outpatient centers will be targeted for services.

iv)   Follow-up services

The Komen-funded Breast Cancer Counselor has been at Flo Okin since February 2004. Part of her responsibility is to make contact with every breast cancer patient seen at Flo Okin and guide them through the system, helping them apply for appropriate insurance, charity care, and other aid programs. No woman is denied services at NBIMC because of an inability to pay. The Breast Cancer Counselor will work with the NP and the Administrative Assistant to help any woman needing services navigate the system.

The Administrative Assistant will be responsible for phoning each woman whose medical chart (from any of the three centers) indicates that she is due for a mammography. This person will also follow-up with women seen in the community to make sure they have scheduled a mammography. Avon funds have been requested for transportation so that no woman misses an appointment due to lack of transportation.

v)   Data collection and reporting

The Cancer Registry at NBIMC collects, analyzes, and distributes data to the National Cancer Database and the New Jersey State Department of Health. The Registry conducts follow-up annually on patients, tracking date of diagnosis and current health status. There are currently 12,517 patients on the Registry. The Cancer Registry office is located directly in the Flo Okin Center, adjacent to the Radiation Oncology Department, to allow easy access to outpatient charts and treatment information.

The target population for this initiative is women over 40 needing diagnostic treatment and case management. One goal of the project is to provide a complete breast cancer screening to at least 65% of all women over the age of 40 seen at any of the three clinics. Progress toward meeting this goal will be tracked by the number of women coming in for yearly mammograms. This overall coordination of services will enhance NBIMC current offerings by ensuring that appropriate referrals are made in a timely fashion.

Finally, project staff will track the number of community workshops and seminars held and the attendance at each. These community events are expected to lead to an increase in women using the health care system as preventative, rather than as emergency care. The community events, combined with a proactive effort to screen all women presenting at the medical clinics, will result in a large increase in the number of women screened at NBIMC. Furthermore, there will be a decrease in the number of T3 and T4 diagnoses with a corresponding increase in the number of women presenting at earlier stages. Over the three-year grant period, the NP and Administrative Assistant will provide information about the project to the Cancer Registry to allow for long-term follow-up of all women identified with breast cancer through this project.

6

3. TIMELINE

October 2004
- Grant announcement; comply with all Avon Foundation requirements.
- Project kick-off announced in conjunction with Breast Cancer Awareness Month and National Mammography Day (third Friday in October)
- Project Director works with Human Resources to publish job description/vacancy announcement, begin recruiting for Nurse Practitioner and Administrative Assistant.

November
- Interview and hire personnel
- Initial consultation between Project Director and Clinical Directors of the Adult Health Center, Women's Health Center, and the Center for Geriatric Health

December
- NP meets at least bi-weekly from now until the end of year 3 with Project Director to assess progress and determine necessary adjustments.
- NP begins seeing clinical patients
- Administrative Assistant identifies and sends letters African-American and Spanish-speaking churches throughout the greater Newark area
- NP attends first meeting with American Cancer Society, ongoing meeting schedule as determined by the ACS.
- NP and Admin. Assistant attend general meeting with staff from the three outpatient centers to discuss ways to improve the referral process between the centers and Flo Okin; quarterly meetings follow
- NP meets with School-based clinic representatives to determine schedule for parent workshops
- Admin. Assistant begins working with Komen-funded Breast Cancer Counselor to ensure women are receiving the help they need in applying for aid and navigating the system

January 2005
- NP meets with SWAT director to determine screening schedule for senior housing buildings
- Admin. Assistant makes follow-up calls to interested churches
- NP attends initial meetings with church leaders
- School-based workshops at those schools with school-based clinics begins, all host a workshops by the end of year 1
- Monthly chart review of women seen at the medical clinics begins, continues throughout grant period

February
- Church-based workshops begin and continue for the remainder of the grant period. At least 10 church-based workshops will be conducted each grant year
- Senior housing workshops begin; at least 7 are conducted each year

7

April
- File 6-month report with Avon Foundation
- NP attends first of 16 health fairs sponsored by NBIMC

May
- NP or Project Director attends National Breast Cancer Awareness Month's Board of Sponsors National Summit in New York

September
- NP begins attending PTA meetings/conducting parent workshops at those Newark schools without school based clinics. These workshops continue throughout years 2 and 3. At least 10 will be conducted each year.
- Schools with school-based clinics will host an additional round of workshops each year.
- Screening referrals from each of the 3 outpatient centers have increased by 15%
- 6-month report to Avon Foundation is completed by the end of the month

October
- Special events and a city-wide screening day are offered in conjunction with National Breast Cancer Awareness month
- Annual personnel evaluation is conducted by Project Director on NP and Admin Assistant
- Church-based workshop schedule is set for year 2

April 2006
- File 6-month report with Avon Foundation

September
- Screening referrals from each of the 3 outpatient clinics have increased by another 15%
- Referral mechanism is institutionalized and operating effectively
- 6-month report to Avon Foundation is completed by the end of the month

October
- Special events and a city-wide screening day are offered in conjunction with National Breast Cancer Awareness month
- Annual personnel evaluation is conducted by Project Director on NP and Admin Assistant
- Church- and School-based workshop schedule and senior housing screening schedule is set for year 3

April 2007
- File 6-month report with Avon Foundation

September
- Screening referrals from each of the 3 outpatient clinics have increased by another 15%
- Final report to Avon Foundation is completed by the end of the month

8

BUDGET
Newark Beth Israel Medical Center

October 1, 2004 to September 30, 2005 YEAR ONE		AVON Foundation Request	*Other Funding Sources	Agency In-Kind	Total Budget
	Assumptions	A	B	C	A+B+C
Personnel					
Medical Director	XXXXX			XXXXX	XXXXX
Administrative Director				XXXXX	XXXXX
Nurse Practitioner	XXXXX	XXXXX			XXXXX
Administrative Assistant	XXXXX	XXXXX			XXXXX
Breast Cancer Counselor	XXXXX XXXXX		XXXXX		XXXXX
Subtotal Personnel		95,600	7,500	38,250	141,350
Fringe @23%		21,988	1,725	8,798	32,511
Personnel total		**117,588**	9,225	47,048	173,861
Equipment					
Other than Personnel Services					
Transportation					
Client Transportation	750 cab fares @$7	5,250			5,250
Educational Materials					
NCI materials	3,000@.10 each	300			300
Other materials (shower cards, Key chains, posters, etc.		1,500		500	2,000
Computer software, hardware (laptop)		1,500			1,500
Subtotal OTPS		8,550	0	500	9,050
Personnel and OTPS sub-Total		126,138	9,225	47,548	182,911
Indirect expenses (@10%)		12,614			12,614
TOTAL		**138,752**	9,225	47,548	195,525

October 1, 2005 to September 30, 2006 YEAR TWO					
	Assumptions	AVON Foundation Request	*Other Funding Sources	Agency In-Kind	Total Budget
		A	B	C	A+B+C
Personnel					
Medical Director	XXXXX			XXXXX	XXXXX
Administrative Director	XXXXX			XXXXX	XXXXX
Nurse Practitioner	XXXXX	XXXXX			XXXXX
Administrative Assistant	XXXXX	XXXXX			XXXXX
Breast Cancer Counselor	XXXXX		XXXXX		XXXXX
Subtotal Personnel		98,780	7,725	39,398	145,873
Fringe @23%		22,719	1,776	9,062	33,557
Personnel total		**121,499**	9,501	48,460	179,460
Equipment					
Other than Personnel Services					
Transportation					
Client Transportation	750 cab fares @$7	5,250			5,250
Educational Materials					
NCI materials	3,000@.10 each	300			300
Other materials (shower cards, Key chains, posters, etc.		1,500		500	2,000
Subtotal OTPS		7,050	0	500	7,550
Personnel and OTPS sub-Total		128,549	9,501	48,960	187,010
Indirect expenses (@10%)		12,855			12,855
TOTAL		**141,404**	9,501	48,960	199,865

	Assumptions	AVON Foundation Request	*Other Funding Sources	Agency In-Kind	Total Budget
		A	B	C	A+B+C
Personnel					
Medical Director	XXXXX			XXXXX	XXXXX
Administrative Director	XXXXX			XXXXX	XXXXX
Nurse Practitioner	XXXXX	XXXXX			XXXXX
Administrative Assistant	XXXXX	XXXXX			XXXXX
Breast Cancer Counselor	XXXXX		XXXXX		XXXXX
Subtotal Personnel		102,032	7,950	40,580	151,562
Fringe @23%		23,467	1,829	9,333	34,629
Personnel total		**125,499**	9,779	49,913	185,191
Equipment					
Other than Personnel Services					
Transportation					
Client Transportation	750 cab fares @$7	5,250			5,250
Educational Materials					
NCI materials	3,000@.10 each	300			300
Other materials (shower cards, Key chains, posters, etc.		1,000		500	1,500
Subtotal OTPS		6,550	0	500	7,050
Personnel and OTPS sub-Total		132,049	9,779	50,413	192,241
Indirect expenses (@10%)		13,205			13,205
TOTAL		**145,254**	9,779	50,413	205,446
3 YEAR PROJECT TOTAL		**425,410**	28,505	146,921	600,836

October 1, 2006 to September 30, 2007
YEAR THREE

Oncology Nurse Practitioner Job Description

Reports to Medical Director and Administrative Director
of the Flo Okin Oncology and Blood Disorders Center

I. Administrative
- Establishes goals and objectives for his/her area in congruence with the Flo Okin Oncology and Blood Disorders Center goals and objectives on an annual basis.
- Participates in review and revision of job descriptions, policies, and procedures.
- Ensures that developmental and intradepartmental policies, procedures, and standards of care are maintained and assists in interpreting these for patients and visitors.
- Promotes philosophy of employer and acts as a role model and resource person for staff.
- Ensures and maintains patient/family confidentiality at all times.

II. Clinical
- Assesses the physical and psychosocial status of clients by means of interview, health history, physical examination, and diagnostic studies.
- Recognizes deviations from normal in the physical assessment.
- Works in collaboration with a physician in formulating treatment plans for health problems and follow-up.
- Writes prescriptions for medication, blood products based upon laboratory results, routine diagnostic and follow-up studies, therapeutic measures, and post-discharge care in accordance with written practice protocols.
- Determines eligibility of patients for entry into clinical trials based on findings.
- Requests written consultation from physicians and other healthcare professionals to ensure appropriate and quality patient care.
- Interprets and evaluates findings of studies/tests.
- Relays appropriate information regarding patient care to the collaborating physician.
- Administers therapeutic measures and obtains specimens as prescribed.
- Evaluates the quality of care provided and recommends changes for improvement.
- Initiates appropriate actions to facilitate the implementation of therapeutic plans that are consistent with the continuing healthcare needs of the client.
- Dictates follow-up letters to referring physicians with summaries of treatment, response, and plan.
- Maintains provision of preventive health services (e.g. screening, risks assessment, immunizations, PAP smears, self-breast exam).
- Dictates or writes patient history, admissions, care plans, progress, and discharge notes.
- Interacts with program assistants and data managers for optimal patient care.
- Assists in the management of family dynamics and coping mechanisms during acute and chronic phases of patient care.
- Conducts or participates in daily multidisciplinary rounds and ensures appropriate and quality care for assigned patient.
- Provides on-call coverage.
- Triages patients; determines the urgency of physician's evaluation.

III. Skills

- Effective verbal and written communication skills to communicate with diverse populations, including physicians, employees, patients, and families.
- Leadership skills to direct others toward the successful treatment of patients.
- Analytical skills to evaluate patient status and healthcare procedures/techniques and to monitor quality of care.
- Fiscal skills to monitor and control costs and revenue.
- Willingness to learn and remain flexible in the changing healthcare environment.
- Ability to assist staff in times of crisis or emergency.
- Ability to conceptualize, develop, and implement new ideas or systems.
- Ability to exercise sound judgement and discretion while performing duties.
- Ability to meet with the public outside the institution and efficiently market and promote cancer treatment.
- Ability to determine work priorities, assign work, and insure proper completion of work assignments.
- Bilingual Spanish preferred

IV. Communication

- Establishes relationships with professional and/or other health-related groups within the community.
- Coordinates screening and diagnostic procedures with the Adult Health Center, The Women's Health Center, and the Center for Geriatric Health Care
- Educates patients and families about the disease process and treatment.
- Provides information to patients and families related to symptom management and psychosocial response to the diagnosis of cancer and related treatment.
- Coordinates care for complex patients through multidisciplinary team.
- Provides consultation to lay groups and other healthcare professionals in the community.
- Shares clinical expertise with professional and supportive personnel.
- Documents and reports care in an accurate, timely manner using appropriate forms and records.
- Works effectively with others. Collaborates with other health disciplines to ensure continuity and quality of care.
- Uses interpersonal skills to work productively with all levels of hospital personnel.

V. Qualifications

- License and current registration to practice in New Jersey
- Graduate from a registered NP program.
- Master's degree in nursing.
- One full-time year of post-licensure clinical nursing experience.
- Oncology experience preferred

A Proposal From

Boys & Girls Clubs of Greater Milwaukee

Milwaukee, Wisconsin

To

The Hearst Foundation, Inc.

New York, New York

Requested amount: $150,000; **Amount received:** $150,000 over three years

Funder's comments:

"When reading a proposal at the Hearst Foundation as I'm sure is the case at other foundations, we like to know right up front what the needs are, what is the dollar amount requested, and to have at least a brief description of how grant funds will be used. The proposal from the Boys & Girls Clubs of Greater Milwaukee provided all of that information in a format that was easy to read and digest.

"We already had a history with this organization, since we had supported it in the past. And a program officer from the Hearst Foundation had made a site visit and met with the executive director. So we were fairly familiar with the organization itself. In addition we had heard very good things about the Boys & Girls Clubs' programs from colleagues and others in the local community.

"With all of this as background, the proposal persuaded us that this was indeed a well run organization and one that we'd like to support. The cover letter was excellent and the project described very clearly with just enough background information. There was a good budget and virtually all the information we needed to make a decision on this grant. All the elements came together in this case to lead one to say 'This is something we want to fund.'"

—*Ilene Mack, Senior Program Officer, The Hearst Foundation, Inc.*

Notes:

The complete proposal included the following attachments: organizational budget, list of major donors, IRS tax-exempt letter, audited financial statement, list of board of trustees, and annual report.

BOYS & GIRLS CLUBS
OF GREATER MILWAUKEE

February 18, 2005

Ms. Ligia Cravo
Hearst Foundation, Inc.
888 Seventh Avenue
New York, NY 10106

Dear Ligia:

Thank you again for your past support of the Boys & Girls Clubs of Greater Milwaukee. With the Hearst Foundation's commitment, we have been able to sustain membership of 8,000 children at all our Milwaukee satellite after-school sites. This enables members to keep coming back day after day and participate in high-quality, life-changing programs.

Our satellite site initiative has been nothing less than a huge success. When we last sought funding, there were 13 satellite sites. We now have 18 satellite sites. Last year, we added *35th Street*, *Cass* and *Townsend Schools* to our growing list of satellite sites. As you are aware, these sites are situated in densely-populated, high-crime areas of Milwaukee.

Our recent, year-end membership total of 28,041 represents the most children ever registered in the Clubs' history. This membership number is up from 22,141, an increase of almost 27 percent from 2002. The increase in Club membership is due in part to massive City and State cutbacks in summer and after-school programs.

Most of our accomplishments would not have been possible without faithful friends like Hearst who believe in the Clubs' mission – *to inspire and empower all young people, especially those from disadvantaged circumstances, to realize their full potential as productive, responsible and caring citizens.*

We fulfill this mission with services (delivered by over 400 employees, 300 volunteers, and over 70 Trustees), that include summer and after-school programs to kids at six central-city branches, 18 satellite sites located in public school buildings, and *Camp Whitcomb/Mason* in Hartland. Six core service areas create a framework for everything we do:

Character & Leadership Development   *Arts & Cultural Education*
Education & Career Development   *Health & Life Skills*
Sports, Fitness & Recreation   *Outdoor/Environmental Education*

The Positive Place For Kids

Mardak Center for Administration & Training • 1558 North 6th Street • P.O. Box 12486 • Milwaukee, WI 53212

The *Literacy Program* is the single most critical feature under the *Education & Career Development* umbrella, unifying the elements of our educational programming into a well-organized, high-priority effort.

Ligia, at this time I ask that you consider a grant of $150,000 over three years in support of the Clubs' *Literacy Program* and the new *Reading First Program* at the Boys & Girls Clubs of Greater Milwaukee. The *Reading First Program* is a critically-needed expansion of our *Literacy Program*, as students of *Milwaukee Public Schools* are trying to meet the requirements of the federal *No Child Left Behind* law.

Last year, annual program participation in the *Literacy Program* ranged from 80 to 150 youth at each of our Clubs, with an additional 7,000 children participating in the program at our satellite sites. The program provides members with a quiet environment, computer access, and the supervision of a trained volunteer or Club staff so that children can succeed in the classroom.

Implementation of the *Reading First Program* will begin this summer, when Club staff will recruit and train volunteers and mentors. These dedicated professionals will provide one-on-one attention to Club members to improve literacy and other academic skills. In the fall of 2005, Club staff and volunteers will work with MPS to identify students in the fourth grade who did not pass or barely met their proficiency exams the previous year. Third grade children who are intent on passing their upcoming proficiency tests will also be identified. These are the children who will be recruited for the *Reading First Program*. The regular participation goal for *Reading First* during 2005 will be 175 children.

By sponsoring the Clubs' *Literacy Program,* and the *Reading First Program*, the Hearst Foundation can support the Clubs while receiving great exposure for its generosity. Milwaukee will see firsthand that the Hearst Foundation is dedicated to promoting literacy, strengthening families, and helping children reach their potential as productive, responsible and caring citizens. Your general support means more than 28,000 children will know a safe place, caring staff, and opportunity to succeed this year.

Thank you, Ligia, for this opportunity to tell you about our exciting new program as well as all of the general success impacting kids' lives in Milwaukee. If you require additional information, please contact me at 414-267-8103

Best regards,

James L. Clark
President & CEO

**BOYS & GIRLS CLUBS OF GREATER MILWAUKEE
SEEKS GRANT OF $150,000 OVER THREE YEARS
FROM THE HEARST FOUNDATION
IN SUPPORT OF THE *LITERACY PROGRAM*
AND THE NEW *'READING FIRST'* PROGRAM**

Thank you for considering a grant of $150,000 over three years in support of the Clubs' *Literacy Program,* including *Literacy Program* enhancements and the new *Reading First Program* at the Boys & Girls Clubs of Greater Milwaukee.

For 117 years, the Clubs have helped Milwaukee's disadvantaged children and youth reach their fullest potential by providing high-quality, after-school and summer programs. Under the guidance of concerned adults, Club members grow and thrive. We are honored to request the Hearst Foundation play a part in our successful and growing *Literacy Program.*

Last year, the Clubs' *Literacy Program* helped 650 Milwaukee children successfully improve their reading skills. The program provides members with a quiet environment, computer access, and the supervision of a trained volunteer or Club staff so that children can succeed in the classroom. Youth can read books, utilize on-line dictionaries, complete on-line professional tutorials, study flash cards, and participate in writing activities depending on each child's needs. Not only is the *Literacy Program* popular with kids, but it has also allowed us to establish a cohesive, consistent, and systematic educational effort among all Club branches.

HOW THIS SPONSORSHIP CAN WORK FOR YOU
By sponsoring the Clubs' *Literacy Program* and the new *Reading First Program*, the Hearst Foundation can support the Clubs while receiving great exposure for its generosity. In short, we want to show Milwaukee that the Hearst Foundation is dedicated to promoting literacy, strengthening families, and helping children reach their potential as productive, responsible and caring citizens.

We plan to highlight your support of *Reading First* in various ways. Our web-site, newsletter, and annual report – which reach thousands of people each year – will contain written mentions about your sponsorship. The Clubs look forward to working with you so that we effectively emphasize Hearst's commitment to children, to the community, and to the future of our city.

WHY LITERACY PROGRAMS ARE CRITICAL TO THE CLUBS

- "There is a persistent achievement gap in Wisconsin between students of different races and socioeconomic classes. Almost two-thirds of African American children in the fourth grade today cannot read at a basic grade level. For white children, that figure is 27 percent." – *U.S. Rep. Tom Petri statement to U.S. Educators on May 12, 2003.*

- Wisconsin Department of Public Instruction (DPI) data shows that on the fourth grade reading test only 50 percent of MPS students scored at a level of proficient or better. This compares with 79 percent of students statewide. A similar percentage of fourth grade MPS students were proficient in language and social studies. However, less than 50 percent of MPS fourth graders were proficient in math and science. This weakness is exacerbated in higher grade levels.

- "Just 41 percent of black students who had started high school in 1996 picked up their diplomas in 2000 in Wisconsin-the worst graduation rate among the 31 states for which there were data-the Manhattan Institute has noted. Dairyland's white graduation rate was more than twice the black rate-the biggest disparity among the states." – *January 26, 2003 Milwaukee Journal-Sentinel*

- "Those without a high school education represent 13 percent of Wisconsin's adults but 46 percent of the state's prison population and 46 percent of the state's welfare program participants." – University of Wisconsin- Milwaukee Center for Economic Development report – *"Stealth Depression, Joblessness in the City of Milwaukee since 1990," by Marc Levine.*

ORGANIZATION INFORMATION

The Clubs' mission is to *inspire and empower all children, especially those from disadvantaged circumstances, to realize their full potential as productive, responsible and caring citizens.* We fulfill this mission with services (delivered by over 400 employees, 300 volunteers, and over 70 Trustees), that include summer and after-school programs to kids at six central-city branches, 18 satellite sites located in public school buildings, and *Camp Whitcomb/Mason* in Hartland. Six core service areas create a framework for everything we do.

Character & Leadership Development	*Arts & Cultural Education*
Education & Career Development	*Health & Life Skills*
Sports, Fitness & Recreation	*Outdoor & Environmental Education*

Notably, the *Literacy Program* is the single most critical feature under the *Education & Career Development* umbrella, unifying the elements of our educational programming into a well-organized, high-priority effort.

Our 2004 year-end membership total of 28,041 represents the most children ever registered in the Clubs' history. This membership number is up from 22,141, an increase of almost 27 percent from 2002. The increase in Club membership is due in part to massive City and State cutbacks in summer and after-school programs. In fact, we are operating on roughly the same level of funding as 2000, while serving many more children. While we remain the preferred youth development agency in Greater Milwaukee, we are no stranger to the difficult economic environment of the last few years. Fortunately, we have been able to maintain a minimal $5 annual membership fee for Club members. Those who cannot afford this fee are given an opportunity to earn their membership through work at the Clubs.

Founded in 1887, the Boys & Girls Clubs remains Milwaukee's oldest and largest youth-development organization. Accolades for the Boys & Girls Clubs include being named one of the nation's top youth charities (2003 *Chronicle of Philanthropy*). We work with kids from Milwaukee's most disadvantaged neighborhoods, spending 80 cents of every dollar on youth programs - a high level of operating efficiency.

THE HOMEWORK FIRST PROGRAM

"After you finish your homework." Many of us heard our mom or dad say those words. There is good reason why adults make a big deal out of homework. Homework helps children learn. We know that getting a good education can help people build the kind of life that they want. Adults can understand the importance of hard work and persistence, but perhaps that is the benefit of hindsight. For children and youth in the middle of various trials and tribulations, the value of those traits may seem less certain.

Because over two-thirds of our kids come from families that earn less than $25,000 annually, they cannot always rely on their parents to read to them, help them with their homework, or talk with them about the importance of succeeding in school. Since these children desperately need extra assistance outside of the classroom to help develop their skills, this is where the Clubs must step in. Our educational programming allows members to grow their reading and mathematical abilities, critical thinking tools, creativity and technological know-how. The lack of these skills, especially reading skills, has dire consequences when these children reach adulthood. Through *Homework First* the cycle of poverty may be broken so that disadvantaged children can become productive and dynamic members of society.

The Clubs' *Homework First* program provides members with a quiet environment, computer access, and the supervision of a trained volunteer or Club staff member so that they can complete their homework assignments accurately and on time. Staff track members' success and review completed homework assignments for accuracy. Eighteen Club sites are attached to schools, putting the Clubs in a unique position to nurture children in their academic studies. The need for programs like *Homework First* is great for Club members, many of whom are MPS students facing great barriers in their lives. Last year, program participation in *Homework First* ranged from 80 to 150 youth at each Club, with an additional 7,000 children participating in the program at Club satellite sites.

CONTINUUM OF PROGRAMS UNDER THE HOMEWORK FIRST UMBRELLA
The Programs Hearst will also be supporting include:

STAR Reading
STAR Reading is a computer-adaptive reading test that quickly and accurately assesses student reading for grades 1 through 12. STAR not only monitors each student's growth at key points in the school or program year, but also provides grade level equivalents, percentile ranks, and instructional reading levels. STAR results give students a "Zone of Proximal Development" (ZPD), which allows educators to appropriately guide students to books within their reading level. The educator helps the student set goals for the marking period, including reading level and point value goals. Program effectiveness is measured through 1) participation and 2) pre and post test in reading competency.

Accelerated Reader (AR)
Accelerated Reader is a computer-based literacy program designed to motivate, measure and manage student reading practice. *Accelerated Reader* is offered to Club members ages 6-18, with special emphasis on youth in grades K-5. Participants take a quick STAR assessment test upon enrollment and every six to eight weeks thereafter to determine their reading level and gauge improvement. Members then select books within their reading "zone" based on a color-coded book organizing system. Next, youth read their selection independently or with the help of a peer or adult. Finally, members take a computer quiz to test their reading comprehension. Members earn points for reading books and completing quizzes, which allow them to buy prizes from an incentive catalog and participate in "celebration events" such as pizza parties and ice cream socials.

CyberPlace Literacy

CyberPlace is more than just a "cool" place to use computers. In addition to books, computers play an important role in the children's learning efforts. Kids utilize the hardware, software, on-line dictionaries and encyclopedia that are available to them in our high-tech *CyberPlaces* to augment their learning. Internet access is also provided for project research. The *CyberPlace Literacy*

Program changes children's lives by helping them discover their potential. The staff notes that many children are improving their reading rate and accuracy, letter sounds and knowledge, speech, and basic math skills. As they successfully read books and pass *Accelerated Reader* tests, participants can also earn rewards. In this program, kids are learning that reading *is fun!*

Reading is Fundamental (RIF)

We offer *literacy programming* consisting of a Reading Club at each branch. Weekly activities include read aloud sessions, individual reading times, and *Stop, Drop & Read*. Books are given as incentives. Progress and reading levels of youth are tracked through the *Accelerated Reader* software, which helps staff and volunteers identify specific education needs of children and how to best help them achieve.

Licensing – As Needed

All youth must become "licensed" to utilize the *CyberPlace*. This ensures that the youth have a basic understanding of computers and the rules of *CyberPlace*. Staff spends one-on-one time teaching the basics such as how to turn on the computer, names of computer parts, and how to navigate in Windows. Youth also go through an instructional CD-ROM created by Boys & Girls Clubs of America (BGCA). This CD-ROM covers: rules for communication and online behavior, the need for online anonymity, how to protect personal information, and how to identify off-limits areas. Additionally, a short test checks members' comprehension of program information.

Tutor.com

Tutor.com brings live homework help through unlimited access points at the Clubs. The tutoring is provided by professional tutors, professors, certified teachers, college students and graduate students from across the globe to our Club technology rooms via the Internet. Core academic assistance is offered in math, science, social studies and English for $4^{th} - 12^{th}$ graders. In 20-minute sessions, Club members have the opportunity to learn one-to-one from subject experts in math (Algebra, Geometry and Calculus), science (Earth Science, Biology, Chemistry and Physics), social studies, and English. Monthly reports are provided to Club staff regarding exactly how many students are using the software, the most popular subjects, the most frequented grade levels, students' ratings and students' comments.

CompassLearning Odyssey

This online reference database improves children's literacy and reading skills and promotes critical thinking and research abilities. *CompassLearning Odyssey* brings together three of the most respected names in education: *Weekly Reader*, *The World Almanac Education Group*, and *Facts on File News Services*. With these online tools and offline materials, students develop a higher order of thinking and become involved in their own quest for knowledge.

2004 LITERACY PROGRAM ENHANCEMENTS

Enhancements to the *Literacy Program* offered, starting in Fall 2004, are *Tutor.com* and *CompassLearning Odyssey's* online reference database. Both of these enhancements to our *Literacy Program* are currently being offered at five Club branches, with the sixth and newest branch, *Daniels-Mardak*, starting the program during 2005.

2005 LITERACY PROGRAM ENHANCEMENTS

Studies show that of the children who are diagnosed with reading problems in the third grade, 74 percent continue with problems into the ninth grade (Fletcher et al, 1994). This shows the importance of learning to read by the third grade. Without intervention, reading problems do not diminish over time, but persist through the school years and into adulthood.

Additionally, difficulty with reading does not just affect a child's ability in school, but carries over as low self-esteem into every aspect of his or her life. A goal of proposed enhancements to the existing *Literacy Program* is to make reading a reality for every Club member, before it is too late.

Literacy and *Education Programs* at our six branches and 18 satellite sites are designed to increase the academic skills and enhance the self-esteem of all club members through a variety of fun, hands-on learning activities that build skills and provide information needed for success in school.

"READING FIRST" PROGRAM

Reading First is a 2005 enhancement of our *Homework First Program*. Since the number of Wisconsin students taking statewide standardized tests will grow by about 80 percent next year, even more students of *Milwaukee Public Schools* are trying to meet the requirements by the federal *No Child Left Behind* law.

All third graders in the state are required to take the *Wisconsin Reading Comprehension Test* each March. The assigned proficiency categories include: advanced, proficient, basic and minimal. The third graders' scores are based on their responses to the comprehension questions.

The *Reading First Program* includes:

- During summer 2005, Club staff will recruit and train volunteers and mentors, including *AmeriCorps* volunteers, for the new *Reading First Program*. An adequate number of bi-lingual volunteers will also be secured for the *Reading First Program*. These volunteers provide one-on-one attention to Club members to improve literacy and other academic skills. Collaborations with University of

Wisconsin-Milwaukee, Marquette University, Alverno College, and Wisconsin Lutheran College provide student volunteers through service learning and work-study placements. The semester-long commitment varies from 20-150 hours and is usually done in connection with a college course. All volunteers receive an on-site orientation and further training to serve in their new role. Tutors will teach Club members how to learn letters and sounds and read for meaning. Children will have opportunities to practice reading with many types of books. By addressing the needs of a child early on, we can prevent reading failure.

- In the fall of 2005, Club staff and volunteers will work with MPS to identify students in the fourth grade who did not pass or barely met their proficiency exams the previous year. Third grade children who are intent on passing their upcoming proficiency tests will also be identified. These children will be recruited for Reading First. MPS will tell the Clubs in what area of reading the children are deficient. Club staff will put special focus on struggling yet motivated youth who display the potential to improve in school. The regular participation goal for Reading First during 2005 will be 175 children.

- Each Club will provide established dedicated space for *Reading First*, referred to as the *Education Room*. This area is comprised of a library and a *Technology Learning Center*; this is the primary area where homework assistance and structured educational activities are available throughout the day. Staff and volunteers will assist fourth grade students with their reading homework and promote recreational reading in a quiet, nurturing environment. During *Reading First* time, from 3 to 5 p.m., all staff and volunteers support quiet, contemplative time for homework completion as well as recreational reading.

- To provide the public and peer recognition so critical for participant motivation, Club staff will recognize the top *Reading First* participants (i.e. those who have made greatest effort and improvement) during the year with special celebrations. To promote family involvement, quarterly *Family Recognition Nights* will be held at each Club, honoring those members who improved their reading skills, verified by assessments. These children will receive recognition awards and the entire family will be treated to pizza and refreshments. This recognition is vital for continued participation and strengthens families in the process.

- Throughout the year, *Reading First* participants will also receive healthy snacks, playing cards, crayons, Uno cards, stuffed animals, basketballs, gift certificates and applause from their peers, staff and volunteers. Additionally, children are allowed to conduct their own internet research and play web games upon completing reading homework. As the coup de gras at the end of the year, star participants are honored in an awards ceremony and banquet.

- Finally, Club staff will follow *Reading First* participants' involvement and success through data provided via our *Clubs Count* tracking system and *Accelerated Reader*. This information will be a key resource to staff, volunteers, and the children themselves. In addition, standardized reading scores will be a future indicator in the Clubs' longitudinal study.

- The Clubs anticipate similar outcomes with *Reading First* to our *Homework First Program*, which reported that 66 percent of Club participants achieved measurable improvement in ability or grade level within two report card grading periods.

EDUCATION ROOM LIBRARIES

Children who have access to attractive, interesting, well-written books in the primary grades are more likely to practice enough to achieve mastery of the alphabetic principle. Since many of the libraries within the Milwaukee County Federated Library System have reduced or eliminated weekday evening hours, the libraries inside each Clubs' *Education Room* are even more vital, and receiving more usage.

The *Reading Library* at each branch is in dire need of new reading material. New reading material must be purchased annually, so that children are regularly stimulated with new words and images. Besides acquiring additional books, the Clubs must also purchase accompanying quiz books, so that each child can be properly assessed for comprehension.

SUMMER READING CLUB

In addition to reduction of hours at all Milwaukee County libraries, nearly all of MPS' elementary schools have limited hours and programs during summer, due to budget cuts. Summer programs to enhance reading and literacy programs are greatly needed in Milwaukee. Staff, volunteers and *AmeriCorps* volunteers will work with young readers at the Clubs. The new *Summer Reading Club* will ensure children continue to learn throughout summer, when schools are closed. Club members will receive an incentive prize – ranging from a toy to an event ticket – for every 60 minutes that they read.

Tickets can be accumulated to purchase larger prizes, such as family passes to the zoo or certificates to purchase ice cream. Children's book authors and illustrators will visit the *Summer Reading Club*; this will include a special visit from a beloved costumed Dr. Seuss character. At least 180 children in our six branches will be enrolled in the *Summer Reading Club*.

Besides the *Summer Reading Club*. During summer, *Accelerated Reader* is offered at all Club *CyberPlace Technologies Rooms*, giving children the opportunity to continue learning while school is not in session.

HOW WE KNOW OUR LITERACY PROGRAM IS MAKING A DIFFERENCE

The Clubs' educational programming changes children's lives. We know that our approach is working, thanks to findings of a longitudinal study. We have committed significant resources to conduct a longitudinal study – which commenced in early 2001 – to show the positive, lasting effects of our work in Milwaukee. The great news is that the latest findings indicate that our youth-development approach is succeeding:

- After becoming Club members, 84 percent of those considered juvenile delinquents avoid further brushes with the law;
- Club members attending MPS average a 13.4 percent higher GPA than their non-Club attending peers; high-school-age members have a 61 percent higher GPA; and
- Club members have a 10 percent higher attendance rate than children who attend the same schools but are not Club members.

Measurements in the area of education are very encouraging. When comparing members who participate in the Clubs' educational programs, such as *Homework First* and *Accelerated Reader*, to Club members who don't participate in educational programs:

- 38 percent achieve a higher grade point average
- 37 percent are less likely to be habitual truants
- 6 percent have a higher school attendance rate

Homework First provides important educational support for Club members. Our latest outcome study also reports that 429 out of 650 youth served by *Homework First* achieved measurable improvement in ability or grade level within two report card grading periods, meaning 66 percent of Club participants met their goal!

These statistics are truly astonishing if you consider that Club members are more likely than other children in Milwaukee to:

- live in a single-parent home or with neither parent; or
- live in foster care; and
- have low incomes.

WHO WE SERVE

As the following demographic profile outlines, our audience is largely central city minority youth, and they hail from predominantly low-income and single parent households.

Member Age		_Gender_	
Ages 6-12	55%	Male	57%
Ages 13-18	45%	Female	43%

Race/Ethnicity		_Household Income_	
African American	70%	$0-$11,999	40%
Hispanic American	19%	$12,000-$14,999	11%
Caucasian	7%	$15,000-$24,999	14%
Asian American	1%	$25,000-$49,999	11%
American Indian	1%	$50,000 plus	3%
Other	2%	Unknown	20%

HOW THE HEARST FOUNDATION CAN PLAY A PART IN OUR SUCCESS

The Boys & Girls Clubs remains extremely pleased with the outcomes of the _Literacy Program_ thus far and, in partnership with the Hearst Foundation, plans to continue to grow both the program as well as its success. We hope to show even more positive outcomes during the next year of our longitudinal study.

Your backing of the _Literacy Program,_ and _Literacy Program_ enhancements including and the new _Reading First Program_ will assist us in reaching this community's neediest children, helping them to develop the skills and sense of responsibility to succeed.

Major Corporate and Foundation Donors

Philip Morris U.S.A
Argosy Foundation
Daniel M. Soref Charitable Trust
Northwestern Mutual Foundation
Payne & Dolan, Inc.
Joy Global Foundation
Miller Brewing Company
David & Julia Uihlein Charitable Foundation
Helen Bader Foundation, Inc.
Badger Mutual Insurance
Richard & Ethel Herzfeld Foundation
Hearst Foundation
Nicholas Family Foundation
Lynde & Harry Bradley Foundation
Marshall & Ilsley Foundation, Inc.
Harley-Davidson Foundation

Boys & Girls Club of Greater Milwaukee
Education & Literacy Operating Budget - 2005

	2005 Budget
Expenses	
Salaries	$ 597,081
Employee Benefits	97,026
Payroll Taxes	67,995
Subtotal Compensation	762,102
Professional Fees And Service	-
Temporary Help	-
Supplies	30,868
Telephone	-
Postage & Shipping	-
Utility & Occupancy	64,262
Printing & Publications	1,969
Local Transportation	-
Training & Conferences	-
Client Assistance	-
Organizational Dues	-
Insurance	46,640
Financing Costs	-
Allocated Administration	117,759
Total Operating Expenses	261,497
Grand Total Expenses	$ 1,023,600

Boys & Girls Clubs of Greater Milwaukee
2005 Operating Budget

	2004 Actuals (unaudited)	2005 Approved Budget
Revenue		
Annual Campaign	$ 3,301,763	$ 3,465,000
Restricted Gifts	265,051	741,000
Government & Other Grants	2,469,998	2,381,000
School Site Grant Funding	2,313,097	2,384,000
Payments for Services & Supplies	314,657	351,000
Facility Use	456,844	519,000
Investment Distribution	825,995	795,000
United Way Allocation	1,261,677	1,275,000
Total Revenue	**11,209,082**	**11,911,000**
Expenses		
Salaries	6,744,395	7,215,000
Employee Benefits	842,999	968,000
Payroll Taxes	719,030	823,000
Subtotal Compensation Expenses	**8,306,424**	**9,006,000**
Professional Fees & Services	309,287	304,000
Temporary Help	191,451	242,000
Supplies & Minor Equipment	831,704	660,000
Telephone	85,305	99,000
Postage & Shipping	39,405	45,000
Utilities & Occupancy	476,432	510,000
Printing & Publications	83,084	89,000
Local Transportation	234,864	228,000
Training & Conferences	79,177	89,000
Client Assistance	61,791	74,000
Organizational Dues	49,778	55,000
Insurance	399,867	474,000
Financing Costs	5,336	6,000
Increase to Bad Debt Reserve	45,000	30,000
Subtotal Non-compensation Expenses	**2,892,481**	**2,905,000**
Grand Total Expenses	**11,198,905**	**11,911,000**
Surplus/(Deficit) from Operations	**$ 10,177**	**$ -**

A Proposal From
Chinatown Community Development Center
San Francisco, California

To
The California Endowment
Woodland Hills, California

Requested amount: $495,000; **Amount received:** $495,000 over three years

Funder's comments:

"At The California Endowment, we do not have a formal application form. We do, however, require that applicants complete a common cover sheet. In the case of the Chinatown Community Development Center request, we first held a meeting with representatives of this group to discuss the general parameters of the project. I always think that it is good practice for a grantseeker to try to engage in an early conversation with a program officer to make sure that you are addressing the foundation's goals. My session with this applicant enabled me to provide advice on how to 'frame' their activities to address our goal areas. By this I mean that I advised them to emphasize certain activities that spoke more about connecting residents to health and social services.

"I view the executive summary as important. I often look to the executive summary to provide a synthesized version of the proposal. If the executive summary does not include the critical components that fit our guidelines, I may read through the proposal more quickly noting that it's probably one we'll decline. If there are references to activities that fit within our guidelines, I will read it more thoroughly. In addition to the executive summary, all of the other proposal components were present.

"The strongest features of this proposal in my opinion were the description of resident education and engagement regarding health and safety issues and the strategy of utilizing residents as peer outreach workers and as advocates for better conditions. The proposal writer articulated very clearly the need to engage senior residents in addressing health issues and the need to employ this strategy to create a sense of community within their buildings. The issue of medication management is a major concern for all seniors, but particularly those who do not speak or read English. Also, non-English speaking seniors are at a major disadvantage in being able to advocate for better health services. This project provided an opportunity to address those issues.

"The writing style and graphic presentation were both fine. Recognizing that not everyone has the luxury of being able to call upon a professional proposal writer, I am not as concerned about presentation as I am about content. The worst thing a grantseeker can do is to submit a proposal that is so vague and general that it becomes difficult for the grants decision maker to comprehend what is it they are asking for. Also, if the proposal is too academic, it raises concerns about whether it is all theory and not grounded in a true understanding of how programs are implemented. Graphically, it needs to be straightforward. Fancy charts and so on are not impressive if they are not relevant to the program. But timeline charts are fine.

"As to the budget, from my point of view, the budget is never set in stone. Usually if there are questions about the budget, I will contact the applicant for clarification. We ask for a budget narrative that explains each line item. If there are items that we cannot fund as a line item—for example, insurance, equipment maintenance, utilities, etc.—I just collapse them in our 15 percent administrative overhead allotment and explain that to the applicant. Sometimes, I will request a revised budget based on whatever changes are necessary. I don't think we needed to do so in this case.

"At The California Endowment we always conduct a site visit, and then we follow up with additional questions. To recommend an applicant for funding, I need to prepare a document where I have anticipated all questions that might be asked by my supervisor or peers. Finally, one item that perhaps would have made this an even better proposal would have been an indication that the City Office on Aging or the MediCal office was willing to be an active partner in this effort."

—*Dianne Yamashiro-Omi, Program Officer, The California Endowment*

Notes:
Proposal written by Louise Cooper, (former) Grants Manager.

Chinatown Community Development Center
華埠社區協進中心

April 25, 2003

The California Endowment
CommunitiesFirst-Grants Administration
21650 Oxnard Street, Suite 1200
Woodland Hills, CA 91367

To Whom It May Concern:

The Chinatown Community Development Center is pleased to submit the following proposal for consideration by The California Endowment's CommunitiesFirst Program. Chinatown CDC is requesting $495,000 over three years to support a comprehensive language access project targeting low-income Chinese, Russian, and Tagalog-speaking seniors of Chinatown CDC's affordable housing projects, as well as other limited English-speaking seniors citywide.

The California Endowment has been a tremendous supporter of Chinatown CDC's senior health advocacy efforts in the past, and we are hopeful that the Foundation will consider providing support for this important new project. Should you have any questions regarding this request, please do not hesitate to contact our Grants Manager, Louise Cooper, at (415) 984-1167, or by email at lcooper@chinatowncdc.org.

Sincerely,

Gordon Chin (cc)

Gordon Chin
Executive Director

cc: Dianne Yamashiro-Omi
        Program Officer
        101 Second Street, 24th Floor
        San Francisco, CA 94105

1525 Grant Avenue · San Francisco, California 94133-3323
415.984.1450 · FAX 415.362.7992 · CRS 800.735.2929
www.chinatowncdc.org

THE CHINATOWN COMMUNITY DEVELOPMENT CENTER
Language Access and Multicultural Health: Building The Knowledge, Advocacy and Leadership Capacity Of Chinese, Russian and Tagalog-Speaking Seniors
A proposal to The California Endowment--April 2003

Executive Summary

The Chinatown Community Development Center is pleased to submit the following request for funding to The California Endowment. Chinatown CDC is requesting $495,000 over three years to address language barriers impacting senior health through improved health communication skills for Chinese, Russian and Tagalog-speaking seniors in San Francisco and advocacy around improved multi-lingual access to Medicare and Medi-Cal information and services. The project will take seniors through a process of (1) increasing their own ability to communicate about their health; (2) teaching their health communication skills to other seniors through a San Francisco-wide housing network; and (3) creating a network of senior advocates to improve language access for Medi-Cal and Medicare services. The project has the following key goals:

1) *Individual Self Improvement: Providing the Tools for Better Health Communication:*
   - To increase the ability of limited-English speaking seniors to communicate better with health professionals, insurance providers, social workers and emergency service personnel through the design and implementation of a tenant-led medical terminology ESL training curriculum for Chinese, Russian and Tagalog-speaking seniors.

2) *Peer Leadership Development: Building Leadership through Peer Health Trainings:*
   - To increase the leadership abilities and public speaking skills of limited-English speaking seniors through peer-to-peer ESL educational efforts and a video project targeting Chinese, Russian and Filipino tenants through a citywide housing network. This effort will build the grassroots base for our policy advocacy (See (4) below.)

3) *Information Access Initiative: Linking Seniors to Existing Services:*
   - To respond to the immediate Medicare/Medi-Cal information needs of limited English-speaking seniors through the provision of multi-lingual informational workshops in partnership with SSA (and potentially DHS), and through the creation of a network of service providers citywide who can assist seniors to more easily access existing resources such as one-on-one benefits counseling/on-line materials.

4) *Policy Advocacy: Creating a Network of Senior Leaders Through Targeted Advocacy:*
   - To increase the ability of limited-English speaking seniors to become health advocates in their communities by working with them to advocate to government agencies such as SSA and DHS for the increased availability of translated health insurance materials for limited English-speaking populations in San Francisco.

This project will build the capacity of our seniors as health advocates and leaders in their communities. It will give seniors the tools to communicate effectively with doctors, social workers and other medical personnel, resulting in more effective and appropriate treatment for health problems and conditions. It will provide seniors citywide with greater access to translated materials ensuring better understanding and utilization of their health benefits. Finally, it will create a broader awareness about the need for dedicated resources to meet the health information needs of non English-speaking Medicare and Medi-Cal recipients, and create a broader spectrum of translated materials available to the wider community. We expect this project to have a positive and lasting impact on multicultural health and language access in our communities.

Background on Issue to be Addressed

For a number of years Chinatown CDC has been addressing issues of multicultural health for its diverse populations of low-income seniors. An established affordable housing provider with projects located in the Chinatown/North Beach, Polk Gulch, Tenderloin and Richmond neighborhoods of San Francisco, Chinatown CDC currently houses more than 1,800 low-income tenants of Russian, Chinese, Filipino, Latino, African American and Caucasian backgrounds. Nearly half of these tenants are low-income seniors. A baseline of educational, recreational, information and referral, and translation assistance are offered to tenants of buildings under our management, with more specialized services available through community collaborations.

In recent years, Chinatown CDC has paid particular attention to the unmet health needs of its senior tenant populations. In 2001 the organization engaged in a partnership with the California Endowment to address the health needs of Chinese, Russian and Filipino seniors residing in three of Chinatown CDC's housing projects. Building on the organization's strong history of community organizing activities among Chinese-speaking tenants, the Senior Health Advocacy and Research Project (SHARP) project successfully engaged seniors in each language group in developing their own senior health advocacy groups. Accomplishments of this project included: building the capacity of seniors to define (for the first time) their own health priorities, working with them to bring in community-based resources to address those priorities through monthly health workshops and screenings; and building tenant-led advocacy through participation in broader, city-wide, health advocacy efforts. In just one example, 69 seniors from the Notre Dame apartments developed a petition advocating for better health and social services for seniors and disabled persons. The petition was presented to the San Francisco Department of Aging at a town hall meeting held in October 2002.

A random survey conducted with project participants in July 2002 found an overwhelmingly positive response to project activities. The survey found that tenants participated regularly in project activities, with 95% of tenants rating health activities as excellent or good. In total:

- 60% of respondents stated that they participated in health workshops on a regular basis;
- 80% of respondents rated the health activities at their buildings as 'excellent', 15% rated them as 'good'. 95% of respondents rated health activities at their buildings as excellent or good.
- 70% stated that health workshops increased their knowledge of health issues and services;
- 65% stated that health activities offered by the project had enabled them to gain a better understanding of their health insurance and available community health resources; and
- 60% stated that had Chinatown CDC not provided these workshops, they would not have accessed health-based resources by themselves. Lack of mobility, language skills and lack of knowledge about where to seek help were all factors in tenants' decisions not to seek help.

A more comprehensive evaluation to determine the impact of project activities on participating tenants is currently being conducted. Information regarding the health behaviors and needs of senior tenants was collected through a baseline 'pre-test' survey conducted with participating resident seniors during March and April 2002. This survey was based on adaptations of the Lehman Quality of Life Scale and General Health Issues Survey and is designed to elicit quality data on health and life behaviors. A follow-up survey is currently being administered to determine whether behavior patterns have changed and knowledge increased as a result of tenants' participation in project activities. Results will be available in July 2002.

2

Program Description

Through SHARP, our senior tenants have helped us to more clearly pinpoint some of the key barriers to accessing and utilizing health services in the community. For example, while tenants clearly benefited from having on-site health workshops offered directly in their buildings, they continue to indicate a lack of confidence to seek medical services in the community, and clearly demonstrate frustration at not having the language skills to communicate effectively in medical situations. In addition, they identified the lack of information about medical benefits in their own language as a key barrier to understanding their own health benefits and services available.

This new project seeks to build upon these learnings as well as the leadership development achievements of SHARP. SHARP has given us a clearer understanding of senior tenant health needs, as well as a greater understanding of the capacity and willingness of our tenants to become motivated around issues they most care about, and to become leaders and decision-makers around health issues in their communities. Residents have commented that SHARP was so informative and valuable for their own health that they are motivated to share this learning with others. Following are some of the key problems to be addressed by the project:

Lack of English language skills: One of the ongoing problems identified by tenants in all three language groups was the inability to communicate effectively with doctors, nurses and paramedics, particularly in emergency situations where translation services are not readily available. Language ability was one of the main reasons cited by seniors in the SHARP project for not seeking outside health services, and according to a 1993 study conducted by the National Adult Literacy Survey (NALS) older people, non-whites, immigrants and those with low-incomes are more likely than other patients to have trouble reading and understanding health-related information. A key objective of this grant therefore will be to address language barriers through development of a tenant-developed ESL training curriculum and video project targeting limited English speaking seniors in each of the three language groups. According to the Center for Health Care Strategies, "Patients with poor health literacy tend to be more responsive to information designed to promote patient action, motivation and self-empowerment than detailed facts." Suggested strategies for helping patients absorb information include diagrams, audiotapes and interactive or instructional videos, of the kind proposed under this project.

Lack of access to translated health materials: A second key problem identified by tenants is the lack of readily available translations of Medicare and Medi-Cal insurance materials. Because of the lack of fully translated materials, tenants have difficulty understanding the full extent of their coverage and often remain unaware of services available. Currently the Social Security Administration (which determines eligibility for Medicare and which serves as the local contact and information source for Medicare recipients) provides complete translations of its social security benefits information in Spanish, with fact sheets about SSI and other social security benefits available online in other languages (including Chinese, Tagalog, and Russian). However none of these translated materials pertain to Medicare benefits coverage specifically, and in any case this is not a realistic solution for our tenants since few have access to online computer resources. At the five Social Security offices located in San Francisco, only one, the Chinatown branch, offers Chinese language assistance over the phone. In addition, of the six Medicare publications made available through the Chinatown, Downtown, Mission, Western

3

Addition and Parkside offices, all are available in English and Spanish only.[1] In addition, all written communications to tenants from SSA are in English, as are all accompanying explanatory materials. Unlike other San Francisco departments, letters to seniors do not include a telephone hotline in Chinese or other languages that seniors can call for assistance. The Dept. of Human Services (which determines eligibility and provides information about Medi-Cal for seniors not receiving SSI) has no language hotlines and no translated information available on its website.

This issue affects tenants across all three language groups: approximately 80% of seniors in our buildings are SSI recipients with Medicare and/or Medi-Cal coverage. It is also an issue that affects thousands of limited English speaking, low-income seniors citywide. In January 2003, there were a total of 25,580 Medi-Cal households in San Francisco. Of these, exactly one quarter (25%) were Chinese, 28% were Latino, 17% were White, and 14% African American. Filipinos formed 6% of the Medi-Cal population and Russians 2%. While the primary language for 47% of these households was English, for 22% of households their primary language was Cantonese; the same percentage for Spanish-speaking households. Tagalog and Russian speaking households each comprised 2% of households. Given the tremendous significance of the Cantonese speaking Medi-Cal population, there is a clear need to give greater attention to the translation needs of this group, as well as to the needs of Tagalog and Russian speakers. Regarding Medicare, it is estimated that racial and ethnic minority Americans will account for one in three Medicare beneficiaries by 2025. Currently 'Other' racial groups (including Asians) account for nearly 10% of the total Medicare population in California (SF data not available). In addition, and according to a 1999 study commissioned by the California HealthCare Foundation (CHCF), 37% of California Medicare beneficiaries surveyed had difficulty understanding their health care coverage, with similar studies confirming that beneficiaries do not know where to go for information, and are frustrated by their inability to obtain the information they want.

While in recent years there has been a greater commitment on the part of federal, state and local agencies to address the language access needs of limited English-speaking populations as they relate to health care and health benefits coverage [2] it is important that during this time of budget cuts and fiscal restraint, we continue to work toward both implementing federal, state and local language access requirements, while also identifying and advocating for cost-effective and realistic language access solutions for our communities. A second objective of this grant

---

[1] These are Medicare & You, Your Guide to the Outpatient System, Medigap Policies and Protections, Choosing a Nursing Home, Choosing a Doctor, and Coverage of Skilled Nursing Facilities and Care. These publications are generated by the Centers for Medicare and Medicaid Services (CMS) a division of the US Dept. of Health and Human Services that runs Medicare and coordinates Medicare information for beneficiaries nationwide. Currently only one of 54 Medicare publications is available in Chinese on their website. Because it is a national agency, CMS has no local offices. As a result the Social Security Administration (which determines recipient eligibility) serves as the only local information resource for Medicare recipients.

[2] The Social Security Administration is in the process of implementing federal requirements to provide meaningful access to limited English-speaking persons receiving its services through provision of qualified interpreter services, public information, and written communications in a number of languages on its website. In 2002, Governor Davis vetoed SB 987 a broad language access bill that would have increased immigrants' access to government services across all state agencies. Instead advocates were successful in incorporating a number of language access provisions into AB3000 a budget trailer bill that will amend the 29-year old Dymally-Alatorre Bilingual Services Act and require departments to design long-term implementation plans for making services accessible to limited English proficient residents in compliance with the Act. In 2000, the San Francisco Board of Supervisors passed the Equal Access Ordinance requiring all city departments that interact with the public to translate their written materials into languages spoken by more than 10% of the city's population and to hire bilingual staff for key positions. (Note: federal departments such as SSA are not bound by city ordinances such as this).

4

therefore will be to harness the leadership capacity that we have developed with our Chinese, Russian and Tagalog speaking tenants to date, to create a city-wide network of seniors who can come together to advocate with the Social Security Administration and other social services networks for availability of health information materials for limited English-speaking residents.

Project Objectives, Activities and Outcomes

Chinatown CDC proposes the following objectives, activities and outcomes to be conducted over a three-year grant period (July 2003- June 2006):

Tenant Self Improvement Initiative: Increase the ability of limited-English speaking seniors to communicate better with health professionals, social workers and emergency service personnel through the design and implementation of a participant-led and replicable medical ESL training curriculum and resource guide for Chinese, Russian and Tagalog-speaking seniors.

Year 1 Objectives: (July 2003 – June 2004):
- Conduct three focus groups with each language group to identify culturally relevant topics for inclusion in curriculum (Curriculum content will likely include such topics such as basic conversation--how to introduce oneself, address emergency contact person, and communicate whether allergic to medications; Ways to express pain and discomfort; How to communicate with 911 operators/paramedics; How to read signs in hospitals and clinics; How to read nutrition labels; Common medical terminologies & Patient's rights.)
- Work with tenants to develop and implement Medical ESL training curriculum for each language group (with technical and translation assistance from consultants such as Self Help and On Lok Senior Health); implement workshops to tenants on a monthly basis;
- Implement pre- and post-tests to measure increase in seniors understanding and use of key medical terms in English. Conduct focus groups with each language group to identify elements of training curriculum most valuable to tenants to incorporate into video project.

Anticipated Outcomes:
- 70% of participating seniors will demonstrate increased understanding and use of basic ESL medical terminologies in medical situations at the end of the one-year period.
- Creation of a permanent medical ESL curriculum and resource guide in Chinese, Russian, and Tagalog to serve as an ongoing resource for tenants and training tool for staff replicable for other community groups. (Year 1)

Peer Leadership Initiative: Increase the leadership abilities and public speaking skills of limited-English speaking seniors through peer-to-peer ESL educational efforts and a video project targeting Chinese, Russian and Tagalog speaking tenants through a citywide housing network.

Year 1 Objectives: (July 2003 – June 2004):
- Provide quarterly leadership training to CCDC tenant leaders from each language group to prepare them as trainers. Leadership training will be provided by Chinatown CDC's community organizing staff and focus on public speaking and presentation skills.
- Investigate options for utilizing in-kind media support to help with the production of ESL video project. Chinatown CDC will investigate opportunities through KTSF Channel 26 (the Chinese Language news channel) as well as through Filipino and Russian networks.

5

- Begin working with CCHO member organizations (the citywide housing network of which Chinatown CDC is a leading member) to identify groups of tenants to be served through the peer-to-peer education project.

Year 2 Objectives: July 2004 – June 2005:
- Recruit in-kind media support (multi-media college interns/media professionals from local news networks) to assist with designing, shooting and editing one 24 minute video;
- Work with Chinatown CDC tenant leaders to develop an ESL training video based on feedback from tenants about which information from the workshops was most useful;
- Conduct three tenant-led ESL training/video presentation workshops with Chinese, Russian and Filipino seniors via the CCHO network of affordable housing providers;

Anticipated Outcomes:
- Creation of one multi-language ESL training video for use as a training tool with seniors;
- Increased leadership and presentation skills among Chinatown CDC's senior leaders;
- Provision of ESL education to a minimum of 50 tenants of CCHO housing projects;

Information Access Initiative: Respond to the immediate Medicare/Medi-Cal information needs of limited English-speaking seniors through the provision of multi-lingual informational workshops in partnership with SSA (and potentially DHS), and through the creation of a network of service providers citywide who can assist Chinese, Russian and Tagalog speaking seniors to more easily access existing resources such as one-on-one counseling services/on-line materials.

Year 1 Objectives: (July 2003 – June 2004):
- Increase seniors' access to available community resources by working with senior social service networks citywide to promote existing multi-lingual public benefits counseling and other services to tenants, and by encouraging these agencies to dedicate resources to printing out translated (online) materials and make them available to their constituents.
- Respond to seniors' existing information needs by working with Social Security Administration (SSA) staff to provide three on-site multi-lingual informational workshops on benefits issues (including Medicare) for Chinatown CDC tenants during the first year of the grant period; Investigate options for conducting similar workshops with DHS staff around Medi-Cal issues.

Year 2 Objectives: July 2004 – June 2005:
- Coordinate with Social Security Administration (SSA) staff to provide informational workshops to senior tenants of the broader CCHO network. A total of three workshops will be held at neighborhood locations throughout the city (such as the Richmond, Excelsior, South of Market and Chinatown) during the second year of the grant period.

Anticipated Outcomes:
- Increased understanding and awareness on the part of seniors about existing translated Medicare/Medi-Cal benefits materials and multi-lingual services available citywide;
- Educational workshops provided to a minimum of 100 seniors citywide (50 Chinatown CDC, 50 CCHO network).

6

Public Policy Advocacy Initiative: Build a broad network of senior health advocates and multi-lingual social services providers who can work together to advocate to city agencies including the Social Security Administration (SSA) for increased availability of translated health insurance materials for limited-English speaking populations.

Year 1 Objectives: (July 2003 – June 2004):

- Begin identifying a network of 10 multi-lingual social services providers throughout the city (6 Chinese-serving, 2 Russian-serving and 2 Filipino-serving) who can work with the project on public advocacy issues around language access needs during the course of the three-year project.

Year 2 Objectives: July 2004 – June 2005:

- Conduct one joint meeting of Chinese, Russian and Filipino seniors from Chinatown CDC and CCHO buildings so that tenants can share their own health advocacy/leadership experiences and encourage participation of CCHO tenants in joint advocacy efforts.
- Recruit up to 5 tenant leaders from CCHO tenant buildings to work with Chinatown CDC tenants in joint advocacy activities at the beginning of Year 3 of the grant period.

Year 3 Objectives: July 2005 – June 2006

- Work with senior tenant advocates to lobby Social Security Administration offices for:
  - 1) Commitment to making available multi-language fact sheets summarizing Medicare information at SSA neighborhood offices;
  - 2) Commitment to including information about SSA's 1-800 telephone translation services and Medicare helpline on correspondence sent out to seniors;
  - 3) Commitment to investigating with CMS opportunities for complete translation of 'Medicare and You' booklets into Chinese and other languages; and
  - 4) Commitment to institutionalizing regular information workshops covering social security and Medicare benefits and changes targeting limited-English-speaking seniors in SF communities. (Conduct a minimum of two meetings between tenant advocates, CCDC and SSA staff during the course of the year);
- Investigate options for similar advocacy efforts with DHS; (Conduct one meeting with DHS staff during the grant period).
- Continue to build a network of support by implementing one letter writing campaign to highlight broad community support for language access issues in San Francisco. Utilize networks of social service organizations and senior advocates created through this project to bring both institutional and individual supporters together to sign on to the campaign;
- Utilize the results of this letter writing campaign and other activities to support broader advocacy efforts (such as those being carried out by Chinese for Affirmative Action and others) focused on enforcement of language access legislation at the city, state levels.

Anticipated Outcomes:

- Creation of broad base of senior advocates and service providers committed to working together to meet the multi-lingual health information needs of low-income seniors;
- Implementation of one broad based letter writing campaign demonstrating significant individual and institutional support for this issue among San Francisco's low-income, multi-cultural communities;
- Increased commitment on the part of the Social Security Administration to address language access needs of Medicare recipients in San Francisco as demonstrated by commitment to implement at least one of the four SSA objectives described above.

7

Addressing CommunitiesFirst Objectives:

The Chinatown Community Development Center's proposed project addresses each of the three CommunitiesFirst objectives as follows:

Access: Given fiscal constraints, competition for resources, and the range of different agencies at the federal, state, and local level responsible for administering public benefits in California, it is not surprising that there are critical gaps in the provision of translated materials for limited English speaking populations. This project seeks to increase access of low-income seniors to information about their own public benefits and health care plans by increasing the quality and availability of translated materials targeting low-income Chinese, Russian and Tagalog-speaking populations. Increasing access will have two dimensions. The first is to better link our tenants (and seniors citywide) to existing available resources made available by public agencies (such as interpreter services made available by SSA) and to services offered by non-profit groups (such as the HICAP multi-lingual benefits counseling services offered by agencies such as Legal Assistance to the Elderly in San Francisco). The second is to advocate directly with city agencies to ensure a greater commitment to cost-effective means of producing translated Medicare and Medi-Cal materials.

Health & Well-Being: This project will promote increased health and well being among low-income seniors in a number of ways: Health-specific ESL trainings will increase feelings of safety, reduce isolation, and help to remove fears associated with having a lack of English language skills in health-related situations. Participating in curriculum development, video production, peer-to-peer training, leadership development, and collective advocacy efforts will promote confidence, increase interaction, and build a sense of community among seniors (all factors likely to reduce the risk of depression and other mental health problems among seniors). Finally, increasing the range of information available to seniors in their own languages about social security benefits, health care coverage and available health care services will promote healthy behaviors by increasing confidence, ensuring better interactions with health care providers, and empowering them to make informed choices regarding their health care needs.

Multicultural Health: Learning materials developed through this project, such as the Medical ESL curriculum and training video, will be culturally specific, designed by tenants, and focused on topics identified by each language group as being most pertinent to the needs of their own population. By focusing on peer-to-peer education efforts, as well as having tenants play a leading role in designing the educational components of this project ensures that materials developed will be accessible to all tenants and delivered in a manner that is sensitive to cultural barriers to health issues experienced by Chinese, Filipino and Russian seniors. At the same time, the information access initiative will seek to more clearly identify (and then link tenants to) the full range of public and private health providers who can help to meet their language access needs of the target groups. Finally, the advocacy component of this project will seek to break down significant barriers in the utilization and understanding of health care coverage by limited English speaking seniors by significantly reducing existing disparities in the quality and quantity of published materials for limited-English speakers.

Evaluation

Chinatown CDC will measure the effectiveness of project activities as follows:

The success of the ESL *Self Improvement Initiative* will be measured by the extent to which participating seniors demonstrate increased understanding of basic ESL medical terminologies.

8

We expect that 70% of participating tenants will demonstrate increased understanding. In order to measure impact on tenants the project will conduct both baseline and follow-up surveys with Chinatown CDC participants. Chinatown CDC's Tenant Services staff will implement the surveys with oversight provided by consultant evaluation specialists familiar with Chinatown CDC's tenant base and health advocacy projects. The success of this initiative will also be measured by the extent to which we are able to create a permanent medical ESL curriculum and reference guide in Chinese, Russian, and Tagalog for broad distribution.

The success of the *Peer Leadership Initiative* will be measured by the extent to which we are able to effectively share the ESL Training/Video workshop with a multi-lingual tenant base beyond Chinatown CDC and build the leadership skills of tenants. The measure of success will be provision of training to a minimum of 50 tenants of CCHO buildings. Leadership development of Chinatown CDC tenants will be measured by the number of Chinatown CDC tenant leaders recruited to conduct workshops with CCHO tenants. We expect a minimum of 5 tenants to be recruited as workshop leaders. The success of the *Information Access Initiative* will be measured by the extent to which we are able to increase access of tenants' to information. Indicators of success will include: the number of education workshops provided by city agencies for participating tenants and the extent to which information received benefits tenants. We expect that a minimum of 6 workshops will be provided by city agencies, and that a total of 50 CCDC tenants and 50 CCHO building tenants will benefit. Indicators for measuring increased understanding of benefits information and coverage include: increased awareness of range of benefits and services provided; and increased awareness of existing multi-lingual services and language access provisions of city agencies and non-profits and how to access them. A post-training survey with workshop participants will be conducted to help measure this understanding.

The success of the *Public Policy Advocacy Initiative* will be measured by the extent to which we are able to generate broad community support for improved translation of public benefit and health care coverage materials benefiting limited English speakers in San Francisco. This will be measured by the number of social service institutions who commit to providing support for the project; the number of individual seniors and institutions demonstrating the importance of this issue by signing on to the language access petition to be developed under this project, and by the extent to which we are able to gain increased commitment on the part of SSA and other agencies to provide translated materials that can benefit Chinese, Tagalog and Russian speakers—as measured by implementation of at least <u>one</u> of the following: 1) Commitment to taking steps to make available multi-language fact sheets summarizing Medicare information at SSA neighborhood offices; 2) Commitment to investigating with CMS opportunities for complete translation of Medicare and You and other booklets in Chinese and other languages; 3) Commitment to including information about SSA's 1-800 telephone translation services and Medicare helpline on correspondence sent out to seniors; and 4) Institutionalization of regular information workshops targeting limited-English-speaking seniors in SF communities.

Challenges of Program

Building the capacity of city agencies to respond to the multi-lingual needs of seniors and other low-income residents who utilize their services remains a challenge of this project, especially in this tight fiscal environment. In order to maximize our ability to achieve the proposed advocacy objectives, we will work directly with the Social Security Administration's Public Affairs Department on joint education and information workshops for our tenants, while also working to

9

build relationships with Administration staff to generate support for the project's advocacy goals. Not only will these workshops enable tenants to gain updated information about benefits coverage in their own language, they will also enable us to assist SSA in their own objective of promoting multi-lingual services available through the department (such as SSA's recently created national telephone interpreter service). Because the Regional Affairs department of SSA has the capacity to make local level decisions around the translation of materials based on the local population base, it is important that we build effective relationships with them (as well as with the Dept. of Human Services where possible) in order for the project to be successful.

Sustainability of Program

Chinatown CDC's three year project will respond to the information and language access needs of limited English-speaking seniors both among Chinatown CDC's multi-cultural tenant base and citywide. We expect that our efforts will result in short-term gains by increasing the knowledge base, communication skills and leadership ability of low-income seniors, while also laying the groundwork for long-term commitments to meeting the language access needs of Chinese, Russian and Tagalog speaking seniors citywide. This project will:

- Enhance community health resources by creating a health-focused ESL training curriculum and reference guide in 3 languages which has the potential for long-term replication and distribution among limited English speaking populations citywide.
- Enhance tenants' advocacy skills, public speaking skills, and knowledge of how to affect change on the local government level connecting them to other seniors across the city so that they will feel empowered as a group to advocate for themselves and their communities for multi-lingual health information, services and policies in the future.
- Create lasting linkages between CCDC tenants, CCHO network tenants, social services providers, and city agencies around the need for sustained efforts targeting the language access needs of senior tenants. It will result in better connections between communities and service providers and offer a broader base of information, materials and knowledge for seniors to access to meet their informational needs and make informed decisions regarding their health care benefits and coverage.
- Have a lasting impact on the availability of translated health coverage materials available through city agencies such as SSA, potentially impacting thousands of residents citywide.

Capacity and Qualifications to Conduct Program

Chinatown CDC has provided community organizing, neighborhood planning, affordable housing development, property management and tenant services to San Francisco residents since 1977. The agency has developed nineteen affordable housing developments (1,343 units) seventeen of which we own and manage (1,200 units). Our affordable housing and property management programs have been nationally recognized with awards including *The National Alliance to End Homelessness Award for Non Profit Sector Achievement (1992)*, a *Fannie Mae Foundation Sustained Excellence Award (1998)* and a *Metropolitan Life Foundation Award for Excellence in Affordable Housing – Property and Asset Management Category (2000)*.

Chinatown CDC has extensive experience implementing the kinds of activities proposed under this project. In addition to the activities of the two-year SHARP program implemented with California Endowment funding, Chinatown CDC was recently awarded a three-year grant through the California Department of Mental Health to provide enhanced health and mental health services to frail seniors at six Chinatown CDC buildings. This is a collaborative project of

10

Chinatown CDC, On Lok Senior Health Services, the Mental Health Association, and the Department of Public Health's Chinatown/North Beach Mental Health Services. In addition, and since its inception Chinatown CDC has provided a range of translation, information and referral and health-related support services to its clients. The organization has consistently partnered with health providers in the community to support enhanced services for its clients through agencies such as On Lok Senior Health, Self Help for the Elderly, and others. The agency has also participated in a number of long-running community collaborations including the Health, Housing and Integrated Services Network, which provides on-site primary health care, mental health and substance abuse counseling, and life skills management training to formerly homeless tenants of our Tenderloin buildings. Chinatown CDC takes an innovative approach to service provision, using an empowerment model in which clients themselves take an active role in defining their needs, developing structures, and taking actions to improve their lives.

This project will be led by staff from Chinatown CDC's Tenant Services and Program and Planning Divisions. Our Tenant Services staff have extensive experience providing a range of multi-cultural and multi-lingual supportive housing services to the more than 1,800 ethnically diverse residents of our seventeen supportive housing projects, while staff of our Program and Planning division are leading experts in multi-cultural community organizing and advocacy, particularly as they relate to housing and health. Both divisions will work together to ensure smooth implementation of project services through the following staff as follows:

The project will be led by *May Wan, Tenant Services Supervisor*. May speaks English and Cantonese, has extensive experience working with older adults from culturally diverse backgrounds and served as the Project Coordinator on Chinatown CDC's Endowment-supported SHARP project. Other Tenant Services staff working on the project will include: *Jhoanna Cruz, Support Services Coordinator* speaks English and Filipino (Tagalog and Pampango) and who will provide coordination and support to the Filipino senior tenants; *Wyland Chu, Director of Tenant Services*, who will provide overall oversight of project activities; and *Lisa Ochev, Support Services Coordinator* who is fluent in Russian and English and provides supportive services to our Russian-language tenants.

Norman Fong, Program and Planning Director, will assist in the provision of leadership and community organizing training for Chinatown CDC tenant leaders and provide overall input and advise regarding the public policy advocacy components of the project. Norman has coordinated our work in the area of community organizing, open space, alleyways, and citywide tenant rights issues for over twelve years and in 2001 was awarded the Vanguard Foundation's Social Justice Sabbatical Award in honor of his community organizing work. Other Program Division staff working on the project include: *Angela Chu, Senior Community Organizer*, who has extensive experience conducting organizing and advocacy initiatives serving the Chinese community, is the main organizer for the Ping Yuen Residents Association; and is a supervising organizer with the SRO Families Collaborative; and *Anna Chang, Senior Community Organizer* who is our main staff liaison with the Community Tenants Association, providing tenant leadership training and helping coordinate communication and tenant education programs for CTA membership.

Chinatown CDC will partner with a number of agencies to implement project services. On Lok Senior Health Services will provide assistance with the health-specific ESL training project and provide consulting assistance regarding the language access advocacy components of the project. A Letter of Agreement between Chinatown CDC and On Lok Senior Health is attached to this

11

proposal. On Lok Senior Health is a not-for-profit community organization established in 1971 as one of the country's first adult day health centers. On Lok operates a fully integrated health plan that delivers medical and long-term care to those looking for an alternative to nursing homes and also offers health related workshops and other services in the community to senior serving, supportive housing providers and other non-profits in the Asian American community. Chinatown CDC is also in discussions with Self Help for the Elderly for the provision of assistance with the design and Chinese language translation of the ESL training curriculum and reference guide. We will also contract with an external evaluator (potentially Davis Y. Ja, PhD, Program Evaluator, from Davis Y. Ja & Associates, Inc. who is serving as the SHARP Health Consultant) or with a similar group with equivalent health-related evaluation experience.

Summary

Through this project, Chinatown CDC hopes to address a variety of language access issues currently standing as critical barriers to the health and well being of our own Chinese, Tagalog and Russian speaking tenants as well to the well-being of limited English speaking seniors citywide. It will provide critical resources and training for our seniors, while also building their leadership capacity and advocacy abilities through engaged, community-wide advocacy efforts. We expect this project to provide seniors with greater access to translated materials ensuring better understanding and utilization of their health benefits, create a broader awareness about the need for dedicated resources to meet the health information needs of non English-speaking Medicare and Medi-Cal recipients, and create a broader spectrum of materials available to the wider community. The California Endowment has been an extremely important partner in Chinatown CDC's health advocacy efforts to date, and we look forward to continuing and building on this partnership in the years ahead.

12

CHINATOWN COMMUNITY DEVELOPMENT CENTER
Building Leadership Capacity of Seniors Around Language Access and Multi-cultural Health
July 1, 2003 - June 30, 2006

	Year One	Year Two	Year Three	Total
Proposed Income				
The California Endowment	$ 165,000	$ 165,000	$ 165,000	$ 495,000
Walter and Elise Haas Foundation	$ 20,000	$ 30,000	$ 25,000	$ 75,000
HCR Manorcare Foundation	$ 20,000	$ 25,000	$ 22,000	$ 67,000
Robert Wood Johnson Foundation	$ 20,000	$ 20,000	$ 20,000	$ 60,000
Total Proposed Income	$ 225,000	$ 240,000	$ 232,000	$ 697,000

	Year One	Year Two	Year Three	Total
Expenses:				
I. Personnel Expenses				
Director of Tenant Services (.25 FTE)	XXXXX	XXXXX	XXXXX	XXXXX
Senior Svc. Supervisor (.60 FTE)	XXXXX	XXXXX	XXXXX	XXXXX
Support Services Coordinator (.60 FTE)	XXXXX	XXXXX	XXXXX	XXXXX
Support Services Coordinator (.60 FTE)	XXXXX	XXXXX	XXXXX	XXXXX
Support Services Coordinator (.60 FTE)	XXXXX	XXXXX	XXXXX	XXXXX
Program Director (.10 FTE)	XXXXX	XXXXX	XXXXX	XXXXX
Sr. Community Organizer (.20 FTE)	XXXXX	XXXXX	XXXXX	XXXXX
Sr. Community Organizer (.20 FTE)	XXXXX	XXXXX	XXXXX	XXXXX
Subtotal Salaries	$ 132,221	$ 137,511	$ 143,012	$ 412,744
Benefits/Taxes (22.3%)	$ 29,485	$ 30,665	$ 31,892	$ 92,042
Total Personnel	$ 161,706	$ 168,176	$ 174,904	$ 504,786
II. Operating Costs				
Health Consultant Sub-Contractors	$ 9,000	$ 4,000	$ 4,000	$ 17,000
Evaluation Consultant	$ 5,000	$ 5,000	$ 5,000	$ 15,000
Evaluation Tool Development	$ 2,000			$ 2,000
Office and Staff Meeting Supplies	$ 1,500	$ 1,500	$ 1,500	$ 4,500
Health Group/Curriculum Supplies	$ 4,000	$ 4,000	$ 4,000	$ 12,000
Translation	$ 4,000	$ 4,000	$ 4,000	$ 12,000
Printing and Copying	$ 1,600	$ 1,600	$ 1,750	$ 4,950
Resident & Peer Leadership Training	$ 1,500	$ 1,500	$ 1,500	$ 4,500
Videography Consultant		$ 5,000		$ 5,000
Video Editing & Production		$ 10,000		$ 10,000
Telephone/Internet	$ 2,000	$ 2,000	$ 2,000	$ 6,000
Travel/Mileage	$ 150	$ 750	$ 750	$ 1,650
Postage	$ 250	$ 500	$ 750	$ 1,500
Total Operating Costs	$ 31,000	$ 39,850	$ 25,250	$ 96,100
Subtotal (Personnel + Operating)	$ 192,706	$ 208,026	$ 200,154	$ 600,886
Administrative Costs (15%)	$ 28,906	$ 31,204	$ 30,023	$ 90,133
Total Expenses	$ 221,612	$ 239,230	$ 230,177	$ 691,019

A Proposal From
Medicare Rights Center
New York, New York

To
Altman Foundation
New York, New York

Requested amount: $160,000 over two years
Amount received: $80,000 for one year

Funder's comments:

"Guidelines for submitting proposals to the Altman Foundation are posted at our Web site. Aside from the necessary attachments, we require a proposal narrative, preferably no more than five pages. In order to comply with the five-page limit, the Medicare Rights Center's proposal packs a lot of material in tightly, almost too much. However, they use a variety of tools to present the narrative—bolding, bullets, headings, and indentations for case studies—that were helpful in breaking up the text. The introduction provides a nice summary, but it would have been helpful to have the amount sought included in the cover letter.

"A proposal must, of course, make a pitch to a prospective funder. One thing this proposal does well is explain how the project will build on work previously funded by the Altman Foundation, tying a new project not only to investments the Foundation has already made, but also to core, ongoing programs. While the organization requested multiyear support, we felt the model was quite new and brought with it several potential challenges. Thus the Foundation approved support for one year with an option to renew, pending first-year outcomes and the development of strategies to address these challenges.

"The proposal does a fine job of presenting the need for the project, moving from the general to the specific, and combining case studies with hard data to good effect. The statistics cited reinforce the applicant's credibility at the same time that the anecdotal material provides more dimension and communicates how the project will benefit the target population. This proposal provides a good example of how anecdotes can be used well—never in place of evaluation, but as a complement to it or as a tool for illustrating the need component of a grant proposal.

"A particularly strong aspect of this proposal is the evaluation section. It is very specific, and the proposed outcomes seem viable. The very clear goals and timeline indicate that the project has been well planned.

"Many foundations, ours included, appreciate projects that may be replicable and/or self-sustaining. Medicare Rights Center makes a good case in these areas, although the rationale for project sustainability could have been more specific—the funding plan is a bit vague. Looking to the budget, there is some indication that other foundations will be contributing to the project. Given the need for other funding, it is always a good idea to update the grantmaker if other funding comes through during the application process, either by means of an addendum or a revised supporters list.

"Submitting a proposal is just one piece of our application process. Applicants also fill out a questionnaire that provides a snapshot of their organization and project. If, after the proposal is reviewed, there is a possibility for support, we meet with the applicants. In this case, the proposal was revised somewhat as a result of the meeting."

—Kate Liebman, Program Officer, Altman Foundation

Notes:

The complete proposal included the following attachments: IRS tax-exempt letter, organizational budget, list of corporate and foundation supporters, list of board members, and audited financial statement.

The Health Buddies project has subsequently been renamed Health LINCS (Linking Individuals in Need to Care and Services).

Proposal written by Rachel Bennett.

Medicare Rights Center

January 20, 2005

Kate Liebman
Program Officer
Altman Foundation
521 Fifth Avenue, 35th Floor
New York, NY 10175

Dear Ms. Liebman:

Enclosed is the Medicare Rights Center's full proposal to the Altman Foundation for the Health Buddies project. Health Buddies would leverage your past support of our education and counseling work (specifically the BEEP'M program) by greatly expanding our—and other organizations'— capacity to reach many more volunteers willing to serve and Medicare consumers in need of good counsel.

As you may know, the Government Accountability Office recently released a report showing that, in an in-depth study, the federal Medicare hotline did not give correct answers to one-third of callers and did not give *any* answers to 10 percent of callers. Health Buddies would decrease reliance on inaccurate and inefficient systems like the federal hotline, instead creating solutions in New York City and other communities that enlist committed people to help others in need.

Health Buddies is a strong salvo against confusion and inaccuracy. Take a look, and let's talk soon.

Best Regards,

Diane S. Archer

Encls:

1460 Broadway, New York, NY 10036 • Tel: (212) 869-3850 • Fax: (212) 869-3532 • www.medicarerights.org

Medicare Rights Center
Proposal to the Altman Foundation
Health Buddies for New York City

Introduction

For three years, the Medicare Rights Center (MRC) has been developing Medicare Interactive as an online compendium of counseling, training, and assistance resources for individuals trying to navigate the complicated health care system. Medicare consumers and professionals throughout New York City and in five other states have received Medicare Interactive with enthusiasm, and currently MRC is further developing the system to respond to the needs of convalescent care and caregiver communities. Furthermore, AARP, the National Rural Electric Cooperative Association, and others have contracted with MRC to make Medicare Interactive available to their millions of constituents nationwide.

Now, MRC wants to take Medicare Interactive to the next level, beginning in New York City. With $160,000 in funding from the Altman Foundation over 24 months, MRC will pilot a cutting edge remote counseling model in New York City. Altman support will allow MRC to develop and roll out the system to New York City companies, community organizations, schools, and government agencies, with the eventual intent of rolling it out nationwide and sustaining it through earned income.

The Problem

Angela: Angela's mother, Crystal, is a 72-year old Queens resident who uses seven prescription drugs and has an income low enough to qualify her for a Medicare Savings Program. Angela has heard about the new Medicare prescription drug benefit that will be offered through private companies but doesn't know if her mother qualifies for any special benefits or how to sign her up. Angela wants a quick and easy way to get answers to her questions, but, between taking care of her mother, working full time, and going to school, she does not have much time to research options. She would like to be able to schedule an appointment with a counselor to determine the best plan for her mother, but she doesn't have time to meet someone face to face. She only has time to call Medicare hotlines after-hours, and she has left messages but no one has yet gotten back to her. She is not sure how to get the information she and her mother need.

Mike: Mike is a retired investment banker living in Manhattan, who spends his time collecting old books, corresponding with friends via e-mail, and taking care of his chronically ill wife. Mike has extra time each day during which he would like to volunteer. He would especially like to give his time to an organization where he is helping real people, rather than entering data or soliciting funds. Mike cannot leave the house for long periods of time because his wife may need him. Even if he could leave, he isn't sure his neighborhood offers many good volunteer opportunities. Mike wants to help but doesn't know how.

The Medicare Rights Center's (MRC's) telephone hotline currently receives more than 75,000 calls a year and is able to respond to some 10,000 new clients annually. While some hotline callers are repeats, the difference between 75,000 and 10,000 calls reflects substantial unmet need. In New York alone, there are over one million individuals with Medicare, the federal program that provides health insurance to adults over 65 and people with disabilities. MRC's hotline operates live five days a week from 9 a.m. to 3 p.m. and is open for call-backs on four afternoons (3 p.m. to 6 p.m.) and two evenings (6 p.m. to 9 p.m.). On average, people like Angela, who call after hours and leave messages for hotline counselors, cannot be called back for a week or more owing to call overload. MRC is one of hundreds of counseling organizations nationwide faced with the difficulty of meeting rising client need.

While MRC's hotline receives thousands of calls from people with Medicare—older and disabled individuals themselves—it is also contacted by caregivers—family members and friends, like Angela—who are responsible for finding health care answers for their loved ones. In the U.S. today, caregivers bear a tremendous burden. More than 52 million people, or 31 percent of the adult

1

Medicare Rights Center's Proposal to the Altman Foundation
December 2004

population, provide care for an elderly, disabled, or chronically ill friend or relative.[1] According to a recent MRC survey, 21 percent of caregivers spend between five and 10 hours each day caring for a relative or friend. Some 52 percent of these individuals report that they sacrifice their own health in order to perform caregiver duties. And 55 percent of caregivers report that in order to provide care for a sick older adult, they made work-related sacrifices, such as working fewer hours, taking an unpaid leave-of-absence, or foregoing promotions.[2] Thus caregivers, as much as people with Medicare themselves, are having to find answers to health care questions affecting their aging and disabled friends and relatives—and the number of questions is only increasing.

MRC engages over 100 volunteers in direct service to people with Medicare, their families, and professionals who have questions about health care rights, benefits, and options. The number of questions has skyrocketed of late as policies related to the 2003 Medicare overhaul bill take effect, privatizing Medicare and expanding the program to cover prescription drugs. Not since Medicare's inception in 1965 have such broad changes been effected in the system. The changes have bred an unprecedented need for fast, reliable information—a need that regular hotline functionality is not capable of meeting. Furthermore, while MRC prides itself on running efficient, accurate hotlines, many other help sources are much less reliable; the dearth of good information available was made glaringly apparent by a recent Government Accountability Office report showing that the federal Medicare hotline provides incorrect information to one-third of callers and cannot assist another 10 percent of callers.[3]

Add to current troubles the fact that the aging population is set to explode—and soon—as the baby boom generation comes of Medicare age. Born between 1946 and 1964, the first baby boomers are already members of AARP, and they will become eligible for Medicare in 2011. Planning for the future must begin now to stem the tide of needs threatening to burst its gates as 42 million people with Medicare become nearly 90 million by 2050.[4]

The Solution

Mike's story, above, is one of millions that evidence the enormous pool of volunteers that are going untapped for a number of reasons—many of which are preventable. In 2003, about 63.8 million Americans volunteered, an increase from 2003.[5] In the Bureau of Labor survey, respondents who had volunteered in the past but not in 2003 cited lack of time (44.7 percent), health problems (14.7 percent), and family responsibilities (9.5 percent) as their reasons for not volunteering.[6] The YMCA asserts, additionally—and MRC can corroborate—that transportation is a significant barrier to volunteering, especially for older volunteers.[7] Presumably, if volunteering could be made more adaptable to individual schedules, more efficient, and less reliant on the caprices of public transportation, people of all ages who would like to volunteer but cannot would join the ranks of volunteers in New York City and throughout the country. MRC relies primarily on older, retired volunteers and finds it difficult to retain younger, working volunteer hotline counselors. For all of volunteerism's growing popularity (consider that, in 2000, 81 percent of companies connected volunteering to their overall business strategies, compared to

---

[1] "Informal Caregiving: Compassion in Action." The Assistant Secretary for Planning and Evaluation and the Administration on Aging of the U.S. Department of Health and Human Services, 1998.

[2] Medicare Facts and Faces. "Easing the Burden of Family Caregivers," Medicare Rights Center, November 2002.

[3] Pear, Robert. "Test Finds Inaccuracies in Help Line for Medicare," *New York Times*, December 12, 2004. "In a test of [Medicare's toll-free hotline]… investigators from the Government Accountability Office found that 29 percent of callers received inaccurate answers, while 10 percent got no answers at all."

[4] "Baby Boomers and Medicare." *Health Affairs*, 23:2, 282-3, 2004: "Projections of the Total Population by Five-Year Age Groups and Sex with Special Age Categories: Middle Series, 1999-2100," U.S. Census Bureau, 2000.

[5] "Volunteering in the United States, 2003." Bureau of Labor Statistics.

[6] Ibid.

[7] YMCA, 2001.

2

Medicare Rights Center's Proposal to the Altman Foundation
December 2004

only 31 percent who did so in 1992[8]), it frequently remains too difficult for would-be volunteers to access opportunities. The proposed Health Buddies project will remedy this problem.

Angela and Mike: Mike learns about a remote volunteer opportunity through a local health care organization. After completing a web-based teletraining and post-training assessment, he is qualified to counsel people with health care-related questions at home using his computer and internet connection. Mike receives an e-mail one day saying that Angela would like to receive live counseling from him. Angela discovered the counseling system on a city agency's web site and e-mailed the address listed to set up an appointment. She was contacted and told that Mike would be calling her, and at what time. At the set time, Mike calls Angela and uses Medicare Interactive to answer her questions. It is not necessary for Angela to be at a computer, but if she is, she can log on, too, and follow along with Mike. Mike helps Angela determine which drug plan is best for Angela's mother and recommends certain publications for Angela to read if she wants even more information. If Angela has a computer, she can download these publications immediately. Angela learns everything she needs and is able to help her mother enroll in the prescription drug benefit, saving her money on drugs. Mike and Angela's conversation was free, and Angela can access Mike again if she has other questions.

Health Buddies will create a web-based system that trains and matches virtual counselors like Mike to clients like Angela and her mother with health care questions, radically increasing volunteer bases, maximum client capacities, and the efficiency of counseling sessions. With two years of Altman support, MRC will pilot this program in New York City, preparing it for launch nationwide.

New York City is the ideal location for the Health Buddies pilot. MRC has strong relationships with organizations that will serve as sources of volunteer counselors and clients. MRC's own volunteers will be the program's first testers. In New York and throughout the country, excellent information on Medicare benefits, rights, and options is available on the internet, though older and disabled individuals do not tend to get their information from this source. Younger, working adults, however, the target counselors for this program, are extremely web-savvy, relying on the internet to meet many of their information needs. One study found, for example, that 82 percent of baby boomers have used computers, not far behind the 86 percent for the 18-37 age group. Even among individuals 57 and up, including all of the current Medicare population, 43 percent have used computers.[9]

Remote counselors in the Health Buddies model could be available as little as a few hours a month, completely at their own convenience and able to provide services from their own homes via phone and using internet-based decision support tools to assist in their counseling. MRC staff will train new virtual counselors remotely. After passing a post-training assessment, virtual counselors will list the times they are available for counseling. A Session Coordinator at MRC will use these times to slot counseling sessions between a client and virtual counselor. The client will either be an individual who has called MRC for assistance and left a message or a client at another New York City community organization who is either looking for assistance herself or being helped by one of that organization's counselors. Health Buddies will become a referral network so that any organization that cannot meet client demand can refer clients to MRC to be slotted for a Health Buddies session. MRC's Session Coordinator will check messages daily and call back clients with the time they should expect to hear from their virtual counselor. The Session Coordinator will also e-mail the virtual counselor with the time to call the client, and the client's number.

At the time of a scheduled appointment, the virtual counselor will call the client. Health Buddies will use Medicare Interactive's scripts and other web tools to provide clients with good information. A Health Buddy relationship could extend over multiple sessions and result in a close relationship, or it could simply be a one- or two-time occurrence. After each session, the virtual counselor will record key

---

[8] "Corporate Volunteer Programs—A Strategic Resource: The Link Grows Stronger." Points of Light Foundation in partnership with the Allstate Foundation, 1999.
[9] Pew Internet and American Life Project.

Medicare Rights Center's Proposal to the Altman Foundation
December 2004

data about the client into a form that will be sent to MRC in order to evaluate system success, recurring issues, counselor and client demographics, virtual counselor activity, etc. Clients will be mailed a post-counseling form on which they can record specifics of their session, their general satisfaction with the Health Buddies model, and any suggestions for its improvement. When clients themselves have e-mail access, they will receive this form from MRC electronically.

MRC will work vigilantly to ensure Health Buddies quality control. Virtual counselors will have access to a counselor at MRC who they can speak to if they encounter difficulties. However, because usability and content accessibility of Medicare Interactive has proven excellent during the system's roll-out in New York City and nationwide, MRC expects that new counselors will have little difficulty finding correct answers and conveying clear information to their clients. MRC will have several gauges in place to effectively measure counselor accuracy and client satisfaction.

Objective and Methodology

During the two-year development and implementation of Health Buddies in New York City, the following objectives will be achieved as outlined below:

1) **Develop Health Buddies tools and consolidate them in one user-friendly online package (Months 1-6).**

The Health Buddies tools will initially consist of training modules for would-be virtual counselors, a post-training assessment for these counselors, and forms for counselors and clients to fill out following a counseling session. Would-be virtual counselors will participate in a web-based teletraining that conforms to a model MRC has already piloted nationwide in partnership with the American Society on Aging. The trainings will accommodate multiple participants at once and will contain everything a virtual counselor needs to know to answer client questions and sign up for counseling sessions. The health care information contained in the trainings will parallel the information contained in the hundreds of live Medicare trainings MRC conducts annually, and, as in the live trainings, participants will be shown how to use Medicare Interactive to find information. Medicare Interactive will be the pilot Health Buddies tool and will be enhanced where appropriate to meet volunteer and client needs. MRC does not expect that significant enhancing will be required because the system has, owing to past support from the Altman Foundation and others, been in development now for over three years, with positive results.

2) **Roll out Health Buddies in New York City, recruiting and training an average of 10 new virtual counselors a month (Months 3-24).**

(A. Months 3-9) The first stage of Health Buddies will take the form of e-mail correspondence between virtual counselors and web-savvy Medicare consumers and their families. Currently, MRC receives scores of e-mails each week from people with questions about health care benefits and options. New MRC hotline volunteers have already begun answering these questions successfully using Medicare Interactive. Thanks to the clarity of Medicare Interactive, the learning curve for new counselors is very short (a few days). This first stage will provide 1) quality control for Health Buddies, as e-mails can be checked for accuracy by senior staff; 2) an assessment of Medicare Interactive's strengths and weaknesses, as the resource should be usable even by someone with no previous health care knowledge; and 3) a means of increasing counseling capacity, as new volunteers will assume responsibilities formerly assigned to other MRC staff.

(B. Months 10-15) Once Medicare Interactive is shown to be suitable for the use of new volunteers, under senior staff supervision, external volunteers will be recruited and trained to use Medicare Interactive to answer e-mail queries. This stage will effectively outsource the task of responding to clients' and their families' health care questions, while maintaining rigorous quality control. External volunteers will be recruited from local companies (for example, MRC has strong relationships with employers like JPMorgan Chase, and MRC's evening hotline is staffed by working

4

professionals who will promote Health Buddies in their workplaces); from the membership of the New York City branch of the AARP (MRC is working closely with NY AARP as part of the local Access to Benefits Coalition); from community-based organizations with which MRC has worked on projects like BEEP'M and CityNET; from senior centers and organizations; from local schools (MRC operates an intergenerational hotline that relies on strong connections to New York City schools, the parents at which would make ideal Health Buddies virtual counselors); and from local government agencies, with which MRC is currently working to make Medicare Interactive publicly accessible.

(C. Months 16-24) The third and final stage in Health Buddies implementation will involve the addition of telephone counseling to purely e-mail counseling. Volunteers from sources like those cited above will be trained to telephonically counsel seniors, people with disabilities, and their families on health benefits, drug assistance programs, and other entitlements. Virtual counselors will be trained using teletrainings outlined above, then assessed, to ensure good knowledge both of key health care information and of proper counseling techniques. Clients seeking virtual counseling will specify in either a phone or e-mail message to the Health Buddies program whether they want to be counseled via telephone or e-mail.

3) **Publicize Health Buddies and prepare it for national expansion (Months 7-24).**

Health Buddies will be publicized through MRC's web site and press releases and, more largely, through city government agency web sites and the materials of local service organizations and companies. MRC's peer counseling program in Westchester (Seniors Out Speaking on Medicare) has had great success recruiting volunteers from local organizations, senior centers, and faith-based institutions; Health Buddies will also be promoted in such locations.

Once the two-year pilot is complete, refined, and successful, the Health Buddies model can easily be expanded to cover a range of topics and employ a variety of web-based tools, including Health Wise and BenefitsCheckUp. MRC foresees that, once tested and honed, Health Buddies will generate self-sustaining earned income as it is marketed and licensed to organizations nationwide interested in increasing volunteer capacity and counseling accuracy and efficiency.

4) **Evaluate virtual counselors, clients served, and overall quality of the Health Buddies model (Months 3-24).**

The counselor and client post-counseling forms, initial screened e-mail conversations between virtual counselors and clients, and other feedback from virtual counselors, clients, and organizations from which counselors are drawn will be used to determine ways in which to improve the Health Buddies system. MRC expects good results in the first two years of roll-out but acknowledges that these years will be a pilot period, with a host of details in need of working out through practical application.

Outcomes

MRC expects that the Health Buddies initiative will produce the following outcomes by the end of 2006:

- Two hundred percent increase in the number of MRC-connected volunteers answering health care questions in New York City (200 new volunteers)
- One hundred percent increase in the number of older and disabled individuals served by MRC-connected counselors in New York City (10,000 new clients)
- Empowerment of at least 50 local health counseling organizations to grow and maintain volunteer bases using Health Buddies tools
- Strengthened connections between New York companies, organizations, schools, and government agencies seeking volunteer opportunities for their employees, retirees, and constituencies and New York organizations seeking volunteers and increased service capacity.

5

Medicare Rights Center's Proposal to the Altman Foundation
December 2004

Medicare Rights Center
Budget to the Altman Foundation: Health Buddies Pilot 2005-6

	Base Salary	% Time	Total Cost Year One	Total Cost Year Two	Total Cost	Total Altman Request*	Other Funding Sources**
I. Personnel							
Diane Archer, Special Counsel	XXXXX	XXXXX	$ 6,000	$ 6,000	$ 12,000	$ 6,000	$ 6,000
TBD, Project Director	XXXXX	XXXXX	$ 40,000	$ 40,000	$ 80,000	$ 80,000	$ -
Monica Sanchez, Director of Education	XXXXX	XXXXX	$ 8,000	$ 8,000	$ 16,000	$ 8,000	$ 8,000
Laura Perry, Health Education Fellow	XXXXX	XXXXX	$ 5,600	$ 5,600	$ 11,200	$ 5,600	$ 5,600
Betty Duggan, Director of Trainings	XXXXX	XXXXX	$ 2,000	$ 2,000	$ 4,000	$ 2,000	$ 2,000
Cathy McElroy, Director of Operations	XXXXX	XXXXX	$ 3,000	$ 3,000	$ 6,000	$ 3,000	$ 3,000
Subtotal Personnel			$64,600	$64,600	$129,200	$104,600	24,600
x Fringe Benefits (27%)			x 1.27	x 1.27	x 1.27	x 1.27	x 1.27
Subtotal Section I			$82,042	$82,042	$164,084	$132,842	31,242
II. Other Direct Costs							
Space			$ 12,000	$ 12,000	$ 24,000	$ 8,000	16,000
Telephone			$ 2,400	$ 2,400	$ 4,800	$ 2,400	2,400
Supplies			$ 1,200	$ 1,200	$ 2,400	$ 1,200	1,200
Postage			$ 1,200	$ 1,200	$ 2,400	$ 1,200	1,200
Duplication and Printing			$ 1,200	$ 1,200	$ 2,400	$ 1,200	1,200
Subtotal Section II			$ 18,000	$ 18,000	$ 36,000	$ 14,000	22,000
Subtotal Sections I-II			$100,042	$100,042	$200,084	$146,842	53,242
III. Indirect Costs (9% Subtotal Sections I-II)			$ 9,004	$ 9,004	$ 18,008	$ 13,216	4,792
IV. Consultant/Contractual Agreements							
Technology Consultant (software development)			$ 10,000	$ 10,000	$ 20,000		20,000
Evaluation Consultant			$ -	$ 20,000	$ 20,000		20,000
Infrastructure and Hosting			$ 23,500	$ 23,500	$ 47,000		47,000
Subtotal Section IV			$ 33,500	$ 53,500	$ 87,000		
Total			$142,546	$162,546	$305,092	$160,058	145,034

*MRC has made initial progress on this project thanks to a public contract from the New York City Council.

**MRC has requested $50,000 a year in funding from the Silverman Charitable Trust, and will be requesting additional funds from the Starr Foundation and the Atlantic Philanthropies, among others, to complete the pilot and begin rolling it out.

Chapter 3

General Operating Support

The proposals in this chapter are requests for general operating support. By definition this type of funding can be used for any operational expenses the organization incurs, such as salaries and benefits, rent, direct program expenses, utilities, and so on. This type of support, sometimes referred to as "basic" support, is much sought after by non-profit organizations because it has the fewest restrictions on the use of funds and can be applied to whatever operating expenses arise. Though many fundraisers consider it difficult to obtain grants for general operating support, according to the most recent information in *The Foundation Directory Online*, more than 16,000 foundations indicate that they award this type of funding.

The writer of a general operating support proposal needs to make the case for the value of the organization overall and not just specific projects or programs that it runs. This task requires condensing the description of an often complex roster of activities into a cogent document that sells the organization itself. Requests for general operating support need to feature persuasive and informative explanations regarding the organization's essential worth to the community.

There are four general operating support proposals presented here, with requests ranging from $5,000 to $25,000. Each does an excellent job of making the case for the organization, its programs, and its mission.

First is a proposal by Boys & Girls Harbor, Inc., of New York, New York, to the New York City-based Adolph & Ruth Schnurmacher Foundation. This proposal seeks a grant of $10,000 for programs benefiting the children and youth of Harlem. The proposal makes good use of quotes and statistics to highlight the organization's many accomplishments and the need for support from the foundation. The proposal's conclusion points out that while much has changed in the time Boys & Girls Harbor has been in existence, the core values of the organization have not, providing a sense of stability for the funder.

The second proposal is from Fresh Start, Inc., which provides shelter and outreach services for homeless women in the Lincoln, Nebraska, area. This proposal for $5,000 in general operating support was submitted to the Cooper Foundation, also of Lincoln, Nebraska. In light of a recent 100 percent staff turnover, including the departure of the executive director, Fresh Start's proposal includes a frank discussion of its recent difficulties and challenges it faces. Because these challenges are presented in an honest and realistic manner, and due to the quality of the proposal itself, the Cooper Foundation's grants decision maker was able to recognize that "the organization was back on track."

The third proposal is a request for $15,000 to The Community Foundation for Greater Atlanta submitted by Literacy Action, Inc., of Atlanta, Georgia. This is an organization that provides literacy instruction for adults with school-age children and effectively engages parents as partners in their children's education. The budget accompanying this proposal includes personnel expenses for salary and benefits as well as funds for supplies. In this case, the foundation is being asked to support only a portion of the costs.

Finally, there is a proposal from Puppies Behind Bars of New York, New York, that requests $25,000 from the Achelis and Bodman Foundations, also of New York. The nonprofit organization has a history of successfully teaching prison inmates to raise guide dogs. This general operating support proposal requests funds to expand programming to include both additional guide dog training and a new Explosive Detection Canines Program that trains bomb-sniffing dogs. The "New Directions" section of the proposal highlights the organization's many accomplishments and makes the case for expansion, since in the post-9/11 era, government agencies need many more trained dogs.

A Proposal From
Boys & Girls Harbor, Inc.
New York, New York

To
Adolph & Ruth Schnurmacher Foundation, Inc.
New York, New York

Requested amount: $10,000; **Amount received:** $10,000

Funder's comments:

"We at the Adolph & Ruth Schnurmacher Foundation have been supporting this organization since 2002. This proposal was a request for renewal and an increase in general operating support. Since we were familiar with the program by virtue of our past association with the organization, for our purposes, the proposal also served as a program update. While the prior year's grant was $7,000, in response to this proposal we made the requested $10,000 increased grant. In our decision-making process, when providing operating support, we view each applicant with the assumption that it may come to be an organization that we will continue to fund for many years. Therefore, our initial grant award may be modest in amount, but very often it is increased in subsequent years, as our board deems appropriate, as financial statements and program reports are received and reviewed to ascertain the financial condition of the organization, how grant funds are used, and the level of need.

"The proposal clearly and concisely sets forth the basic culture of the organization, its mission, the characteristics of the constituency served, the problems facing the constituents and the programs designed to respond to those problems. We were impressed with the descriptions of the program components designed to help children learn and develop skills that create opportunity. And even if we had not had prior contact with this organization, the proposal alone would have provided sufficient information for a meaningful evaluation of whether or not to make a grant.

"The need was well stated. It made it clear that although the program had expanded to serve more individuals, there was no diminution in the quality of service provided, thereby justifying the request for a grant increase. Information was presented in an organized and logical manner. It was not necessary to reread any portion in order to grasp the essence of what was being stated, and we had no difficulty making inferences relevant to our decision-making process.

"In my opinion, the strongest feature of this proposal was the ease with which the material could be read and understood. This is important to board members who have to review numerous proposals for discussion at a meeting. The attachments were helpful. In addition to a budget, audited financial statements and an annual report were also submitted so that we could get a good picture of the financial condition of the organization and be able to determine if an increase was warranted. This application was so thoroughly put together that we did not have to go back to Boys & Girls Harbor for further information or for clarification. Indeed we had all the information that was necessary for our positive grant-making decision."

—*Fred Plotkin, Secretary and Treasurer, Adolph & Ruth Schnurmacher Foundation, Inc.*

Notes:
Proposal written by Jane Lindberg, Grant Writer.

BOYS & GIRLS HARBOR, INC.

Educating Children To Be Their Best

PROPOSAL TO THE

Adolph and Ruth Schnurmacher Foundation

HARBOR GENERAL OPERATIONS

November 18, 2004

One East 104th Street, Room 544, New York, NY 10029-4495 ● http://www.theharbor.org
(212) 427-2244, ext. 548

Introduction

Boys & Girls Harbor is a nurturing environment where young people of low-income families are encouraged to learn and grow to become their very best. We proudly serve the Harlem community with preschool and afterschool educational programs, behavioral health services, performing arts, technology-based entrepreneurial training, career and college preparation, and an environmental education center and summer camp.

With deep gratitude for the Adolph and Ruth Schnurmacher Foundation's past generosity, and to help us continue to provide effective educational, cultural and social services that our families so greatly need, the staff and children at Boys & Girls Harbor request a renewed and increased grant of $10,000 to support our general operations.

About Boys & Girls Harbor

The mission of Boys & Girls Harbor is to empower children and their families to become full, productive participants in society through education, cultural enrichment, and social service. We help our students develop a positive self-image and a keen awareness of cultural heritage. Each year we help over 4,000 individuals gain the skills and confidence necessary for long-term success in education, careers, and positive family and community life. We believe in the shared responsibility of the Harbor and the broader community to advance the quality of life and future options of its children and young people. We help our students develop a positive self-image and a keen awareness of cultural heritage.

Founded in 1937 by Anthony Drexel Duke, who continues to serve as president, the Harbor is based at One East 104th Street in East Harlem and operates seven additional sites in Harlem and in East Hampton. Boys & Girls Harbor is a member of the United Neighborhood Houses of New York. Our constituents are 56% African-American, 35% Latino, and 9% of other heritage. Predominantly they are residents of Harlem and the South Bronx. We serve youth between eighteen months and twenty-three years old, with 75% between six and seventeen years old. 10% of our staff is comprised of former Harbor students and many of them later enroll their own children in our programs. In countless ways, the Harbor is a family.

From our modest beginning in Boys & Girls Harbor has grown to seven sites:

- Boys & Girls Harbor, *our main facility* – 1 East 104th Street
- Harbor Oasis Day Care – 2211 First Avenue
- Harbor Family Horizons and Playing2Win – 1330 Fifth Avenue
- Harbor Grant Day Care Center – 1299 Amsterdam Avenue
- Harbor Morningside Children's Center – 311 West 120th Street
- Harbor Harriet Tubman Day Care – 138 West 143rd Street
- Harbor Camp and Environmental Research Center – East Hampton NY

Boys & Girls Harbor helps children and their families overcome the educational and social obstacles surrounding poor and working-poor households. Ours is a holistic approach serving the wide needs, interests, and talents of children with:

- Harbor Daycare for preschoolers in six locations in East and Central Harlem;
- Harbor After-School programs;
- Harbor Literacy Center;
- Harbor Conservatory for the Performing Arts and the Raíces Latin Music Collection;
- Harbor College Preparation Services;
- Playing2Win, Harlem's first community technology center;
- Harbor Behavioral Health Services; and
- Harbor Camp and Environmental Studies Center, in East Hampton.

Most Harbor programs have waiting lists of youth eager to participate, evidence of the fine work performed by our staff, and of the scarcity of resources.

About the People We Serve

East Harlem is one of New York City's three greatest-risk neighborhoods for children[1].

Poverty limits opportunities and pulls many families into a continuing downward cycle.

- Over 47% of East Harlem children live below the poverty level. [2]
- 66% of East Harlem children under 18 live in a household headed by a single parent, and of these children, nearly half live with a parent who is not in the labor force.[3]
- East Harlem has the second highest number of public assistance recipients in Manhattan[4]

In under-resourced public schools, the potential within many students is not met.

- At the Harbor's neighboring public schools, more than 70% of elementary students failed standardized tests in mathematics in 2004.[5] That year, more than 65% of 4th and 8th graders at these schools could not meet the city and state standards in English Language Arts.[6]
- Only one third of the local population has graduated from high school. Less than 10% are college graduates.[7]

The health and the futures of many children and young people are at-risk.

---

[1] Citizens' Committee for Children of New York, Inc., *Keeping Track of New York City's Children* (2002, New York, NY) 29
[2] Federal Census 2000, QT-P34 Poverty Status in 1999 of Individuals; Summary File 3 (SF3) Sample data for geographical area 10029
[3] Federal Census 2000, QT-P46 Age of Own Children Under 18 in Families and Subfamilies by Living Arrangement (SP3) Sample data for geographical area 10029.
[4] Community Board Eleven Borough of Manhattan, *District Needs Fiscal Year 2006*, (2004, New York, NY): 14
[5] The NYC Department of Education, City-CTB Mathematics Tests; *District 4*, June, 2004
[6] The NYC Department of Education, combined average of 4th and 8th grade scores in State ELA Tests; *District* 4, June 2004
[7] Community Board Eleven Borough of Manhattan, *District Needs Fiscal Year 2005*, (2003, New York, NY): 17

- 15.2% of births in East Harlem are to teen mothers.[8]
- 1,448 children in East Harlem were reported abused and/or neglected in 2001. [9]
- 1,107 East Harlem children were placed in foster care in 2001.[10]
- East Harlem ranks third of communities with the greatest number of felony arrests.[11]
- In East Harlem, Harlem and the South Bronx in 2001, 486 youth between the ages of 12-16 were incarcerated. They accounted for over 10% of all juvenile incarcerations that year, even though youth in these community districts are less than 0.8% of the City's juvenile population.[12]

These statistics are alarming. Yet, here at Boys & Girls Harbor there is hope.

- More than 85% of students being tutored at the Harbor Literacy Center are measurably improving their skills.
- In 2004, 90% of the children served by our Foster/Kinship Care Clinic were stabilized in their homes with their adoptive/foster parents.
- Virtually all high school students exposed to higher education through the Harbor's college prep programs successfully enter college after their senior year.
- *And much more...*

Boys & Girls Harbor helps children and their families develop the skills and the character, strength and resilience they need to overcome the barriers they encounter on the way to the realization of their dreams.

Helping Children Learn

"I thank and commend you for your devotion and commitment to children, creating programs which allow children to tap into their own resources which allow them to fly."
From a mother's letter to the Harbor about our after-school programs

Harbor Day Care and Enrichment Services:
Year-round, we build upon school day learning with activities that include homework help, classes in various disciplines, art, youth leadership projects, science projects, sports and athletics and other social skill building activities, all in a stimulating, stable, loving and supportive environment.

These programs consist of the Infant/Toddler Program for eighteen month to two year olds, preschool for children aged two and a half to six, afterschool Junior Education for six to nine year olds, and afterschool Senior Education for nine to thirteen year olds.

---

[8] Citizens' Committee for Children of New York, Inc., *Keeping Track of New York City's Children* (2002, New York, NY), 29
[9] *Ibid,* 29
[10] *Ibid, 215*
[11] Citizens' Committee for Children of New York, Inc., *Keeping Track of New York City's Children* (2002, New York, NY): 203
[12] Farquee, Mishi, Correctional Assoc. of NY; *Rethinking Juvenile Detention in New York City,* (New York, NY 2002): Appendix B

Preschool: More than 350 young children (80% of whose families use New York City ACD vouchers) enjoy year-round programs, Monday through Friday from 8:00 am – 6:00 pm. Infants and toddlers are given attentive and loving care at the Harbor's two nurseries. Our daycare centers, for children two and one-half to six years old, are well-equipped, pleasant, safe, and stimulating surroundings where there are three instructors in each class and an average class size of 23. Music and movement, storytelling, reading, creative play and trips help prepare our young charges with the emergent literacy and math skills they need to succeed in grade school. In January 2004, the National Association for the Education of Young Children accredited the Harbor's preschool at One East 104th Street, making it one of *only two* accredited preschool programs in our area.

Afterschool: In a typical semester, over 400 children are enrolled in *Junior Education*, for six to nine year olds, and *Senior Education*, for nine to thirteen year olds from 3:00 pm to 6:00 pm Monday through Friday, and all day during the summer and on school holidays. Students receive homework help and academic enrichment, and are encouraged to explore their individual talents and creativity through performing and visual arts, team sports, science and computers, and debating classes. To bolster their literacy and math skills, all learning is project-based. Recent themes have included the peoples and cultures of other nations, ecology, the environment, and economics. Making the most of the wonderful cultural opportunities in New York City, we partner with the Metropolitan Museum of Art, Lincoln Center's Young People's Orchestra, El Museo del Barrio, and the American Museum of Natural History, among many others.

MicroSociety: In this popular aspect of the Senior Education portfolio, children nine to thirteen years old create their own society. Micro-citizens mimic the adult world by holding jobs and playing other roles in their community. While improving their math and writing abilities they hone their social skills, learn how to negotiate, work as a team, bring ideas into end results, to assume responsibility for their choices, and to advocate. MicroSociety gives valuable insights on how society operates and the rigorous social rules that govern adult life. Beginning with the Fall 2004 term, we have added a Financial Literacy curriculum to this program, which gives Micro-citizens hands-on experience with banking, credit, debit and investments.

Urban Princess Project: Young women ages 12 to 18 develop positive values through workshops and other personal development activities that encourage them to respect their bodies and themselves. Field trips and lectures from progressive and successful women focus on concerns such as teen pregnancy, low self-esteem, STDs, illiteracy, nutrition, and other important issues.

Harbor Literacy Center
In a community where a good education is the surest, if not only, path to a self-sufficient adulthood, the Harbor Literacy Center is an important resource. We teach children and young people to read, spell, and write with fluency. Literacy Center staff work closely with all Harbor programs, training teachers to incorporate literacy skill-building into every activity. Literacy Specialists assess skill levels and devote extra attention to students who

struggle with reading. We are pioneers in the use of the Orton-Gillingham approach for students who are at-risk, dyslexic, or otherwise disadvantaged.

Our Early Childhood Literacy program helps Harbor preschoolers gain the fundamental literacy skills they will need to be ready to read once they enter kindergarten. School-age children who are new to the Harbor come to us with a variety of individual needs and varying levels of proficiency. Literacy Center Specialists work with remedial students in small groups, patiently helping them to read and write with greater fluency and confidence.

Clearly we are benefiting the children and young people in our care. Last year, 95% of referred students who were categorized as "below average" moved to at least "average status" and 75% of school age remedial students read and comprehended connected text with greater fluency and accuracy. Because of our unusual expertise in the Orton-Gillingham approach, the Literacy Center gives training to outside teachers and to school administrators who are eager to emulate our techniques and our success.

Harbor Conservatory for the Performing Arts
Established in 1970, the Harbor Conservatory of the Performing Arts is the only multi-disciplinary performing arts school serving the East Harlem community. Most of Boys & Girls Harbor's educational, recreational and after-school programs receive performing arts training through the Conservatory. We offer low-cost, high-quality instruction in vocal and instrumental music, dance and drama to over 1,300 children and teens and 300 adults, after school and on Saturdays throughout the year.

While our Conservatory offers training in a broad array of styles in music, dance and drama, all divisions follow comprehensive sequential curricula modeled on NY State School Music Association guidelines. Students are required to master the fundamentals of a particular form before moving on to more advanced work. The Conservatory hosts a variety of ensembles, master classes, and workshops that offer students hands-on learning opportunities, and also produces regular public performances to expose students to the challenges of performing before an audience. Over the years the Conservatory has collaborated on a variety of projects with organizations such as the Caribbean Cultural Center, the American Symphony Orchestra, ArtsConnection, The Museum of the City of New York, Central Park SummerStage, Lincoln Center Out-of-Doors, HOSTOS Center for Arts and Culture, the Metropolitan Museum of Art and the South Street Seaport Museum.

With the founding of the Raíces Latin Music Collection in 1979, the Harbor leads in the preservation and documentation of New York's Latin music legacy. Raíces ("roots" in Spanish) is New York's largest collection of materials tracing and documenting the Afro-Caribbean roots and the subsequent evolution of Salsa and Latin Jazz, and is an affiliate of the Smithsonian Institution.

Harbor Camp and Harbor Environmental Research Center
Every year more than 300 children of low-income families discover the joys of nature at our sleep away summer camp in East Hampton. Set on 28 acres, our property encompasses a forest and a harbor beach opening into Gardiner's Bay and the ocean. Through our special focus on environmental exploration and navigation, youth improve their literacy, math, and

science skills while lifetime friendships are forged. Boating, tennis, swimming, basketball, performing arts, and arts and crafts: all these and more are available during 12 day sessions than pass much too quickly. The *Harbor Environmental Resource Center* offers hands-on lessons in forest and marine ecology for teachers and students of Suffolk and Nassau Counties and New York City. During the spring, fall and winter, more than 600 young people come to our camp for environmental education and for the *Harbor Adventure Program*, which offers age-appropriate games and physical tests that encourage personal confidence, problem solving and teamwork.

Developing the Skills that Create Opportunity

"I learned so much in such a short time, not only did I learn about academics, I also learned about how to be responsible for myself."

From a student's letter to the Harbor about our College Prep programs

<u>Harbor College Preparation Services</u>
In our East Harlem neighborhood, only one third of the local population has a high school education and less than 10% are college graduates.[13] Since 1992, our college preparatory programs, including College Tours and Summer College, have helped thousands of young people achieve their very best. More than 95% of those who take part go on to college.

The Harbor's College Preparation Services consist of Talent Search, Upward Bound, Math and Science Upward Bound, College Tours, and Cornell Summer College. Participating students are in grades nine through twelve, most of whom represent the first potential generation to attend college. These programs represent the culminating Harbor experience for minority youth in Harlem, and a very precious opportunity.

Talent Search offers important SAT prep classes, tutoring and homework assistance as well as counseling. In 2003-04 we helped over 900 young people, in grades six through twelve, matriculate and complete their post-secondary education. We offer useful workshops on study skills and time management, provide homework assistance, career counseling and exposure to colleges and corporate professional life through field trips.

Upward Bound and *Math and Science Upward Bound* offer services similar to those of Talent Search, but provide more concentrated class work and remediation. In these rigorous programs, promising high school students come to the Harbor every afternoon after school for college preparation classes, workshops in test taking strategies, writing skills and library research, and assistance with the often-daunting college admissions process. We also offer mentoring, internship opportunities, career education, special cultural activities and activities for parents. *Math and Science Upward Bound* is offered daily over the summer for students in need of intense tutoring in these key areas.

College Tours help Harbor youth lay the building blocks of their academic success. By visiting campuses, our students can see what the college environment is really like and begin to picture themselves as college students. Our tours range from one day to one week in

---

[13] Community Board Eleven Borough of Manhattan, *District Needs Fiscal Year 2005*, (2003, New York, NY): 17

duration. Each summer, students embark on a weeklong tour where they visit six to seven campuses. Participating young people gain a new perspective on education as they begin to identify what possibilities lay ahead of them after they graduate high school.

Cornell Summer College provides a valuable preview of college life to high school sophomores and juniors selected from our College Prep programs. Summer College participants benefit from a strong support system throughout their summer experience, including tutoring where needed and a designated faculty mentor who carefully follows their progress. They live in a dormitory, attend classes, and interact with other students from around the country and the world. Graduates of Summer college also receive an immediate academic advantage: up to six college credits that can be applied toward an undergraduate degree at another institute of higher learning.

Harbor Mini-College
Through this highly structured and sequential GED program, low-income high school dropouts get a valuable second chance. In daylong classes Monday through Friday, youth are given individual attention as they improve their academic skills and work/study habits. Course work is enhanced by computer literacy, financial literacy and workforce skills development, leadership development, counseling, and mentoring.

First Work
In two 10-week sessions per year, First Work helps young people from many Harbor programs to land their first job. Combining workshops on business etiquette, resume writing and personal finance with career counseling, visits from successful businesspeople and tours of corporations throughout Manhattan, First Work counselors closely mentor young men and women from their initial entrepreneurial projects and summer internships in various Boys & Girls Harbor departments, through their job search, the interview process, and eventual hire. Counselors continue to offer support and encouragement after placement, helping these young workers to eventually become young leaders.

Playing2Win
Playing2Win is Harlem's oldest community technology center, and is open year-round. Through independent study, group workshops, and one-on-one instruction, young people and adults gain experience in web design, digital art and video, music production, e-business, and an array of other marketable skills. We teach a wide range of advanced technologies including HTML and Java, desktop publishing, computer-aided design, and other technology fields. The Technology Jobs Initiative prepares young adults for entry-level positions as technical support and help desk personnel in public schools, small businesses and community-based organizations.

Supporting and Empowering Individuals and Families

"'Thanks,' is not enough for what we have learned from the staff and the counselors."
From a mother's letter to the Harbor about our Strengthening Families program

Many of the children and families who come to the Harbor need support in their journey to be their very best. Here at Boys & Girls Harbor we offer comfort, support, guidance, and programs and services that support personal and interpersonal skills, improve communications within the family, build resilience and foster hope.

Harbor Behavioral Health Services

Strengthening Families: This is a highly structured national model program of weekly sequential family skills training and counseling sessions that strengthen the bond between parent and child, promotes positive communication and parenting, reduces delinquency and substance abuse, and helps to keep families together. In addition to group workshops, all participants meet individually with their Harbor counselor to discuss issues raised in the groups and also other concerns. We anticipate 90% of participating families to complete the course, and to enjoy stronger familial bonds, and be able to express thoughts and wishes with greater effectiveness, appropriateness, and empathy.

Foster/Kinship Care Program: Here we help to reinstate feelings of trust and attachment in foster and adoptive children who have been abused and neglected. We give training, guidance and support to parents/caregivers that helps them to interact better with their children and to prevent future incidents of abuse or neglect. Our methods are an effective answer to the problems of the families we serve. Through family participation in our program, last year *all* children have remained in their current home; *none* have experienced a failed relationship with their adoptive/foster parents.

The Clinic for Adolescents and their Families: We support young people between the ages of 13 and 21 who are truly at a turning point: they have begun using alcohol and illegal drugs, and many have been referred to us by the Department of Probation. Our social workers help approximately 125 youth and their families each year, guiding them to better conflict resolution and family communications. Intensive group work leads young people to positive ways to manage anger, to succeed in healthy relationships and stay with No Use techniques.

Program for Adolescent Choices and Transitions (PACT): By replicating the Children's Aid Society's National Adolescent Sexuality Training Center model, we intend to minimize the high rate of teen pregnancies and births by offering compelling alternatives for the future, and the tools that young people need to achieve those goals, all within a nurturing and respectful environment. For eight years, 60 young people (now ages 12 and 13) learn, work, and share with this "second family", receiving tutoring, lifetime sports, job club and financial literacy, medical and dental care, mentoring and intense counseling that includes sexual education in an age- and stage-appropriate manner.

Genesis: For nearly 30 years, the Harbor's Genesis program has offered leadership development, tutoring, mentoring, counseling, sports, and visual arts to youth who face high exposure to factors that lead to risky behavior, substance abuse, and trouble with the law. Genesis creates positive peer networks, helping young people grow to be their best possible self.

CONCLUSION

Over six decades, much has changed at the Harbor while much has stayed the same. Although we have steadily grown from our modest beginning as a simple summer camp to our current multi-site organization that serves 4,000 individuals each year, the Harbor's core values have not changed. We feel the same strong dedication to everyone who passes through our doors, the same commitment to excellence, and the same respect for the talents and aspirations, dreams and desires of the children and families who have come to us.

Boys & Girls Harbor is committed to empowering children and their families to become full, productive participants in society through education, cultural enrichment, and social service. Ours are timely and creative responses to the forces that threaten the stability of our families and children.

We are deeply grateful for your past generous support. A renewed, and increased grant of $10,000 from the Adolph and Ruth Schnurmacher Foundation will help needy and hopeful children, young people, and families continue to gain the skills and the strength they need to meet the challenges and the opportunities that await them. Thank you for your consideration.

Boys Girls Harbor, Inc.
July 1, 2004 - June 30, 2005

	Food Services	Pre/After School Edu. Services	Counseling	Performing Arts	Education	Camp	Total
Revenues							
Contributions				125,000			125,000
Foundation Grant			247,000	254,000			501,000
Benefit Income						550,000	550,000
Program Contract Revenue	442,866	4,389,136	1,693,732		939,201		7,464,935
Government Grants				224,478			224,478
Camp Fee Income							
Performing Arts Program Fees				480,009			480,009
Program Fees		404,500		30,000		123,000	557,500
Medicaid Income			384,781				384,781
Investment Income & Dividends							
Gains & Losses on investments							
Other Income	0	40,300	38,930			25,000	104,230
Total Revenues	442,866	4,833,936	2,364,443	1,113,487	939,201	698,000	10,391,933
Operating Expenses							
Personnel Costs							
Administrative Salary	22,000	596,027	188,134	303,775	113,077	85,000	1,308,013
Staff Salaries	43,000	2,664,097	1,544,467	669,000	372,819	215,000	5,508,383
Fiscal Salaries		62,131	4,750		18,413		85,294
Support Salaries Clerical		53,148			47,394		100,542
Support Salaries Other		176,920		20,000			196,920
Program Consultants		1,200	60,870	18,500	5,000		85,570
Total Direct Salaries & Wages	65,000	3,553,523	1,798,221	1,011,275	556,703	300,000	7,284,722
Fringe Benefits	13,000	710,705	359,644	202,255	111,341	60,000	1,456,944
Non-Direct Personnel							
College Work Study					2,900		2,900
Stipends			22,040		45,409		67,449
Services To Clients							0
Total Non-Direct Personnel			22,040	0	48,309	0	70,349
Total Personnel Costs	78,000	4,264,228	2,179,905	1,213,530	716,353	360,000	8,812,016
Office And Operational Expenses							
Rent & Utilities	0	365,052	122,922	110,034	83,013	41,000	722,021
Telephone	500	12,425	22,544	11,264	7,866	6,500	61,099
Postage	50	100	2,972	9,907	3,016	1,500	17,545
Printing & Xeroxing	50	400	3,400	58,800	3,194	1,500	67,344
Office Supplies & Advertising		22,031	16,755	51,000	13,755	4,500	108,041
ADP Expense	200	2,852	2,301	750	5,762	2,500	14,365
Dues & Subscriptions		2,295	575	650		300	3,820
Messenger & Delivery				1,600		500	2,100
Administrative Conference		2,050			3,500	3,000	8,550
Professional Fees		172,676	8,407			3,500	184,583
Audit Fees	200	11,853	9,000		8,096		29,149
Computer Expense		500		7,000	2,000	6,000	15,500
Other Expenses			0	2,000	250	5,000	7,250
Insurance Expense			15,500	1,500	7,960	5,000	29,960
Custodial Service Provided		2,000	0				2,000
Workshops/ Seminars Staff		36,505	12,000		150	2,000	50,655
Parents Assoc. Expenses		4,763	500				5,263
Agency Admin Allocation			79,364		18,547		97,911
Food Costs	347,536	1,000	16,520	2,000	7,369	50,000	424,425
Classroom Supplies		69,864	0	3,000	588		73,452
Other Program Supplies	6,400	30,445	27,944	64,700	14,600	13,500	157,589
Total Office & Operational Expenses	354,936	736,811	340,704	324,205	179,666	146,300	2,082,622
Other Operating Expenses							
Transportation Costs	100	24,705	45,363	9,100	31,484	50,000	160,752
Equipment Expense		16,895	8,000	3,000			27,895
Repairs & Maint Equipment	6,000	19,329	12,500	29,500	6,816	35,000	109,145
Camp Expense				3,000	10,778	18,500	32,278
Equipment Leasing		2,930	8,314	8,000		2,000	21,244
Repairs & Maint Boats						9,000	9,000
Fund Raising Printing & Postage						7,500	7,500
Direct Benefit Costs						252,150	252,150
License & Permits	250					1,500	1,750
Int. Exp., Bank Charges & Invest. Fees				3,536			3,536
Scholarships				3,336			3,336
Misc. General Expenses		4,264	14,472				18,736
Total Other Operating Costs	6,350	68,123	88,649	59,472	49,078	375,650	647,322
Total Costs Before Depreciation	439,286	5,069,161	2,609,258	1,597,207	945,097	881,950	11,541,959
Net Surplus or (Loss) before Dep.	3,580	(235,225)	(244,815)	(483,720)	(5,896)	(183,950)	(1,150,026)
Depreciation Expenses							
Net Surplus/(Deficit)	3,580	(235,225)	(244,815)	(483,720)	(5,896)	(183,950)	(1,150,026)

Boys Girls Harbor, Inc.
July 1, 2004 - June 30, 2005

| | --------- Supporting Services --------- | | | | Actual |
	Management and General	Fundraising	Total	Fiscal 2005 Total	Fiscal 2004 Total
Revenues					
Contributions		700,000	700,000	825,000	823,817
Foundation Grant		999,000	999,000	1,500,000	1,023,237
Benefit Income		2,220,000	2,220,000	2,770,000	2,330,019
Program Contract Revenue				7,464,935	7,724,988
Government Grants				224,478	173,865
Camp Fee Income				0	0
Performing Arts Program Fees				480,009	388,587
Program Fees				557,500	604,350
Medicaid Income				384,781	332,654
Investment Income & Dividends	150,000		150,000	150,000	139,428
Gains & Losses on Investments	250,000		250,000	250,000	353,193
Other Income	30,000		30,000	134,230	381,064
Total Revenues	**430,000**	**3,919,000**	**4,349,000**	**14,740,933**	**14,275,202**
Operating Expenses					
Personnel Costs					
Administrative Salary	491,900		491,900	1,799,913	1,908,924
Staff Salaries	493,220	285,000	778,220	6,286,603	6,006,844
Fiscal Salaries				85,294	230,624
Support Salaries Clerical	52,832		52,832	153,374	37,345
Support Salaries Other				196,920	171,977
Program Consultants				85,570	360,805
Total Direct Salaries & Wages	**1,037,952**	**285,000**	**1,322,952**	**8,607,674**	**8,716,518**
Fringe Benefits	**207,590**	**57,000**	**264,590**	**1,721,535**	**1,732,124**
Non-Direct Personnel					
College Work Study				2,900	902
Stipends				67,449	82,933
Services To Clients				0	1,092
Total Non-Direct Personnel				**70,349**	**84,927**
Total Personnel Costs	**1,245,542**	**342,000**	**1,587,542**	**10,399,558**	**10,533,568**
Office And Operational Expenses					
Rent & Utilities	448,396		448,396	1,170,417	1,136,326
Telephone	52,900	8,250	61,150	122,249	133,902
Postage	8,746	9,750	18,496	36,041	27,076
Printing & Xeroxing	2,600	15,000	17,600	84,944	27,231
Office Supplies & Advertising	17,540	45,000	62,540	170,581	129,969
ADP Expense	86,004	3,000	89,004	103,369	68,263
Dues & Subscriptions	5,500		5,500	9,320	13,421
Messenger & Delivery	250	2,000	2,250	4,350	11,429
Administrative Conference		0	0	8,550	5,549
Professional Fees	46,000	159,250	205,250	389,833	646,179
Audit Fees	65,851		65,851	95,000	111,425
Computer Expense	67,000	12,750	79,750	95,250	413
Other Expenses	7,500	4,300	11,800	19,050	42,586
Insurance Expense	123,540		123,540	153,500	89,821
Custodial Service Provided				2,000	7,355
Workshops/ Seminars Staff	20,000	2,000	22,000	72,655	101,962
Parents Assoc. Expenses				5,263	868
Agency Admin Allocation				97,911	58,302
Food Costs	1,000	2,250	3,250	427,675	481,334
Classroom Supplies				73,452	81,692
Other Program Supplies		25,700	25,700	183,289	160,568
Total Office & Operational Expenses	**952,827**	**289,250**	**1,242,077**	**3,324,699**	**3,335,672**
Other Operating Expenses					
Transportation Costs	3,900	1,900	5,800	166,552	218,782
Equipment Expense	2,900	1,000	3,900	31,795	36,112
Repairs & Maint Equipment	11,150	3,000	14,150	123,295	29,861
Camp Expense				32,278	24,778
Equipment Leasing	50,000	10,500	60,500	81,744	96,049
Repairs & Maint Boats				9,000	14,563
Fund Raising Printing & Postage		62,500	62,500	70,000	89,068
Direct Benefit Costs		299,486	299,486	551,636	345,730
License & Permits	7,000	850	7,850	9,600	9,552
Int. Exp., Bank Charges & Invest. Fees	110,492		110,492	114,028	51,713
Scholarships		44,240	44,240	47,576	64,783
Misc. General Expenses	1,000	3,000	4,000	22,736	37,162
Total Other Operating Costs	**186,442**	**426,476**	**612,918**	**1,260,240**	**1,018,153**
Total Costs Before Depreciation	**2,384,811**	**1,057,726**	**3,442,537**	**14,984,496**	**14,887,393**
Net Surplus or (Loss) before Dep.	**(1,954,811)**	**2,861,274**	**906,463**	**(243,563)**	**(612,191)**
Depreciation Expenses	**200,000**		**200,000**	**200,000**	**184,890**
Net Surplus/(Deficit)	**(2,154,811)**	**2,861,274**	**706,463**	**(443,563)**	**(797,081)**

A Proposal From

Fresh Start, Inc.

Lincoln, Nebraska

To

Cooper Foundation

Lincoln, Nebraska

Requested amount: $5,000; **Amount received:** $5,000

Funder's comments:

"This proposal was submitted using the Lincoln/Lancaster County Grantmakers Common Application Form, which we require. The application was complete, and all the budget figures stated were correct and matched the supporting documentation.

"What makes this application stand out is the candor with which it was presented. This is an agency that had recently had major changes, including the departure of the founding executive director and 100 percent staff turnover. There was no attempt to minimize the difficulties that the agency faced, including the fact that other funders were concerned, and that some funding was in jeopardy. This candor allowed them to plainly address each area of concern and clearly state the actions they had taken, or were planning to take, to solve the problems.

"The application is very readable, with longer sections of information organized by bullets or as short tables. They included enough, but not too much, information from their new strategic plan, and there is a clear and measurable evaluation plan. The high quality of the application and apparent thoughtfulness that went into compiling it convinced us that the organization was back on track."

—*Victoria Kovar, Grants Administrator, Cooper Foundation*

Notes:

The proposal was written using the Lincoln/Lancaster County Grantmakers Common Application Form.
Proposal written by Tiffany L. Mullison, Executive Director.

Lincoln/Lancaster County Grantmakers
Common Application Form

Foundation Applied To:	The Cooper Foundation
Application Date:	November 15, 2003
Federal Tax I.D. Number:	36-3785810

I. ORGANIZATIONAL INFORMATION:
Provide the following information in two pages using this format.

A.	Organization Name	Fresh Start, Inc.
B.	Address/9-digit Zip Code	2323 F Street
		Lincoln, NE 68510-2931
C.	Telephone Number	402.475.7777
D.	Fax Number	402.475.7779
E.	E-Mail Address	tmullison@inebraska.com
F.	Website	www.freshstarthome.org
G.	Chief Executive Officer	Tiffany L Mullison
H.	Contact Person and Title	Tiffany L Mullison, Executive Director

I. Purpose of Request

A one-paragraph summary of the amount requested and its purpose.

Fresh Start Home is requesting $5,000 from the Cooper Foundation to assist in supporting general operational expenses to maintain the current level of programming for women who are homeless. Fresh Start, Inc has experienced its own "fresh start" in its 11th year. The agency experienced severe budget cuts in 2001, which continued to impact the operating budget through 2003. A 100% staff turnover occurred in 2002, and resulted in former employees drawing unemployment far in excess of budget projections. New funds were received from several sources after the transition; however, these funds still lag behind the level of services necessary for attaining the agency's mission. Monies from the Cooper Foundation are requested to allow Fresh Start Home to move beyond short-term stability to focus on sustainability. Requests to two additional foundations are pending; the monies requested are designated for the continuation of overnight staffing and for commercial refrigeration.

1

Lincoln/Lancaster County Grantmakers
Common Application Form

J. Budget Summary for This Proposal

1. Applicant's Contribution from Operating Funds, if any $ 157,765.00

2. Applicant's Contribution from Reserve Funds, if any $ -0-

3. Amount of This Request $ 5,000.00

4. Amount of Other *Pending* Requests, if any $ 21,701.27

Sisters of Charity Ministry Foundation	$17,249.00
Building Strong Families Foundation	$ 4,452.27

5. Amount of Other *Confirmed* Requests, if any $ 29,859.50

Community Health Endowment	$16,531.50
Woods Charitable Fund	$ 6,664.00
Lincoln Community Foundation	$ 6.664.00

6. **Total** Income (1.+ 2.+ 3.+ 4.+ 5.= 6.) $ 214,325.77

7. **Total** Expense $ 208,494.18

8. Balance: (6. – 7. = 8.) $ 5,831.59

(Explain positive or negative balances under II. B.3. referenced on the following page.)

K. Income & Expense Summaries for the Organization

	Actual	**Budget**	**Budget**
	Last Fiscal Year Ending: 12/31/02	Current Fiscal Year Ending: 12/31/03	Next Fiscal Year Ending: 12/31/04
Income	$143,308	$163,958	$214,325.77
Expense	$139,767	$156,924	$208,494.18
Net	$3,541	$7,034	$5,831.59
Net Assets	$113,465	$120,499	$126,330.59

Wayne Svoboda, Board Chair   Tiffany L Mullison, Executive Director

2

Lincoln/Lancaster County Grantmakers
Common Application Form

II. PROPOSAL NARRATIVE:
   A. FUNDING REQUEST
      1. The amount requested.
Fresh Start Home is requesting $5,000 from the Cooper Foundation.

      2. The purpose of your request (the need, problem or opportunity).
Fresh Start incurs the day-to-day general operating expenses in running a transitional shelter. To be able to provide for the residents' needs, Fresh Start must be able to support these expenses. An award of $5,000 will provide for the increasing operational expenses and address the potential deficits in the 2004 budget.

In the past two years, Fresh Start Home experienced a number of challenges due to severe budget cuts. These cuts began in 2001 with the elimination of full-time overnight coverage and included the loss of health insurance benefits for all employees and a reduction in the salary for the Executive Director. The Joint Budget Committee withdrew funding on a temporary basis; the United Way expressed strong concerns regarding the agency. The agency's founding Executive Director resigned in May 2002. From May to August, the Resource Coordinator assumed the dual roles of direct service provider and Interim Executive Director. The Board of Directors submitted and received funding to support the reinstatement of health insurance, restoration of the Director's salary, and explore avenues to provide overnight staffing for residents through the attainment of funding from the Lincoln Community Foundation, the Woods Charitable Fund, Inc. and KENO monies. The new Executive Director began in August. Thereafter, a 100% turnover in staffing occurred. The Director was hired with the understanding her focus was on securing future funding for programming, operations and staffing. Due to the turnover, the Director was responsible for direct services, maintaining a safe facility, and recruiting three full time employees and two on-call positions. By December 2002, a full team was trained and health insurance benefits restored for the four full time employees.

With a new, energetic staff team, Fresh Start Home began re-establishing relationships with area agencies. Many community based organizations had strong concerns about collaborating with Fresh Start due to the agency's reputation. For example, the former Outreach Coordinator was repeatedly delinquent in her reporting which resulted in a sanction where Fresh Start residents could not be added to the HUD Homeless program; Cornhusker Place Detox had severed ties with Fresh Start; and, the Community Mental Health Center was reluctant to schedule assessments with residents.

During her first year, the Director focused her time on the following:
  ♦ Securing a competent, compassionate, consistent staff team;
  ♦ Revising the *Women's Guidelines* and all in-house forms to convey a model of empowerment, not a punitive model for women;
  ♦ Cultivating relationships with area agency Directors for support;
  ♦ Developing a new logo which reflects the hope, strength and resiliency of women who are homeless;

3

- Designing a *Team Member Manual* to serve as a guide for current and new team members;
- Enhancing the facility, including safety issues, reducing operating expenses, and creating a positive environment within the home;
- Submitting successful proposals to new funders [Community Health Endowment Fund, Emergency Food & Shelter Program, NEBHANDS];
- Submitting pending proposals [Sister of Charity Ministry Foundation, Building Strong Families Foundation, SuperNOFA];
- Seeking leadership roles in the Lincoln Continuum of Care [Co-Chair] and Director's of United Way Agencies [Secretary];
- Actively attending meetings to further promote Fresh Start; and,
- Developing relationships with funders.

The Director is currently focusing on the following: securing funding sources, rebuilding a donor base, and educating the community about the need and scope of services. The opportunities facing Fresh Start Home are vast and include a strong vision for the future. With this future orientation, and much of the arduous work completed, the agency must move beyond struggling for short term funding and design a plan for sustainability. This process is not expeditious and requires funding support from the Cooper Foundation.

The Board of Directors appears pleased with the progress made by the new staff team and continues to be a strong source of support. A strategic planning session was facilitated by Marie Fischer in March 2003 and will serve as a road map toward achieving both short and long term agency goals. With many of the initial steps completed, Fresh Start is dependent upon funding from Cooper in the coming year to truly move forward. Funding from the Lincoln Community Foundation and Woods Charitable Fund, Inc. were received in the past two years, therefore the agency is unable to apply for future funding at this time.

3. *The population you plan to serve including numbers, location, socio-economic status, race, ethnicity, gender, sexual orientation, age, physical ability and language.*
Fresh Start Home provides simplistic services to complex consumers. The most basic services include shelter and outreach services to women who are homeless who do not have children in their custody. Services are offered to women ages 19 years and older. Fresh Start does not determine acceptance on sexual orientation. Fresh Start is not accessible by the physically handicapped. Future expansion plans include physically handicapped accessibility. English is the only language spoken by Fresh Start staff team on a daily basis.

Women who are in need of transitional housing, are invested in a two-month stay in shelter, and interested in developing residency in Lincoln are considered a strong match for shelter services. Intake interviews are conducted face to face at the shelter and in the correctional facilities in Lincoln and York, Nebraska. Additional criteria for admission include: a woman's willingness to develop an *Individual Goal Plan* which addresses her unique precursors to homelessness and steps to reach self-sufficiency; compliance with prescription orders from her medical provider; and actively addressing issues of alcohol or other drug addiction.

4

Based on 2002 data, 62% of women had been diagnosed with a mental illness; 62% reported involvement in an abusive relationship; 76% reported an addiction to alcohol or other drugs; and 15% presented a physical disability. One-hundred [100%] percent of residents had income levels below the federal poverty guidelines. Based on demographics from prior years, Fresh Start Home is estimating residential services will be provided to ninety-one [91] women in 2003.

Year	Number of Women Sheltered
1999	85
2000	83
2001	91
2002	103*
Total	362
Average # Served Per Year	91

* This figure may be higher due the staff turnover and lack of consistency during the year.

Please refer to demographic information below for demographic information from 2002.

AGES SERVED

Range	Number	Percent
19-25 years	22	21%
26-35 years	27	26%
36-45 years	38	37%
46 years and above	16	16%

ETHNICITY/RACE

Caucasian	78	76%
Hispanic	1	< 1%
African-American	17	17%
Native-American	6	6%
Asian	1	< 1%
Bi-Racial	1	< 1%

4. The effect your action will have on need, problem or opportunity.
The women served by Fresh Start Home need and deserve services from a competent, consistent, compassionate staff team. To maintain the level of services to women, operational and staffing expenses must maintained. Funding for merit increases to team members upon their anniversary dates must also be provided as a tool to retain qualified staff. All team members, except the Executive Director, received a four percent increase in salary upon their one-year anniversary. Salary increases are included in the 2004 budget, with a four percent increase for the eight women currently on the payroll.

5

Fresh Start responds to the residents' basic needs for shelter, food, clothing, and medical care. Case management is vital in keeping the women on the road to self-sufficiency. Developing new skills and obtaining knowledge about community programs empower the women to attain self-sufficiency. Providing these services and ensuring a safe place to live is the foundation of Fresh Start and supports the agency mission to *"ensure the provision of services to women who experience barriers in their lives and to assist restoration of these women to the community."*

5. *Strategies you will employ to implement the project, including, if applicable, collaborations with other agencies (include a work-plan with key dates and actions).*

Due to the basic nature of the request, few strategies are needed for successful implementation of the project. Through the securing of financial support, Fresh Start Home will be in a stronger position to request increases in funding from current supporters and actively pursue new funding sources on a local, state and national level.

The $5,000 request will help cover operational expenses, such as utilities, administrative costs, insurance, and ongoing repairs. These expenses will occur throughout the year. Fresh Start has pledged and pending funding from other sources, but also, relies on the generosity of the Cooper Foundation to meet obligations and support our growth.

6. *The names and qualifications of those who will direct the project.*

The Executive Director, Tiffany L. Mullison, will direct the project with supervision from the Board of Directors. Ms. Mullison has served as Executive Director since August 2002. Her areas of expertise include: shelter services, domestic violence and sexual assault, desktop publishing, volunteer and staff supervision, grant writing, serving high risk populations, advocacy, public speaking and program evaluation. Since 1990, Ms. Mullison has worked exclusively for non-profit agencies serving marginalized populations. She is responsible for reporting to the Board of Directors, funders, and offering guidance to the staff team.

7. *The impact of your project on diversity, if applicable.*

The proposed project will not have an impact on diversity. Fresh Start Home serves women of diverse backgrounds and ethnicity. The agency has adopted a *Human Diversity Statement of Intent*, which affirms a commitment to cultural diversity.

6

B. FINANCIAL PLAN

1. When funding would be needed, and if multiple annual payments would be appropriate.

Fresh Start Home would benefit from receipt of ½ of the funding upon completion of the necessary documentation to be eligible for the award. Fresh Start would accept the second ½ of the payment in July 2004.

2. Explanation of positive or negative balances if shown under I.J.8. on the cover sheet.

With the inclusion of two pending funding request, Fresh Start Home has a positive balance of $5,831.59. The request to the Sisters of Charity Ministry Foundation will address the cost for overnight staffing from July – December 2004, and serve as replacement monies for the Community Health Endowment Fund award received in July 2003. The request to the Building Strong Families Foundation will allow for the purchase of a commercial refrigerator and freezer. Notification of both awards is anticipated in January 2004.

Projected funding from donations and fundraisers [$28,300] is approximately 14% of the operating expenses. Funding from renewal sources is estimated at a flat or slight increase, with many of these funders operating on a July – June funding cycle. Due to economic uncertainty, Fresh Start Home must strive to not only have a balanced budget, but to have a cash reserve. If the agency receives increased funding from individual and corporate contributors, funds would be channeled into shelter renovations and public awareness.

3. Outline of your development plan for securing funding for this proposal now and, if applicable, in the future

The Fresh Start team has worked conscientiously this year to increase awareness in the community. Team members have attended an average of 20 meetings each month. They also provide speakers at community meetings to provide for the exchange of information about homelessness in Lincoln and the services provided by Fresh Start Home.

Fresh Start Home is at a crossroads with regard to funding. The agency has worked diligently to re-establish relationships with funders. With the temporary loss of Joint Budget Committee funds and risk of losing United Way funding, the agency was not in a position to craft a development plan; rather, the agency was operating in a crisis mode. Current funders expressed strong concerns regarding the departure of the agency's founding Executive Director in May 2002. As a result of these factors, the new Director was not aggressive in increasing the amount of each request to current funders. Following renewed confidence in the organization by funders, additional monies will be sought when available. This futuristic vision will allow the agency to grow slowly, via sustainable dollars.

Fresh Start Home has relied on local foundations and local renewable funding sources. Funding will not be available from the Lincoln Community Foundation or Woods Charitable Fund, Inc. in the next cycle, due to two years of financial support.

Fundraisers will be further evaluated and those with potential will be conducted. Participation in the Younker's Charity Benefits on three occasions has proven successful, with minimal efforts of team and board members. The *Gala of Stars Chocolate Party* and Annual Rummage Sale will also be included in the development of future funds, although these events require a greater time

7

commitment. Local charitable organizations will also be solicited for funds [i.e., faith communities, fraternal organizations]. Friends of Fresh Start will continue to solicit funds from individuals and refine their plan to embark on a Capital Campaign. The Capital Campaign will assist in the renovation of the duplex next door to be utilized as additional shelter beds. The campaign was originally slated for 2002, and has been delayed due to the transition phase at the current facility.

4. Evidence of financial ability, stability, and planning with reference to the project budget, operating budget, and the organization's long-range development plan.

Fresh Start Home has an eleven-year history of providing services to this marginalized population. The agency owns the present shelter site and has been able to expand the number of beds available to sixteen. The agency is capable to provide the services because the Board of Directors, staff team, volunteers and community supporters understand, appreciate and embrace the importance of the mission statement. These ambassadors to the agency recognize the value of the services offered and how these services are essential to address chronic homelessness in the Lincoln community. The Executive Director has a thirteen-year history in women's issues. She has experience in program delivery, client advocacy, grant writing and supervision.

A strategic planning session occurred in March, engaging board and staff members. The impetus of the session was to propel the organization away from short-term stability to long-term sustainability. The full Board of Directors [13] and the full staff team [5] convened in March to develop a strategic plan. Below are five areas of focus and a summary of each.

1. *Community Relations* – focus on increasing visibility of the agency among providers, community members, and recruitment of new board members.
2. *Employee Issues* – focus on securing funding for overnight staff [new position] and supporting current staffing level [4.2FTE]; staff training, development and recognition; and, revising Personnel Policy.
3. *Programming* – focus on defining our niche; revising guidelines and criteria for admittance and continuation of residents; fostering strong relationships with community based organizations; and, deciding which services to offer on-site to best meet resident need without duplication of services.
4. *Facility* - focus on enhancing the appearance of the facility; creating a safe, welcoming atmosphere for residents; devising a plan to maximize limited space; and, embarking on a capital campaign.
5. *Finances* – focus on diversifying funding sources; identifying effective fundraisers; maintaining positive relationships with current funders; developing a cash reserve; and, moving from short term financial stability to long term sustainability.

8

C. EVALUATION

1.   ***The criteria and plan for measuring the proposed objectives during the grant period.***

Fresh Start Home has established measurable goals for the current funding year; these goals are consistent with the Lincoln/Lancaster County Comprehensive Human Services Action Plan – Basic & Emergency Needs Coalition. Fresh Start Home's mission *"to ensure the provision of services to women who experience barriers in their lives and to assist restoration of these women to the community"* remains consistent; it is our methods of measurement that have been enhanced to better reflect the agency's progress toward this mission.

Fresh Start Home will measure program results with regard to support services:
- Maintain the number of case managers at the agency;
- Maintain the number of call for service;
- Document the number of calls for service answered between 12AM-9AM (no baseline established);
- Maintain the number of meetings attended by team members;
- Improving tracking regarding the number of meetings, contacts and training opportunities between team members and other agencies (no baseline established); and,
- Document the number of referrals provided to residents (no baseline established).

Fresh Start Home will measure program results with regard to shelter services:
- Maintain the number of beds available and filled;
- Maintain the number of women receiving services;
- Increase the number of women unable to be served due to presenting needs exceeding our level of services;
- Document the number of women receiving services at another agency (baseline currently being established); and,
- Increase the number of women receiving outreach and supportive services following departure.

2.   ***Names of those who will be involved in evaluation.***

Tiffany L Mullison, Executive Director, will be responsible for the evaluation component.

9

D. BACKGROUND OF THE ORGANIZATION

1. A brief description of your agency's history and mission.

In 1991, community leaders began meeting to discuss the lack of services to single homeless women who did not have children in their custody. As a result of these meetings, Fresh Start Home began operation in March 1992. During the program's decade of service to women, logistics have altered, leadership has evolved, financial support had ebbed and flowed, and the demand for services continues to exceed the supply. Fresh Start Home was designed following the guidelines of a Canadian transitional housing in Calgary. The name "Fresh Start" came to mind when someone spoke of giving women a "fresh start in life". To address the mission, Fresh Start Home offers a safe, structured, alcohol and drug free environment for women invested in attaining self-sufficiency. Fresh Start Home serves homeless women who do not have children in their custody. Services are offered to women ages 19 years and older. With a stay of up to one year, women are able to create an *Individualized Goal Plan* and receive the supportive services necessary to implement their program and reduce the barriers that precede homelessness.

The organization is synonymous with the programs offered. Transitional housing and supportive services are the entryway for women to reclaim self-sufficiency and lessen barriers to success. The organization's primary method of service delivery is transitional shelter. Upon intake, women are encouraged to commit to a two-month stay. While in shelter, women are matched with a team member based on the team member's area of expertise, much like an on-site case manager. During the intake process, each potential resident completes an Individualized Goal Plan. This plan is implemented by the resident and supported by the staff team. As a part of programming, residents are to donate four hours of service to a community-based organization each week, attend educational workshops at the house, and perform household responsibilities. Additional programming may include: supervised child visits, attendance at AA/NA, participation in domestic violence support groups, individual counseling, alcohol or other drug treatment/relapse prevention, compliance with Drug Court and the justice system, seeking and maintaining employment, medication monitoring, and attaining medical care.

An outreach position was created in 1999. This addition has permitted Fresh Start Home the opportunity to continue serving a portion of women after successful departure. The current Community Outreach & Support Coordinator conducts home visits with former residents and attends the weekly HUD Homeless Committee meeting.

2. The needs, problems or opportunities your organization addresses if different than A.2. above.

According to the National Coalition for the Homeless, there are approximately 760,000 people who are homeless in the United States on any given night. On the local level, the Lincoln *Point in Time Count* from November 2002 revealed a homeless count of 1,812. These figures may be inaccurate due to those who remain uncounted (i.e., persons who access no services, persons who live with friends or family members, persons who live in cars). The regional recap of people served July 1, 2002 through June 30, 2003 through the Nebraska Homeless Assistance Program stated there were 3,204 homeless people receiving services from seven agencies in Lincoln. Fresh Start is the only transitional shelter that serves only women ages 19 and over who are

10

unaccompanied by children. Since January 2003, Fresh Start Home has served 84 women. Currently, the wait to move into Fresh Start Home is approximately one month long.

3. *Current programs and accomplishments emphasizing achievements of the past year.*
Please read below for a summary of accomplishments in the past year.

- Five team members have celebrated their one-year anniversary at Fresh Start since August 2003. The sixth will celebrate her one-year anniversary on December 4, 2003.
- Fresh Start has re-organized as transitional housing, not emergency shelter. Programming has reflected that change.
- In February 2003, workshops have been available to the residents twice a week. These workshops cover a variety of subjects, including budgeting, medical issues, nutrition, legal aid, area human service agencies, abusive relationships, conflict resolution, goal setting and car care.
- In July 2003, overnight staffing became a reality. The overnight team has provided security for the residents, access to medications, and served as a sounding board for any nighttime traumas.
- In fall 2003, nine residents took advantage of the Vision Improvement Project offered through Matt Talbot Kitchen, where Fresh Start Home is a collaborative partner.
- In 2003, 21 women have completed the *Life Skills* six sessions offered by Matt Talbot Kitchen, and each received a $100 voucher from Shopko.
- The Community Outreach and Support Coordinator has transitioned two women from a HUD voucher to a Section 8 voucher; she currently maintains contact with thirteen former residents.
- The facility has been enhanced and beautified, establishing a more home like feeling. Six of the eight bedrooms have been repainted, along with every common area in the house.
- An 'enchanted garden' was installed in April 2003 to provide a healing environment for women, thanks to generous donations and volunteer labor.
- The four bathrooms were renovated with $4,700 of donations, three mini-grants, and the impetus of four eight grade students who united youth and adults in this volunteer endeavor.

4. *The population your agency serves if different from A.3. above.*
Same as A.3.

5. *Number and composition (racial-ethnic-gender) of full and part-time staff, board and volunteers.*
The eight full and part-time staff members are non-Hispanic white females. The board consists of 5 men (4 non-Hispanic white and 1 non-Hispanic African American), and 8 women (all non-Hispanic white). The volunteers who pick up the food from the Food Bank are a non-Hispanic white couple (man and woman), and the volunteer taking care of the storage unit used to house donations is a non-Hispanic white woman. The Fresh Start volunteer drivers are 2 non-Hispanic white women and one non-Hispanic white man. The volunteer who picks up the donated clothing from the consignment shops is also a non-Hispanic white woman. The facilitators of the weekly in-house AA group are a non-Hispanic white female and a non-Hispanic African American female.

11

Fresh Start Home
REVENUE

	2004	2003	2002	2001
Donations				
Individual Contributions	$5,000.00	$10,000.00	$14,000.00	$12,000.00
Friends of Fresh Start	$4,000.00	$5,000.00	$0.00	$0.00
Donor Mailing	$1,000.00	$1,200.00	$1,200.00	$2,000.00
Church Donations	$4,000.00	$4,000.00	$4,000.00	$4,800.00
Corporate Contributions	$2,000.00	$3,000.00	$2,400.00	$2,400.00
Clubs	$2,000.00	$1,200.00	$1,200.00	$1,200.00
total	$18,000.00	$24,400.00	$22,800.00	$22,400.00
Fundraisers				
Chocolate Party	$2,800.00	$2,500.00	$1,500.00	$3,000.00
Rummage Sale	$2,500.00	$2,500.00	$3,000.00	$7,500.00
Younkers	$1,500.00			
Floral/V-Day/Misc	$1,500.00			
Improv Contract	$2,000.00			$78,000.00
total	$10,300.00	$5,000.00	$4,500.00	$88,500.00
Grants/Contracts				
JBC	$7,875.00	$7,500.00	$17,800.00	$17,656.00
United Way	$12,232.00	$11,000.00		
LHA	$52,608.00	$52,608.00	$52,608.00	$52,608.00
NHAP	$25,200.00	$28,900.00	$20,900.00	
ESG	$14,800.00	$0.00	$15,100.00	
Woods	$6,664.00	$13,400.00		
Lincoln Community Fdn	$6,664.00	$9,000.00		
Cooper	$5,000.00			
SC Ministry Foundation	$17,249.00			
KENO	$0.00	$3,750.00		
CHE	$16,531.50			
Building Strong Families	$4,452.27			
EFSP	$1,000.00			
NebHands	$5,000.00			
CFC	$500.00			
Outsourcing	$3,250.00			
total	$179,025.77	$126,158.00	$106,408.00	$70,264.00
Misc Revenue				
Laundry	$1,000.00	$2,400.00	$2,400.00	$1,800.00
Resident Rent	$6,000.00	$6,000.00	$7,200.00	$6,000.00
total	$7,000.00	$8,400.00	$9,600.00	$7,800.00
Total Revenue	$214,325.77	$163,958.00	$143,308.00	$188,964.00

Fresh Start Home

EXPENSES	2004	2003	2002	2001
Employee Expenses				
Salaries	$137,107.46	$104,750.00	$86,000.00	$104,820.00
Payroll Taxes	$10,488.72	$8,013.00	$6,579.00	$10,776.00
Retirement	$0.00	$0.00	$0.00	$2,100.00
Health Insurance	$12,000.00	$7,875.00	$0.00	$18,624.00
Worker's Comp	$2,000.00	$1,300.00	$775.00	
Unemployment	$1,637.00	$2,500.00	$3,333.00	
Employee Life Insurance	$0.00	$0.00	$0.00	$240.00
Workshop Fees	$0.00	$360.00	$400.00	$480.00
Conferences & Education	$800.00	$500.00	$0.00	$2,500.00
total	$164,033.18	$125,298.00	$97,087.00	$139,540.00
Staffing Expenses				
Dues & Subscriptions	$395.00	$200.00	$320.00	$600.00
Equipment Purchases	$0.00			$5,000.00
Copier	$2,200.00			
Office Supplies	$2,000.00	$3,000.00	$3,000.00	$4,500.00
Mileage	$360.00	$480.00	$1,800.00	$2,400.00
License & Permits	$116.00	$66.00	$66.00	$60.00
General Insurance	$5,000.00	$6,050.00	$7,400.00	$6,960.00
total	$10,071.00	$9,796.00	$12,586.00	$19,520.00
Financial Expenses				
Dana Cole - Audit	$1,000.00	$1,200.00	$1,000.00	$1,000.00
Outsource - payroll	$480.00			
Outsource - books	$3,500.00			
total	$4,980.00	$1,200.00	$1,000.00	$1,000.00
Household Expenses				
Wells Fargo - mortgage	$1,200.00			
Wells Fargo - interest	$5,100.00		$1,020.00	$1,080.00
Contract Labor -Ron	$350.00	$350.00	$324.00	$324.00
Food	$3,000.00	$3,000.00	$6,000.00	$6,240.00
Household Supplies	$1,500.00	$480.00	$1,200.00	$1,200.00
Household Repairs	$2,400.00	$2,400.00	$2,400.00	$2,400.00
total	$13,550.00	$6,230.00	$10,944.00	$11,244.00

Program Expenses

Bus Passes	$300.00	$0.00	$0.00	$0.00
Drug Testing	$550.00	$0.00	$0.00	$0.00
total	$850.00	$0.00	$0.00	$0.00

Publicity Expenses

Postage	$2,400.00	$1,200.00	$1,200.00	$1,200.00
Bulk Mail Permit	$150.00			
Newsletter	$3,000.00	$600.00	$1,000.00	$1,800.00
Fundraising Expenses	$1,200.00	$1,200.00	$1,000.00	$3,340.00
total	$6,750.00	$3,000.00	$3,200.00	$6,340.00

Utilities

		$6,300.00	$6,300.00	$6,000.00
Alltel	$2,160.00	$3,600.00	$4,800.00	$3,840.00
Alltel - resident line	$504.00			
D&D Refuse	$480.00			
LES	$3,500.00			
Lincoln Water System	$1,200.00			
Time Warner Cable	$216.00			
total	$8,060.00	$9,900.00	$11,100.00	$9,840.00

Misc Expenses

Line of Credit	$200.00	$5,000.00	$6,000.00	$5,280.00
Loan Principal Payments	$0.00	-$3,500.00	-$2,150.00	

Total Expenses	$208,494.18	$156,924.00	$139,767.00	$192,764.00
Total Cash Flow	$5,831.59	$7,034.00	$3,541.00	-$3,800.00

Literacy Action, Inc.
Atlanta, Georgia

To

The Community Foundation for Greater Atlanta, Inc.
Atlanta, Georgia

Requested amount: $15,000; **Amount received:** $15,000

Funder's comments:

"The Community Foundation for Greater Atlanta requires applicants to the Competitive Grants Program to use the Competitive Grant Application form, a form we created. Many Competitive Grants Program applicants will call before submitting their application to ask program officers questions about the form and about how their organization might fit within our program areas and priorities. The application process is open to any nonprofit organization that meets our eligibility criteria, and applicants are not required to submit a letter of inquiry. There was no discussion with staff at Literacy Action prior to the submission of this proposal.

"While a cover letter is one of the attachments required of applicants, the purpose of the letter is to let us know that the board chair/president endorses the organization's application for funding. Occasionally, organizations will provide additional information in their cover letters. Literacy Action's cover letter met our needs but did not provide additional information. All expected components were included in the application packet, and the proposal was well balanced.

"Literacy Action's need statement provides vital information about the rationale for their project. It mentions the barriers associated with low parental literacy levels, the need for parents to be able to support their children's education, and the success the organization has had in implementing its strategy. The plain writing style makes it very easy to understand. With regard to formatting and graphic presentation, applicants are limited to what and how much they can present because of our application form.

"Literacy Action also did a good job at providing solid, succinct answers to our questions. Going into the in-depth review process, we did have a few questions about the budget, but all items were clarified, allowing us to make a positive funding decision. It is critical for applicants to learn how to state their case and describe their program concisely. This proposal's strongest feature is the answer describing the in-kind support for the project. Not only did they describe tangible items that had been donated, but they also named program volunteers. Besides having monetary contributions for programs, we feel it is critical for organizations to secure volunteers and other in-kind donations.

"As part of our Competitive Grant Application form, we require applicants to submit certain attachments. Literacy Action submitted all required attachments. Literacy Action also provided additional materials about its board of directors at the site visit. Before any decision is made, program officers of The Community Foundation for Greater Atlanta conduct site visits with applicants. We request that the organization's executive director and board chair/president be present, in addition to program staff if relevant to the request. In addition to meeting with the above named individuals, our foundation's staff members were able to observe the program in action and spoke to several participants. Such opportunities provided staff with valuable information about the program.

"Finally, one element that might have made this an even better proposal would have been if Literacy Action had provided more detailed information about its strategies. Applicants sometimes find it difficult to determine how much information is enough in response to a funder's question. While we encourage applicants to be brief in their answers, some are often too brief or too vague, while still not utilizing all of the space allowed.

"Here are some additional general comments I'd like to share with grantseekers:

- In our communications with nonprofit organizations, we encourage potential applicants to contact us with questions prior to submitting their applications and following a declination. We want to help organizations put their best foot forward. When a funder says something like this, take them up on their offer.

- Follow directions—if the application instructions tell you to submit a certain document or not to submit other documents, do as they say.

- Sometimes applicants know their subject so well that they think everybody else knows it just as well. Do not include terminology that is very specific and hard to understand; simplify your writing. We often suggest to applicants that they have someone outside the organization read the proposal and give them feedback. That person should be able to point to jargon and other areas that need clarification.

- While application forms often only allow for a certain amount of space for answers, thus encouraging brevity, use the space provided to adequately describe your organization, program, successes, and so on."

—*Lita Ugarte, Program Officer, The Community Foundation for Greater Atlanta, Inc.*

Notes:
The proposal was written using The Community Foundation for Greater Atlanta, Inc.'s Competitive Grant Application. The complete proposal included the following attachments: IRS tax-exempt letter, list of board of trustees, principal staff biographies, and organizational budget.
Proposal written by Mattie H. Eley, President.

101 Marietta Street
Suite 200
Atlanta, Georgia 30303
(404) 818-READ (7323)
Fax No. (404) 818-7322

July 15, 2004

Ms. Alicia Philipp
The Community Foundation for Greater Atlanta, Inc.
The Hurt Building
50 Hurt Plaza, Suite 449
Atlanta, Georgia 30303

Dear Ms. Philipp:

As chairman of the 2004 Board of Trustees, I am writing to authorize the enclosed grant request to help fund Literacy Action's " Better Readers Build Better Futures" program. The purpose of this grant is to increase parental involvement and boost academic achievement in the children of adults enrolled in Literacy Action's adult literacy program.

Thank you for your consideration of this application

Sincerely,

Herron Weems
Chairman, 2004 Board of Trustees

THE COMMUNITY FOUNDATION
FOR GREATER ATLANTA, INC.

2004-2005 COMPETITIVE GRANT APPLICATION

Please maintain the original font (Verdana) and use 10-point type. Do not change the margins (0.5" all around) or split tables over a page break.

I. GENERAL INFORMATION

Organization Name: Literacy Action, INc.	**Application Deadline:** July 16, 2004
Mailing Address: 101 Marietta Street Suite 200 **City, State, Zip Code:** Atlanta, GA, 30303	**Executive Director/President:** Mattie H. Eley
Phone Number & Extension: 404-818-7323	**E-mail Address:** meley@literacyaction.org
Website Address: www.literacyaction.org	**Current Year's Organization Budget:** $650,991
Project/Program Budget: $35,000	**Amount Requested:** $15,000
Date of 501(c)(3) Certification: June 12,1968	**Federal Tax ID #:** 58-1053728
Purpose of Proposal (Refer to your answer to question 3.7 and state the purpose of your proposal/request in one sentence): The purpose of the proposal is to help fund the salaries and materials for Literacy Action's "Better Readers Build Better Futures" project.	
Program Area (check the Application Guidelines and mark the program area that best applies to this proposal): ☐ Arts & Culture ☐ Community Development ☒ Education & Youth Development ☐ Health ☐ Human Services	

II. ORGANIZATION BACKGROUND

2.1 Mission & History:
Literacy Action, Inc. (LAI) is a mature organization that was founded in 1986 to teach functionally illiterate adults how to read. the organization began in the basement of Central Presbyterian Church across from the capitol with two volunteers teaching a handful of adults, some of whom simply wanted to learn how to read the bible, understand medical regimen and prescriptions for their children or read stories to their children or grandchildren. Today the organization helps 700-1,000 adults each year, including hundreds of parents, to improve their literacy skills, employment opportunities, educational opportunities and quality of life. Our mission is to build better futures for our students, by teaching undereducated adults literacy, life and work skills that empower them to reach their potential as self-sufficient individuals, parents, employees, and citizens. The LAI curriculum and program results have attracted the attention of leading family literacy and adult literacy advocates such as former First Lady Barbara Bush and Cal Ripken, Jr. Recently, the agency was awarded an unsolicited grant from The Oprah Winfrey Angel Network Fundation.

2.2 Programs: Using bullets, list the organization's main programs/projects with a sentence to describe each one.

- Adult Basic/Workplace -teaches basic reading, writing, thinking skills
- Computer Skills-teaches basic computer and work related skills
- Survival Math Skills-covers basic math skills that relate directly to everyday activities
- GED Preparation-prepares studeents to take and pass all 5 sections of the GED exam
- Parenting Skills-integrated in basic reading, writing, thinking skills and monthly workshops

2.3 Population served by the Organization (during the last fiscal year): Indicate the number of people served by the organization according to race and gender. In the column marked "*% (race)*", indicate the percentage of the individuals served in that row (i.e. Caucasian females) as a percentage of the entire population served. In the row marked "*% (age)*", indicate the percentage of individuals served in that column (i.e. individuals ages 0-5) as a percentage of the entire population served.

RACE & GENDER		0-5	6-11	12-14	15-18	19-63	64+	Total	% (race)
						AGE			
African	Females				9	458	2	469	62%
American	Males				15	251	1	267	35%
Asian/Pacific	Females					2		2	.2%
Islander	Males								
Caucasian	Females					6		6	.8%
	Males				1	8	1	10	1%
Hispanic/	Females					3		3	.4%
Latino	Males					5		5	.6%
Multi Racial	Females								
	Males								
	TOTAL				25	733	4	762	100%
	% (age)				3.3%	96.2%	.5%	100%	100%

2.4 List characteristics that are important to note, but are not defined by race, gender or age (such as disabilities, homelessness or sexual orientation):
1. Over 10% of LAI's population has experienced homelessness.
2. Approximately 20% of LAI's students exhibit common characteristics of learning disabilities.
3. 400 children served indirectly

2.5 Counties served by the Organization (during the last fiscal year): Indicate the number and percentage of people served in the following counties.

Name	Number	%	Name	Number	%	Name	Number	%
City of Atlanta	470	62	DeKalb	160	21	Morgan		
Barrow			Douglas	5	.4	Newton		
Bartow			Fayette			Paulding		
Butts			Forsyth			Pickens		
Carroll			Fulton	83	11	Rockdale		
Cherokee			Gwinnett	5	.6	Spalding		
Clayton	25	3.2	Hall			Walton		
Cobb	14	1.8	Henry			Other		
Coweta						**TOTAL**	762	100

2.6 List all grants received from The Community Foundation for Greater Atlanta since January 1, 1999:

Program	Year	Amount	Purpose
Workforce DEV	1999	$5,000	Matching funds for UPS grant
Workforce Dev	2000	$7,500	Matching funds for UPS grant
Workforce Dev	2001	$10,000	Program Expenses
21 Century Workskills	2002	$12,500	Program integration (work skills into basic skills instruction)

2.7 Describe the composition of your Board and Staff

RACE/ETHNICITY	BOARD			STAFF		
	Females	Males	TOTAL	Females	Males	TOTAL
African American/ Black	5	3	8	7	1	8
Asian/Pacific Islander						
Caucasian	6	12	17	5		5
Hispanic/Latino		1	1			
Other (specify):						
TOTAL	11	16	27	12	1	13

III. PROJECT/PROGRAM DESCRIPTION
This section of the application provides you with flexibility on the length of each of your answers. However, your answers in this section may not exceed 3 pages including the tables below. Please do not split tables over a page break.

3.1 The Issue: Describe the issue or situation the grant will help to address.

Literacy is a legacy that can be passed from parent to child, from generation to generation. Children whose parents lack basic literacy skills and education often grow up to face multiple barriers associated with low literacy and inadequate education: poverty, unemployment, low self-esteem, school failure and many related social ills. Evidence abounds that children who fall behind in the early grades are at increased risk of falling further behind and dropping out of school entirely.

The "No Child Left Behind Act" mandates national education reform in K-12 public schools to improve academic performance, test scores, and high school graduation rates. Parental involvement, the ability to support grade level performance and academic achievement, is a critical component of school success. However, many parents are at risk of being left out of the education reform process by functional illiteracy, and thus, they are unlikely, without a helpful intervention, to be able to provide the level of involvement and academic support needed to prevent their children performing below grade level.

Currently, LAI serves hundreds of custodial parents of school age children. Our data show that in 2003, 400 school age children benefited from their parents' participation in LAI's classes. This grant will be used to teach parents how to become partners in their children's education.

3.2 The People: In a short paragraph, describe the population that is the focus of the proposal.
The target population for this proposal includes LAI basic literacy students (parents/caregivers) and their children in grades K-8. who attend City of Atlanta, Fulton and Dekalb County schools.

3.3 Population served by the Proposal (during the last fiscal year): Indicate the number of people served by the proposal according to race and gender. In the column marked "*% (race)*", indicate the percentage of the individuals served in that row (i.e. Caucasian females) as a percentage of the entire population served. In the row marked "*% (age)*", indicate the percentage of individuals served in that column (i.e. individuals ages 0-5) as a percentage of the entire population served.

		AGE							
RACE & GENDER		**0-5**	**6-11**	**12-14**	**15-18**	**19-63**	**64+**	**Total**	**% (race)**
African American	Females								
	Males							—	
Asian/Pacific Islander	Females								
	Males								
Caucasian	Females								
	Males								
Hispanic/ Latino	Females								
	Males								
Multi Racial	Females								
	Males								
	TOTAL								
	% (age)								100%

3.4 Counties served by the Proposal (during the last fiscal year): Indicate the number and percentage of people served in the following counties.

Name	Number	%	Name	Number	%	Name	Number	%
City of Atlanta			DeKalb			Morgan		
Barrow			Douglas			Newton		
Bartow			Fayette			Paulding		
Butts			Forsyth			Pickens		
Carroll			Fulton			Rockdale		
Cherokee			Gwinnett			Spalding		
Clayton			Hall			Walton		
Cobb			Henry			Other		
Coweta						**TOTAL**		100

3.5 The Strategy: State specifically how the grant will help to address the issue or situation.

The grant will help address the issue of illiteracy in the home/family by supporting the cost of class instruction, monthly workshop activities and procurement of special print materials and software related to LAI's goal of increasing parental involvement and boosting academic achievement in the children of adults enrolled in Literacy Action's basic literacy program.

Grant funds will specifically be used to identify, recruit and enroll parents in a special project to improve the reading comprehension and academic achievement of their children.

Our strategy is as follows:
- identify and recruit participants (parents with one or more children enrolled in grades 3-8)
- provide adult literacy activities
- provide weekly class activities and monthly parenting classes focusing on school achievement of children and other parenting activities
- develop survey instrument for summative evaluation
- compile outcomes data on academic gains of parents and their children
- develop evaluation report

3.6 Outcomes: How will your project/program, if funded, "make a difference?" List two outcomes that you predict will take place, and how you will know (measure) that changes took place. Please refer to the Guidelines for Competitive Grants for further instructions.

1. 50% of Parents/caregivers will increase literacy levels, **measured by** pre-post ABLE & course tests.

2. 30% of children of LAI students will improve school performance, **measured by** pre-post questionnaries and a portfolio of performance samples of children's school work.

3.7 Project Expenses (2004-2005): Complete the Project Expenses table with dollar amounts for the Project for which you are requesting funding. If your request is for operating support, complete the table with your organization's financial information.

Personnel Expenses	Paid by TCF Grant	Paid by other sources	TOTAL
Salaries & Wages	10,000	20,000	30,000
Benefits & Payroll Taxes		510	510
Project Expenses			
Building Maintenance			
Consultants/Professional Services			
Insurance			
Marketing			
Membership Dues			
Office Supplies			
Postage/Mailings			
Printing			
Program Supplies	5,000		5,000
Rent			
Rent & Maintenance of Equipment			
Staff Development			
Technology/Computers			
Telephone			
Travel/Mileage			
Utilities			
Other (specify):			
TOTAL PROJECT EXPENSES	15,000	20,510	35,510

3.8 Who has committed funds for THIS project, and who is considering a request for funding? If you need additional space, please hit Return in one of the existing rows and continue typing.

Name Source	Funds Already COMMITTED to this Project/Program	Funds Currently PENDING for this Project/Program
Ronald McDonald House Charities		$15,000
TOTAL		**$15,000**

3.9 In-kind Support: Describe in-kind support for the project, including volunteer activities and contributions received for items such as office space, office equipment, program supplies, etc.

The following groups have agreed to provide in-kind support for LAI's "Better Readers Build Better Futures" project: Midtown Atlanta Rotary Club (Childrens' books); Delta Kappa Gamma Society (Children's books); Atlanta Dogwood Chapter of the Links, Inc. (volunteer lectures, family workshops and annual "Becoming Your Best Self" Symposium); Public Broadcasting Atlanta (workshops on parent interaction with children's TV programs and free children's books); IBM (Reading Recognition software); IBM 10 station computer lab to support "Reading Recognition " project; Chapter 11 (25% discount on purchase of books for children and LAI students); Public Service Announcements by Kenny Leon and Judge Glenda Hatchett (encouraging parents to participate in Literacy Action's adult literacy programs; Youthfest (providing venue and opportunity for LAI to give books to children).

3.10 Future Funding: The Competitive Grants Program does not commit to continued funding. Outline your plan to secure funding support, once Foundation grant funds are expended. Be as specific as possible, including the names of particular institutional funders or foundations, and your history of mobilizing funds from these sources.

As reflected in its history, LAI has always realized a majority of its support from a broad base of corporate contributors and individuals, and to a very limited degree from the United Way of Metro Atlanta. Even in the recent economic downturn, we have been able to obtain sufficient program and general operating funds to provide the full range of services needed. Our goal for continuation of the "Better Readers Build Better Futures" project is to go beyond the base level of funding by appealing to NEW donors interested in literacy and basic educational gains, community building and quality of life issues, workforce development, and pathways out of poverty for women and children, low income families and minority males. Our plan includes:
- Increasing efforts to secure new and larger contributions from individuals (including LAI trustees) with whom we established support over a number of years.
- Submitting grant applications to the Barbara Bush Foundation, Bell South Foundation, United Way of Metro Atlanta, The UPS Foundation and other sources of direct and indirect public support.
-Continuing our ongoing efforts to solicit in-kind donations of computer hardware and software: i.e., we are seeking a donation of 15 laptop computers for parents to use with their children at home. At present, we have one technology request pending from a court ordered settlement benefiting children in Georgia that if awarded could be used to procure both the laptop computers and the educational software for children.
- Submitting new requests to foundations for program continuation and expansion/intergration of direct children's services into LAI's ongoing core program. We are targeting several independent foundations (Ronald McDonald House Charities, Dollar General).
- Seeking multi-year commitments from selected companies, foundations and high net worth individuals

IV. ACKNOWLEDGEMENT OF THE COMMUNITY FOUNDATION'S APPLICATION POLICIES:

The Executive Director has reviewed this application and understands and assures that:

- The applicant is eligible for funding and requests support for activities eligible for funding. (Please see the Application Guidelines for details);

- All End of Grant Reports for previous grants have been filed before submitting this Application;

- This application is complete according to *Grant Application Checklist* (attached). The complete application package is either postmarked on or before the deadline date (July 16, 2004 and January 28, 2005), or will be delivered to The Community Foundation's offices by 5 P.M. on the deadline date. Incomplete or late proposals will not be reviewed. The Community Foundation's staff is NOT authorized to extend an application deadline;

- Grant requests range from $5,000 to $25,000;

- This application is part of an open competition. Although all eligible applications will be reviewed, a limited number will be selected for more detailed examination and funding consideration;

- The Community Foundation selects applications for more detailed evaluation **based on the contents of this application form**. The applicant has clearly and completely described its mission, programs, populations served, request for funding, strategy and anticipated outcomes on this form; and

- Organizations that are declined may apply again by the next deadline, if they wish. Organizations that are funded, including all programs under the same 501(c)(3) number, are not eligible to apply again for twelve months from the date of the grant award.

_____   July 15, 2004
Executive Director/Authorized   _____
Organization Representative   **Date**

CONTACT PERSON FOR THIS GRANT:

_____Mattie H. Eley_____   _____President_____
Name   **Title**

_____404-818-7323_____   _____meley@literacyaction.org_____
Phone Number & Extension   **E-mail Address**

A Proposal From
Puppies Behind Bars
New York, New York

To
The Achelis and Bodman Foundations
New York, New York

Requested amount: $25,000; **Amount received:** $25,000

Funder's comments:

"While the Achelis and Bodman Foundations do not have our own application form, we do accept the New York/New Jersey Area Common Application Form if a grantseeker chooses to submit one. In this case, the proposal was referred to us by our president, who was introduced by a trustee of the Puppies Behind Bars organization to its founder, Gloria Gilbert Stoga.

"The cover letter accompanying this proposal quickly reminded us of the success of our first grant to this organization, which enables both male and female prison inmates inside correctional institutions to train puppies to become guide dogs for the blind. After 9/11 and especially for New York City, there is an obvious need for a much greater number of properly trained bomb-sniffing police dogs. So the stage was set for our foundation to be receptive to another idea: to help raise bomb-detection police dogs.

"Everything we needed to make a decision regarding this grant request was included in the full proposal with attachments that Puppies Behind Bars submitted. The Explosive Detection Canines section made specific reference to the organization's collaboration with the New York Police Department and the U. S. Bureau of Alcohol, Tobacco, and Firearms, which lends substantial credibility to the proposal. And in addition to the organization's board of directors, there is evidence of a strong advisory board. The project description includes extensive details in support of the assertions being made. The wide use of volunteers—both inmates and civilians who help "socialize" the dogs to get them used to city and street life—is impressive. The strongest feature of this proposal in my view is the level of specificity and the many facts provided. There were very few 'glittering generalities.' The single-lined, two-page budget was detailed enough and gave us confidence that the organization would be spending our grant funds appropriately.

"As to the attachments, the outside articles with photographs and testimonials from trainers were helpful and cast the proposal in a larger light than just paper text. In particular the articles they included from the *Smithsonian* magazine, the *New York Times*, and Delta's *Sky* magazine all helped to enhance the proposal by offering personal testimony from the participants. The financials and audit report were also fine.

"With most nonprofit organizations that we are seriously considering for grant support, we often go back for further details or for clarification. Such was the case with Puppies Behind Bars. The Web site of Puppies Behind Bars and GuideStar were helpful in providing additional information on the organization itself. As the organization matures and the dogs are used more by both visually impaired people and police/law enforcement agencies for bomb detection, even more testimonials from the actual beneficiaries would further strengthen the future depiction of their important endeavors.

"The Achelis and Bodman Foundations, two separate grantmaking entities, have only two full-time program staff, plus one part-time secretary, for a total staff of three people, to run both foundations. With 30 or more proposals under consideration for each of our three board meetings every year, it is impossible to devote extensive time and resources to each individual proposal being considered. In the case of Puppies Behind Bars, the complete proposal with attachments gave us quick confidence that we could move ahead in supporting this venture. As a very rare exception, we did not conduct a site visit to this particular project, since accessibility would be complicated, and it would take a full day to visit a prison site where inmates were training puppies."

—*Joseph Dolan, Secretary and Executive Director, The Achelis and Bodman Foundations*

Notes:
The complete proposal included the following attachments: organizational budget, list of foundation and corporate supporters, list of outstanding grants, list of board members, IRS tax-exempt letter, audited financial statement, and newspaper clippings.
Proposal written by Gloria Gilbert Stoga, President and Founder; Annie Losey Teillon, Director of Development; and Lori Gevalt, Board Member.

PUPPIES BEHIND BARS

training inmates to raise puppies to be dog guides for the blind and explosive detection canines for law enforcement

99 Madison Avenue, 2nd floor
New York, New York 10016
telephone: 212–924–7404
fax: 212–689–9330

April 3, 2003

Mr. Joseph S. Dolan
Executive Director
The Achelis and Bodman Foundations
767 Third Avenue, Fourth floor
New York, New York 10017

Dear Mr. Dolan:

I am writing to update the Achelis and Bodman Foundations on the progress Puppies Behind Bars has made since the Achelis and Bodman Foundations issued it a grant in December 2000, to describe a new initiative we are undertaking, and to ask your continued support. I am hopeful that after reading this proposal you will consider granting $25,000 to support our ongoing work and our expanded mission.

Goals and Objectives of Organization

As the Achelis and Bodman Foundations are aware, since July 1997, Puppies Behind Bars (PBB) has been training prison inmates to raise guide dogs for the blind. Our puppies, all specially bred Labrador Retrievers donated by guide dog schools, enter prison when they are eight weeks old and live there, with their inmate "puppy raisers," for the next 16 months. The inmates who volunteer for the program (in addition to the arduous task of raising a guide dog puppy the inmates must retain their mandatory prison jobs) are completely responsible for all aspects of caring for, and training, the puppies. In order to participate in the program, inmates must meet stringent criteria established by PBB and must be willing to dedicate 16 months to produce the best trained dogs they can. Once inmates pass the screening and are interviewed by PBB staff, they must attend six hours of PBB classes each week, complete homework assignments and take regular tests and quizzes, they must come together as a team, working toward a unified goal (prison life emphasizes a mentality of everyone for himself; learning to work together with other people is actually a huge undertaking for many of the inmates, and provides social skills necessary for life on the outside); and, what is most important, they become primary caretakers for a live being totally dependent upon them.

Once the puppies are ten weeks of age, they start leaving prison for outside socialization trips with volunteers. More than 200 volunteers take the pups into their homes and communities to expose them to situations they are unable to encounter in prison: riding in cars, busses, and taxis; walking down congested sidewalks and streets; and hearing regular household noises such as doorbells, telephones, dishwashers, and coffee bean grinders.

Mr. Joseph S. Dolan
April 3, 2003
Page two

Every weekend PBB runs one or two "puppy shuttles" from the prisons into Manhattan where we have more than 70 volunteer "city weekend sitters" who socialize our pups to city life.

As the pups mature into guide dog candidates, the inmates mature as well. Perhaps for the first time in their lives they have undertaken a serious responsibility and stuck with it; they have acted as loving caretakers dedicated to the dogs' well-being; they have learned to work together as a team to achieve a common goal; they have experienced the uplifting possibilities of giving and receiving unconditional love; and they are showing themselves and society that even though they have made serious mistakes in their lives, they are still capable of contributing to society, rather than taking from it.

PBB is now very much in demand. While there are other prison/dog programs in the country, it is PBB dogs that blind people want; it is the PBB program that New York's and other states' correctional departments are requesting; and it is PBB that guide dog schools are asking to raise its dogs. The most dramatic and newest of these requests has come from the New York Police Department Bomb Squad and the bureau of Alcohol, Tobacco, and Firearms (ATF), seeking our help in raising explosive detection dogs.

New Directions

Explosive Detection Canines
Because of the events surrounding September 11, 2001 and its aftermath, ATF and NYPD Bomb Squad's needs for dogs have increased. ATF is currently training 52 dogs a year and is mandated to increase that to 100; NYPD has 13 dogs in the bomb squad (one of which was raised by PBB) and is increasing to 16. *All 51 of these dogs will be raised by PBB.* Our organization is honored to have been selected to meet this challenge and is designing a new initiative specifically designed to provide the NYPD Bomb Squad and local law enforcement agencies with the best explosive detection dogs in the country.

Since September 11th, a number of individuals and companies have gone into the business of training explosive detection dogs, but they have done so with very little knowledge of how to accurately train such dogs and with little regard of the quality of life the dogs have. As a result, dogs that are improperly trained, worked too hard and with too many different handlers, or are "cross-trained" (trained to sniff both bombs and drugs, for example) are making their way into public life. It is probably just a matter of time before one of these dogs misses a bomb or makes a wrong decision which could have serious consequences. By comparison, PBB is honored to work with the NYPD Bomb Squad and ATF because we have visited both agencies' training headquarters, we have seen the love between handlers and their dogs, we have seen the conditions under which the dogs live while they are being trained and we know that the dogs, once trained, do not live in kennels but live at home with their trainers.

Mr. Joseph S. Dolan
April 3, 2003
Page three

In addition, both an agent from ATF and two bomb technicians from the NYPD Bomb Squad made separate visits to the Edna Mahan Correctional Facility for Women in Clinton, New Jersey, to meet and thank the women for the work they are doing. One of the bomb sniffing dogs currently in the NYPD Bomb Squad, "Sheeba," was raised at the Edna Mahan Facility and came back with her handler, Police Officer Paul Perricone, as a graduate of the NYPD's program. My abiding memory of that morning was looking over my shoulder and seeing an NYPD police officer sitting side by side with an inmate, deeply engrossed in conversation about the dog that lay at their feet. At that moment, it wasn't a police officer talking to an inmate; it was a bomb technician who spends his days making New York City safe for private citizens – and who depends on his dog to make the right decisions – speaking with the young woman who raised this incredible dog. All labels and barriers were nonexistent as two people discussed the pride and joy who sat between them, eagerly wagging her tail and looking up at people she loved dearly.

Educational Opportunities for Inmates
Only a very small percentage of inmates are successful in finding employment upon release from prison, so PBB is now offering higher educational opportunities to inmates in our program in the hopes that this will help make them more employable upon release. In April 2002, PBB began offering qualified inmates the opportunity to take a correspondence course, offered by Education Direct, which earns them a diploma as Veterinary Assistants. In order to qualify for the course, inmates must have been in the PBB program for at least one year, must have at least six months left before their parole board hearing, and must have a high school diploma or a GED. Twenty-five inmates are currently enrolled in the course and seven have earned their diploma; a brochure describing it is enclosed.

Evaluation

In terms of evaluating our program, during the course of PBB's six years of operation, we have created a "win-win-win" formula, which has earned national prominence: guide dog schools have gained a valuable training source; blind adults are given excellent guide dogs; and inmates have gained a strong sense of purpose and accomplishment while making a contribution to society. Our new initiative creates another win-win situation: more prisons and more inmates can participate in PBB's successful puppy training program and NYPD and ATF are given the most highly-trained, healthy, and happy-to-work bomb sniffing dogs available. Going one step further: PBB gives inmates the opportunity to do something positive for law enforcement agencies and for law enforcement to see that inmates can do something right.

Currently, PBB has thirty-eight working dogs in the field — twenty-one of our dogs lead their blind users through city streets and down country roads, preserving their sense of independence and dignity, ten PBB-raised dogs work daily with the NYPD and ATF to make our cities safe

Mr. Joseph S. Dolan
April 3, 2003
Page four

and seven others have bettered the lives of blind children by functioning as companion and therapy dogs. Our true test will be how many more dogs we can graduate next year and if we can raise the bar and further increase the graduation rate.

Another measure of our progress — and one of which we are extremely proud — is that the New York State Department of Correctional Services recently recognized PBB as a "Merit Time" program, one of only three such programs in the state. The Merit Time program allows certain non-violent inmates to earn a 1/6th reduction in their minimum sentence by completing a qualified program and by maintaining a good disciplinary record. When designating PBB as a Merit Time program, the Department of Corrections cited the community services that we provide the public, our stringent program standards, and the educational opportunities we offer (in addition to the Veterinary Assistant course, the New York State Department of Labor recognizes all PBB graduates as certified "Animal Caretakers").

Enclosed please find the additional information requested by the foundation, including our annual organizational budget, list of 2002 funding sources, 501 (c)(3) letter and latest audited financial report. In addition, I am also enclosing a copy of a newspaper article that appeared in a New Jersey newspaper the day following the Bomb Squad visit to the prison.

It is a strange irony that it has taken prison – and puppies – to enable people to do well in their lives. Thank you for helping us help them in this transformation.

Sincerely,

Lori S. Gevalt
Board Member

enclosures

Puppies Behind Bars
2003 Projected Budget
1 New Jersey Prison, 3 New York Prisons and
1 Federal Prison in Danbury, Connecticut
65 dogs and 135 inmates

Salaries
    Administrative
President (in office 3 days/week) — XXXXX
Managing Director (in office ½ day/week) — XXXXX
Instructor (in office 1 day/week) — XXXXX
Administrative Assistant — XXXXX
Instructor (in office 2 days/week) — XXXXX
Development Officer — XXXXX
  Subtotal for Administrative Costs — **$165,000**

    Direct Services
President (in prison teaching 2 days/week) — XXXXX
Managing Director (in prison teaching 2 ½ days/week) — XXXXX
Instructor (in prison teaching 4 days/week) — XXXXX
Instructor (in prison teaching 3 days/week) — XXXXX
Drivers (Part Time) x 2 — XXXXX
  Subtotal for providing Direct Services — **$129,000**

Benefits (18%) — **$52,920**
  Subtotal — **$346,920**

Other Administrative Expenses
Office Equipment & Supplies — $16,000
Professional Fees-Book Keeping & Accounting — $13,000
Telephone — $12,000
Rent *($1,500/month x 12)* — $18,000
Office Mail — $12,000
  Subtotal — $71,000

Insurance
Auto — $6,000
General Liability — $4,000
Worker's Compensation — $4,000
  Subtotal — $14,000

Public Outreach and Education
Newsletter (3x/year) — $3,500 per issue — $10,500
Newsletter Postage — $1,900 per issue — $3,060
Brochures and Advertising Materials — $1,500
Website Maintenance — $1,000
  Subtotal — $16,060

Transportation		
Gasoline		$27,000
Maintenance (3 vehicles)		$6,000
Parking		$2,400
Animal Transport-Van (including special equipment)		$30,000
Subtotal		$65,400
Dog Supplies for 65 dogs		
Food₁	$40/month/dog x65 dogs	$31,200
Toys & Other Miscellaneous	$300/dog	$19,500
Subtotal		$50,700
Veterinary Expenses for 65 dogs		
Basic Care₂	$400/dog	$26,000
Spaying & Neutering	$200/dog	$13,000
Emergency Treatment	$750/dog	$48,750
Medication (including tick and flea preventive)		$11,700
Subtotal		$99,450
Inmate Education		
Videos, books, puppy raising manuals, photographs		$10,000
Veterinary Assistants Training Course $550 per inmate x 45 inmates		$24,750
Subtotal		$34,750
Total		$698,280
(Noncash Expenses)₃		(22,000)
Total Cash Expenses		$676,280

1: $14,000 worth of dog food provided through a grant from the Iams Company

2: Basic care for 20 dogs provided *pro bono* from Guiding Eyes for the Blind

3: Total sum of 1 and 2

Chapter 4

Capacity Building

Funding requests for capacity building are intended to strengthen an organization in order to improve its performance and impact. Capacity building grants enable the organization to better accomplish its mission and often lead to stronger fiscal sustainability for the future. Capacity building grants are not meant to save failing projects or organizations, but rather to make good programs even more effective. Capacity building proposals typically focus on building skills and leadership potential among the organization's staff and board. These grants may include funds for technical assistance provided by the grantmaker or a consultant in such areas as financial management or fundraising.

The writer of a capacity building proposal must depict the organization's capability to grow and expand to the next level, given additional funding. Proposals for capacity building funds often include a presentation of long-term goals for the organization as well as well-thought-out specifics on how the organization intends to enhance its impact in the community by means of capacity building funds, while still maintaining its ongoing services.

The proposal included here is from Year Up, a Boston, Massachusetts-based non-profit youth organization. It requests a capacity building grant over five years from the Richard and Susan Smith Family Foundation, of Chestnut Hill, Massachusetts. The funding would enable Year Up to expand its intensive training program for low-income, recent high school graduates in urban areas. While the proposal does not contain an "ask" (e.g. request for a specific amount of grant dollars), it has many of the correct elements of a capacity building proposal, including a description of the organization's five-year goals, a list of capacity building needs, a sustainability plan, profiles of its management team and board members, benchmarks and program evaluation, a listing of strategic partnerships, future funding plans, and a five-year capacity building plan as a "discussion document."

A Proposal From
Year Up
Boston, Massachusetts

To
Richard and Susan Smith Family Foundation
Chestnut Hill, Massachusetts

Requested amount: Not specified; **Amount received:** $1,000,000 over five years

Funder's comments:

"At the Richard and Susan Smith Family Foundation, we establish guidelines for our funding programs and publish them on our Web site. Our guidelines include instructions on what we ask applicants to cover in their applications. In the case of Year Up, I invited this proposal as well as proposals from about 18 other groups, based on their reputation for excellence.

"The cover letter and executive summary helped us make an initial assessment of the program. And all the components that one would expect in a proposal were present in this one. Particularly well developed were the descriptions of the group's current accomplishments and how our funds would enable them to grow. The need statement was clear and crisp. The budget was presented clearly with the appropriate level of detail that we needed in order to make a funding decision. In my opinion the strongest feature of Year Up's proposal is its strategy for growth.

"While Year Up included all the attachments required, before making a final decision we did invite their leadership and one of their clients in for a meeting with our trustees. In the end we were delighted to fund this excellent proposal."

—*David Ford, Executive Director, Richard and Susan Smith Family Foundation*

Notes:

Proposal written by Matt McCann, Director of Development. Because any successful proposal is a product of the organization, Matt McCann would like to thank the Year Up staff, students, and graduates.

David Ford
Executive Director
Richard and Susan Smith Family Foundation
Suite 100
1280 Boylston Street
Chestnut Hill, MA 02467   September 16, 2002

Dear David,

It was great to see you again at the New Profit session and we appreciate your suggestions.

I am delighted to have this opportunity to submit a proposal to the Smith Family Foundation for your consideration. We ask that you consider supporting Year Up through a multi-year capacity building relationship. This will help us to grow the organization to serve more urban young adults and to prove the scalability of our model.

We believe that Year Up's program fits well with the Foundation's focus on increasing education and development opportunities for youth. We are also very compatible with your approach of tying annual contributions to benchmarks.

Year Up is founded on the belief that everyone deserves a chance to realize his or her potential. Our one-year, intensive training program combines hands-on skill development and real work apprenticeships with educational stipends. Year Up provides a critical transitional year that enables urban young adults to successfully pursue careers and college.

Over the past year, we have had a great deal of success. Ninety-two percent of our founding class successfully completed six months of full time classes along with six month paid internships with local companies to gain valuable work experiences. All have plans to pursue full time jobs and/or higher education upon completing our program. Over seventy percent have already received job offers averaging over $30,000. The hard work of these students is making our vision a reality.

Attached is a proposal that outlines our program, along with a set of attachments. Please don't hesitate to contact me if you need any additional information at all. Thank you very much for your time, interest and consideration.

Many kind regards,

Gerald Chertavian
Executive Director, Year Up

----
93 SUMMER St 5th Fl BOSTON, MA 02112 **PHONE** 617.542.1533 **FAX** 617.542.1539 **www.yearup.**

E M P O W E R I N G   U R B A N   T A L E N T   T O   R E A C H   T H E I R   P O T E N T I

Proposal to the Richard and Susan Smith Family Foundation

empowering urban talent to reach their potential

▶ Organizational Data

Year Up, Inc.
93 Summer Street, 5th floor
Boston, MA 02110

Phone:	617-542-1536
Fax:	617-542-1539
Contact:	Gerald Chertavian, Executive Director
Email:	gchertavian@yearup.org

Years in Existence:	Incorporated in November 2000
Fiscal Year:	June 1 – May 31

▶ Social Need and Rationale

In 2001, unemployment for urban young adults exceeded 40 percent. Over 1,000,000 jobs employing young adults have been eliminated since September 2001, wiping out the employment gains of the previous ten years for this age group. At the same time, the Information Technology Association of America estimates that more than 500,000 Information Technology positions will go unfilled in 2002. However, low-income, urban young adults are virtually unrepresented in IT careers. In fact, many of these young adults do not have the skills and knowledge needed to succeed in a variety of areas, including IT. This represents a *digital* and *economic divide* in our society – a gap between those who have and do not have the skills and knowledge needed to succeed. Without the proper guidance and opportunities, these young adults will continue to face enormous challenges in transitioning from high school to successful careers and higher education.

A Big Brother mentor since 1985, Gerald Chertavian understands first hand the positive impact of individual mentoring and education on urban youth. After graduating from Harvard Business School and founding and growing a highly successful technology firm, Gerald recognized that technical and professional skills could transform the lives of urban youth. He founded Year Up in October 2000 as a one-year intensive education and internship program. Gerald has made a personal commitment to Year Up of at least ten years and $500,000 to help ensure a successful program.

Year Up believes that we have designed and tested a scalable, sustainable model to provide young adults with the skills, experience and support to make successful transitions into the 21st century economy. Our goal is to expand this model first within Greater Boston and then nationally in order to empower 10,000 lives over a ten to fifteen year period.

1

Proposal to the Richard and Susan Smith Family Foundation

► Business Concept and Program Overview

Our mission is to provide urban young adults with a real opportunity to achieve economic self-sufficiency through well-paying careers in technology and further education. We achieve this mission through an innovative program that derives the majority of its revenue from internships. We believe that Year Up can significantly close the "Urban IT Gap" that exists for urban young adults. Our ability to place entry-level IT interns at near market rates is an important aspect of our scalable and sustainable business model.

Our customized, project based curriculum targets low-income high school graduates and GED recipients 18-23 from Greater Boston area neighborhoods. The program model combines four elements. Year Up places a particular emphasis on **support** and **guidance**, as we believe a supportive environment builds confidence and encourages better learning. Educational stipends, staff advisors and mentors are an essential part of this support. Classroom-based **education** focuses on technical and professional skills, using project-based teaching methods. Students then gain valuable **experience** during paid internships.

During the first six months of the program, students choose one of two focus areas:

- *Desktop User Support/IT Helpdesk*
- *Web Production and Design*

The second six months consist of paid corporate internships with a local partner company and a transitional process leading to permanent employment and higher education.

► Community Served

Our target population is low income, urban young adults 18-23 in Greater Boston. Based on data from our first two classes, our key demographics are summarized below:

Gender		Neighborhood	
Male	72%	Dorchester	20%
Female	28%	East Boston	16%
Ethnicity		Mattapan	10%
African-American	32%	Lynn	8%
Southeast-Asian	32%	Roxbury	6%
Hispanic/Latino	23%	Cambridge	6%
Caribbean	13%	Chelsea	6%
Caucasian	9%	Jamaica Plain	6%
Language		Everett	4%
Native English Speaking	58%	Hyde Park	4%
English as a Second Language	42%	Allston	2%
Age		Boston	2%
18-19	54%	Malden	2%
20-21	26%	Quincy	2%
21-23	20%	Other	6%

2

Proposal to the Richard and Susan Smith Family Foundation

▶ Business Plan

Year Up has a strategic business plan in place. As part of the launch of Year Up, Gerald Chertavian wrote the initial version in the fall of 2000. The plan was updated slightly in the summer of 2001 and more extensively in the spring of 2002 with input from the staff members, the Board and the Catalyst team. It was most recently modified in the summer of 2002 to reflect our learning from our first year and our latest strategic thinking. We feel that the current version, covering the next three years of our growth, adequately describes our business model and program. We will continue to refine it based on our experience as an organization. Year Up would welcome any feedback on the plan.

▶ Five Year Goals

By 2006, Year Up will expand its program in Greater Boston to train more than 200 students per year. To achieve this, we must demonstrate the scalability of our model. In essence, this means serving more students, at a lower cost per student, while maintaining high quality standards. The Cambridge College Expansion Project represents the first opportunity to scale beyond our existing Boston location in Downtown Crossing.

In July of 2002, the Boston class size expanded from 20 to 30; this lowers the program cost per student and allows Year Up to positively affect more young people. Beginning in January 2003, Year Up intends to grow the program further by:

- Increasing the number of students served at the current Boston site from 30 to 60 per year. The site will accommodate two classes of students, beginning in February and in July.
- Opening a second site at Cambridge College to accommodate 40 students per year, increasing to 60 students per year following the first cycle of training.
- Begin planning for a third site in the Greater Boston area to accommodate another 60 students per year. Through partnerships, our intention is to replicate the Cambridge College model, enabling Year Up to open new sites without having to lease costly infrastructure.

After proving our model in Greater Boston, we will expand to other cities in New England. We are currently in discussions with businesses and supporters in Providence, RI. Once we have successfully expanded locally, we will expand further, most likely to the New York area. Our goal is to create a sustainable program that can scale to empower 10,000 lives over a ten to fifteen year period.

More qualitatively, we believe Year Up can be an agent of change for corporations, education and the community. We can change corporate views of urban talent and develop a "virtuous cycle" which ultimately closes the "Urban IT Gap". We have already seen evidence of this with our internship partners. We can also strengthen communities by increasing the earnings potential of residents, creating role models and building valuable social networks. Finally, we believe we can help lead education reform by creating new pathways for urban young adults to transition from high school to careers and further education.

3

Proposal to the Richard and Susan Smith Family Foundation

▶ Capacity Building Needs

To achieve our growth objectives, we will need to make considerable investments in capacity and infrastructure. The most significant of these will include, but are not limited to:

- Additional staff members for new sites and Boston site
- Staff member development
- Infrastructure for new sites
- Public funding expertise
- Fundraising and financial management software
- Intranet and extranet hardware and software
- Automated systems for program evaluation, admissions, student contract administration, etc.
- Marketing and public relations

Year Up would benefit significantly from participation by the Smith Family Foundation. Although we have been fairly successful in our fundraising to date, the challenge increases as our program scales. We see four primary advantages to the funding approach taken by the Smith family Foundation:

- Focus on capacity building that is essential to a young, growing organization
- Significant multi-year investment
- Negotiated benchmarks to ensure the appropriate results
- David Ford's youth development program experience augments Year Up's own expertise

▶ Sustainability

Year Up believes it will successfully sustain its work and grow its program after support from The Smith Family Foundation ceases. We base this upon three primary factors:

➤ *Economics*

Year Up has a unique financing model that will enable the organization to generate internally more than half of its operating costs. In year one, Year Up was able to generate more than 30% of its operating costs through the paid internship program. In short, the revenue from the six-month paid internship entirely offsets the educational stipends that students receive over the twelve months of the program. As our program expands and reaches scale, we believe we can generate over 50% of our operating costs through internship revenue. We are also exploring other revenue streams such as placement fees. Over the past year, Year Up has proven that it can teach urban young adults the requisite technical and professional skills to succeed as paid-interns in entry-level technology jobs. Despite a poor economic climate, Year Up placed these paid interns into the region's most well regarded companies. Feedback from our internship partners is very favorable.

Year Up will continue to lower our operating costs through partnerships with organizations that can provide us with cost-effective infrastructure, such as Cambridge College. In addition, Year Up is finalizing the details of an articulation agreement that will allow Year Up graduates to earn up to a semester's worth of college credit during the Year Up program. This in turn will enable us to apply for federal funding in the form of Pell grants. In addition to federal student aid, we are actively researching public funding opportunities for Year Up's program. We realize that accessing public funds will require additional focused resources as part of our capacity building and we expect to obtain public funding within the next two years.

4

Proposal to the Richard and Susan Smith Family Foundation

➤ *Strategy*

Year Up focuses on creating and maintaining a unique and competitive position in the market for helping urban young adults transition to careers and higher education. We are diligent about identifying and incorporating the best practices of similar organizations. We continue to develop effective partnerships with organizations and individuals that add value. For example, our relationship with Cambridge College (www.cambridge.edu) is a pioneering model of how a youth training program can tightly integrate with a college. This has tremendous implications for curriculum development, fundraising (especially on the federal level) and cost control. Our strategic partnership with Jobs For the Future (www.jff.org) provides significant help with evaluation, best practices, organizational scaling, and access to both national foundation and public funds. We were also selected by Catalyst Alliance (www.catalystalliance.org) as one of ten national partners with the most potential to create social change. This award provided us with several months of pro bono strategic consulting by Harvard Business School students and Accenture consultants.

➤ *Operations*

Year Up's staff has highly relevant expertise in areas such as education and training, non-profit organizational development, business management, technology and fundraising. Year Up's founder previously co-founded and rapidly grew a software start-up into a 150-person company with four offices in three countries. Our approach is to grow the program in a controlled manner, testing new approaches before introducing them on a broad scale.

▶ Management Team and Board Members

Management Team

Gerald Chertavian, *Founder and Executive Director,* brings a life-long commitment to working with urban young adults. As a Big Brother mentor, Gerald understands the positive impact of individual mentoring and education on urban youth. Prior to founding Year Up, Gerald co-founded and managed Conduit Communications, an Internet strategy-consulting firm. From 1993 to 1998, Conduit ranked as one England's 15 fastest growing companies with offices in London, Amsterdam, New York and Boston. Gerald has a B.A. in Economics from Bowdoin College and an MBA with honors from Harvard Business School. He also serves as a Trustee of Cambridge College and Bowdoin College. Gerald was recently recognized by Boston Business Forward magazine as one of "Boston's 40 most promising individuals under the age of 40."

Linda Swardlick Smith, *Director of Community Partnerships and External Affairs,* has more than 15 years of training and community leadership experience. Linda also served as the Vice President for Business Development at WorkSource Staffing Partnership and for more than a decade, Linda was the Executive Director of Training, Inc., a Boston-based, not-for-profit job training organization in seven U.S. cities. Linda holds a B.A. from the University of Vermont and a M.S.W. from the University of Michigan, specializing in community organization and resource capacity building.

Tom Berté, *Director of Corporate Partners and Operations,* has a strong background in technology and relationship management. He joined Year Up most recently from Digitas, one of the nation's leading interactive agencies where he worked as a consultant in their digital strategy group and as an account manager. Prior to Digitas, Tom worked as an analyst for Andersen Consulting. Tom has a B.A. in Economics from Duke University.

5

Proposal to the Richard and Susan Smith Family Foundation

Richard Dubuisson, *Learning Director,* comes to Year Up with an extensive background in education, technology, and teaching urban youth. Richard is responsible for the development and delivery of the six-month technical course curriculum. He is also responsible for evaluating teaching methodologies, student assessment tools, and overseeing the SAT preparation classes and certification requirements. Richard has a B.A. in History and French from Duke University.

Nicolette Patti, *Office Manager/Instructor,* comes to Year Up with keen organizational skills and several years of teaching ESL and literacy in urban settings. Fluent in Spanish, she designed a comprehensive business communication curriculum to improve writing, grammar and public speaking skills in a neighborhood-based youth program. Nikki has a B.A. in English from Boston University.

Mary McLaughlin, *Director of Information Technology,* has worked for over ten years as a systems administrator and software tester for small to enterprise-sized businesses and non-profits. More recently, she has designed, developed and written curricula for telecommunications and data communications technologies and has taught at Northeastern University. Mary is certified in and has taught many technologies including Microsoft, Symantec, Compaq, and Lucent. She has a B.A. in business economics from Bentley College.

Matt McCann, *Director of Development*, brings a 20-year career in technology to Year Up. As a Client Partner at Razorfish and i-Cube, he managed large consulting teams for major clients. As Partner and General Manager for Conduit Communications in Boston, he was responsible for strategic direction and day-to-day operations. Matt has held senior positions in software development, marketing, sales, product management, direct marketing and purchasing at Sun Microsystems, PC Connection, Data General and Wang Laboratories. He has a B.A. in Philosophy from Dartmouth College and has done graduate work in Multinational Commerce at Boston University.

Bella Graffam, *Instructor*, comes to Year Up with extensive experience in both training and technology. As a freelance web developer, she has used her skills to create websites for a variety of Boston area businesses. Before joining the Year Up team, she worked for New Horizons Computer Learning Center as a Web Technology Instructor. Bella earned her B.A. in Political Science and Communications from Webster University in St. Louis, MO.

Board of Directors

- **Gerald Chertavian,** *Founder and Executive Director*
- **Eileen Brown,** *President, Cambridge College*
- **Constance Davis,** *President, C.R. Davis and Associates*
- **Tim Dibble,** *Managing General Partner, Alta Communications*
- **Nick Gleason,** *President and CEO, CitySoft*
- **Pamela Trefler,** *Director, Trefler Foundation*
- **Craig Underwood,** *President, Underwood Consulting*

Board of Corporate Advisors

- **James Ireland Cash, Jr., Ph. D.** *Professor of Business Administration and Senior Associate Dean, Graduate School of Business Administration Harvard University*
- **Martin J. Mannion,** *Managing Partner,* Summit Partners
- **John R. Muse,** *Chief Operating Officer* and Partner, Hicks, Muse, Tate and Furst
- **John Simon,** *Co-Founder and Partner*, General Catalyst Partners

6

Proposal to the Richard and Susan Smith Family Foundation

▶ Benchmarks and Program Evaluation

Year Up uses four primary criteria to ensure the quality of its program:

- **Internship Placement and Employer Feedback** -Year Up interns provide a range of technical services to partner companies. The quality of these services is measured directly by feedback collected from corporate partners and indirectly by the amount Year Up is able to charge partners for these services and their willingness to accept trainees from future classes.
- **Graduation Rate** - One important measure of Year Up's effectiveness will be its ability to retain individuals throughout the year and successfully graduate them from the program.
- **Job Placement and Further Education** - A key measure of success will be Year Up's ability to place individuals into living-wage jobs and further education within three months of completing the program. Year Up's goal is to enable students to earn a minimum of $15 per hour with prospects for career advancement.
- **Post-Year Up Tracking** - Once students have transitioned from Year Up to jobs and/or further education, we will continue to track students' earnings and employment history and academic record over time compared to a control group of individuals.

Results

Student Outcome	Measurement	Goal	Actual
Placement in paid 6 month internships	Internship placement rate	100%	100%
Positive internship feedback	Internship partner survey data	85% meet/exceed expectations	90%
Graduation from Year Up	Graduation rate	85%	92%*
Placement in full/part-time or contract positions	% of students placed within three months of graduation	100%	75% to date**
College Applications	% of all students admitted to two or four year college or university	25% - 35%	70%***
Significant earning potential	Salary level	≥ $15/hour	$18/hour

*One of the students left for financial reasons prior to graduation and was able to secure a $30,000/year position using the skills she learned at Year Up. Although we don't count her in our results, we still view this as a success.

** The remaining 25% are actively engaged in the job search and interviewing process, with considerable support from Year Up. We are working hard to place the remaining students by our target date of end of September 2002.

*** 100% of all students who applied to college were accepted. The majority will be attending part-time in addition to working.

▶ Strategic Partnerships

Year Up works closely with more than 30 community-based organizations, training organizations, local high schools, and community and four-year colleges. We develop value-added partnerships with existing organizations to avoid duplication of efforts and take advantage of existing intellectual capital in relevant areas. Year Up is diligent about identifying and incorporating the best practices of similar organizations. We continue to develop effective partnerships with organizations and individuals that add value. Key partnership examples include:

7

Proposal to the Richard and Susan Smith Family Foundation

- **Cambridge College** - Year Up is finalizing an agreement with Cambridge College (www.cambridge.edu) that will allow our graduates to receive up to a semester's worth of college credit. In addition to saving our students time and money, this will enable us to apply for federal funding such as Pell grants. Year Up will continue to lower our operating costs through partnerships with organizations that can provide us with cost-effective infrastructure. The Cambridge College relationship also enables us to lower our operating costs significantly by utilizing their infrastructure for our second site.

- **Jobs For The Future** - Our strategic partnership with Jobs For the Future (www.jff.org) provides significant help with best practices, organizational scaling, and access to both national foundation and public funds. Through this relationship, we develop, document and refine an operating model that can ultimately achieve both scale and systemic impact. We are also working actively with JFF to define and execute a five-year evaluation methodology for our program.

- **Teen Empowerment** (www.teenempowerment.org) is a non-profit organization that employs youth ages 14 - 20 to work as catalysts for social and institutional change. Year Up works closely with Teen Empowerment, applying relevant aspects of their model to our admissions and behavior management processes.

- **The Bottom Line** (www.bottomline.org) is a community-based educational counseling program whose mission is to increase the number of Boston students earning college diplomas. This partnership provides expertise and assistance to Year Up students with college selection, application and the completion of financial aid packages.

- **Catalyst Alliance** (www.catalystalliance.org) selected Year Up as one of ten non-profit organizations in the Boston and San Francisco areas to receive 16 weeks of pro-bono consulting. A Catalyst Alliance Team, made up of consultants from Accenture and five Harvard Business School students worked with Year Up to help research and develop the organization's strategic growth plan.

▶ Funding

Year Up recognizes the need to develop sustainable sources of operating capital. We are explicitly managing this to reduce our reliance on private funding. Our internship program will generate upward of 50% of our revenue in the future. In addition, Year Up has raised funds from foundations, individuals and corporations. We are also actively researching public funding opportunities for Year Up's program. We expect to obtain public funding within the next two years.

Our goal within the next three years is to cover at least 75% of our operating expenses through internship revenue and public funding. The remainder would come from foundations, corporations and individuals. To date, our funding breakdown is as follows:

Funder Type	Total Grants	% of Total
Individuals	$800,000	50%
Foundations	$534,000	33%
Corporations	$159,000	12%
Public	$80,000	5%

We are not currently building an endowment, although we expect to begin this process once we have proven multi-site, multi-city capability. We are working toward a goal of having four to six months in cash on hand at any given time and are on track to hit this goal by January 2003. Lastly, we have made arrangements to put in place a mid-six figure line of credit as a backstop, although we do not expect to use this facility.

8

Proposal to the Richard and Susan Smith Family Foundation

In terms of multi-year capacity building funding, Year Up has received the following multi-year grants from foundations:

Granter	Amount per year	# of years
Barr Foundation	$10,000	3
Hunt Foundation	$10,000	2

These grants have helped us grow the program within the Boston site.

Many grants were awarded to Year Up with the expectation that we would apply for funding the following year. Organizations that have awarded us a second round of funds or invited us to apply for a second year include the Boston Foundation, FleetBoston, Trefler Foundation, Hyams Foundation, Citizens Bank and State Street Bank. In addition, several individual donors with annual amounts ranging from $1,000 to $15,000 have made commitments of three to four years.

▶ Additional Comments

It is impossible to adequately convey an organization's passion in a proposal. The roots of Year Up's passion are Gerald Chertavian's experience as a Big Brother in New York City. He became convinced that lack of opportunity was the single biggest obstacle for low-income urban youth and vowed to eventually do something about it on a larger scale. After gaining broad experience and achieving success in the for-profit world, Gerald has applied his business skills to this social challenge. His belief in the importance of Year Up is underscored by his commitment of a minimum of ten years and $500,000. Critically, he has assembled a team that shares his passion for challenging the status quo and working closely with urban youth. The Year Up team combines considerable for-profit, non-profit and education expertise with an unshakable conviction that urban youth deserve the same opportunities for success as their more advantaged counterparts.

Year Up recognizes that effective collaboration is essential to young organizations. We have placed a particular emphasis on establishing a few truly deep and innovative partnerships. Our growing relationship with Cambridge College has generated national interest as well as tangible results. By allowing us to locate our second site on their campus, Cambridge College will allow us to save considerable planning time and infrastructure cost. They have already awarded four full scholarships to Year Up graduates, the first time this was done in 14 years. We are especially excited by the articulation agreement we are finalizing that will allow Year Up graduates to earn up to a semester's worth of college credit during the Year Up program. This in turn will enable us to apply for Pell grants. Several other avenues of collaboration are being actively discussed with Cambridge College. This relationship is strengthened by the fact that Year Up's Executive Director and Cambridge College's President sit on each other's Board of Directors.

Year Up has received feedback from a wide range of sources that our mission is compelling, our program design innovative, our team well rounded and our business model sound. We believe our biggest challenge is one of execution: expanding our program without sacrificing quality. To facilitate successful expansion, we will need to develop deep, long-term relationships with strategic funders. To be truly transformative, these relationships need to transcend the financial aspect to incorporate a consultative dimension. We believe that these funders should help shape strategic direction and define results that meet the objectives of both organizations. We hope to have the opportunity to establish just such a relationship with the Smith Family Foundation.

9

Year Up 2003 Capacity Building Plan – *Discussion Document*

	Item	Benefits	Est. Cost	Benchmark(s)	Comments
Human capital development	Program Director	• Allows increase in student intake while ensuring program quality and consistency across sites • Enables Exec. Dir. to focus on fundraising, board development and strategy	XXXXX	• Hired by end of Q3 • Portable curriculum by end of Q4 • Maintain ≥ 80% positive overall responses from internship partners	XXXXX XXXXX XXXXX XXXXX
	Public Funding Consultant	• Ensures a cost-effective approach to pursuing public funding	$20,000	• Consultant(s) in place by end of Q1 • Submit at least 2–4 public funding proposals by end of Q4 with an aggregate value of at least $400,000	• Planning, research, grant writing and editing
	Outreach Coordinator	• Ensures sufficient quality and quantity of applicants to meet growth targets	XXXXX	• Hired by end of Q1 • Maintain ≥ 2:1 ratio of applicants to accepted students	XXXXX XXXXX XXXXX XXXXX
Curriculum development	On-line remediation tools	• Enables English improvement for ESL students	$10,000	• License fee negotiated by end of Q1	• For site license

12/16/2002

Year Up 2003 Capacity Building Plan – Discussion Document

Item	Benefits	Est. Cost	Benchmark(s)	Comments
Infrastructure and information systems				
Define needs and research systems	• Ensures appropriate selection of software that can accommodate Year Up's future needs	$6,000	• Complete assessment by end of Q1	
Systems for Cambridge College	• Enables expansion from 20 to 30 students/year	$20,000	• Source and install by end of Q2	
Fundraising software	• Supports more efficient donor management	$15,000	• Source, install and migrate data by end of Q3	
Financial management software	• Supports more efficient financial planning and management	$10,000	• Source, install and migrate data by end of Q4	
Program evaluation	• Defines the evaluation metrics and methodology for the next five years • Positions YU to receive government and national foundation grants	$15,000	• Complete high level strategic plan by end of March 2003	• Part of a larger initiative • Need to identify best partner(s) to work with
Marketing and PR — Enhanced brochure and outreach materials	• Enables Year Up to present itself more effectively to potential funders, partners and students	$10,000	• Produce two brochures by end of Q2 for: 1) funders & partners and 2) general outreach	
Total		**$200,000**		

12/16/2002

Year Up 2004–2007 Capacity Building Plan

	Item	2004 Benchmarks	2005 Benchmarks	2006 Benchmarks	2007 Benchmarks
Student Impact	# students touched per year	120	150	180	200+
	Student retention rate	≥85%	≥85%	≥85%	≥85%
	% of students placed in full and/or part-time positions w/in 4 months	≥85%	≥85%	≥85%	≥85%
	% of students admitted to higher education w/in 1 year of graduation	≥50%	≥50%	≥50%	≥50%
Corporate Impact	% of students meeting/ exceeding expectations for technical skills	≥85%	≥85%	≥85%	≥85%
	% of students meeting/ exceeding expectations for professional skills	≥80%	≥80%	≥80%	≥80%
Organizational Capacity Building	Assess and refine curriculum development	Technical Advisory Board in place and contributing to curriculum refinement	Continue to assess market demand and refine curriculum to meet that demand	Continue to assess market demand and refine curriculum to meet that demand	Continue to assess market demand and refine curriculum to meet that demand
	Information Technology	• Intranet • Finalize needs for site 3	• Finalize needs for site 4 • Plan for site beyond Boston	Plan for/implement site beyond Boston	Implement site beyond Boston
	Program evaluation	• Work with 3rd party to validate system design • Begin implementation of evaluation system (data collection and analysis)	Continue implementation of evaluation system	Evaluation system refinement	Evaluation system refinement

1/2/2003

Year Up 2004–2007 Capacity Building Plan

	Item	2004 Benchmarks	2005 Benchmarks	2006 Benchmarks	2007 Benchmarks
Human Capital	Hire key people to build capacity	• Alumni Support and Job Placement Coordinator • Internship Partner Manager	• Fundraising Associate • IT Manager	• Accounting and Finance Manager	
	Professional development	Create professional development plan	Implement professional development plan	Refine professional development plan	Refine professional development plan
Financial Stability	Develop a public revenue stream	Obtain at least one source of public funding	Continue to develop potential sources of public funding	• Continue to develop potential sources of public funding • Public funding becomes a significant source of operating revenue	• Continue to develop potential sources of public funding • Public funding becomes a significant source of operating revenue
	Achieve overall revenue targets	$3,000,000	$3,750,000	$4,500,000	$5,000,000

1/2/2003

Chapter 5

Building/Renovation

Grants in this category make possible the building, renovation, remodeling, or rehabilitation of property. Because these projects tend to be quite large in scope, no one funder typically takes on the entire cost of a construction project. Grants from several supporters may be sought simultaneously. Sometimes, as is evident in the two proposals presented here, the construction projects are part of a larger capital campaign. As with other types of funding requests, contributors to building and renovation projects will want to know which other funders have or are being asked to contribute, and how much. The amounts requested of funders of construction projects may vary in size, with certain funders taking a lead role. And some funders may pay for only particular aspects of the project, such as a playground or auditorium. In such instances there may be a "naming" opportunity inherent in the request.

Depending on the funder's requirements, proposals for building and renovation may include specific and definitive plans, such as architects' renderings and specifications, engineers' reports, design schematics, blueprints, and other technical documents, frequently handled as attachments.

As in other types of proposals, the need for a construction project is best expressed in terms of those in the community who will ultimately benefit, not just enhancements for the organization and its staff. The writer of this type of proposal succeeds by demonstrating how the new or renovated facility will improve the programs that serve an audience that the funder cares about. Both building and renovation proposals included here, one for $25,000 and the other for $200,000, accomplish that goal quite effectively.

The first proposal is from Inner Harbour for Children & Families, of Douglasville, Georgia, and requests $25,000 from The Community Foundation for Greater Atlanta as part of a campaign to construct a residential facility for emotionally troubled pre-adolescent males and cognitively challenged youth.

The second proposal is from the Methodist Home for Children and Youth of Macon, Georgia, to the Peyton Anderson Foundation, also of Macon, Georgia. The request is in the amount of $200,000 toward the construction of a $6 million, 53,000 square-foot Intergenerational Activity Center. The cover letter includes information on how much funding has been committed by other donors to the campaign and points out that a gift from the Peyton Anderson Foundation will help the organization obtain a $1 million challenge grant.

A Proposal From
Inner Harbour for Children & Families
Douglasville, Georgia

To
The Community Foundation for Greater Atlanta, Inc.
Atlanta, Georgia

Requested amount: $25,000; **Amount received:** $20,000

Funder's comments:

"Inner Harbour's proposal letter provided a lot of details that were not included in its application form, primarily due to the fact that The Community Foundation's Competitive Grant Application form has limited space for answers. The additional details supplied in this letter, while not required, were very helpful in our initial assessment of the application. All expected components were included in the application packet. Components of Inner Harbour's application that were well developed were the attachments detailing the project budget and the funds raised to date. Since Inner Harbour's request was for support for a capital campaign, it was especially good to see what other local, regional, and national foundations had committed their support and to learn that the organization's board of directors had committed significant funds to the campaign.

"My impression of the proposal letter's need statement ('Extend the Healing' section) is that it is concise and that each sentence provides critical information about the need for the project. It discusses the high number of children needing services, the low number of providers who can address those needs, and how Inner Harbour's project will support the community's needs. Inner Harbour did an excellent job of providing good, succinct answers to our questions. They clearly indicate how a grant from our foundation combined with their strategies will have a positive impact in addressing the community's needs. And the budget was very clear and provided all the detail necessary to make a positive funding decision.

"Inner Harbour submitted all required attachments in addition to several key attachments relating to their capital campaign. Since the additional attachments directly related to their request, they were very helpful. Before any decision is made, program officers of The Community Foundation for Greater Atlanta conduct site visits with applicants. We request that the organization's executive director and board chair/president be present, in addition to program staff if relevant to the request. I visited Inner Harbour and gained a lot from that visit. As I was preparing my funding recommendation, I did contact the organization to get an update on the status of their capital campaign. I was pleased to receive a prompt response."

—Lita Ugarte, Program Officer, The Community Foundation for Greater Atlanta, Inc.

Notes:

The proposal was written using The Community Foundation for Greater Atlanta, Inc.'s Competitive Grant Application. The complete proposal included the following attachments: IRS tax-exempt letter; list of board of trustees; staff biographies; organizational budget; audited financial statement; capital campaign project budget; list of foundation, corporate, and individual supporters; outcomes report; and newspaper clippings.

Proposal written by Lynn Merrill, Vice President for Charitable Giving.

TURNING HURT INTO HOPE

The Campaign for Inner Harbour

July 15, 2004

Ms. Alicia Philipp
President
Community Foundation for Greater Atlanta, Inc.
50 Hurt Plaza, Suite 449
Atlanta, Georgia 30303

Dear Alicia:

For over forty years, Inner Harbour has provided a highly effective treatment program and healing refuge for emotionally and psychologically troubled children and teens in metropolitan Atlanta. Now, the organization is seeking help from the community as we conduct our first capital campaign in over two decades to build a new facility on our Douglasville campus. On behalf of the Board of Directors of Inner Harbour, we respectfully request a grant of $25,000 from the Community Foundation for Greater Atlanta toward our $4.16 million *"Turning Hurt into Hope"* Capital Campaign.

We originally launched a $3 million campaign in January to raise funds to completely finish the first story of the new building, with the second story to be completed at a later time as funds were available. In April, the Robert W. Woodruff Foundation made a $750,000 grant with another $250,000 as a challenge grant if Inner Harbour expanded their vision to complete the second floor of the new building. Following Woodruff's example, the John H. and Wilhelmina D. Harland Charitable Foundation made a $150,000 grant with a $50,000 challenge for an expanded campaign. The development staff and campaign leadership carefully reviewed the implications of raising the campaign goal to be sure to proceed in the most thoughtful manner. After an analysis of the positive response of the community to date and the remaining prospects, the Board of Inner Harbour voted to raise the goal to $4,160,000 to respond to the tremendous opportunity presented by these challenges. To date, Inner Harbour has raised $2,168,026 toward the revised goal.

Background

Inner Harbour has grown in stature to become one of Georgia's leading providers of quality residential and community-based services for severely troubled children and adolescents, offering the broadest array of services for youth in the state. We are the only therapeutic youth treatment center in Georgia accredited by the Southern Association of Colleges and Schools, the Joint Commission on Accreditation of Health Care Organizations and the Association for Experiential Education. As the state's largest youth intensive residential treatment center, we are a sought after training site for psychiatric medical residents from the Schools of Medicine at Emory University and Morehouse College, as well as students from a wide variety of other disciplines, including recreational and experiential therapy interns from 50 colleges and universities located throughout the United States and Canada.

Using our own resources or in partnership with other agencies, Inner Harbour strives to provide a full continuum of mental health services, from preventive care to after-care for youth ages 6 to 18 years. The Douglasville campus is the site of the intensive residential treatment program for males and females with problems ranging from depression to serious aggressive behaviors to other psychological disorders. Most residents begin in the more clinical, restrictive environment, with a goal of progressing to live in outside units with more privileges. A second campus in Rockmart for male juvenile offenders and males with sexual behavior disorders completes our residential service programs. Over 1,000 youth are served each year through these treatment programs including after-school programs in Fulton and Douglas Counties and on-campus group homes. In addition, Inner Harbour provides individual and family therapy, psychological testing, and community presentations on mental health issues through its outpatient center.

Healing Through Experience

Inner Harbour uses a unique combination of conventional treatment and experiential, activity-based therapies to help children, teens and their families address serious behavioral or emotional problems. Early on, Inner Harbour pioneered the use of outdoor wilderness experiences, such as hiking, caving, canoeing, climbing and camping to help troubled adolescents learn how to build relationships, trust others and resolve conflict. Our natural woodlands in Douglas County provide an ideal setting for young people to learn critical life skills by interacting with highly trained staff, family members and peers during carefully structured outdoor projects.

Inner Harbour continues to add new programs to respond to the increasingly complex needs of the children it serves. Art, music, pet therapy and our model horsemanship program complement the outdoor adventure programs in helping these young people develop trust, build self-esteem, reduce stress, and become receptive to the intensive psychiatric treatment they receive. For example, our unique West African drumming program is highly effective in helping youth heal and offers a means to provide community service through workshops and performances. Education at Inner Harbour is also geared to each student's individual needs. Inner Harbour's specially trained teachers weave educational objectives into every activity whether it occurs outdoors or in the traditional classroom setting.

The positive results are evident. Inner Harbour successfully discharges 93% of its patients into lower levels of care. Only 2% of all 2003 admissions consisted of former patients – a very low number considering Inner Harbour's commitment to serve any previous patients requiring readmission into intensive residential care. Psychiatric measurements for patients who completed the program, as defined by the Global Assessment of Functioning (GAF) and Child and Adolescent Functional Abilities Scale (CAFAS), indicate that all patients achieved higher levels of functioning abilities and exhibited less aggressive behavior, emotional problems and substance abuse. In our most recent follow-up surveys with parents, guardians and caregivers, 100% of them expressed satisfaction with the treatment their child received and 94% were satisfied with the progress their child made in Inner Harbour's care.

Extending the Healing

In today's world, children and adolescents comprise the fastest growing segment of the population with mental illnesses, yet they are the least likely to be treated for them. Current national studies reveal that 20% of youth between the ages of 9 and 17 years, or 15 million young people, have diagnosable psychiatric disorders and that four million have such serious emotional disturbances that their daily lives are disrupted. According to the 2000 census and the U.S. Surgeon General's Report on Mental Health, nearly 195,000 children in Georgia have a severe emotional disturbance requiring treatment – far more than Inner Harbour and Georgia's other youth residential treatment providers *combined* can offer.

To address these needs and to continue to lead the way in providing mental health services for Georgia's youth, the board and staff of Inner Harbour recently completed an in-depth strategic plan in which improving and expanding facilities is recognized as a major goal for the organization. The first priority is to address urgent housing needs on the Douglasville campus. Most of the residential facilities have not been updated since the 1970s and are camp-like shelters originally designed to house older boys for short stays. Over the years these structures have become longer-term "homes" for many of Inner Harbour's younger residents. As Inner Harbour serves youth with more specialized needs, its facilities must be improved to meet these needs.

As a first step, Inner Harbour financed the construction of a children's building for boys, ages 6-10, which opened in March 2003. This building is the first new construction at Inner Harbour's Douglasville site in 25 years and was completed under budget and on schedule. The next priority is to address the housing needs of two distinct populations needing residential care and treatment: pre-adolescent male patients, ages 10-14 and cognitively challenged male and female patients, ages 13-17. In order to serve these youth, Inner Harbour will construct and furnish a new 17,373 square foot, two-story residential facility, which will include private rooms for each resident; common spaces for living and dining; four classrooms; two nurse/staff stations; and administrative offices. The building will be configured to include four separate ten-bed units that can be adapted to respond to changing service needs. The total cost of the building is $4.16 million.

Currently, the pre-adolescent boys, ages 10-14, are housed in rustic individual cabins with no indoor plumbing or in a multi-resident bunkhouse. This setting presents numerous clinical and safety challenges. Experience has shown that lack of privacy and sharing of small cabins can create conflicts if roommates' personalities are at odds, and may increase a child's level of frustration and the need for staff intervention. Based on current research and the study of other treatment programs, it is clear that boys at this vulnerable age respond better to treatment in a more controlled and centralized setting. Consolidating the housing for these pre-adolescent boys will offer a number of clinical advantages that will enable Inner Harbour's staff to serve these children more effectively and efficiently.

Residential space for cognitively challenged youth is the number one need of the Department of Juvenile Justice and a primary need of Georgia's MATCH (Multi-Agency Team for Children) program in which Inner Harbour participates. With severe psychiatric problems and a typical IQ of 60-75 points, these youth do not respond to traditional therapies and must be treated in a highly structured environment. Currently, there is only one other designated facility in Georgia addressing this population. Again, by being able to offer private rooms and treatment in a centralized location, these youth will be served more effectively and efficiently.

Impact of a Grant from the Community Foundation for Greater Atlanta

Inner Harbour has diligently prepared itself for this capital campaign, and we are very appreciative of your willingness to receive this funding request. A grant of $25,000 from the Community Foundation at this time would serve as a strong endorsement of the importance of Inner Harbour to the community and help us leverage other significant contributions. With your support, we can help these young people reclaim their lives and *turn hurt into hope*.

If you have further questions, please call any of us or Lynn Merrill, Development Director at Inner Harbour, (770/942-2391, ext. 366) to provide additional information. We thank you in advance for your consideration.

Sincerely,

Robert F. Clayton
Board Chair

Lewis Holland, Sr.
Campaign Co-Chair

Ronald J. Scroggy
Chief Executive Officer

THE COMMUNITY FOUNDATION
FOR GREATER ATLANTA, INC.

2004-2005 COMPETITIVE GRANT APPLICATION

Please maintain the original font (Verdana) and use 10-point type. Do not change the margins (0.5" all around) or split tables over a page break.

I. GENERAL INFORMATION

Organization Name: Inner Harbour, Ltd.	**Application Deadline:** July 16, 2004
Mailing Address: 4685 Dorsett Shoals Road **City, State, Zip Code:** **Douglasville, Georgia 30135**	**Executive Director/President:** Ronald J. Scroggy, Chief Executive Officer
Phone Number & Extension: 770-942-2391	**E-mail Address:** ron.scroggy@innerhabour.net
Website Address: www.innerharbour.org	**Current Year's Organization Budget:** $23,933,476
Project/Program Budget: $4,160,000	**Amount Requested:** $25,000
Date of 501(c)(3) Certification: May 1964	**Federal Tax ID #:** 58-0873694
Purpose of Proposal (Refer to your answer to question 3.7 and state the purpose of your proposal/request in one sentence): To construct a $4.16 million residential facility for emotionally troubled pre-adolescent males and cognitively challenged youth.	

Program Area (check the Application Guidelines and mark the program area that best applies to this proposal):

☐ Arts & Culture   ☐ Community Development   ☒ Education & Youth Development
☐ Health   ☐ Human Services

II. ORGANIZATION BACKGROUND

2.1 Mission & History:
For over 40 years, Inner Harbour has provided a highly effective treatment program and healing refuge for emotionally and psychologically troubled children and teens in metro Atlanta. Inner Harbour's mission is to help young people build upon their strengths to overcome life's most difficult challenges by providing a continuum of behavioral and educational services.

2.2 Programs: Using bullets, list the organization's main programs/projects with a sentence to describe each one.

- School--The accredited school's specially trained teachers weave educational objectives into every activity both outdoors and in the classroom.
- Therapy--Youth receive intensive individual, group and family therapy to address a variety of emotional and behavioral issues.
- Outdoor programs--Troubled adolescents hike, cave, canoe, climb and camp, teaching them to build relationships, trust others and resolve conflict.

- Horsemanship--A nationally accredited therapeutic horse program teaches youth about responsibility, empathy, trust and relational self-reliance.
- Drumming--West African drumming engages youth in building and playing drums, improves hand-eye coordination, and stimulates brain activity.

2.3 Population served by the Organization (during the last fiscal year): Indicate the number of people served by the organization according to race and gender. In the column marked "% *(race)*", indicate the percentage of the individuals served in that row (i.e. Caucasian females) as a percentage of the entire population served. In the row marked "% *(age)*", indicate the percentage of individuals served in that column (i.e. individuals ages 0-5) as a percentage of the entire population served.

RACE & GENDER		0-5	6-11	12-14	15-18	19-63	64+	Total	% (race)
					AGE				
African American	Females		10	22	18			50	12
	Males		42	43	46			131	31
Asian/Pacific Islander	Females		1					1	<1
	Males								
Caucasian	Females			23	43			66	16
	Males		21	53	81			155	37
Hispanic/ Latino	Females			1	2			3	<1
	Males		1	3	4			8	2
Multi Racial	Females				3			3	<1
	Males		2	1				3	<1
	TOTAL		77	146	197			420	
	% (age)		18	35	47				100%

2.4 List characteristics that are important to note, but are not defined by race, gender or age (such as disabilities, homelessness or sexual orientation): Of the children served, approximately 75% are victims of physical, sexual, and/or mental abuse.

2.5 Counties served by the Organization (during the last fiscal year): Indicate the number and percentage of people served in the following counties.

Name	Number	%	Name	Number	%	Name	Number	%
City of Atlanta	136	32	DeKalb	19	5	Morgan	0	0
Barrow	1	<1	Douglas	19	5	Newton	0	0
Bartow	5	1	Fayette	5	1	Paulding	7	2
Butts	2	<1	Forsyth	2	<1	Pickens	1	<1
Carroll	7	2	Fulton	unknown		Rockdale	0	0
Cherokee	7	2	Gwinnett	23	5	Spalding	7	2
Clayton	2	<1	Hall	2	<1	Walton	0	0
Cobb	30	7	Henry	1	<1	Other	136	32
Coweta	8	2				**TOTAL**		100

2.6 List all grants received from The Community Foundation for Greater Atlanta since January 1, 1999:

Program	Year	Amount	Purpose
N/A			

2.7 Describe the composition of your Board and Staff

	BOARD			STAFF		
RACE/ETHNICITY	Females	Males	TOTAL	Females	Males	TOTAL
African American/ Black	2	0	2	95	124	219
Asian/Pacific Islander	0	0	0	1	1	2
Caucasian	4	13	17	211	124	335
Hispanic/Latino	0	0	0	1	1	2
Other (specify):						
TOTAL	6	13	19	308	250	558

III. PROJECT/PROGRAM DESCRIPTION
This section of the application provides you with flexibility on the length of each of your answers. However, your answers in this section may not exceed 3 pages including the tables below. Please do not split tables over a page break.

3.1 The Issue: Describe the issue or situation the grant will help to address.

Today, children and adolescents comprise the fastest growing segment of the population with mental illnesses, yet they are least likely to be treated for them. Current national studies reveal that 20% of youth, ages 9-17, or 15 million young people, have diagnosable psychiatric disorders and that 4 million have such serious emotional disturbances that their daily lives are disrupted. According to the 2000 census and U.S. Surgeon General's Report on Mental Health, nearly 195,000 children in Georgia have a severe emotional disturbance requiring treatment--far more than Inner Harbour and Georgia's other youth residential treatment providers combined can provide.

To address this issue and continue to lead the way in providing mental health services for Georgia's youth, Inner Harbour is committed to providing top-quality services for its residents. Through this campaign, Inner Harbour will construct and furnish a new 17,373 square foot, two-story residential facility which will include private rooms for 40 residents; common spaces for living and dining; four classrooms; two nurse/staff stations, and administrative offices. The building will be configured to include four separate ten-bed units that can be adapted to changing service needs.

3.2 The People: In a short paragraph, describe the population that is the focus of the proposal.

Inner Harbour is seeking to address the housing needs of two populations needing residential care and treatment: pre-adolescent males, ages 10-14 and cognitively challenged males and females, ages 13-17.

3.3 Population served by the Proposal (during the last fiscal year): Indicate the number of people served by the proposal according to race and gender. In the column marked "*% (race)*", indicate the percentage of the individuals served in that row (i.e. Caucasian females) as a percentage of the entire population served. In the row marked "*% (age)*", indicate the percentage of individuals served in that column (i.e. individuals ages 0-5) as a percentage of the entire population served.

RACE & GENDER		0-5	6-11	12-14	15-18	19-63	64+	Total	% (race)
					AGE				
African American	Females								
	Males		—3	4				7	37
Asian/Pacific Islander	Females								
	Males								
Caucasian	Females								
	Males		6	6				12	63
Hispanic/ Latino	Females								
	Males								
Multi Racial	Females								
	Males								
	TOTAL		9	10				19**	
	% (age)		47	53					100%

**Cognitively challenged youth will be a new population for Inner Harbour and as such, there is no historical data.

3.4 Counties served by the Proposal (during the last fiscal year): Indicate the number and percentage of people served in the following counties.

Name	Number	%	Name	Number	%	Name	Number	%
City of Atlanta			DeKalb	1	5	Morgan		
Barrow	1	5	Douglas	2	11	Newton		
Bartow			Fayette			Paulding	1	5
Butts			Forsyth	1	5	Pickens	1	5
Carroll	1	5	Fulton	2	11	Rockdale		
Cherokee			Gwinnett			Spalding	1	5
Clayton			Hall			Walton		
Cobb	3	16	Henry			Other	5	26
Coweta						**TOTAL**	19**	100

**Cognitively challenged youth will be a new population for Inner Harbour and as such, there is no historical data.

3.5 The Strategy: State specifically how the grant will help to address the issue or situation.

The new facility is designed to offer a warm, child-friendly environment that will create a new sense of safety for these youth. Currently, the pre-adolescent boys are housed in rustic individual cabins with no indoor plumbing or in a multi-resident bunkhouse. This setting presents numerous clinical and safety challenges. Experience has shown that lack of privacy and sharing of small cabins can create conflicts if roommates' personalities are at odds, and may increase a child's level of frustration and the need for staff intervention. Based on current research and the study of other treatment programs, it is clear that boys at this vulnerable age respond better to treatment in a more controlled and centralized setting.

Residential space for cognitively challenged youth is the number one need of the Department of Juvenile Justice and a primary need of Georgia's MATCH (Multi-Agency Team for Children) program in which Inner Harbour participates. With severe psychiatric problems and a typical IQ of 60-75 points, these youth do not respond to traditional therapies and must be treated in a highly structured environment. Currently, there is only one other designated facility in Georgia addressing this population. Consolidating the housing for this group of adolescents and the pre-adolescent males will offer a number of clinical advantages that will enable Inner Harbour's staff to serve these children more effectively and efficiently.

3.6 Outcomes: How will your project/program, if funded, "make a difference?" List two outcomes that you predict will take place, and how you will know (measure) that changes took place. Please refer to the Guidelines for Competitive Grants for further instructions.

1. 25% more**% of** the residents in the new building **will** be able to participate in school classroom interaction. Currently, children on precautions (those requiring constant monitoring) cannot leave their housing unit. Because classrooms are housed in the new facility, children on precautions will be able to attend school rather than receive individual tutoring, **measured by** the increase in classroom attendance.

2. 50**% of** the amount of time residents spend on precautions and in seclusion and restraints **will** be reduced, **measured by** the improvement in residents' behavior and increased ability to function in a group setting because of the design and function of the new building.

3.7 Project Expenses (2004-2005): Complete the Project Expenses table with dollar amounts for the Project for which you are requesting funding. If your request is for operating support, complete the table with your organization's financial information.

Personnel Expenses	Paid by TCF Grant	Paid by other sources	TOTAL
Salaries & Wages			
Benefits & Payroll Taxes			
Project Expenses			
Building Maintenance			
Consultants/Professional Services		90,000	90,000
Insurance			
Marketing			
Membership Dues			
Office Supplies			
Postage/Mailings			
Printing			
Program Supplies			
Rent			
Rent & Maintenance of Equipment			
Staff Development			
Technology/Computers			
Telephone			
Travel/Mileage			
Utilities			
Other (specify): Construction**Please see Project Budget, EXHIBIT F.	25,000	4,045,000	4,070,000
TOTAL PROJECT EXPENSES	25,000	4,135,000	4,160,000

3.8 Who has committed funds for THIS project, and who is considering a request for funding? If you need additional space, please hit Return in one of the existing rows and continue typing.

Name Source	Funds Already COMMITTED to this Project/Program	Funds Currently PENDING for this Project/Program
Board of Directors	184,388	
Staff	29,052	
Corporations	24,250	
Individuals	295,505	
Foundations	1,542,720	1,190,000
Miscellaneous	92,111	
TOTAL	**2,168,026**	**1,190,000**

3.9 In-kind Support: Describe in-kind support for the project, including volunteer activities and contributions received for items such as office space, office equipment, program supplies, etc. In-kind support includes the volunteered time of the campaign committee and their sponsorship of committee meetings and cultivation events. We will also seek in-kind contributions for building materials, furnishings and fixtures.

3.10 Future Funding: The Competitive Grants Program does not commit to continued funding. Outline your plan to secure funding support, once Foundation grant funds are expended. Be as specific as possible, including the names of particular institutional funders or foundations, and your history of mobilizing funds from these sources.

To date, we have raised $2,168,026 from foundations, individuals, and corporations. We continue to submit requests to foundations and are preparing to launch a campaign specifically targeted at the Douglasville community. We do not anticipate significant increases in operating costs as the new facility will realize greater efficiency and utlity costs. Currently, 91% of patients are paid for by the Department of Juvenile Justice and Georgia MATCH funds and these funds will be used to pay for ongoing operating expenses. The remaining resident revenue is funded by fees for managed care and private pay residents. This capital campaign will also serve as the catalyst for instituting an ongoing annual campaign as outlined in our strategic plan to increase private support for Inner Harbour.

IV. ACKNOWLEDGEMENT OF THE COMMUNITY FOUNDATION'S APPLICATION POLICIES:

The Executive Director has reviewed this application and understands and assures that:

- The applicant is eligible for funding and requests support for activities eligible for funding. (Please see the Application Guidelines for details);

- All End of Grant Reports for previous grants have been filed before submitting this Application;

- This application is complete according to *Grant Application Checklist* (attached). The complete application package is either postmarked on or before the deadline date (July 16, 2004 and January 28, 2005), or will be delivered to The Community Foundation's offices by 5 P.M. on the deadline date. Incomplete or late proposals will not be reviewed. The Community Foundation's staff is NOT authorized to extend an application deadline;

- Grant requests range from $5,000 to $25,000;

- This application is part of an open competition. Although all eligible applications will be reviewed, a limited number will be selected for more detailed examination and funding consideration;

- The Community Foundation selects applications for more detailed evaluation **based on the contents of this application form**. The applicant has clearly and completely described its mission, programs, populations served, request for funding, strategy and anticipated outcomes on this form; and

- Organizations that are declined may apply again by the next deadline, if they wish. Organizations that are funded, including all programs under the same 501(c)(3) number, are not eligible to apply again for twelve months from the date of the grant award.

_____
**Executive Director/Authorized
Organization Representative**

7/15/04
Date

CONTACT PERSON FOR THIS GRANT:

Lynn W. Merrill
Name

Director of Development
Title

770-942-2391
Phone Number & Extension

lynn.merrill@innerharbour.net
E-mail Address

EXHIBIT F

INNER HARBOUR
"Turning Hurt Into Hope"
Capital Campaign

Project Budget

Design and Construction	$	3,215,000
Site Development and Landscaping	$	335,000
Furnishings, Fixtures & Equipment	$	365,000
Project Management	$	90,000
Fees and Contingency	$	155,000
TOTAL	$	**4,160,000**

A Proposal From

The Methodist Home for Children and Youth
Macon, Georgia

To

The Peyton Anderson Foundation
Macon, Georgia

Requested amount: $200,000; **Amount received:** $200,000

Funder's comments:

"An original and five copies of the PAF2 Proposal Form fully completed and signed by a responsible officer are required for submission to the Peyton Anderson Foundation. In this case, after receiving a telephone call request, the foundation mailed the form to the grant applicant. A representative of the Methodist Home then called to set up an appointment between the organization's president and the executive director of the Peyton Anderson Foundation. The project was outlined during the meeting, and the president described the ways in which the Intergenerational Activity Center fits with the overall services of the Methodist Home.

"The cover letter and need statement were among the strongest features of this proposal. The cover letter summarized the need and clearly stated what was requested of the foundation. The letter also emphasized the substantial amount of support already committed to the project and the importance of the Intergenerational Center to the organization's mission of serving children who require an alternative to their home environment.

"The statement of need was particularly strong because it addressed the broader concerns of child welfare and then focused in on the specific construction project as an important resource for current foster children in the group home, as well as the necessity for preventative programs. This need statement presents a thorough look at the reasoning behind the proposal. The entire proposal is built around the case for a new facility and the resulting benefits that would be brought about by the completion of their capital campaign. The need statement highlights a community problem of abused and neglected children and offers a project to benefit current group home children and assist in preventative outreach services.

"The proposal contained all the required information. The content of the proposal is weighted toward the organization's financials, most of which are required items for submission to our foundation. The breakdown of history, need statement, project and program descriptions, and facilities/staffing information makes for a readable proposal where information is easy to locate. The floor plans and booklet for the

Intergenerational Center provide an adequate amount of detail about the building without overloading the proposal.

"The writing is clear and concise. The presentation is constructed in a logical manner and flows smoothly. The graphics and charts are easily understood and present relevant information in a direct manner. As to the budget, labeling the existing programs and the new areas that require funding helps avoid confusion. The budget also addresses the organization's plan for additional operating costs and furnishing and equipment needs. The attachments are appropriate as well. Architectural drawings are very helpful in determining the scope and components of a project. Capital campaign materials are relevant in assessing the organizational structure and fundraising capacity.

"During the meeting with the president of our foundation, the organization's representatives spoke of the benefits of having youth and senior citizens interacting at the same facility and the nurturing environment that is created by such an arrangement. The proposal itself, however, lacked information about the benefits of this concept. Because the project is an innovative one, the proposal might have been even better if it had also provided more details about the programs made possible by the Intergenerational Activity Center that include the neighboring senior facility. A one-page construction budget breakdown would have also strengthened this proposal."

—*Michele Pritchard, Grants Administrator, The Peyton Anderson Foundation*

Notes:

The complete proposal included the following attachments: The Peyton Anderson Foundation Proposal for Grant Cover Sheet, list of trustees, informational brochure, annual report, floor plans, IRS tax-exempt letter, audited financial statements, and supplementary financial information.

Proposal written by Dr. Laudis H. "Rick" Lanford, Vice President for Development, and Steve L. Rumford, A.C.S.W., President and Chief Executive Officer. Contributions to the proposal made by Bruce Stanfield, Vice President for Finance, and Dr. Edwin Chase, Director of the Family Institute.

The Methodist Home For Children and Youth

304 Pierce Avenue • Post Office Box 2525 • Macon, Georgia 31203-2525 • 478-751-2800
Fax: 478-738-0201 • E-Mail address: information@themethodisthome.org

May 7, 2002

Steve L. Rumford, A.C.S.W.
Diaconal Minister
President/CEO

Laudis H. "Rick" Lanford, D. Min.
Vice President
Development & Public Relations

Jeffery D. Lawrence, L.S.W.
Vice President
Programs & Services

Bruce Stanfield, C.P.A.
Vice President
Finance

Board of Trustees
Executive Committee

M. Creede Hinshaw, M. Div.
President

J. Russell Lipford, Jr., C.P.A.
Vice-Chairperson

James E. Swanson, M. Div.
Secretary

John T. Farmer, Jr.
Treasurer

Ms. Juanita T. Jordan
Executive Director
The Peyton Anderson Foundation
577 Mulberry Street, Suite 1015
Macon, Georgia 31201

Dear Ms. Jordan;

The Methodist Home for Children & Youth is a multifaceted residential care home providing a continuum of specialized treatment programs that address the needs of abused and neglected children. Over the last 130 years, the Home has provided a safe haven and impacted the lives of more than 7,000 Georgia children. As we begin the new millennium, the Home is in the final phase of a capital campaign that strengthens its capacity to serve the growing number of children needing an alternative to their home environment. The Board of Trustees respectfully requests that The Peyton Anderson Foundation consider a grant in the amount of $200,000.00 towards the building of the Intergenerational Activity Center.

The Methodist Home is affiliated with the South Georgia Conference of the United Methodist Church and is independently governed by a Board of Trustees. The Home's purpose is to offer security, education and hope, in a Christian environment, that supports needy children through their transition into adulthood. In addition to basic residential care, the Home provides short-term residential programs to assess and treat physical abuse, sexual abuse, and behavior disorders. The Home serves 110 children daily and in the last year served 350 children.

The Home has never seen a greater demand for its services. In May of 1998, the Board of Trustees launched a $7,000,000.00 capital campaign to meet the Home's critical need for two new facilities. The main focus of this campaign is the $6,000,000.00 Intergenerational Activity Center, a 53,000 square-foot, multi-purpose complex to be built on the Home's Macon campus. This

Affiliations
South Georgia Conference, United Methodist Church • United Methodist Association of Health and Welfare Ministries
Georgia Association of Homes and Services for Children • Macon Chamber of Commerce • Licensed by State of Georgia, Certified Intermediate
Treatment An "EAGLE" accredited agency by the United Methodist Association of Health and Welfare Ministries

building will include a new and expanded dining room and kitchen, a gymnasium with an elevated walking track, a racquetball court, a conference center with a multi-media auditorium, a resource center, and a suite of offices for prevention programs. Groundbreaking was held on January 31, 2002, and the building will be completed in 18 months.

To date, $6,000,000.00 has been pledged or received toward the total campaign goal. This figure includes the offer of a $1,000,000.00 challenge grant from the Saint Marys UMC Foundation, Inc., which is paid when the Home raises a final $1,000,000.00. A gift from The Peyton Anderson Foundation will help meet the Saint Marys Foundation challenge grant.

The Intergenerational Activity Center will be a defining moment in the history of The Methodist Home. We hope that The Peyton Anderson Foundation will join with us to impact the lives of children across South Georgia for years to come. We would like to invite you to visit our Macon campus as soon as time permits. Thank you for your time and thoughtful consideration of this request.

Sincerely,

Steve L. Rumford, A.C.S.W.
President

The Methodist Home for Children and Youth
Intergenerational Activity Center

Organization History

The Methodist Home for Children and Youth originated as the Bibb County Widows and Orphans Home in 1856. Sixteen years later, Bibb County sold the Home to the South Georgia Conference of the Methodist Church for one dollar, and the organization began its journey from an orphanage to a true "Home" that provides shelter as well as enriches and prepares children for successful lives. Over the last 128 years, the Home has evolved from a 92 acre working farm with a few small buildings to a beautiful residential campus situated among Macon's most charming homes, in the historic Ingleside neighborhood. While the landscape around the Home has changed dramatically, the Home remains in its original place and focused on the dignity and worth of children.

In the 1950's the Home faced a new type of challenge. Homes providing residential care for children and youth were seen as dreaded institutions, and as a result, state agencies began chasing a series of failing panaceas. Consequently, the number of children served at the Home decline significantly. By the mid-1980's foster care, adoption, and other state programs were overwhelmed, and the degree of abuse and neglect experienced by children needing placement was at its most severe. The Home recognized that to best serve children and youth, it must offer a continuum of specialized, treatment programs addressing the needs of seriously abused and neglected children.

Bold initiatives resulted from these new challenges. In the last fifteen years, three residential cottages, two short-term treatment centers, and a school for children with emotional and behavioral disorders have been constructed. The Home has also implemented programs that assess and treat physical and sexual abuse, behavior disorder, and abuse reactive syndrome. In addition, the Home has built and staffed group homes in Americus and Valdosta to meet the needs of children in South Georgia. To date, the Home has provided a safe haven to over 7,000 Georgia children.

As we enter the new millennium, the Methodist Home is lengthening its continuum of services to include prevention programs. The new Family Institute strengthens families by supporting the parents of at-risk children. With the addition of the Family Institute's outreach programs, the number of children and families that the Home can serve is no longer limited to the space available on campus. The Methodist Home for Children and Youth looks forward to another century of offering security, hope and a future to abused and neglected children.

Statement of Need

Over the last four years, the incidence of child abuse and neglect has been steadily increasing in Georgia. A record high, 20,349 Georgia children were in foster care in 2000. In 1999, there were 26,888 substantiated incidents of child abuse and neglect. Of these incidents, 85% occurred in the child's home and in 82% the child's biological parents were the maltreaters. The state of Georgia placed 752 foster children into group homes in 1999. The need in Georgia for specialized service providers to treat children who have been seriously abused and for effective prevention programs that reduce the incidence of abuse by equipping parents with resources and skills to successfully care for their children is critical.

Through its programs and services, the Methodist Home for Children and Youth is addressing both of these needs. However, the Home's ability to impact child abuse and neglect in Bibb County and throughout Georgia is limited by the adequacy of its facilities. Program growth and increases in children served have resulted in a serious need for facilities. In addition to space for operating programs, the Home currently does not have an indoor recreational facility or a sufficient dinning hall to meet the needs of its children.

The Home's capacity for preventative outreach to serve children and families in the community is also limited by inadequate facilities. The Home's Family Institute, which prevents children from entering the welfare system by providing resources and equipping parents with the skills to care for their children lacks training or resource material space. And, the current day care facilities are located in mobile trailers that do not have the capacity to train other professional childcare providers.

The Intergenerational Center will meet the Home's critical need for facilities. Through providing office and training space for expanding programs and services, enrichment opportunities (arts/crafts, drama, and puppet theater) and indoor recreational areas, and a model environment to teach childcare providers best practices for caring for at-risk children, the Intergenerational Center will strengthen the Home's ability to impact child abuse and neglect in Georgia. Thus, the Home's capital campaign does not only build buildings, it's an investment in the families and children of Georgia.

Project Description

The Intergenerational Activity Center, a 53,000 square-foot, multi-purpose complex to be built on the Home's Macon campus. This building will include new and expanded dining room and kitchen, a gymnasium with an elevated walking track, a racquetball court, a conference center with a multi-media auditorium, a resource center, and a suite of offices for prevention programs.

Programs and Services

The Methodist Home for Children and Youth provides a continuum of specialized treatment programs that address the needs of abused and neglected children. In addition to basic residential care, the Home provides intermediate treatment in the form of short-term residential programs to assess and treat physical abuse, sexual abuse and behavior disorders. The Home serves 110 children daily and in the last year served 350 children. The following is a description of programs and services offered at the Home.

The Main Campus Program provides residential treatment services in a cottage setting that address the unique needs of emotionally troubled youth in a community-based setting. Services include basic care, intermediate treatment, medical treatment, psychiatric supervision, therapy, on-campus education and recreational and enrichment activities.

The Assessment Program is a 90-day program that provides a comprehensive assessment of children ages 6-17 and secures placement based on the treatment goals and recommendations set during their initial evaluation.

H.O.P.E. (Helping Others in Parenting Environments) is a therapeutic foster care program that offers individualized treatment in a safe and loving home setting to youth with a variety of emotional and behavioral problems.

The Specialized Treatment for Abuse Reactive Syndrome Program (S.T.A.R.S.) provides intermediate residential treatment for young males (ages 6-12) who have a history of sexual, physical and emotional victimization, which results in the children having sexual behavior problems. This 12-18 month program treats each child's sexual behavior problems.

The Genesis Program provides positive life choices for women facing crisis pregnancies. Services include a crisis hotline, counseling, mentoring, and education.

The Family Institute's purpose is to prevent children from entering the welfare system by educating and empowering parents and by assisting communities in providing innovative, quality programs for at-risk children and youth.

Facilities

The Methodist Home for Children and Youth is a 26-acre residential campus. Arranged like a traditional neighborhood, the campus consists of five residential cottages, two treatment centers, three administrative buildings, a daycare center, a school, a staff house, and a chapel and dining facility. An additional administration building is located two blocks from the main campus. The Home provides a variety of recreational opportunities for its residents with a playground, ball field, swimming pool, ropes course and basketball and volleyball courts. In addition to the Macon Campus, the Home operates group homes in Americus and Valdosta, and an outdoor retreat in Rochelle, Georgia.

Staffing

The Methodist Home for Children and Youth provides exceptional care with a full-service staff totaling 175. The majority of employees deliver direct services to the children through the Home's range of specialized programs. The Home employs a comprehensive support staff including administration, food services, maintenance, nurses and teachers to meet the needs of our children onsite.

The Home maintains strong leadership and a highly qualified staff to provide the best quality care. Nearly half of the Home's staff hold higher education degrees. Mr. Steve Rumford, president of the Home, has a master's degree in social work and more than thirty years experience in the childcare field. A diversified board of directors, that accurately reflects the community, governs the Home.

The following is a description of the direct childcare positions and qualifications. *Cottage Directors* are responsible for the management of an individual cottage, for providing prescriptive care for each child, and for serving as the liaison between the Home and the child's guardian. Cottage Directors are master's level therapists. *Team Leaders* oversee the routine operations of a cottage and are required to have at least a bachelor's degree. *Childcare Counselors* provide daily care and supervision of the children and must have prior experience in the childcare field. *Clinical Therapists* provide counseling for children and families and have a college degree in their area of expertise. *Recreational Specialists* oversee all campus life activities for the children including indoor and outdoor physical education activities.

INTERGENERATIONAL ACTIVITY CENTER
Anticipated Budget

The Intergenerational Activity Center will be the home for both existing and new programs for the Home. Therefore, the budget will itemize both existing and new program areas.

Existing/Current Funding

•	The Family Institute Dr. Chase, secretary, conference wide church consultation and various projects – funded by Pitts Trust	$222,000
•	The Parenting Academy Includes the Director of Community/ Professional Education and programs – funded 2001-2 by Pitts Trust	$ 75,000
•	Dining Hall staff/food funded by Operations	$361,000
•	Recreation/Campus Life funded by Operations	$112,000

Additional Funding Required
Staff

‣	Maintenance worker	$ XXXXX
‣	Receptionist	XXXXX
‣	Community Activities	XXXXX
‣	Center Director	XXXXX
		93,000
	Benefits	18,000
		$ 111,000
‣	Utilities	30,000
‣	Materials/Support	6,000
‣	Phone	6,000
‣	Grounds	8,000
‣	Spiritual events/activities	12,000
	Total above current budget	$ 173,000

Beginning with budget year 2001-02, the Home is budgeting $200,000 for the Pitts Trust to offset additional operation costs. The amount accumulated in two years ($400,000) will fund all new furnishings and equipment for the center XXXXX.

Chapter 6

Evaluation

The term evaluation is used in several different contexts when referring to a grant proposal. The evaluation section, that is the part where the grantee explains what concrete steps the organization will take to ensure that goals and objectives are met, is an important component of the project description in any proposal, and one many funders pay special attention to. Many of the proposals in this guide have excellent evaluation sections, including the one in the Southeast Community College proposal and in the Cleveland Scholarship Programs proposal, both in Chapter 1.

Grantmakers occasionally provide funding to nonprofits to evaluate a project or programs they run. The purpose of such funding is to assess the success of the nonprofit's current strategies and methods and to determine to what degree these programs accomplish what they set out to do. Evaluation grants may also address the question of whether or not programs are being conducted in the most effective and efficient manner.

The proposal included here is a request from Kids Voting Central Ohio, of Columbus, Ohio in the amount of $23,625 submitted to The Columbus Foundation and Affiliated Organizations. The mission of Kids Voting Central Ohio is to increase informed voter participation by involving youth in school and community based citizenship activities. This request is for funding to help implement a long-term evaluation of the impact of the organization's curriculum on students in central Ohio. As noted in the cover letter, the grant is part of an overall capacity building effort that would be used to "attract future funders and also to focus. . . future efforts on those aspects of the program that are having the greatest impact."

A Proposal From
Kids Voting Central Ohio
Columbus, Ohio

To
The Columbus Foundation and Affiliated Organizations
Columbus, Ohio

Requested amount: $23,625; **Amount received:** $23,500

Funder's comments:

"At the time this proposal was submitted we required a two-page cover sheet, but not the formatted application form we subsequently instituted. The proposal from Kids Voting Central Ohio was submitted under our discretionary grantmaking cycle in Urban Affairs. My initial assessment of the program was that it was an innovative concept. Kids Voting Central Ohio made a strong case for supporting this project as a way to increase civic engagement of school-age children.

"Overall it was a well-developed proposal. The implementation strategies and expected outcomes in particular were clear and concise. The writing style was also clear and factually based. They submitted a detailed budget and an explanatory narrative as well as a list of other funders and the status of those requests. The strongest features of this proposal in my view are the detailed description of the evaluation plan and the supporting materials. They actually included more attachments than we expected. We did perform a site visit as we do with every applicant, so we used that as a chance to secure whatever additional information we needed."

—Emily Hunter Savors, Director of Community Research and Grants Management,
The Columbus Foundation and Affiliated Organizations

Notes:

The complete proposal included the following attachments: IRS tax-exempt letter, authorization letter from the board of directors, list of board members, audited financial statement, detailed project description, sample curriculum, letters of endorsement, and project materials. The foundation was formerly named the Columbus Foundation.

Proposal written by Suzanne C. Helmick, Executive Director. Research for the proposal conducted by Dr. William P. Eveland, Jr., The Ohio State University.

Today's Youth Tomorrow's Future

Kids Voting Central Ohio
191 W. Nationwide Blvd., Suite 300-A
Columbus, OH 43215
Tel: 614/224-3555 Fax: 614/629-5705
kidsvoteohio@earthlink.net
www.dispatch.com/kidsvoting

★　　★　　★　　★　　★　　★　　★

September 3, 2004

Mr. Douglas F. Kridler
President and CEO
The Columbus Foundation
1234 East Broad Street
Columbus, OH 43205-1453

Dear Mr. Kridler:

The Kids Voting trustees sincerely appreciate the generous contributions we have received from the Columbus Foundation over the past 3 years. Those grants made it possible for us to bring Kids Voting to all 62,000 students in the Columbus Public School system.

On behalf of the Board of Trustees of Kids Voting Ohio/Central Region, we now ask approval of this application for $23,625 for 2005 so that we may move the program to the next level. To develop sources for future financial support, Kids Voting would like to conduct a comprehensive evaluation of the effectiveness of the program on the political knowledge, attitudes and political participation of students and adults, in the Columbus schools.

The results of this evaluation would be used to attract future funders and also to focus our future efforts on those aspects of the program that are having the greatest impact.

Again, the support The Columbus Foundation has show in the past three years. The vote of confidence you have given us has made it possible for Kids Voting to attract new partners and additional funders for our efforts.

Your consideration of this request for 2005 is very much appreciated!

Yours truly,

Suzanne C. Helmick
Executive Director
Kids Voting Central Ohio

Lisa C. Bateson
Chair, Kids Voting Central Ohio
Board of Trustees

Kids Voting Central Ohio
Request to The Columbus Foundation

Kids Voting History

Kids Voting Central Ohio is a nonprofit, nonpartisan 501(c)(3) civic education organization affiliated with Kids Voting USA. It was created to increase informed voter participation by involving youth in school- and community-based citizenship activities.

Kids Voting USA was founded in Arizona in 1988 to help students learn about responsible citizenship and the democratic process using award-winning curriculum activities developed by citizenship education professionals and classroom teachers. The program is designed to supplement classroom teaching by bringing together community organizations and neighbors to help give students an authentic learning experience by voting at actual polling places with adults on Election Day.

Kids Voting USA came to Ohio in 1992. In ten years, Kids Voting programs in 17 Ohio counties reach more than 450,000 students, 15,000 teachers and 7,000 volunteers. Kids Voting was established in Central Ohio in 2000. In four years the program has expanded to reach more than 130,000 students in ten districts – including the Columbus Public Schools.

Specific Accomplishments. Since 2000, Kids Voting Central Ohio has —

★ Recruited more than 248 schools to participate; including all schools in the Big Walnut Local, Canal Winchester, Columbus, Dublin, Gahanna, Hilliard, New Albany-Plain Local, Upper Arlington, Westerville and Worthington school systems.

★ Provided "Civics Alive" curriculum materials to 3,500 area teachers grades K-12.

★ Motivated more than 53,000 students to vote in the last four elections, in spite of record low adult voter turnout.

★ Conducted numerous teacher training seminars as part of Columbus Public and other districts' "in-service" training sessions for teachers, including three annual workshops for teachers from all participating districts. Evaluation comments have been very positive.

★ Held three "Youth Summit" events for 200+ high school students focusing on political involvement and the potential impact of young adults.

★ Introduced new "Destination Democracy" curriculum designed to encourage community service for high school students.

★ Recruited and trained more than 1,000 students and community volunteers who staffed more than 350 polling locations for Kids Voting last year on Election Day — more than 4,000 volunteer hours on Election Day alone! (This volunteer effort has grown each year, from staffing 100 polls for the 2000 election to staffing more than 450 polls for November, 2004.)

"Kids Voting sows the seeds of participation in our democratic process. It is one of the only organizations in our area encouraging individuals to accept personal responsibility for the success of our democracy."
Michael B. Coleman
Mayor, City of Columbus

1

Basic Elements of the Kids Voting Program

Kids Voting Central Ohio facilitates collaborations among educators, parents, community leaders, civic organizations, elected officials and election boards to develop citizenship and self-government skills in youth. **The program encourages lifelong habits of participating in the civic life of the community.** At the same time, national research shows that the program's "trickle-up" impact empowers students to improve their political knowledge and skills, while motivating adult members of their households to do the same.

The program has four main components:

★ Hands-on K-12 school and family based activities that build citizenship skills and also track state and national social studies academic content standards,

★ Effective teacher training,

★ Real-life voting experience on Election Day that starts the habit of civic participation, and

★ Community service activities and collaborations between schools, neighbors, civic groups, businesses, elections officials, and volunteers to provide unique opportunities for students to exercise citizenship skills in addressing the needs in the community.

Key Steps in Operating the Program

1. School Districts are Recruited. Kids Voting staff meet with administrators, curriculum specialists, and teachers in area school districts to describe Kids Voting lesson activities, and outcomes. The district superintendent commits to participate in Kids Voting in every school building and at every grade level. Annual meetings are held to reconfirm district participation and strengthen program implementation.

2. Teachers Receive Materials and Training. Kids Voting provides social studies teachers with curriculum supplements at no cost to the schools. These materials show teachers how to use the lessons in the classroom and how they tie in with Ohio's new social studies academic content standards at each grade level. This instruction takes place at the Kids Voting annual teachers' workshop and in individualized sessions at participating schools. (More information about the Kids Voting curriculum and sample lessons are included in Attachment F.)

3. Election Day Preparation Begins. Kids Voting gives students an authentic learning opportunity on Election Day. Thanks to legislation passed by the Ohio General Assembly, Kids Voting is permitted to operate special voting tables at the official poll locations on Election Day. Kids Voting staff develop and print "optical scan" ballots for students and distribute samples to schools so students can study the candidates and issues before the election. Kids Voting works with the County Board of Elections to identify all poll locations within the school districts participating in the program. These locations are then staffed by Kids Voting volunteers (mostly high school students).

4. High School Teachers and Student are Recruited. Kids Voting meets with high school teachers and students to promote Kids Voting community service activities and recruit student volunteers to work at one of the hundreds of Kids Voting poll locations after school on Election Day. One teacher at each participating high school is recruited to serve as the contact person for the building and help coordinate training for student workers, organize students for each location, and distribute ballots and supplies. Immediately after the polls close, the teacher coordinates the return of the ballots and supplies and may organize students to help count results.

2

5. Parent and Community Outreach is Conducted. A portion of the Kids Voting activities take place in students' homes, where they discuss candidates and issues, political ideology, and other topics with adults in their households. For Kids Voting to succeed, adults must take their children with them to the polls after school on Election Day. Without this adult link, most students are unable to vote, since Ohio law requires students under age 14 to be accompanied at the polls by an adult. Participating schools send letters to parents about Kids Voting and ask that they talk with their children about the candidates and issues and take their kids to vote after school on Election Day. This opportunity helps build a lifetime habit of voting and, at the same time, increases adult voter participation. Kids Voting staff also meet with parent and community organizations to alert them to the unique opportunity they have to take their students with them to the polls. By modeling voting behavior, parents can pass this essential civic value on to their children. Volunteer training for student and adult volunteers is provided by Kids Voting.

6. Students Vote on Election Day. Kids Voting provides volunteers with ballots, supplies, maps and instructions so that Kids Voting polling stations can be open from 3:00 to 7:30 p.m. Ballots then are collected and taken to a location where they are counted. Kids Voting adult and student volunteers have contributed 2,000 hours of time on Election Day alone in each of the last four general elections. (A sample ballot for 2004 is included in Attachment H.)

7. Results are Tabulated and Reported. Kids Voting staff identify an organization to scan and tabulate the tens of thousands of student ballots cast on Election Day. The results are posted the next day on the Kids Voting web site and distributed to the media. Teachers and students then are able to compare their votes with those cast by adults.

8. KV Activities are Ongoing. Events are held throughout the year to reinforce the importance of civic participation and provide other opportunities for building citizenship skills. These events include the Kids Voting Youth Summit for high school students, the Kids Voting Pledge for Democracy, voter registration efforts, and other activities to keep students engaged.

"I am proud to support Kids Voting because it actually gets young people excited and involved in the democratic process. Current events have illustrated how precious our freedom is and Kids Voting helps instill an appreciation for such thing in our youth.

Patrick J. Tiberi
Member of Congress, 12th District

3

The Problem Addressed by Kids Voting USA

Civic disengagement is a national and local dilemma. Voter participation is one of the key measures of civic engagement. It is strongly correlated to community vitality, quality of education, and the responsiveness of democratic institutions in meeting community needs.

The right to vote is the cornerstone of our representative democracy. Yet, in practice, voting is increasingly viewed as a meaningless gesture:

★ voter turnout in Franklin County has declined 24% in less than 30 years and ranked 85th out of 88 counties in 2003;

★ 50% of eligible citizens do not participate in presidential elections;

★ 70-80% do not participate in local elections;

★ less than half of 18 and 19 year olds are registered to vote and, at best, 20% will vote by age 21; and

★ more than half of all children now live in a household where no adult votes.

The decline in political participation has been uneven. It is greatest among those who are disadvantaged in terms of education, economics, and influence. For example, in Franklin County, over the past 50 years, voter turnout (among those registered) has been significantly lower among Columbus residents than suburban residents. In 2000, this difference was 24% (52% vs. 76%).

The drop in voter participation also is not uniform across age groups. Participation is poorest among those under age 35. This is especially relevant given that young adults age 25 - 34 make up the largest age group in Columbus (19.6%) and in Franklin County.

Kids Voting Central Ohio has been working for the past four years to try to turn today's youthful non-voters into tomorrow's active adult voters. Kids Voting Central Ohio has subscribed to the idea expressed by Warren Miller and Jay Merrill Shanks in their book, <u>The New American Voter</u>, that those who become comfortable voting at a young age continue to do so throughout their life, making voting a habitual practice. On the other hand, they write, **"those who do not vote as young people continue to avoid going to the polls later in life"**.

Kids Voting Central Ohio works to give students the skills and motivation to become productive adult citizens. As the only program in the nation that combines civics education in the classroom with the actual experience of voting alongside adult citizens, we strive to provide a long-term solution to voter disinterest. National research has shown that children who participate in Kids Voting tend to have a positive influence on the political participation of adults with whom they live and tend themselves to become more active voters than their peers who are not exposed to a Kids Voting program.

"I have been privileged to observe the Election Day activities and other educational events of Kids Voting on several occasions with both High School and elementary-age students. The interest and enthusiasm shown by both age groups was remarkable. The fact is that students are enjoying the program while at the same time learning critical information. They are developing skills that help them succeed in school, and that will help our democracy thrive for years to come."

Jeff Cabot, Member
Columbus Board of Education

4

Priorities of The Columbus Foundation

The Columbus Foundation places a high priority on educational projects, especially those that serve disadvantaged students and those that strengthen educational institutions. Based on the financial support the Foundation has provided over the past three years, Kids Voting Central Ohio has been an excellent match with these areas of interest. (Combined contributions from funds within the Columbus Foundation and contributions from the Ingram-White Castle Foundation have totaled $60,000 in 2002, $45,000 in 2003 and $40,000 in 2004.)

In its 2003 annual report, The Columbus Foundation emphasizes its mission to strengthen and improve the quality of life in central Ohio. **The report also underscores the Foundation's commitment to create and sustain the momentum of change its financial contributions support.**

Since its inception, Kids Voting Central Ohio has collected evaluations of its programming from teachers and students who have participated in various programming or attended Kids Voting events. However, a more thorough evaluation of the impact the program is having in the community is beyond the capabilities of our staff.

Results of the proposed study would enable Kids Voting Central Ohio to make our case for support more effectively to future funders. At the same time, this detailed evaluation would enable us to increase our emphasis in the years ahead on those aspects of our program that are demonstrated to be having the greatest impact on the civic participation of our local youth.

Request for 2005 Support/ Project Description

Kids Voting Central Ohio is requesting a grant of $23,625.00 to begin a long-term evaluation of the impact of the Kids Voting USA curriculum on students' civic knowledge, communication with peers and family members, and political participation. We hope to use the information gained through this evaluation to demonstrate to future funders the value of the program and its ability to impact students' citizenship participation for the long-term.

A central component of the Kids Voting program is our K-12 curriculum, designed to involve students in politics through teaching the use of political information (news and advertisements) and encouraging political discussion. Kids Voting uses the classroom to encourage behaviors that take place in the home and in interactions with peers and family members. An additional goal is to see that changes in political behavior persist beyond the time the students spend in a Kids Voting classroom or school.

At the national level, program evaluations in several communities have been conducted and have reached positive conclusions, indicating the students become empowered as "change agents" in the home, motivating parents to become more informed and more active and showing that students are more active citizens after reaching age 18.

Most of these evaluations have focused on student and teacher evaluations of the program and limited "exit polling" of parents rather than directly measuring the impact of the program by measuring outcomes such as knowledge and attitudes of the students, parents and siblings. Limited information also has been gathered on the long-term impact of the program once the student has graduated and is able to vote officially.

5

To complete this program evaluation, Kids Voting Central Ohio would commission a political communications expert at The Ohio State University to survey groups of students and teachers in the Columbus Public School system to determine students' exposure to Kids Voting classroom activities on political communications and behaviors over a period of several years. This specific request of the Columbus Foundation is to begin this research process. Other sources of funding will also be explored for continuation of this evaluation through the 2008 election cycle.

Measurable Data to be Collected. The following types of information will be gathered and evaluated. More detail is included in the project description included as Attachment E.

★ Basic Demographic Information

★ Frequency of Use of News Media

★ Political Discussion

★ Family Communication Patterns

★ Factual and Civics Knowledge

★ Attitudes and Participation

Specific expenditures for this grant are outlined in the section following the overall Kids Voting Central Ohio budget and budget narrative.

"The Kids Voting organization and its staff work hard at getting the facts and information to children about the voting process. The children participating get excited about the program and the opportunity to see how it really feels to cast your vote. I commend the Kids Voting organization for its efforts in teaching our children the importance of participating. This program can only enhance our children's education of the political process."

Dewey R. Stokes, President
Franklin County Board of Commissioners

6

Implementation Strategies

To complete this multiple-year evaluation process, Kids Voting Central Ohio (KV) will use the following strategies:

Staffing: The work for this evaluation will be completed by Suzanne Helmick, Kids Voting Central Ohio Executive Director, Dr. William P. Eveland and a graduate research assistant under his supervision.

Identification of Study participants: Working with administrators in the Columbus Public Schools (CPS), we will identify 9th, 10th and 11th grade teachers and students who are using the Kids Voting curriculum in the fall of 2004 and a comparable group who are not. This group will provide our baseline information.

Information Gathering 2005 *: Kids Voting will again work with CPS to identify 9th - 12th grade teachers and students who are using the Kids Voting curriculum in the fall of 2005 and a comparable group who are not. Dr. Eveland and his research assistant will survey as many of the students as possible as well as the primary caregivers of this group of students. The information gathered will be compared with data from the 2004 efforts to assess the impact of the Kids Voting curriculum in these ways:

(A more detailed description of the research proposal is included as Attachment E.) The information gathered about these students' participation in Kids Voting in 2004 and 2005 will be combined with the data gathered in the student and parents surveys to assess the impact of the Kids Voting curriculum in the following ways: (a) the impact of Kids Voting on students who received the program in 2004 but not 2005; (b) the impact of Kids Voting on students who received the program in 2005 but not 2004; (c) the impact of the Kids Voting program on students who received the program in both 2004 and 2005; and (d) the impact of the Kids Voting program on students who received the program in neither 2004 nor 2005. Such an analysis of the relative impact of single versus repeated exposure to Kids Voting – and the ability of the program's impact to extend from one election season to the next – has never been conducted.

* (This is the portion of the project for which we currently are seeking funding from the Columbus Foundation.)

Information Gathering and Analysis 2006: Kids Voting Central Ohio will again work with CPS to identify 9th - 12th grade teachers and students who are using the Kids Voting curriculum in the fall of 2005 and a comparable group who are not. Dr. Eveland and his research assistant will survey as many of the students as possible as well as the primary caregivers of this group of students. The information gathered will be compared with data from the 2004 efforts to assess the impact of the Kids Voting curriculum in these ways:

Data will be gathered in 2006 in exactly the same manner as in 2005, except 9th graders (class of '10) will not be interviewed and we will make every attempt to track down members of the class of 2006 and their parents outside of the school context for reinterview. The importance of the 2006 data collection is twofold. First, it provides the first opportunity to gather data on individuals who received Kids Voting in school and who have now left school and are eligible to vote (class of 2005). Second, unlike 2005, 2006 will have a number of statewide elections on the ballot and thus will provide a higher interest election context in which to identify the effects of Kids Voting compared to the 2005 election. We may apply for funding for the November 2006 data collection during the Columbus Foundation's 2005 funding cycle.

7

No Information Gathering or Analysis 2007:
No data will be collected during this time period; no funding will be necessary.

Information Gathering and Analysis 2008:
Data will be gathered in 2008 in exactly the same manner as 2005 and 2006, except only 12th graders (class of '09) will be interviewed in the classroom. We will also make every attempt to track down members of the classes of 2006, 2007, and 2008 and their parents outside of the school context for reinterview. The importance of the 2008 data collection is primarily the ability to assess the impact of repeated exposure to the Kids Voting program in high school on voting in a presidential election among young adults. No study has ever evaluated the Kids Voting program in this manner, but most assumptions about the value of Kids Voting rely precisely on the program having impact on the students once they become adults. We do not expect to solicit funding from the Columbus Foundation for the 2008 data collection effort. Instead, we believe that with the data gathered in 2004, 2005, and 2006, funding will be available from foundations outside the Columbus area.

Expected Outcome/Impact

By September 2006 we will have completed a written report on the short-term effects of the Kids Voting program (compared to the control group) on both communication behaviors as well as traditional political socialization outcomes such as efficacy and knowledge.

The report will discuss:
- ★ The differences in the parents of Kids Voting and non-Kids Voting students in terms of communication behaviors, efficacy, knowledge, and participation.
- ★ The relative impact of the program on various socio-demographic groups, which will speak to the ability of the program to reduce social inequalities. (This should be more methodologically sound data regarding the short-term effectiveness of Kids Voting than most of the prior national research.)

Of course, the larger outcome of this project will be to the extent that it serves as a foundation for later data collection that can evaluate the long-term impact of Kids Voting on individuals and on social inequalities in political involvement within our community.

It certainly is our hope that the evaluation will show that the Kids Voting program in Central Ohio mirrors the impact that has been demonstrated in many other Kids Voting communities around the state and the country: effectively increasing the level of informed voter participation among young voters and their families.

Armed with this information, Kids Voting Central Ohio will be able to make a more compelling case for financial support for maintaining and expanding our program throughout this part of the state!

Individuals Responsible for Implementing the Project

Suzanne Helmick, Executive Director of Kids Voting Central Ohio has directed all phases of the operations of Kids Voting in Central Ohio since 1999. She will be the coordinator of the proposed research project and, initially will serve as the primary liaison between the research team and the Columbus Public Schools.

8

Ms. Helmick's previous experience includes:

- Vice president of PR firm where her projects won national and regional awards.
- Government Relations Officer at Nationwide Insurance Company, managing state and federal lobbying activity and political education programs for employees.
- Staff member in the Ohio Senate and Ohio House of Representatives.
- Graduate and Board Officer of Leadership Columbus and several community boards.

Dr. William P. Eveland, Jr., Associate Professor, School of Communication at The Ohio State University teaches undergraduate and graduate courses in research methods, political communication and the effects of mass media.

Dr. Eveland will oversee the design, collection, and analysis of the data gathered in November 2005 and will write the report to the Columbus Foundation at the completion of the 2005 data collection phase. Eveland received his bachelor's and master's degrees in communication from the University of Delaware and his Ph.D. in mass communication from the University of Wisconsin-Madison. Eveland served as Associate Researcher and later co-head of the National Institute for Science Education's Communicating with Mass Audiences team. He was a faculty member in the Department of Communication at the University of California at Santa Barbara, where he was the founding director of the Social Science Survey Center and Benton Survey Research Laboratory.

Eveland's research focuses on the role of mass mediated (including new technologies like the Internet) and interpersonal communication in politics and public opinion. He is particularly interested in what motivates both children and adults to use news media, how they process this mediated information, and what factors increase or decrease what they learn about politics from the news. Much of Eveland's work has been in the area of evaluation research. He was part of a team of researchers who evaluated the Kids Voting San Jose program in 1994, and he spent four years doing evaluation research on science Web sites for the National Institute for Science Education. In each of these cases, his work focused on issues of the effects of communication on learning.

Eveland has regularly served as an expert source in the popular press, including the *Washington Post*, *USA Today*, the *Dallas Morning News*, the *Columbus Dispatch*, the *Toledo Blade*, and various local radio and television programs throughout the country. His research has been recognized with numerous awards from major academic and professional associations in the areas of journalism, communication, and public opinion, such as the Association for Education in Journalism & Mass Communication, the National Communication Association, the International Communication Association, and the World Association for Public Opinion Research. In 2003, Eveland was presented with the Young Scholar Award by the International Communication Association in recognition of outstanding early career research.

9

Kids Voting Central Ohio — Operating Budget 2004

Expense/Item	Amount
Office Expense (phone, copier, Web, parking, mileage, insurance, audit)	$6,250.00
Supplies	$5,750.00
Salaries-Executive Director, Program Coordinator, Community Coordinator	$101,000.00
Consultant Fees-Education Coordinators, Admin. Asst., other consultants	$20,100.00
Program Fees (KVUSA fee and annual meeting)	$4,000.00
Fundraising (printing and postage)	$500.00
Education/ Teacher Workshops	$10,000.00
Volunteers/Community Coordinators	$4,000.00
Ballots and Tabulation	$6,000.00
Printing	$10,000.00
Youth Summit	$3,000.00
Audit	$2,000.00
Expense Total	$172,600.00

Anticipated Income	
Balance Brought Forward	$25,000.00
Columbus Foundation/ Ingram-White Castle Foundation	$40,000.00
Grange Insurance (In-kind printing)	$10,000.00
Nationwide	$5,000.00
Anthem	$3,500.00
Time-Warner	$2,000.00
Columbus Bar Auxiliary	$8,000.00
Columbia Gas	$5,000.00
Rotary Club Contributions	$15,000.00
Other Foundations/Corporations	$25,000.00
Franklin County/Board of Elections	$15,000.00
Cols. Dispatch/Wolfe Enterprises	$15,000.00
Fundraising Event	$15,000.00
Board Donations	$2,000.00
Workshop Fees	$2,500.00
Adopt-A-Poll	$ 7,500.00
Other Income Anticipated	$4,000.00
Anticipated Total Income	$199,500.00
Anticipated Total Expenses	$172,600.00
Total Remaining	$26,900.00

2005 Kids Voting Evaluation — Project Budget

Program coordination for Kids Voting XXXXX	XXXXX
Research Director (1 mo. Salary)	XXXXX
Printing and mailing of consent forms and questionnaires (12,000)	XXXXX
Graduate Assistant (working for 1 Quarter)	XXXXX
Total	$ 35,204.00

10

Project Budget Narrative

The total request to The Columbus Foundation is for $23,625.00 for the first phase of this evaluation. The breakout of these costs, as well as other costs that will be generated from other sources are described below.

1. **Project Management** — Suzanne Helmick will work with the Columbus Public School administrators to gather data in 2004 and 2005 regarding teachers who are and who are not implementing Kids Voting in their classrooms. She also will monitor expenses incurred with this project to assure that a full report can be made to the Columbus Foundation at year end.

2. **Research Director** — William P. Eveland, Jr. will design the study, prepare the questionnaire, oversee the data collection and entry, and analyze the results. He will also provide a report of the results for the Columbus Foundation and Kids Voting Central Ohio. Although the value of his time is listed above, he has agreed to provide his time in return for the ability to use these data for academic purposes, including publishing the results in the form of academic articles or books, with acknowledgement of the contributions of the Columbus Foundation and Helmick.

3. **Graduate Assistant** — The graduate research assistant (GRA) will assist during the Fall quarter of 2005 in the administration of the survey (delivery of consent forms and surveys to schools, mailing of surveys to parents, maintenance of participant data base) and entry of questionnaire data collected.

4. **Materials, Printing, and Postage** — Our goal is to identify 50 participating classrooms that are using Kids Voting materials and another 50 that are not for each grade level in our evaluation. We further assume that each classroom has at least 25 students, and that there will be a combined student/parent return rate of the consent forms of 10-20%. A 10% return rate should produce an individual sample size of approximately 1000 and a sample size of 100 classrooms at each grade level. This sample size is necessary given expected attrition after multiple waves of interviewing (i.e., 2005, 2006, 2008).

If we realize a 20% return rate of the consent forms, the entire amount budgeted for this piece of the project would be needed. If our return rate is only 10%, our cost to evaluate the responses would be half of this budgeted amount. A full report will be given to The Columbus Foundation, and should we not need this entire budgeted amount, the actual amount of our funding request would be smaller and the extra amount budgeted would not be drawn down.

The estimates below are the expenses for materials, printing, and postage for the consent forms and mailings to parents and students:

Adult Consent Form (includes envelope, postage, & SASE*)	10,000[3]	$0.50	$5000
Student Questionnaire	2000	$1.50	$3000
Adult Questionnaire (includes envelope, postage, & SASE*)	2000	$3.50	$7000

* SASE: self addressed stamped envelope

11

Kids Voting — Current and Anticipated Income

So far in 2004, Kids Voting Central Ohio received its most significant financial and in-kind contributions from these sources:

The Sayer Charitable Fund of The Columbus Foundation — A grant of $30,000 was received from the foundation for Kids Voting Central Ohio expansion efforts in 2004.

The Ingram-White-Castle Foundation — A grant for $10,000 was received from the foundation for efforts in 2004.

The Columbus Dispatch/Wolfe Enterprises — Since 2000, we have received annual grants of $15,000. The Dispatch also created and hosts our Web site; ran special features for educators prior to the election featuring Kids Voting lessons; donated free color advertising space; and, actively served on the Kids Voting Central Ohio board. *A request for continued sponsorship of $15,000 for 2005 will be submitted.*

Grange Insurance Company — Since 2000, Grange has printed more than 3,000 sets of curriculum, at an estimated value in excess of $30,000. In addition, Grange has provided graphic design assistance each year, designing posters, fact-sheets and color ads for Kids Voting Central Ohio to encourage parents to take their children to the polls and vote, to thank supporters, and to print election results. In 2004, Grange printed curriculum, a 4-color brochure, a 4-color newsletter, 2-color letterhead, materials for our Youth Summit and Teacher Workshop and will print materials for over 1,000 Election Day volunteers. Grange hosted two events at their offices for Kids Voting, a May reception for our 2004 Poster Project with the League of Women Voters and a fundraising reception in June. Grange has committed to continue as a sponsor in 2005.

The Franklin County Board of Elections (BOE) — Since 2000, we have received annual grants of $15,000. This funding for Kids Voting Central Ohio has been incorporated into the BOE budget for 2005, which has been approved by the Franklin County Commissioners.

The Coalition of Central Ohio Rotary Organizations — Since 2000, Kids Voting Central Ohio has received financial backing ranging from $1,000 - $2,000 from local Rotary Clubs in Dublin and Worthington. In 2003, a new contribution was received from the downtown Columbus Rotary Club. In 2004, a newly-formed coalition of 15 local Rotary clubs committed to raise $15,000 for Kids Voting for the 2004 election efforts. More than $10,000 has been received and additional contributions are expected.

Kids Voting Central Ohio Fundraising Event — In June 2004, Kids Voting held its first fundraising event. It was hosted at Grange Insurance Company by CEO Phil Urban. Event chairs were U. S. Congressman Patrick Tiberi (R) and State Representative Joyce Beatty (D). The event raised $12,000. A similar event will be held in 2005.

Buckingham, Doolittle and Burroughs — Since 2002, the law firm generously donated office space (for five persons) in the Arena District to Kids Voting Central Ohio, valued at about $10,000 per year. This space is donated for 2005 as well.

The Nationwide Foundation — In 2000, 2001, 2002 and 2003 the foundation contributed $5,000.00. In addition, Nationwide donated two parking passes for the Arena Grand Parking garage, which is attached to our new office space downtown. This contribution is valued at about $2,000 per year. In 2004, the foundation contributed $2,500 and continued the donated parking spaces. *An application for support for 2005 has been submitted.*

Anthem Blue Cross and Blue Shield — In the last four years, Anthem has donated a total of $19,000.00 to Kids Voting Central Ohio. *A $5,000 contribution for 2004 will be requested.*

12

The Columbus Bar Auxiliary — The Columbus Bar Auxiliary contributed $3,000 in 2001, $5,000 in 2002 and $6,000 in 2003 and 2004. *A $7,000 contribution will be requested for 2005.*

Fifth-Third Bank/ Jacob G. Schmidlapp Trust — A contribution of $7,500 has been recommended for Kids Voting Central Ohio for 2004 from the Jacob Schmidlapp Trust, administered by Fifth-Third Bank. It is anticipated in September 2004.

Honda of America — A contribution of $5,000 was received for 2004.

Columbia Gas of Ohio/NiSource — A donation of $1,000 was received in 2004. A request for $15,000 for 2005 has been submitted. *A decision is pending.*

Sprint — Sprint contributed $2,500 for 2004.

Time Warner Cable — Time Warner has contributed $2,000 annually since 2002. *A request for 2005 will be submitted.*

Adopt-A-Poll — The Kids Voting Central Ohio Board of Trustees has set a target for raising at least $10,000 in 2004 through an aggressive Adopt-A-Poll solicitation. In 2002, we raised more than $4,000 from local businesses to adopt polling locations on Election Day. These funds were raised from only Westerville and Dublin. The plan for 2004 is to expand significantly on this effort in every Kids Voting community.

Plans for Project Continuation

At this time, we are seeking funding from The Columbus Foundation only for the 2005 data collection and analysis portion of this project. As is apparent from the above information, our intention is to continue gathering data through the fall of 2008. We will begin soliciting funding from other sources beginning with the 2006 data collection efforts, however, we may solicit the Foundation's assistance for a portion of that phase of the project. Out intention is that by the 2008 data collection phase, Dr. Eveland will be able to attract funding from foundations outside of the Columbus area for that part of the project.

Project Evaluation

This proposed project in itself is a comprehensive evaluation of the Kids Voting Central Ohio program.

In order for The Columbus Foundation to evaluate the impact of funding this project, **Kids Voting and Dr. Eveland will prepare a written summary of the information collected in 2005 and a description of how it will be used in modifying or improving our project** going forward and how it will be used to attract potential future funders of Kids Voting Central Ohio program operations.

13

Chapter 7

Equipment

Nonprofits need equipment to run their organizations and related programs. Some funders are willing to provide grants to cover these needs. Grant requests for equipment may be to acquire, update, or replace equipment such as telephones, photocopiers, computers, machinery, vehicles, or anything else of a substantive nature that a nonprofit organization needs in order to execute its mission. These funds may be for purchase or for lease of such equipment. Depending on the nature of the request, proposals that seek funding for equipment may be somewhat shorter than other types of proposals, since the project description component, often the longest section of a grant proposal, tends to be quite compact. The statement of need and the budget, on the other hand, are critical determining factors in equipment proposals.

The four proposals in this chapter ask for a dental X-ray machine, a replacement van, a computer system for breast cancer screenings, and adaptive technology to assist individuals with disabilities using computers in a library. The grant amounts range from nearly $5,000 to more than $350,000. Each proposal included here makes a strong case as to how new equipment will help the organization better fulfill its mission.

The first proposal presented in this chapter is from the Food Project of Lincoln, Massachusetts to the Richard and Susan Smith Family Foundation, of Chestnut Hill, Massachusetts. The full request is for $48,375 to repair an aging and damaged building and to replace a cargo van that the proposal writer points out plays an essential role in transporting tools, harvest crates, and produce safely and efficiently between three urban gardens and farmers' markets that the Food Project operates. The proposal emphasizes the urgent need for the purchase of a van in order for the organization to continue providing much needed services to Boston's youth. After some consideration, the foundation decided to fund only the van in the amount of $25,000.

The next proposal is a brief one submitted by the Foundation Center–Washington, DC, to the Mitsubishi Electric America Foundation, of Arlington, Virginia, for $4,875 to purchase adaptive computer technology. This adaptive equipment includes a scanner,

Kurzweil reader, and two other software programs that allow library users who are blind or have limited vision to read and navigate print and electronic materials and databases in the Foundation Center's Washington, DC, library. The proposal was submitted subsequent to conversations with an expert recommended by the foundation.

The third proposal, from the Nassau Health Care Corporation/Nassau University Medical Center of East Meadow, New York, requests $352,500 from the Avon Foundation's Supporting the Safety Net program to purchase breast cancer screening equipment and a computer system that would increase the number of women screened and would speed diagnostic time. This proposal effectively incorporates statistics to back up the need for the services of the medical center and to demonstrate how a lack of equipment (along with staff shortages) has caused serious delays in mammogram appointments and delivery of test results.

The final equipment proposal in this chapter is from the Tuscarawas County Health Department in Dover, Ohio, to the Austin-Bailey Health and Wellness Foundation in Canton, Ohio. Along with funding for a part-time hygienist, the proposal asks for a panoramic X-ray machine to replace a nearly 30-year old piece of equipment. In interim communications with the grantseeking organization the funder requested clarification on the purpose and value of a panoramic X-ray machine as compared to conventional X-ray technology, and the grantee's responses (included here) served to convince the foundation's board of directors of the benefits of the requested equipment.

A Proposal From

The Food Project

Lincoln, Massachusetts

To

Richard and Susan Smith Family Foundation

Chestnut Hill, Massachusetts

Requested amount: $48,375; **Amount received:** $25,000

Funder's comments:

"The Richard and Susan Smith Family Foundation establishes guidelines for our programs, and we publish these on our Web site. Our guidelines include instructions on what we want applicants to cover in applications. In the case of The Food Project, I had actually met their CEO at a meeting, and informed her about our 'small capital grants' program, to which she subsequently applied.

"In the case of this particular proposal the description of why the requested equipment was important for the organization and the community it serves was compelling. The need statement was especially clear. The writing style, presentation, and formatting were all fine and made the proposal easy to read. The budget was succinct, which is not surprising since this was primarily a request for money to replace an aging passenger van.

"Before our trustees made a final determination, I visited The Food Project and we discussed their need for a van as opposed to other organizational needs. We were pleased to fund this capital proposal."

—*David Ford, Executive Director, Richard and Susan Smith Family Foundation*

Notes:
Proposal written by Joshua Solomon and Rebecca Benefiel.

The Food Project

March 25th, 2004

Mr. David S. Ford
Executive Director
Richard & Susan Smith Family Foundation
1280 Bolyston St, Suite 100
Chestnut Hill, MA 02467

Dear Mr. Ford:

Please convey my thanks to the Trustees of the Smith Family Foundation for selecting our request for further consideration. At this time, we would like to sharpen the focus of our earlier request, which outlined the range of our capital needs. We respectfully invite the Richard and Susan Smith Family Foundation to invest $48,375 in critical repairs to our Lincoln building, and in the replacement of an aging cargo van which supports our urban agriculture, hunger relief, and youth development programs. Because many funders are reluctant to invest in the supporting infrastructure of nonprofits, your capital grant will meet vehicle and facility needs that would otherwise go un-met, providing our youth and agriculture programs with exactly the dollars we find most difficult and cumbersome to raise. While all of our capital needs are pressing, the van and building repairs must be carried out to ensure successful operations in 2004.

This is an exciting time for The Food Project. In 2003, we completed a strategic business planning process with the Bridgespan Group of Bain Consulting. The resulting five-year plan laid out several key goals, including doubling our youth programs and land base in the next five years, and improving our basic infrastructure and management systems to ensure sustained excellence in program delivery as we grow. The central components of this infrastructure are our fleet of five passenger and cargo vehicles and the buildings that house our offices. We hope that you will partner with us through supporting the most crucial of these projects, which improve our financial sustainability, and our ability to deliver innovative programs serving Boston's youth and communities.

<u>Organizational Profile</u>
The Food Project was founded in 1991 with 20 youth, two acres of land and a powerful and transformative vision: to create personal and social change through sustainable agriculture. Since then, The Food Project has engaged over 550 Greater Boston youth in structured work, service, and learning through our youth development programs and collaborated with almost 10,000 student and adult volunteers to grow 1.1 million pounds of fresh produce. Half of this harvest has been donated to a network of 10 local soup kitchens and homeless shelters, including the American Red Cross and the Greater Boston Food Bank. The Food Project has put down deep roots in Boston and Dorchester, where our youth and staff have turned 2.5 acres of trash-strew vacant lots into productive urban gardens, launched farmers' markets serving 2,000 customers a year, and partnered with Boston public schools to educate 350 elementary school students using a garden-based curriculum. The Food Project is an IRS 501 (c) (3) nonprofit with an annual operating budget of $2,328,512.

In 2003, The Food Project completed a five-year comprehensive evaluation of our programs with support from an independent evaluator and the W.K. Kellogg Foundation. We also finalized our five-year strategic plan, developed through a six-month consulting process with the Bridgespan Group of Bain & Company. In 2002, we received The President's Community Volunteer Award, the nation's highest honor for organizations dedicated to solving critical social problems, from the Points of Light Foundation, and were highlighted in *Learning Outside the Lines*, a W.K. Kellogg Foundation-funded publication that profiled six innovative youth programs from across the country.

<u>Needs Addressed</u>
Engaging youth in service and keeping them involved over time
Students who report being consistently engaged in school-based or community-based extracurricular activities between 8th and 12th grade are 2.5 times more likely to enroll in college, two times more likely to volunteer, and almost two times as likely to vote in their twenties, according to a recent Child Trends analysis of the National Educational Longitudinal Survey. Results from the 2001 Massachusetts Department of Education's Youth Risk Behavior Survey also revealed that students who participated in at least one hour of volunteer work or community service in an average month had significantly lower rates than their peers of smoking and illegal drug use. Each year, more youth apply to stay at The Food Project for multiple years, through our after-school and internship programs. Because we keep young people involved over an extended period of time, we form strong relationships with youth that enable them to deepen skills and achieve the positive outcomes listed above. Through mentorship and structured curricula, youth gain valuable life, job, public speaking, and communication skills, which increase their success in school and careers.

Building healthier communities
The Food Project's urban work is centered in the Dudley Street neighborhood of Dorchester. This community has an average per capita income almost half that of the rest of Boston and has an unemployment rate almost twice that of surrounding areas. Fully 32 percent of the people living here fall below the poverty level and African-Americans, Latinos, Haitians, and Cape Verdeans make up 93 percent of the population. Their neighborhood contains 840 vacant lots, poor access to fresh vegetables, a severe lead contamination problem, and 54 declared hazardous waste sites. The neighborhood contains over 160 backyard gardens and not enough gardeners know that it is unsafe to grow many kinds of vegetables in unremediated urban soil. Of the 60 gardens The Food Project has tested for soil contamination, ninety percent exceed the Environmental Protection Agency's safety standards of 300 parts per million of lead. The Food Project recruits youth from the neighborhood, farms on two acres of formerly idle neighborhood land, runs a weekly farmers' market that provides fresh vegetables at a subsidized rate, engages local elementary school children in hands-on learning, and provides backyard gardeners with resources and information to avoid health risks from soil contamination.

<u>Project Description</u>
Vehicles: Cargo Van, estimated cost $25,000. Our current cargo van, a 1995 Dodge with 83,262 miles is unlikely to last through this growing season. This van plays an essential role in transporting tools, harvest crates, and produce safely and efficiently between our three urban gardens and our farmers' market. Last year the van broke down several times on the way to the market, raising numerous concerns both in ensuring timely running of the markets, and also delaying the take-down of the market, which keeps our teenagers in Dorchester after dark. We hope to replace the cargo van with a passenger van that could transport youth between our work sites, improving our work efficiency, while still having adequate space to transport tools and produce. Located in the heart of the inner-city, our urban gardens produce 20,000 pounds of organic produce to be sold at a subsidized rate to inner-city residents and supplied to area shelters and food pantries. These gardens are also an important training ground in urban agriculture for over 100 youth and 800 community volunteers each year.

Physical Improvements to Facilities, estimated cost $23,375: In 2001, The Food Project purchased our office building in Lincoln. We will finish paying off the building loan in the first quarter of 2004. In order to fully leverage the value of this space, we need to make significant physical improvements to our facilities in 2004, including repointing the front of the building, replacing decaying mortar between bricks, addressing external and internal water damage, and retrofitting an aged alarm system to meet new safety standards. If improvements to the 90-year old external structure of the building are not carried out, damage will increase significantly and repair costs will rise. These are not aesthetic renovations; we need to replace our alarm system or we will be in violation of new town codes. Our Lincoln facility provides adequate workspace for staff, meeting space for youth, and a constant revenue stream to support our programs. This building also solidifies our presence in Lincoln, where we rely on town-owned land to raise 200,000 pounds of healthy produce, which is distributed to shelters, and a subsidized farmers' market in Dorchester, and sold via enterprise projects that provide further financial stability for our youth and agriculture programs.

Project Staffing and Management in Future Years

The Food Project's Business Manager, Lis Cahill, brings 30 years of experience in accounting and fiscal management to her oversight of the physical improvements to our Lincoln facility and the maintenance and expansion of our vehicle fleet. We use a five-year fleet depreciation method and our building improvements are depreciated similarly. We replace vehicles when necessary to assure safety and the uninterrupted implementation of our programs.

Program Expansion in 2005 and beyond

The Food Project's five-year business plan outlines ambitious long-term objectives and concrete steps to reach these goals. We have documented demand for growth of our local programs and national interest in replicating our model. We also have strong relationships in place with peer organizations, city agencies, and several key funders. We hope that you will play a key role in enabling us to reach these goals by 2008, through investing in our critical infrastructure.

- Double the size of our local youth development programs by offering 215 positions per year in a tiered progression that will serve and engage youth aged 14-18.
- Double the size and impact of our local food system work by raising our annual harvest from 200,000 to over 350,000 pounds, creating a local food policy council, and partnering with producers, distributors, and city officials to increase the amount of healthy food available to urban residents;
- Replicate in one to three locations, starting with Summer Programs serving 10-30 youth per location.
- Create local and national networks and resources to engage and train young people as practitioners and leaders in sustainable food system creation. Opportunities will include conferences, exchange programs, internships, jobs, academic programs, skill certification programs, and collaborative action;

Thank you again for the opportunity to apply for this grant. We hope that you will choose to provide support for the capital needs described above, both of which are critical to The Food Project's infrastructure and program growth. Please feel free to call me at (781) 259-8621 if I can provide any additional information or answer any questions.

Sincerely,

Patricia Gray
Executive Director

The Food Project
Budget and Timeline for Capital Projects 2004

Project	Cost	Completion Date
New Fire Alarm System	$8,200	By 4/15/04
Repointing, Caulking and Waterproofing for Lincoln Building	$4,300	By 6/15/04
Installation of New Windows for Lincoln Building	$9,750	By 7/1/04
Replace Front Retaining Wall for Lincoln Building	$1,125	By 7/15/04
Purchase Passenger Van to Replace Urban Agriculture Cargo Van	$25,000	By 6/1/04
Total Cost	$48,375	

The Foundation Center–Washington, DC

Washington, DC

To

Mitsubishi Electric America Foundation

Arlington, Virginia

Requested amount: $4,875; **Amount received:** $4,875

Funder's comments:

"We generally require grantseekers to fill out an application form and provide supporting materials, such as an annual report, board list, qualifications of staff, etc. But for small requests such as this one, we need only a letter outlining the purpose for which the funds are sought and providing a brief background description of the organization, and one or two attachments (in this instance the organizational budget). In the case of this equipment request from the Foundation Center, there was a preliminary letter, followed by a phone call and a visit to the organization by one of our outside advisors, who was to make recommendations.

"As opposed to a full proposal, this was a letter request, so it was brief. But all the main points were covered. Within this context, all of the expected components were present and well balanced in terms of length, level of detail, and content. The need for this grant to assist visitors with disabilities to access the Foundation Center's library was clearly articulated. The writing is straightforward, concise, and cogent—logically ordered with not a word wasted. And given the letter format, the budget was simple and self-explanatory.

"I was particularly impressed with the research and preparation that had already been done, demonstrating the organization's deep commitment to improving accessibility for people with disabilities. This also reassured me, as a prospective funder, that the equipment to be purchased with grant funds would be quickly and efficiently installed and ready for use. Another notable feature of this request was the dissemination plan, which ensured that the target population would be made aware of the new resources.

"Once our advisor confirmed that the proposed technology purchases were appropriate and well chosen, we were ready to approve the grant. One suggestion as to what would have made this an even better proposal would be an assurance that the organization would make every effort to maintain the equipment and to evaluate its usage. One more note: As a corporate foundation, we appreciate mention of the company in publicity materials. Although not included in the request letter, the Foundation Center on its own gave the Mitsubishi Electric America Foundation ample recognition in its announcements about the new equipment."

—Rayna Aylward, Executive Director, Mitsubishi Electric America Foundation

Notes:
The complete proposal included the following attachment: organizational budget.
Proposal written by Anita Plotinsky, Director, The Foundation Center–Washington, DC.

May 7, 2004

Ms. Colleen Maher
Program Officer
Mitsubishi Electric America Foundation
1560 Wilson Boulevard, Suite 1150
Arlington, VA 22209

Dear Colleen:

Thank you again for coming over to visit the Foundation Center–Washington, DC We appreciated the opportunity to bring you up to date on our programs and services, and are particularly grateful for your willingness to receive a proposal for support of our efforts to make our resources more accessible to people with disabilities.

Our proposal is enclosed. As you will see, we are requesting a grant in the amount of $4,875 in order to purchase equipment and computer software to assist library patrons who are blind or have limited vision. If you have questions or need any additional information, please let us know.

Sincerely,

Sara L. Engelhardt   Anita H. Plotinsky
President   Director
The Foundation Center   Foundation Center–Washington, DC

Enclosures

The Foundation Center–Washington, DC

Proposal to the Mitsubishi Electric America Foundation

For Equipment to Assist People with Disabilities

May 7, 2004

Organizational Background

The mission of the Foundation Center is to strengthen the nonprofit sector by advancing knowledge about U.S. philanthropy. Founded in 1956, the Foundation Center has provided services in Washington, DC, for 40 years.

As one of four field offices, the Foundation Center–Washington, DC, provides library resources and services; offers educational programs in foundations, grantseeking, and nonprofit management; and conducts outreach to nonprofits throughout the national capital region.

Purpose of Request

Each year, about 15,000 people use our library/learning center at no charge. They come to take classes, borrow books, read periodicals, use Foundation Center directories and databases to identify prospective funding partners, engage in dialogue with grantmakers, participate in InfoBreakfast discussions on nonprofit "best practices," and attend presentations on philanthropy and nonprofit management by some of the world's most distinguished scholars.

Some of these people have disabilities, and we seek your assistance in making it possible for them to use our resources. To date, we have equipped two computer stations--one in the library and one in the computer lab--with keyboards with enlarged lettering, trackball mice, and keyboard wrist rests. Lumbar support pads were added to the chairs at the workstations with the assistive technology. The Foundation Center provided tuition assistance for our Senior Librarian to take classes in American Sign Language so that she can assist library visitors, and we have engaged ASL interpreters for our educational programs upon request. Our Reference Librarian participates in the Foundation Center's Task Force for Services to the Disabled, attends workshops to learn more about assistive technology, and is currently taking the tutorial Accessibility Basics for Librarians developed by the American Library Association. In fact, a current organizational goal is to improve our overall services to people with disabilities.

The next step is to install equipment and computer software that will enable patrons who are blind or who have limited vision to read books and articles in our library, and to use the Foundation Center's CD-ROM and Web-based funding research databases. The equipment and software we wish to purchase have been tested at the Foundation Center's New York headquarters to make sure that they are compatible with our systems. We have also discussed compatibility issues with Olegario "Ollie" Cantos, VII, General Counsel and Director of Programs of the American Association of People with Disabilities.

We respectfully request a grant from the Mitsubishi Electric America Foundation in the amount of $4,875 in order to purchase the following:

- Kurzweil reader, which enables blind people to read print materials
- Scanner for Kurzweil reader
- JAWS, which enables blind people to use computers
- ZoomText, which enables people with reduced vision to use computers

Dissemination

The director of the Foundation Center–Washington, DC, met with Mr. Cantos to determine how we can work together to raise awareness of the Center resources and services among people with disabilities. It was clear from the meeting that the Center's commitment to accessibility would be furthered by bringing our resources to AAPD affiliates, which serve people with disabilities. As part of this new collaboration, we will send information about the Foundation Center, with appropriate Web links, for dissemination to AAPD members. In addition, the director of the Foundation Center–Washington, DC, will speak at an AAPD conference call with approximately 40 AAPD coordinators to provide an overview of the resources at our libraries, Cooperating Collections, and content-rich Web site.

Organizational Capacity

The Foundation Center is widely recognized as the nation's leading authority on philanthropy and is dedicated to serving grantseekers, grantmakers, researchers, policymakers, the media, and the general public. The Center collects, organizes, and communicates information on U.S. philanthropy; conducts and facilitates research on trends in the field; provides education and training; and ensures public access to information and services through its Web site, print and electronic publications, five library/learning centers, and a national network of 230 cooperating collections.

The Foundation Center–Washington, DC, has a state-of-the-art library and learning center, including a multipurpose training room and computer laboratory. A summary of our staff members' responsibilities and qualifications is enclosed.

Project Budget

Kurzweil reader	995
Scanner for Kurzweil reader	500
JAWS	2,190
ZoomText	1,190
TOTAL	4,875

Organizational Budget

A copy of the Foundation Center–Washington, DC's 2004 budget is enclosed.

A Proposal From

Nassau Health Care Corporation/
Nassau University Medical Center

East Meadow, New York

To

Avon Foundation

New York, New York

Requested amount: $352,500; **Amount received:** $352,500

Funder's comments:

"Nassau University Medical Center used the Avon Foundation application form, after first approaching us by means of our RFP process for 'safety net' gifts. The cover letter was somewhat brief, summarizing the program quickly, but a full program description later on in the proposal provided a more comprehensive overview. This section was especially well developed, describing in depth the facilities available at Nassau University Medical Center, its place in the local healthcare landscape, and the shortage of qualified radiologists to address the needs of the area.

"All components that one would expect to find were present. The various components of this proposal are somewhat long, however, and sections of this proposal might have benefited from being broken down slightly. The writing style is dense at times, due to the level of detail in each section, but it is still clear and accessible, even to those not in the medical or scientific professions.

"The need statement persuasively states the problem, and demonstrates how the mission of the Nassau University Medical Center dovetails with that community's need. The budget is well-written and presented clearly. All budgetary elements are represented, making analysis easy. They included all necessary attachments, and all were helpful. As already alluded to, in my view, the strongest feature of this proposal is the level of detail provided in the program description. But I do think that perhaps breaking up the dense nature of the body of the proposal into more specific subsections would have made it easier on the grants decision maker."

—*Mary Quinn, Senior Manager of Operations, Avon Foundation*

Notes:

The proposal was written using the Avon Foundation grant request cover sheet and guidelines. The complete proposal included the following attachments: program timeline and three-page overview of the Nassau University Medical Center and its Breast Screening Program.

Proposal written by Christine D. Mancuso, R.N., Breast Cancer Screening Program, and Mel Praissman, Ph.D., Director, Office of Grants Management.

THE AVON FONDATION "Supporting the Safety Net": Application Cover Sheet

Organization Name: ___ Nassau University Medical Center ___
Street Address: ___ 2201 Hempstead Turnpike ___
City/State/Zip: ___ East Meadow , New York 11554 ___
Contact Name/Title: Christine Mancuso PHN II, Director, Breast Cancer Screening Program
Telephone: 516-572-3300 Fax: 516-572-0066 E-mail (required): cmancuso@numc.edu

Proposed use of funds description (one sentence only):
This proposal is for funds to purchase equipment and a computer system in order to maximize the number of women screened and receiving care within a system with limited resources.

Population to be served (age, ethnicity, income level):
The population Nassau University Medical Center Breast Cancer Screening Program serves is predominately minority women over the age of 40 years who are uninsured or underinsured.

Geographic area to be served: Nassau County

Exact amount of funding requested: $ __352,500__ Timeline for use of funds: Oct, 2004-September 2005

What is the annual operating budget of your hospital $292,000,000.00

Have you previously received funding from the **Avon Foundation or Avon Foundation Breast Care Fund**?

___Yes _X_No

If yes, provide date(s) of funding: _____

Statement of Applicant
By signing in the space below, the representative of the gift applicant (a) affirms that he or she is an authorized representative of the applicant; (b) affirms that the information in this application is complete and accurate; (c) agrees to provide additional information to Avon and to be available for site visits by Avon, if requested; (d) understands and agrees that funding decisions are made by Avon at its sole discretion and are final, and that Avon shall have no responsibility to any applicant not selected for receipt of a Fund grant; and (e) if selected for funding, agrees to provide semi-annual reports in the format to be specified, to sign a gift agreement stipulating certain terms and conditions of funding and to cooperate with Avon Foundation in local and national publicity about the "Supporting the Safety Net" initative and the gift received from this initiative.

Unless this sentence is crossed out by the applicant, applicant gives Avon permission to share the applicant's contact information and program objective, solely for information exchange purposes.

Nassau University Medical Center   By _____
Name of Organization   Signature of authorized representative

Name: _Christine D. Mancuso,RN_ Title: Director Program Director BCSP Date: _3/31/04_____

Completed applications must be received by mail, express or hand delivery only, **on or before Thursday, April 1,2004, by 5pm Eastern Time**, at the Avon Foundation , 1345 Avenue at of the Americas, New York, New York 10105. Attention: Lisa Morehouse

Nassau University Medical Center   "Supporting the Safety Net"
April 1, 2004   Avon Foundation

Narrative

A. *Assessment*

The geographic area that Nassau University Medical Center (NUMC) serves includes the priority Communities of Elmont, Freeport/ Roosevelt, Hempstead, Inwood, Westbury/New Cassel, Long Beach and Uniondale; these are the same communities in which the Community Health Centers are located along with the ambulatory care center at NUMC. Nassau County is a suburban community located on Long Island bordered by Queens County of New York City on the west and bordered on the east by Suffolk County. Nassau County is one of the most populous counties in New York State.

According to forecasting information from the New York Metropolitan Transportation Council, Nassau County's population is projected to increase gradually from an estimated 1,303,231 in 1995 to 1,433,600 by the year 2020, approximately a 10% increase over 25 years. The county's population is becoming more diverse in that non-white population increased by approximately 50% between 1980 and 1994 and according to the 2000 Census count reported a population of more than 1.3 million persons with nearly 23% of the county's population as minority.

Although income characteristics in Nassau County are reported to be above the national average, a growing number of residents with predominantly multicultural backgrounds are living below the poverty level in a cluster of communities. This "Targeted population" lives in the immediate area surrounding either the Medical Center or residing within a short distance from one of the six Community Health Centers which surround the Medical Center.

The patient population at the Medical Center and the six community centers mirrors that of the communities of greatest need, including designation by the State of New York as areas with low access to healthcare, specifically 80% Black African Americans, 17% Non-Black Hispanics and 1.5% Others including Orientals and White Americans.

The characterization of the residents living within these communities is reflected on Nassau Health Care Corporation, specifically statistics of the Medical Center. For example, 57% of patient contacts were Black, 35% were White and 7% Hispanic. Similarly, the method of payment to the Medical Center is consistent with other demographic data, whereas Medicaid payments represent only 11.5% of patients of other Long Island hospitals; figures from the Medical Center indicate that approximately 45% of the patients at NUMC are Medicaid recipients. These figures do not reflect statistical information about the patient population, which currently utilizes the community health centers, the geriatric center, the satellite health center, or population demographics for the Nassau County Correctional Facility.

Nassau Health Care Corporation is the major health care provider serving these patient populations, offering inpatient and ambulatory services in all primary care specialties, as well as numerous sub-specialties such as the Breast Imaging Center.

The County of Nassau previously owned all of the above facilities. As a result of a recent merger in late 1999, these county-owned institutions were combined under the auspices of a new public benefit corporation called the Nassau Health Care Corporation. The mission of the Nassau Health Care Corporation is to serve the health care needs of all people of Nassau County without regard to the individual's ability to pay. More than 80,000 people annually are treated in the Medical Center's Department of Emergency Medicine and 178,000 in its more than 85 specialty clinics. Approximately 30,000 patients are seen annually throughout the community health center network. As such, the Nassau Health Care Corporation is the largest provider of medical care to the indigent population in Nassau County. The New York State Bad Debt and Charity Pool has determined that the Nassau Health Care Corporation has the greatest need of any health care provider in Nassau County. The Nassau University Medical Center is the only *Safety Net*

1

Nassau University Medical Center   "Supporting the Safety Net"
April 1, 2004   Avon Foundation

Hospital in Nassau County and on Long Island. We serve all of Nassau County, Western Suffolk County and Eastern Queens County residents who are unable to afford health care.

The Breast Imaging Center of Nassau University Medical Center is the referent for the Community Health Centers located in Elmont, Hempstead, Freeport/Roosevelt, Inwood, Westbury/ New Cassel, and Long Beach. Three of these facilities provide Breast Cancer screening including a clinical breast examination with instruction in breast self-exam and mammography. Our Mobile program supports the Communities that do not have screening services located within the health centers. All of the films are read at NUMC in the Breast Imaging Center by our board certified radiologists. The Breast Imaging Center provides all of the follow up and diagnostic services along with the same screening services as the Mobile and Community Health Centers.

The Centers For Disease Control National Breast and Cervical Cancer Education and Screening Program support this Breast Cancer Screening Program. The Nassau County New York State Partnership Program is located in Nassau University Medical Center. We have been a recipient of this grant funding to provide education, screening and diagnostic follow up services to underserved women since the inception of the program in 1989. Additionally, grant funded staff at NUMC has been trained to complete and submit Medicaid applications for the clients screened and diagnosed with breast cancer through this program.

The Breast Cancer Screening Program (BCSP) of NUMC screens more than 6,000 women a year, many of whom are under insured or have no insurance. Of these 6,000 women screened more than 900 women will be referred for additional diagnostic work up and of those women approximately 400 will be referred for some surgical consultation or biopsy. In 2003, 66 women were diagnosed with Breast Cancer at NUMC nearly all of these women were under or uninsured.

The Breast Imaging Center along with the Breast Surgery Clinic at NUMC is responsible for all of the diagnostic and follow-up Radiological and Surgical services. The Partnership Nurse Case Manager provides the coordination of these services thereby assuring that no patient will fall through the cracks. This is accomplished with the assistance of Registered Nurses, who manage the follow up to screening services by:
- Notification of all women their results either by telephone and/ or mail
- Follow-up to resolution or referral for biopsy

This extremely busy BIC is supported by 1 full time Radiologist and 2 part time Radiologists. The documented shortage of Radiologists who read mammography films has impacted on the mammography facilities within Nassau County and in particular the NUMC BIC.

The American Cancer Society reports that in the year 2000 in Nassau County the Breast Cancer Screening rates of women 40 and over who have had a mammogram in the past year at 68.2% [1]. We know that women who have health insurance are more likely to have annual health screenings and that women without such health coverage will ignore their health care. The funds we are requesting will allow our BIC to provide the screening service more effectively and reduce the delay to follow–up that we experience within a system with limited resources. The NYSDOH Breast Screening Program is reaching approximately 2,500 women per year, the additional equipment and upgrades to our existing BIC will enable the BCSP to reach out to more women in Nassau County and provide them with quality care in a more efficient time frame. The upgrades to our existing service will assist the Department with clearing some of the delays we are experiencing in having our screening mammograms interpeted in a more timely manner.

---

[1] Source: CDC-BRFSS, CDC-YRBSS, CDC-YTS

2

Nassau University Medical Center   "Supporting the Safety Net"
April 1, 2004   Avon Foundation

According to the American Cancer Society Eastern Division Nassau County Community Assessment Tool the average annual breast cancer cases (1997 – 1999) 1166 cases were diagnosed with 258 breast cancer deaths occurring in the same time period. [2]

B. *Program Description*

The Medical Center's Breast Imaging Center (BIC) is an American College of Radiology accredited facility, as well as a Center of Excellence of the Nassau University Medical Center. Since 1989, Nassau County's Executive has been in the forefront of breast cancer awareness and early detection efforts. Nassau County was the first municipality in the country to provide free mammography screening to all women in the county. Indeed, the continuation of this effort to alert residents of the important role early detection plays in breast cancer has been adopted by every member of the county legislature regardless of party affiliation.

As part of the county's early detection programs, every household in Nassau County is informed by mail of: the importance of early detection, instructions on performing monthly self breast examination, emphasizing the need for annual mammograms for women over 40 and in high risk groups and the availability of "no out of pocket cost" mammography screening program at any of the Nassau Health Care Corporation Facilities.

The Breast Imaging Center performs screening mammograms for any female Nassau County resident upon request, with no out-of-pocket expense. We have also been approved by the New York State Department of Health to accept self-referred patients, that is patients with no connection to a health care provider. These two points are important factors that allow and encourage the community, especially the underserved and low-income populations, to obtain health care at our facility.

This fully diagnostic Imaging Center contains two dedicated mammography LoRad M IV (2001), units and an ATL dedicated breast ultrasound machine. Our stereotactic breast biopsy procedures are performed in the Center weekly through United Medical Systems under the direction of our Radiologists. The Center is capable of performing fine needle aspiration biopsies and large core needle biopsies. All patients are taught breast self-examination. From the inception of the Breast Imaging Center in 1989, over 70,000 mammography studies have been performed through all of our facilities.

In addition to the stationary sites, Two Mobile Mammography Vans can be dispatched to any area within the county, and are staffed by teams consisting of a nurse, a mammography technician and a clerk. These mobile units, which screen more than 1,700 women a year provide access to mammograms as well as education on self-examination and clinical breast examination to senior citizens, the handicapped, and other members of the underserved, uninsured population at conveniently located sites countywide throughout the year.

The Breast Cancer Treatment Center at Nassau University Medical Center has been designated as a Center of Excellence. The Breast Cancer Team includes a radiologist, a pathologist, a breast surgeon, nurse case manager, a medical oncologist, a radiation oncologist, nurses certified in performing breast exams and the bilingual patient navigators. This multidisciplinary approach is used for treatment of benign and malignant breast diseases starting with the initial mammography screening exam and continuing through treatment. On average, 35 patients are referred to the team for breast evaluation each week. Patients are seen in an outpatient setting by a team of breast surgeons and surgical residents who are trained in treating and diagnosing breast diseases. A Board Certified Breast Imaging Radiologist reviews all mammograms and determines

---

[2] Source: CDC-NCHC, New York State Cancer Registry, and CDC-NPCR-CSS

3

Nassau University Medical Center <u>"Supporting the Safety Net"</u>
April 1, 2004   Avon Foundation

if additional radiology procedures, like sonograms and other special X-ray views, are needed to aid the surgeons in a final diagnosis. When further tests are indicated the team aims to schedule them in a timely manner, should the pathologist need to perform fine needle aspiration on suspicious masses, these procedures are also scheduled on the same day.

With rapid response, our patients' fears can be allayed, definitive diagnosis can be made and treatment can be provided to women needing attention. This is a one-stop rapid diagnostic area for breast evaluation where the patient enters with a question and leaves with an answer. The nurse case manager and patient navigator as well as the professional staff in the Breast Imaging Center are available to assist the breast surgeon and the patients both during their visits to Breast Clinic, the BIC and on the telephone.

With the early diagnosis of breast cancer, the surgeon in many instances can perform breast conservation surgery. Our women are given extensive information regarding their choices. This allows them to make decisions regarding which treatment plan might be the best option due to the type and stage of their cancer. The importance of mammography and breast self-examination in the early detection of breast cancer is emphasized.

The Breast Imaging Center and Breast Treatment Clinic works closely with other medical service departments, including Primary Care, Family Practice, OB/GYN and Plastic Surgery. Every attempt is made to maximize the accessibility of medical specialists available to the patient within the Medical Center.

The Nassau University Medical Center is fully accredited by the Joint Commission on Accreditation of Healthcare Organizations and is approved by the New York State Department of Health and the Accreditation Council for Graduate Medical Education.
It has been designated a Level I Trauma Center and is accredited by the Commission on Cancer For Teaching Hospital Cancer Programs as well as being a designated AIDS Center.

The Nassau University Medical Center is a major affiliate of the Health Sciences Center of the State University of New York at Stony Brook. The affiliation of these two outstanding institutions forms a partnership that provides excellence in healthcare education, comprehensive clinical investigation and research, and the highest quality care to patients in Nassau County and the region.

The Health Sciences Center of the State University of New York at Stony Brook serves as a regional resource for advanced education, patient care and research. It is the mission of the School of Medicine to educate medical students, train residents and provide continuing education for physicians.

Graduate medical education at the Nassau University Medical Center plays an important role in its mission. Scholarly activity, research productivity and high standards of patient care at both institutions are all fostered by our affiliation and students, residents, faculty and the public at large are the beneficiaries. Highly qualified faculty, modern, well-equipped facilities and strong graduate medical education programs offer the prospective house officer teaching hospital responsibilities and experience with a broad patient population.

4

Nassau University Medical Center   "Supporting the Safety Net"
April 1, 2004   Avon Foundation
C. *Use of Funds from the Avon Foundation "Supporting the Safety Net" Initiative.*

Increase the level of service and improvement in the quality of care offered to underserved patients. In conjunction with the outreach efforts of the Nassau Partnership for Healthy Communities, Health Community Access Program (HCAP) grant the Breast Cancer Screening Program will increase the number of underserved women screened by 20% in the Community Health Centers, Breast Imaging Center and Mobile Program. This will allow us to expand our services to screen an additional 500 underserved women annually.

This proposal is requesting funds to purchase equipment to maximize the number of women screened and receiving high quality of care within a system with a limited number of Radiology resources. This funding will allow the BCSP to expand our screening services by:
- Reducing the delay to screening and follow-up
- Alleviate the manual tracking of our abnormal patients
- Allow for computer generated follow-up and recall letters to be sent to our existing clients

The Computer Aided Diagnostic System is a computer-aided detection (CAD) system that digitizes a mammogram and analyzes it using a proprietary signal processing software, which highlights areas on the mammogram, which contain features associated with cancer. After the radiologist reviews the original mammogram they then review the areas that the CAD has marked as areas of concern. This is like a "Spell-Checker" for mammography. The CAD helps reduce observational oversights and aids radiologists with the early detection of breast cancer. This system will assist our patients in receiving the second review of their films. The BIC is unable to provide double reading of mammograms as many of the facilities in the New York City area are doing at this time. Our uninsured patients would thereby be provided with the same standard of care as many women receive in the private setting. Additionally this service would expedite the reading of the screening films allowing the Radiologist to be more efficient and the patient notification process to begin sooner. This will alleviate some of the concerns and fears that many women experience when they have a mammogram.

The BIC currently has two Motorized Mammography Alternator Viewing Systems. The original system was purchased at the inception of the BIC in 1992. According to their manufacturer these viewing systems have a life expectancy of film belt for about 10 years. A replacement for this unit would provide the tools to speed and enhance mammography film interpretation. This replacement will assist the reading Radiologist with a state of the art technology to provide optimum care for our patients by providing better care in less time.

Funds to purchase a Mammography reporting system with voice recognition. This computerized system will assist the Radiologist reading in that she can dictate her exam and have it ready for approval at the same time and will assist our staff with the tracking of our patients. Currently, our Nurses and Nurse Case Manager manage this required patient tracking with a filing system and logbooks. This cost effective tool will improve operational efficiency as well as aid with the meeting of the Mammography Quality Standards Act (MSQA) requirements for any facility performing mammography and other breast-related procedures. This system will generate the radiologist exam report, the patient result letter, it will track problem cases and generate follow up letters and provides the medical audit and practice management statistical reports. Many of these functions are currently being performed by the BIC staff without the assistance of a computer-based system. This upgrade will allow our staff to provide the "hands on" support and follow up that our patients require since they will not be spending their valuable time on clerical issues.

5

Nassau University Medical Center   "Supporting the Safety Net"
April 1, 2004   Avon Foundation

The purchase of this equipment will increase the efficiency of the BIC and reduce the delay to diagnosis or notification of their mammogram exam that our screening patients are currently experiencing.

Follow-up Services

The NUMC Breast Imaging Center provides all of the follow-up care for the women screened in our screening facilities. We are the recipients of the CDC/NYS Department of Health Breast and Cervical Screening Program which allows women who are underserved to be screened and followed-up for Breast Diseases. This program is totally dedicated to provide these services and we are the only hospital in Nassau County mandated to care for the indigent. All women receiving care in our facilities are notified of their outcome according to the MSQA guidelines, additionally women requiring additional diagnostic work up are notified on the telephone or in person by a registered nurse who will explain to them the reason for the necessary additional tests. Women who should require biopsy are transferred to our Nurse Case Manager will remain in contact with them until they receive their diagnosis. The bilingual patient navigators, who support the BCSP and the Breast Surgical Clinic, assist the professional staff with these functions.

Data Collection and Reporting

Currently the BCSP maintains data on our patients through a combined manual tracking and computer based system. Our Radiology System is able to provide the number of patients screened at our sites. These patients are then followed up through a manual tracking system that includes maintaining follow-up files and log books of patients referred for biopsy or surgical consultation. As previously discussed these tracking systems would be monitored by the new mammography tracking system.

The data regarding the outreach efforts by the peer educators will be collected through the HCAP funding initiative this is discussed in the section on the Hospital Information. This tracking will allow us to evaluate the effectiveness of our outreach efforts.

The Office of Development has initiated fund raising efforts to renovate and remodel the BIC. The Breast Imaging Center was established and opened in 1991. The needs of patients have changed since that time and the unit should reflect those changes. In February an event was held to kick off our fund raising plan. We hope to be starting our renovation within a few months. We feel that these changes will allow our patients to be treated with privacy, respect and allow the staff with the space to counsel and educate our patients in a comfortable setting.

6

NASSAU HEALTH CARE CORPORATION
BREAST CANCER SCREENING PROGRAM BUDGET
OCTOBER 2004 TO SEPTEMBER 2005

PERSONNEL	ASSUMPTIONS	AVON REQUEST	OTHER SOURCES	AGENCY
Program Director	1 FTE	0	XXXXX	
Registered Nurses	3 FTE	0	XXXX	XXXX
Case Manager	1 FTE	0	XXXX	XXXX
Resource Interviewer	1FTE	0	XXXX	
Clerk	.5 FTE	0	XXXX	XXXXX
Patient Navigater	1FTE @ XXXXX	0	XXXXX	
Patient Navigater	.5 FTE @ XXXXX	0	XXX	
Mammography Technologists	3.5 FTE	0	XXXXX	XXXXX
Subtotal Personnel			XXXXX	XXXX
Fringe @ 30%			XXXXX	XXXX
Subtotal Personnel			$260,862	$467,712
Equipment				
Computer Aided Diagnostic		$115,000.00		
Mammography Reporting System		$200,000.00		
Moterized Alternator		$35,000.00		
Other Than Personnel Services				
Travel			$3,600.00	
Breast Cancer Conference		$2,500.00		
Sub-total		$352,500.00		
Personnel & OTPS Total			$264,462	
Indirect Expenses				
Total		$352,500.00	$264,462	$467,712
Other Sources include Funds from NYS Dept of Health and EIF Revlon Walk/Run for Women				

A Proposal From
Tuscarawas County Health Department
Dover, Ohio

To
Austin-Bailey Health and Wellness Foundation
Canton, Ohio

Requested amount: $40,960; **Amount received:** $48,000

Funder's comments:

"Austin-Bailey had put forth an oral health initiative in January of 2002. The Tuscarawas County Health Department responded, and received a $25,000 grant in June of 2002. I then visited the facility in February of 2004, and subsequently invited their executive director to speak to our board of directors at the March 2004 board meeting. Tuscarawas County Health Department was told at that time to consider Austin-Bailey for future oral health needs. Thus their grant request in February 2005.

"The Tuscarawas County Health Department used our grant cover sheet as instructed. The complete request was clear and concise. The letter in response to our questions was very clear and direct, and it was particularly instrumental in our decision-making process. Our board of directors concur that oral health care is a major need for low-income families served by the Tuscarawas Health Department and could see the value in hiring a dental hygienist on a part-time basis. They also could understand the real benefits of the Panoramic X-ray machine.

"The need statement was well thought out and well presented, and the writing style and presentation were all well done. While in the end we had enough detail in order to make a funding decision, perhaps a more thorough description initially of the strong benefits of the Panoramic X-ray machine as compared to a conventional one would have been helpful."

—*Don A. Sultzbach, Executive Director, Austin-Bailey Health and Wellness Foundation*

[Editor's note: In an interim communication after review by its Grant Screening Committee, the funder asked for further explanation concerning the superiority of the requested Panoramic X-ray machine compared to conventional X-ray equipment and raised the possibility of providing funding to make the requested dental hygienist position full- rather than part-time with the portion of the grant for X-ray equipment in the form of a challenge grant. The health department responded fully and in detail in writing about the equipment and explained that a full-time hygienist position, including benefits, would be more than they could afford. In the end the foundation's board of directors approved a grant in the amount of $48,000, the total cost of the project as opposed to a partial challenge grant. We have included relevant correspondence as examples of this type of interaction between grantmaker and grantee.]

Notes:

The proposal was written using the Austin-Bailey Health and Wellness Foundation grant request cover sheet and guidelines. The complete proposal included the following attachment: one-page mission statement.

Proposal written by Linda J. Fanning, Executive Director, and Christopher J. Herrick, DDS.

**AUSTIN-BAILEY HEALTH AND WELLNESS FOUNDATION
GRANT REQUEST COVER SHEET**

<u>**Applicant Organization**</u>

Name ___Tuscarawas County Health Department___

Mailing Address ___897 East Iron Avenue___

City ___Dover___ State ___Ohio___ Zip ___44622___

Telephone ___(330) 343-4928___ Fax ___(330) 364-8946___

Executive Director ___Linda J. Fanning___

Chairman, Board of Trustees ___Terry A. Hiller___

Contact Person ___Linda J. Fanning___ Title ___Executive Director___

Total Amount Requested ___$41,000___ No. of years ___83___ Counties Served ___Tuscarawas and limited Carroll___

Project Title ___Dental Program -- Access to Dental Care___

<u>Circle Your Tax Exempt Status – (Circle One)</u>
Charitable Organization 501 (c)(3)   (Government)
Educational Institution   Other Tax Exempt

<u>**Required Attachments**</u>
➢ Tax Determination Letter from IRS (if applicable)   N/A – government agency
➢ Mission Statement
➢ Prior Year's Audited Financial Statement
➢ Current Year's Budget
➢ Board of Directors

In the remaining space on this page, provide a brief description of your organization. Then on a separate <u>SINGLE</u> sheet, discuss the project or purpose for which the grant dollars would be used, including a specific break out of how the dollars requested will be spent.

The Dental Program -- Access to Dental Care is in the Tuscarawas County Health Department (TCHD). It is part of a public, non-profit, community-based local health department. The dental activities can be described as a safety-net dental care program. In 2003, with two-part-time dentists, the program had 1,108 patient visits. In 2002, when the program had a full-time dentist, there were 2,445 patient visits. We are unable to accommodate all the demands we receive for dental care! Most of the patients are at or below the federal poverty level. One of the commendable features of the project is the policy to allow individuals to receive services regardless of their ability to pay.

Signature ___Linda J. Fanning___ Title ___Executive Director___

Print Name ___Linda J. Fanning___ Date ___06-30-2004___

January 2003

- **Description of the Organization and its Activities**

The Dental Program--Access to Dental Care is located in the Tuscarawas County Health Department (TCHD). The TCHD is a public, non-profit, community-based local health department. The appointment book is always full for the Dental Program. The extent of poverty being faced by some of our patients is inadequately described as tremendous. Our goal is to attempt to get patients the dental work or items they need to live a normal life.

There are several other programs at the TCHD that emphasize prevention and treatment of disease. The facility implements programs dealing with safety, substance abuse, nutrition, family planning, tobacco use, food-borne illness, and other public health issues. Medicare and Medicaid designate the Tuscarawas County Health Department as a Rural Health Clinic.

- **Oral Health Needs this Project will Address**

This proposal would expand personnel with the addition of a part-time contract dental hygienist, and create evening hours for the dental division of the TCHD. This proposal would also add the diagnostic feature of panoramic x-ray to the existing array of services. Our existing x-ray machine is a marginal and outdated unit from the 1970's. The new equipment will enhance service quality, delivery, and diagnostic capability.

There are thirty dentists in Tuscarawas County. Only 10% accept the medical card! Of those three in the county, one is a part-time dentist. The Ohio Department of Health, Bureau of Oral Health Services, indicates the ratio of dentist to patient in Tuscarawas County is 1 : 2,841. Tuscarawas County is 37% below the state average in patient to dentist ratio. It is significant to note the southern part of Tuscarawas County is designated as a shortage area for health professionals in general.

- **Amount of Funds and Fiscal Year**

A request of $40,960 in calendar year 2004, from the Austin Bailey Health and Wellness Foundation, would significantly reduce the financial burden created by serving dental needs of the uninsured, underinsured, poor, children, single parents, the addicted, and the aging. A contract dental hygienist would be XXXXX annually (for a half-time basis, which is equivalent to 20 hours per week). The Panoramic X-Ray Machine is $24,960 and the required Developer equipment is $3,000.

In addition to the efficient prevention capability a dental hygienist would provide, we feel this proposal would be a wise and prudent expenditure of funds to equip the dental program with comprehensive diagnostic tools. Our agency assures that any financial assistance will benefit many individuals who have no other treatment option but the health department.

The needs of our dental patients are great. Anything the Austin-Bailey Health and Wellness Foundation can do to assist us will be put to good economic and social use. Our organization thanks you for considering this proposal.
aji:Word®/Austin-Bailey 1 Page--2004

DEPARTMENTAL BUDGET FOR THE YEAR 2004   -1-
TUSCARAWAS COUNTY GENERAL HEALTH DISTRICT

APPROVED BY:_____

FUND: ALL FUNDS

Jun-2004 RECEIPT CLASSIFICATION	RECEIPTS 2002	APPROPRIATION 2003	APPROPRIATION 2004
BCMH	$34,713.76	$34,000.00	$30,500.00
CAPITAL IMPROVEMENT	$25,000.00	$25,000.00	$25,000.00
CONTRACTS	$473,364.69	$466,000.00	$410,500.00
DENTAL	$44,576.82	$43,000.00	$17,000.00
GRANTS	$831,244.24	$804,500.00	$872,500.00
HEALTH LEVY	$862,013.28	$850,000.00	$915,000.00
INSURANCE	$54,497.04	$49,500.00	$46,500.00
MEDICAID	$278,708.69	$258,500.00	$255,000.00
MEDICARE	$57,016.43	$53,200.00	$38,200.00
MOSQUITO PROGRAM	$8,732.85	$5,000.00	$7,000.00
OTHER	$43,921.85	$16,400.00	$32,300.00
PATIENT PAY	$173,682.45	$166,000.00	$176,000.00
PERMITS & LICENSES	$397,400.63	$355,350.00	$343,250.00
SPEECH THERAPY	$13,325.08	$11,000.00	$5,000.00
STATE SUBSIDY	$24,529.55	$24,000.00	$21,000.00
SUBDIVISION SHARE	$25,000.00	$25,000.00	$25,000.00
TB REGISTRY	$5,600.00	$5,600.00	$5,600.00
VITAL STATISTICS	$63,480.00	$59,000.00	$63,000.00
SAFE KIDS	$0.00	$5,000.00	$16,000.00
TRANSFERS	$45,669.69	$0.00	$0.00
*TOTAL RECEIPTS:	$3,462,477.05	$3,256,050.00	$3,304,350.00

FUND: ALL FUNDS

EXPENDITURE CLASSIFICATION	EXPENDITURE 2002	APPROPRIATION 2003	APPROPRIATION 2004
CAPITAL IMPROVEMENTS	$9,236.04	$25,000.00	$25,000.00
CONTRACTS	$486,424.27	$438,850.00	$541,960.00
DEFICIT TRUST FUND	$0.00	$0.00	$0.00
EQUIPMENT	$26,220.79	$26,500.00	$44,845.00
LIFE INSURANCE	$3,034.24	$3,639.00	$3,490.00
MAINTENANCE/VEHICLES	$23,290.00	$3,000.00	$3,650.00
MEDICAL INSURANCE	$315,818.96	$336,314.00	$328,085.00
MEDICARE INSURANCE	$19,731.90	$23,856.00	$21,495.00
OTHER	$28,527.41	$17,486.00	$22,625.00
PERS	$222,668.70	$236,225.00	$229,450.00
REMITTANCE TO STATE	$150,930.55	$94,500.00	$108,600.00
RENT	$8,300.00	$8,300.00	$15,000.00
SALARIES	$1,663,357.79	$1,738,728.00	$1,648,455.00
SUPPLIES	$203,244.95	$196,405.00	$219,380.00
TRAINING	$0.00	$0.00	$5,400.00
TRAVEL/TRAINING	$34,444.48	$50,750.00	$31,155.00
UNEMPLOYMENT	$1,225.70	$2,050.00	$1,795.00
WORKERS' COMP.	$11,487.29	$54,447.00	$53,965.00
TRANSFERS	$47,742.00	$0.00	$0.00
*TOTAL EXPENDITURE:	$3,255,685.07	$3,256,050.00	$3,304,350.00

Austin • Bailey
HEALTH AND WELLNESS FOUNDATION

August 5, 2004

Ms. Linda J. Fanning, Executive Director
Tuscarawas County Health Department
897 East Iron Avenue
Dover, Ohio 44622

Dear Linda:

Our Grant Screening Committee has reviewed your recent grant request, and has asked me to communicate with you about their initial meeting. During our discussion about your request, it was felt that clarification of several areas would be helpful to us. Therefore, please respond to the following:

➢ Please give us information that explains how the Panoramic X-ray machine is superior to conventional X-ray equipment, and how will it enhance the service that you provide?

➢ If funds were available, could you employ a dental hygienist full time rather than part time? If so, would it help if we funded $26,000 for a full time hygienist and a portion of the Panoramic X-ray unit making that portion a challenge grant?

In order to ensure fair and equitable review of all grant applications, the Austin-Bailey Health and Wellness Foundation must receive your response to these questions **by noon of August 19, 2004.** Please submit six (6) copies of your response.

Please be assured that all proposals are thoroughly and prudently evaluated. Submission of a proposal, however, does not guarantee approval of a grant request. If you have any questions or concerns about this request, please contact me at 330-580-2380.

Sincerely,

Don A. Sultzbach
Executive Director

2719 Fulton Drive, NW
Suite D
Canton, Ohio 44718
330.580.2380
fax 330.580.2381
email abfdn@cannet.com

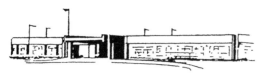

TUSCARAWAS COUNTY HEALTH DEPARTMENT

897 East Iron Avenue., P.O. Box 443
Dover, Ohio 44622-0443
Fax #: (330) 343-1601

Main Office: (330) 343-5555 or 1-800-860-8302	*Administration*	*Environmental Health*
Family Planning or Dental: (330) 364-5718	*(330) 343-4928*	*(330) 343-5550*
Well Child or Family Practice: (330) 364-4979		

Web page: www.ccthealth.org.

August 19, 2004

Don A. Sultzbach
Executive Director
Austin Bailey Health & Wellness Foundation
2719 Fulton Dr., NW, Suite D
Canton OH 44718

Dear Don:

Thank you and your committee for reviewing our recent request for dental grant funds. This letter will address the Grant Screening Committee's concerns.

- *The following is an explanation of the panoramic x-ray machine compared to the conventional x-ray machine. The panorex x-ray is a multi purpose diagnostic tool used in many areas of dentistry. It is an x-ray that gives the doctor a view of the patient from ear to ear and chin to eyes. The x-ray measures 4 inches by 12 inches in size. It allows you to evaluate the patients' whole mouth at one time. It is a great tool used to locate the root size and shape of teeth for extractions. Also, you can study the bone height around each tooth to help determine the patients' periodontal condition. It is ideal for identifying any bone abnormalities such as cysts, tumors or malignancies. One cannot perform a thorough oral cancer examination without one. Also, from the insurance or Medicaid authorization standpoint, one panorex x-ray can be submitted for that process. Unlike now, at the clinic we are required to take a full mouth series. The full mouth series of x-rays consists of fourteen individual x-rays. One can realize the benefit of less radiation exposure to the patient by receiving one x-ray instead of fourteen.*

Because of the need for this unit in patient care prevention we would be willing to accept a portion of financial responsibility in the form of a "challenge grant".

- *Our office would not have the funds to continue employment of a full time dental hygienist position after one year. A full time position would be forty (40) hours per week requiring fringe benefits to be paid. We could however hire a hygienist for up to thirty (30) hours per week on a contract basis for XXXXX.*

If you have any questions regarding any of the above, please contact me at 330-343-4928. Thank you for your considerations regarding this matter.

Sincerely,

Linda J. Fanning

Linda J. Fanning
Executive Director

Linda J. Fanning
Executive Director

"Equal Opportunity Employer/Equal Provider of Services"

Austin • Bailey

September 15, 2004

Ms. Linda J. Fanning, Executive Director
Tuscarawas County Health Department
897 East Iron Avenue
Dover, Ohio 44622

Dear Linda:

Your request for $40,960 has been reviewed by our Board of Trustees, and they concur that oral health care is a major need for low-income families served by your health department. After reviewing your response to my August 5 letter, the Board could see the value in hiring a dental hygienist on a part time 30 hours per week basis. You indicated that the cost would be XXXXX. They also could understand much better the real benefits of the panoramic x-ray machine. The cost of this is just under $25,000 plus $3,000 for a needed developer. Total cost for this project is $48,000.

I am writing to advise you that the Board of Trustees has approved a grant in the amount of $48,000 to support your dental clinic in the ways described above. We feel that by funding the full cost we can enable you to more quickly enhance the services you provide as opposed to a challenge grant approach as outlined in my August 5 letter.

Thank you for inviting us to continue to support the Tuscarawas County Health Department oral health program. Enclosed please find a blank copy of the grant agreement for your review. We will contact you soon to make arrangements to come to our office to sign the agreement.

Thank you again and good luck in your continuing efforts with this valuable program.

Sincerely,

Don A. Sultzbach
Executive Director

2719 Fulton Drive, NW
Suite D
Canton, Ohio 44718
330.580.2380
fax 330.580.2381
email abfdn@cannet.com

Chapter 8

Seed Money

Usually defined as grants to start, establish, or initiate new projects or organizations, these grants may also be called "start-up" funds, and they cover salaries and other operating expenses. Sometimes in subsequent years this funding translates into general operating support for the organization, but more often than not it does not. Funders that award seed money grants expect the organization or project, once up and running, to find other means to support itself and not be dependent on repeat funding from the very same grantmakers that supported it initially.

Awarding seed money entails a greater exposure to risk for a foundation than does giving to more established organizations, since often the organization requesting the funding is new, without an established history and evidence of success. Consequently, it is much more difficult to find foundations willing to fund in this area. Grantseekers who are just beginning to formalize their nonprofits' programs need to focus on establishing the best possible match. They need to search for foundations interested in their subject field, their community, and/or the population group they serve, who will also consider awarding seed money grants.

Where possible, grantseekers in start-up situations should take extra care in the body of the proposal to reassure the funder by mentioning prominent board members, experienced staff, community support, and well-thought-out strategies for achieving results early on. The three seed money proposals included in this chapter are all to initiate programs of benefit to underserved members of the population. Unique audience needs and how these new projects will respond to them are well highlighted in the body of these proposals.

The first proposal included here is a seed money proposal from Reentry Solutions of Oakland, California to Echoing Green of New York, requesting $60,000 for an initiative to reintegrate offenders and exoffenders into their families and communities. The proposal, which was submitted online at Echoing Green's Web site, describes in a number of ways how this organization is well positioned to carry out its programs. The fact that this is a truly grassroots organization with exprisoners training exprisoners in leadership development made a compelling argument to the funder.

The second proposal in this chapter is from the San Diego Military Counseling Project (SDMCP), a support organization for military service members who express opposition to the military's role or to their own role in the military. This proposal, seeking $2,000 from the Agape Foundation of San Francisco, California, establishes the organization's need to expand into larger quarters. In this instance, the Peace Resource Center acted as the fiscal sponsor for the newly formed SDMCP. For a brand new operation, or one that does not have 501(c)3 status, fiscal sponsorship may be a good approach to broaden eligibility for funding.

The final seed money proposal in this chapter was submitted by Summer Search New York City to the Blue Ridge Foundation New York. Summer Search, a leadership development organization for low-income students, already has branches in other parts of the country, but this proposal was specifically to start a new branch in New York City. The purpose of the grant is to provide summer educational experiences, mentoring, and college counseling to New York City youth. Unusual in a proposal of this nature (and not necessarily recommended), there is no request for a specific amount of money in this proposal, although the cover letter alludes to a shortage of $205,000. As the grants decision maker notes in his commentary, awarding funding for seed money often hinges on the qualifications of the people who run the program. And the foundation's trustees seem impressed with the leadership of this organization.

Reentry Solutions
Oakland, California

To

Echoing Green
New York, New York

Requested amount: $60,000 fellowship; **Amount received:** $60,000 fellowship

Funder's comments:

"Echoing Green requires an initial short application, after which applicants that best meet the Echoing Green fellowship criteria are invited to submit a full proposal. All applications are submitted through our Web site. For second-stage applications we ask applicants to submit a budget, innovation matrix, and three letters of recommendation. The questions in the online application directly relate to the criteria used in evaluating the proposal; here, as with any proposal, it is important that the applicants are careful to answer the questions that are asked and keep the criteria in mind as they are developing the proposal.

"Echoing Green provides seed funding and support to launch social change organizations around the world. This proposal's need statement was compelling in that it built a case for why a new organization must be created, versus a new program in an existing organization. It is also directly connected to the proposed strategy—there is a seamlessness between the scope of the problem and the scope of the project. In addition, the need statement makes effective use of statistics, including references to reputable sources.

"The proposal's strongest feature is its theory of change, because it pulls together the mission with a model. The text is very clear, with the applicant's well thought-out opinions related to change coming through in the writing. While this approach can be risky, it can also connect with the funder in an important way.

"The proposal writer communicated a sense of timeliness, demonstrating that there was a window of opportunity for creating this organization. Overall, the proposal exhibits consistency, maturity, and thoughtfulness."

—*Lara Galinsky, Vice President, Strategy, Echoing Green*

Notes:

The proposal was written and submitted via online application at Echoing Green's Web site. Proposal written by Mark Toney, Executive Director.

Project Name:	Reentry Solutions
Have you applied to Echoing Green before?	No
Where will the project be based?	Oakland, California United States
How did you hear about the fellowship?	Fellow or former Fellow

What is the breadth of the geographic coverage of your project?

National

How long has your project been in existence?

Less than one year

What is the one category that most accurately describes your project?

Civil and Human Rights

What is the one population served that best fits your constituency?

Offenders and Ex-Offenders

What is the change that you want to see in the world? What is your new idea for driving this change? When and how did you come up with it?

Reentry Solutions is a two-year pilot community reentry project that promotes racial justice by organizing to eliminate employment, housing, education, voting and other forms of discrimination exercised against ex-prisoners and their communities.

Reentry Solutions seeks to build organizational networks, provide leadership training to former prisoners, and initiate reentry justice organizing campaigns in California, Texas, and New York, which together account for more than one-third of all former prisoners in the U.S.

I developed the concept behind Reentry Solutions after a year of community-based research on criminal justice issues while I worked at Center for Third World Organizing, which identified community reentry as a critical issue to which few resources have been devoted. CTWO was not interested in reentry work beyond the research phase, so I decided to initiate a new reentry project after departing CTWO at the end of 2003.

As specifically as possible, demonstrate the need for your organization. Use statistics and references.

A record number of parolees are returning home to their communities. The Bureau of Justice Statistics estimates that the number of former prisoners has risen to 4,300,000 and that an additional 630,000 persons will be released from state and federal prisons in 2004. Yet few resources support community reintegration or challenge institutional roadblocks.

Discrimination against former prisoners in employment, housing, education and benefits contributes to high rates of recidivism. Bureau of Justice Statistics reports that 67% of released prisoners are rearrested within three years. This discrimination has a racial dimension. The Sentencing Project reports that Blacks constitute 13% of all drug users, but represent 35% of arrests for drug possession, 55% of convictions, and 74% of prison sentences.

Yet, change is possible. The passage in bell-weather state California of Proposition 36 in 2000 suggest that public support can be built nationally for alternatives to incarceration.

Why have you chosen your specific approach to addressing the need defined above? What is you theory or premise about how to create real and lasting social change that underlies the vision for your organization.:

For Reentry Solutions to build a movement to restore the economic and political rights of ex-prisoners:

1) Grassroots organizations and churches in low-income communities of color where most ex-prisoners reside must be motivated to adopt community reentry as a priority issue. Movement building requires mobilizing a base of people willing to take action.

2) The leadership capacity of a core group of former prisoners must be developed for them to emerge as leaders in local campaigns for community reentry policy reform. A key premise of organizing is that people mose impacted by an issue must take leadership in achieving solutions.

3) Organizing campaigns to challenge job, housing, and voting discrimination must be launched to increase the economic and political participation of former prisoners. While each state network will have to prioritize policy proposals based upon local conditions, campaigns in each state will all reinforce common messages of fair treatment and racial justice.

Innovation is important to Echoing Green. Explain how your approach to addressing the need defined above is truly innovative or unique. Provide specific examples of innovative activities or strategies that will make your approach more effective than approaches taken by other organizations. (Note that you must also complete the innovation matrix; this matrix will provide you to opportunity to present side-by-side comparisons with other organizations working in your field.)

Reentry Solutions is innovative because it is transformative in its approach to:

1) Guiding key grassroots organizations through a process of political education and power analysis in which communtiy reentry as a top priority. Campaigns for jobs, housing, and political representation if prison records no longer render a sizeable portion of community residents ineligible.

2) Developing the capacity of former prisoners to emerge as leaders and staff of organizing campaigns for fair community reentry policies. While a few former prisoners are involved in writing, speaking, and research, even fewer are involved in developing organizing strategies to develop policy reforms.

3) Initiate organizing campaigns to develop and advocate for the adoption of model community renetry proposals that reduce discrimination and increase opportunity for former prisoners. With the notable exception of voting rights, there remains little organizing for the economic and political rights of ex-prisoners.

Identify your long term desired outcomes. Describe the activities and/or services that your organization will engage in to deliver these outcomes:

1) Document barriers to ex-prisoners in employment, housing, benefits, education, and voting.

a) Identify discriminatory policies and practices.

b) Interview former prisoners.

2) Create networks of organizations committed to reentry policy work.

a) Develop self-assessment tools for grassroots organizations.

b) Measure local racial impact of disenfranchisement and diversion of funding.

3) Elevate ex-prisoners into policy debates on issues of community reentry.

a) Sponsor 3-day leadership development training for 12 ex-prisoners.

b) Provide on-going consultation to ex-prisoner leaders.

4) Draft policy proposals designed to reduce barriers to community reentry.

a) Publish policy briefing kits.

b) Develop core messages and communications strategy.

5) Implement a model organizing campaign to reduce barriers to community reentry.

a) Recruit ex-prisoners, families, service providers, political leaders, and others.

b) Implement press events, testimonials, direct actions, publications.

How will you measure the impact of your work in the communities that you serve?:

1) Generate 3-4 media stories on barriers to community reentry in each state within 6 months of publishing report documenting discrimination against ex-prisoners.

2) Recruit one organization to serve as network coordinator and 5-10 partner organizations in each state who are committed to participating in organizing campaigns promoting the civil rights of former prisoners.

3) Train and provide on-going development to five ex-prisoners in each state to exercise leadership in their networks and organizing campaigns.

4) Develop 3-5 specific model policy proposals to reduce barriers to community reentry for former prisoners.

5) Convene over 100 people at major hearings and direct actions that promote policy reform.

Why you? Why now? How are you uniquely qualified to take on this challenge? What personal or environmental factors are driving you to make this commitment at this time?

As an Echoing Green Fellow, I would bring a track record of founding successful organizations, a wealth of experience to share with other Fellows, and the motivation to make the most of the experience and resources possessed by other Fellows.

My greatest accomplishment during my eight years as Founding Executive Director of Direct Action for Rights & Equality in Providence, was to provide the staff and leaders sufficient development that the organizations continues to thrive ten years after my departure.

I offer other Echoing Green Fellows considerable experience from twenty years of developing leaders, building organizations, and developing social change organzing campaigns.

Starting an organization today is more difficult than at any time during the past twenty years. Financial resources and peer support from Echoing Green would greatly enhance the prospects of a successful launch and long term sustainability for Reentry Solutions.

Describe your experience with the proposed constituency or community. Describe your experience in providing the proposed services and/or working within the program area.

Last year, I led an ex-prisoner health needs research project that consisted of interviews with service providers and former prisoners. Key findings included:

1) Drug rehabilitation is critical in addressing the issue of reentry and reducing recidivism.

2) Housing and transportation are essential in order to access basic health services.

3) Lack of adequate job skills, education, and training, as well as discrimination by employers and legal restrictions, prevent many from finding a job.

Last summer I supervised an ex-prisoner in CTWO's organizer internship, learning that changes are needed to train ex-prisoners to be effective policy advocates and organizers.

1) Issue-specific training sessions focusing on reentry barriers and policy alternatives.

2) Internship placements in ex-prisoners' local communities instead of being placed out of state.

3) Crisis intervention systems need to be put into place to help ex-prisoners deal with housing emergencies or parole system requirements.

On the organizational budget form you have identified the financial resources that you have secured to date as well as the resources you estimate you will need to build and run your organization over the next two years. For most applicants, there will be a gap between resources currently on hand and resources required. As specifically as possible, explain how you plan to close that gap for your organization.

As an independent project in its start-up phase, Reentry Solutions has no current funding commitments or proposals pending. However, in exploratory discussions, program officers from Open Society Institute, the Jeht Foundation, and The California Endowment have expressed interest in supporting the principles underlying the project as it develops.

Seed funding from Echoing Green can provide initial resources necessary to jumpstart Reentry Solutions project activities, as well as leverage funding from major foundations and donors.

Describe the major challenges and obstacles that you anticipate for this organization and how you will overcome them.

Organizing former prisoners brings with it the unique challenge of doing so without violating conditions of parole, which prohibit parolees from associating with other people with prison records. Since parole violations account for half of the two-thirds of parolees who are rearrested within three years of being released, recruiting former prisoners to attend meetings and join organizations with other former prisoners can be risky. It will be necessary to meet with parole officers to gain for their parolees the same kind of exemption to meet with other former prisoners as service providers receive.

Overcoming the negative stigma associated with former prisoners is another key challenge faced when recruiting grassroots organizations as Reentry Solutions partners. This shall be addressed by conducting workshops and getting media coverage highlighting that 75% of prisoners are incarcerated for nonviolent crimes.

A Proposal From

San Diego Military Counseling Project (SDMCP)

San Diego, California

To

Agape Foundation

San Francisco, California

Requested amount: $2,000; **Amount received:** $2,000

Funder's comments:

"At the Agape Foundation, we require each grantseeker to complete a cover sheet that includes the organization's contact information and mission, the amount requested, and the purpose of the grant. The San Diego Military Counseling Project complied with this requirement neatly and legibly. While all of the components one would expect to find in a proposal were present, the section on the grant amount requested and its proposed use was particularly well written. SDMCP also incorporated into this section the methods they would employ to evaluate the effectiveness of the grant. The remaining components were well balanced and they provided the content that we requested in the appropriate number of pages. They did not include a cover letter or attachments because they are not required.

"The writing style was cogent, tight, and free of jargon. The proposal was easy on the eye. By way of formatting, the proposal writer made sure to indent each paragraph and left plenty of white space on the page. The use of headings made it easy to determine that they had addressed all of the required areas, responded to questions, and covered all topics. The budget included just the right amount of information and reflected the programs outlined in the narrative of the proposal.

"The strongest features of the proposal in my view were the quality and style of writing. They also managed to tell two brief, one-paragraph stories that spoke to their effectiveness and the need for their program.

"We did have some questions for this group after the proposal was submitted. But this is standard procedure for our foundation. Our board of trustees always returns to the grantee with questions, regardless of the quality of the proposal. At least two board members as well as the staff review each proposal. And after a board member reviews a proposal s/he completes a brief questionnaire for use in the evaluation process. At that point the proposal reviewer is asked what question(s) s/he would like to ask the applicant. Unfortunately, I no longer have a copy of the questions that the board asked of this particular applicant."

—*Karen Topakian, Executive Director, Agape Foundation*

Notes:
The proposal was written using the Agape Foundation grant request cover sheet and guidelines.
Proposal written by Michelle Raymond, Organizer and Counselor.

AGAPE FOUNDATION BOARD OF TRUSTEES GRANTS - FALL 2004

Name of organization and/or project: San Diego Military Counseling Project (SDMCP)

Year founded: 2003   **Tax-exempt status (circle):** Y/N/Pending
Fiscal Sponsor: Peace Resource Center, P.O. Box 15307, San Diego, CA 92175
          (501c3 established 1980)

Summarize the organization's mission

San Diego Military Counseling Project empowers, encourages, and supports service members involved in individual and collective expression of opposition to the military's role and their participation in it, who challenge the moral and political bases of their orders, who refuse to continue in the roles to which they have been assigned, and who find themselves at odds with or mistreated by their commands.

Purpose of the grant

A grant from Agape will establish a permanent location as a center for anti-militarism in central San Diego. The center will be a safe place for service members to gather, learn about their rights, and organize cooperatively from the inside in opposition to the military. The center will also function as a gathering place for people working in anti-military organizations.

Total organizational budget (current year): $ 8,800
Grant amount requested: $ 2,000

Director: Leadership is shared among all members.
Contact person & title: Michelle Raymond, Volunteer Counselor and Organizer
Address: P.O. Box 15307   **City, State, Zip code:** San Diego, CA 92175
Telephone: (619) 280-3586   **Fax number:** (619) 293-9345
E-mail: info@sdmcp.org   **Website:** www.sdmcp.org
Please tell us how you heard about us: Referred by SDMCP Volunteer Counselor and Organizer Carol Jahnkow from the Peace Resource Center.

To be filled out by Agape staff (please do not write below this line).

Granting history with Agape:
Staff Review: ___Proposal incomplete   ___Budget >$100   ___>5yrs old   ___Outside CA
          ___ Does not fit Agape's priorities   ___Not on topic (Spring only)

1st Board review by: _____ Accept___ Reject___ Re-apply? ___
____Other comments - If rejected, why:

2nd Board review by: _____Accept___ Reject___ Re-apply? ___
____Other comments - If rejected, why:

Amount granted: $ _____   Fund: _____

Amount granted: $ _____   Fund: _____

San Diego Military Counseling Project (SDMCP)
Contact Person: Michelle Raymond
Address: P.O. Box 15307, San Diego, CA 92175
Telephone: (619) 280-3586
Email: info@sdmcp.org

Grant amount and its proposed use

A $2,000 grant will establish a two (or more) room office as a permanent center. The center will function on three fronts: for military service members, for San Diego Military Counseling Project (SDMCP), and for other organizations in the anti-military community. First, the center will be a safe place for service members to gather, learn about their rights, and organize cooperatively from the inside in opposition to the military. Second, the center will be used for the nightly walk-in and phone session, as a training center for new counselors/organizers, and as a location for organizational meetings. Finally, we will use the location to host outreach events and forums on GI Rights issues and to collaborate with local activist and community organizations.

SDMCP is outgrowing the current meeting locations. Currently, we host a two-hour per week walk-in session in a donated single room at a church. The session averages two to three service members per week and is increasing. The room gets very noisy, crowded, and there is no privacy. Also, since it is a church it may be uncomfortable for people who are not religious or are of another faith. There have been a few nights when the room was not available due to other events at the church. Additionally, organizational and collaborative meetings are held in SDMCP volunteers' living rooms, which are becoming inadequate as we increase the number of counselors/organizers and work with other organizations.

The office will serve as a center for anti-militarism, so it will be centrally located, convenient to military personnel, and could easily be a shared office for use during the evening and weekends. We anticipate acquiring an office in December and expect the cost to be $4,000 per year or about $350 per month. We presently donate $25 per month to the church location. For 2004, our office rent will total around $650. A grant from Agape of $2,000 will fund the center for the critical first 6 months from December 2004 through May 2005.

This campaign will be evaluated by monitoring the number of service members getting involved, the number of new counselors/organizers, and new relations with local activist and community organizations. Success will be indicated by increasing the number of service members to the walk-in session from two to five per week, to increase the number of counselors/organizers from seven to 12, and to host four events with affinity groups over the next year. Additionally, phone calls will increase from 50 to 100 per month and emails will increase from five to 15 per month.

San Diego Military Counseling Project mission statement

Project volunteers are currently working on finalizing a mission statement. Presented here is the interim draft of our mission statement.

San Diego Military Counseling Project empowers, encourages, and supports service members involved in individual and collective expression of opposition to the military's role and their participation in it, who challenge the moral and political bases of their orders, who refuse to continue in the roles to which they have been assigned, and who find themselves at odds with or mistreated by their commands.

How San Diego Military Counseling Project practices and promotes nonviolence

Nonviolence advocates initiated the Military Counseling Project in recognition that service members are potentially the greatest advocates of nonviolence. We empower service members who challenge and directly oppose war, preparations for war, and military policy, culture, and injustice. We encourage and support service members involved in protest activities, organizing campaigns, and we promote collaborations with peace organizations. We work with service members to stand up to the military, tell their stories, and to fight back with dignity and honor.

Organization description and history: major accomplishments, purpose, decision making process, and number of and diversity of volunteers

San Diego Military Counseling Project was initiated by members of the Peace Resource Center, the National Lawyers Guild - San Diego Chapter, the San Diego Coalition for Peace and Justice, and the Military Law Task Force. Five people, including two who are experienced counselors/organizers, collaborated to host a one-day training and recruiting session in June 2003. A core group of seven people continued to meet for training and organizational development. Phone counseling commenced in November 2003 and walk-in counseling commenced in January 2004. SDMCP now provides information five nights a week to GIs in the San Diego and Camp Pendleton area about their rights in the military, regulations, and procedures on topics ranging from discharge applications and right of service members to dissent to procedures for filing formal complaints against command abuse or mistreatment.

The San Diego/Camp Pendleton region is home to the largest military installation in the world with 95,000 active-duty military in San Diego County. 1/5 of the service members who went to Iraq were from this area. Furthermore, the National GI Rights Hotline Network responds to over 36,000 calls a year, with more than 800 calls originating from the San Diego area. The calls to the national 1-800 number are routed directly to SDMCP. Through handling these calls and establishing a local presence, the Military Counseling Project provides an important connection for service members to anti-war efforts in our community and gives voice to the anti-war sentiment and discontent amongst service members and their families.

The structure of San Diego Military Counseling Project is non-hierarchical, democratic, and decisions are made by consensus. During business meetings volunteers decide which projects and activities to pursue and participate in. There are two monthly business meetings that are overseen by the facilitator. The role of facilitator rotates once a month among volunteers. Decisions are made and priorities are set on a modified consensus basis. Every effort is made to achieve decisions on a consensus basis, however, when all parties feel they have sufficiently contributed their views, but consensus has not been achieved, a vote may be held.

The Military Counseling Project is staffed on an all-volunteer basis and consists of 7 members. Presently, the counselor/organizer demographics do not directly reflect the service member constituency that we work with. One counselor, Hal, is a Navy veteran. We are constantly building relationships with service members, several of whom have expressed some interest in becoming counselors/organizers. We will have several veterans and service members attend the training session in September.

SDMCP is working with activists in the Mexican community and to improve the availability of counseling in Spanish. One counselor, Lynn, is a fluent Spanish speaker. We are teaching counseling skills to Fernando Suarez del Solar and several other members of the San Diego Chapter of Military Families Speak Out who speak Spanish as their primary language. We are also having outreach materials translated to Spanish.

Rationale and work of your organization

As the occupation of Iraq and Afghanistan drags on, active duty military service members are in a state of unrest. Increasingly they are suicidal, questioning their roles in the military, wanting to avoid war-related assignments, and looking for alternatives to completing their obligations to the military. One example is D, a constituent of SDMCP:

D reported to boot camp just eight weeks before. He had sustained a knee injury, was depressed, and was suicidal. D had attempted suicide, but the Marines psychologist reported that the suicide was merely an attempt to get out of the military and sent him back to his unit. The counselor, Lynn, worked with the local congressional military liaison to begin an inquiry into the case and also enlisted help from a psychologist to draw up a full psychological evaluation to present to the Marines psychologist and the congressional liaison. Within a week Lynn heard from D. He was granted a discharge and was calling from home in Oklahoma.

The Military Counseling Project provides support and resources to military service members who have come to oppose their mission as enforcers of American Imperialism, who are questioning the moral and political basis of the orders they are being forced to carry out, and who can't continue for reasons that they are as yet unable to articulate. SDMCP assists service members in saying no to war, refusing war related assignments, and seeking military discharges.

Conscientious Objectors who work with counselors/organizers increase their likelihood of a discharge from 14% to 94%. Currently we are working with several Objectors on developing their discharge applications. We have also begun working with a group of Objectors from the one unit who served together in the Iraq war. They are taking a powerful position of standing up collectively to their command. Objectors often become the strongest advocates of peace because they must thoroughly justify their beliefs as deeply felt and sincere.

We empower service members who have been mistreated, maligned, harassed, and discriminated against. We support and encourage service members to speak out publicly regarding military culture and injustices. One young client, J, teared up as he told us:

> "The military is the most racist, sexist, homophobic organization I've ever seen; it's *horrible.*" J had sustained a back injury while in the Coast Guard. He was presented the paperwork for discharge, which didn't recognize his injury and would cut his veterans benefits. He decided to fight for his benefits and enlisted our assistance to do so. Through our efforts, J was discharged with full recognition of his injury and veterans benefits. Since then, J has been actively speaking at rallies, to service members, and to military families about the military injustices he witnessed both against himself and others.

Volunteers are working on many programs to build relationships with service members and local communities. Our Fund-a-Bus campaign will place advertisements on local transit buses to outreach to service members. We are developing a relationship with the local chapter of Military Families Speak Out (MFSO) that we anticipate will serve as a model for the national MFSO and GI Rights organizations. We are collaborating with MFSO to begin a bimonthly newsletter that will host articles written by and for service members and their families about issues that most concern them. The first newsletter will be completed by mid-August and distributed locally in military communities and leafleted at military bases and events. We are also establishing relationships with members of the Psychological Association of San Diego, who we will co-host events with to educate families, communities, service members, and counselors/organizers on post-traumatic stress disorder. Finally, we are developing a recruiting and training program to expand the pool of counselors/organizers.

Funding priorities and statement of philosophy of social change

Volunteers of San Diego Military Counseling Project are organizers within various local peace groups, working against militarism, war, and in the interest of social justice. We empower, encourage, and collaborate with service members who challenge and directly oppose war, preparations for war, and military policy and culture. Since we actively work against the interests of the military, it is unlikely that we will secure funding from traditional sources or government funding. Future counselor/organizer recruitment will be to peace, veteran, minority organizations, and to constituents of the Military Counseling Project.

A collective, growing discontent within the military can help to change U.S. domestic and foreign policy. When service members increasingly exercise their rights to benefits and discharge, they are evidence of the growing discontent within the military. Supporting service members in their fight against military cruelty in a public and outspoken way has the potential to alter the public view of the military. This leads to public pressure on policymakers to change U.S. domestic policy. Military counseling seeks to assist in cases resulting in changes in military policy. With respect to foreign policy, the GI movement helped to end the Vietnam War and can help to end present military operations and preparations for war in the future. We support, celebrate, and honor anti-war service members and encourage them to speak out publicly about the realities of war and military service.

Key Members/Leaders and their occupations

Hal Brody: Navy veteran. Mechanical engineer acting as Project Coordinator for the construction of the environmentally sensitive Friends Center (non-profit building in San Diego).
Larry Christian: Electrical engineer, designing electrical systems for buildings.
Kathleen Gilberd: Paralegal counselor in the area of military administration for 30 years. Co-chair of the National Lawyers Guild, Military Law Task Force and co-editor of its publication, On Watch.
Lynn Gonzalez: Bilingual elementary school teacher for 12 years.
Carol Jahnkow: Executive director of the Peace Resource Center of San Diego for 22 years.
Katherine Miller: Life-time community and youth activist, retired administrative assistant.
Michelle Raymond: High school math teacher.

Funding Sources

- $500 from San Diego Foundation for Change, Granted September 2003
- $50/month stipend from National Lawyers Guild – San Diego Chapter, Granted November 2003
- $3000 from Resist, Granted May 2004
- $1500 from AJ Muste, Granted June 2004
- Two fundraisers, February 2004 and December 2004
- Individual donations for the Fund-a-Bus campaign
- SDMCP volunteer cash and in-kind donations
- SDMCP will seek FY 2005 funding from Resist, San Diego Foundation for Change, Samuel Rubin Foundation, Inc and submit letters of inquiry to several other potential funders.

Financial Statement and Budgets

San Diego Military Counseling Project was founded in June 2003 and began a budget in November 2003. Therefore, SDMCP does not have an established financial statement for the previous year. The current annual organizational income and expense budgets are attached.

ORGANIZATIONAL INCOME (PROJECTED)
FY 2004

Major Gifts	$0
Membership	$0
Sale of products	
Manuals	$100
Special Events	
Fundraising Event	$750
Individual Donations	$2,435
Fees for Service	
Foundations	
Resist	$3,000
AJ Muste	$1,500 *
National Lawyers Guild	$600
Agape	$2,000 **
Other (specify)	
In-kind contributions	$500
Training donations	$315
TOTAL	$11,200

* $750 of the AJ Muste grant will be used in FY 2004 and $750 of the AJ Muste grant will be used in FY 2005.

** $350 of the Agape grant will be used in FY 2004 and $1650 of the Agape grant will be used in FY 2005.

ORGANIZATIONAL EXPENSE (PROJECTED)
FY 2004

Personnel Expenses	$0
Total Personnel Expenses	$0
Office Expenses	
Office Rent	$650
Office Equipment	$0
Telephone	$1,800
Office Supplies	$200
Printing/Photocopy	
Brochures	$400
Envelopes	$50
Mail Appeals	$0
Annual Report	$0
Newsletters	$600
Stationary	$0
Other: Stickers, bus ads	$300
Total Printing	$1,350
Postage	
First Class	$400
Total Postage	$400
Miscellaneous	
Web Services	$400
Promotion/Outreach	$4,000
TOTAL	$8,800

A Proposal From

Summer Search New York City
Brooklyn, New York

To

Blue Ridge Foundation New York
Brooklyn, New York

Requested amount: Unspecified; **Amount received:** $130,000

Funder's comments:

"Blue Ridge Foundation New York supports start-up nonprofits in New York City with funding, back office support, and management assistance. Summer Search, although it operated in several cities already, applied to us for funding to support the launch and development of its first office and programs in New York. Blue Ridge Foundation New York, like many funders, makes decisions based on two overarching considerations: the people and the idea.

"Summer Search's application only briefly described New York's leadership team, but what it said was important. The founding executive director had started and run a Summer Search program in another city, and the associate director was an alumna of the program. These were important characteristics to highlight and demonstrated the managerial capacity of the people applying, as well as their commitment to the organization. Key details that speak to the abilities and passion of the leadership team should always be included.

"The rest of the application also provided clues about the people behind the proposal. It was well written, and this is critical—it speaks to the organization's ability to fundraise from other sources, since most fundraising occurs through grant writing, and almost all foundations want to give to organizations that will find support from other sources as well. The writing also suggested a team that was strategic and thoughtful; rather than simply describing the program activities, the application took pains to explain why the model is organized as it is. This approach, although it added to the overall length of the proposal, conveyed thoughtfulness and reflection on the part of the organization.

"The proposal presents the 'idea' of Summer Search well because it draws a very clear connection between the problem Summer Search is trying to address and the strategy it pursues. The narrative puts Summer Search's model of intensive mentoring and experiential learning in the context of research about adolescent development and the factors that influence college-going behavior; it convincingly makes the case that Summer Search's activities are precisely what is required by the problem the proposal identifies. The detail contained in the proposal leaves the impression that the idea is viable and the team is prepared to follow it through.

"Finally, Summer Search's application references the outcomes that the organization tracks. As has been well documented, foundations are giving increasing weight to measurable outcomes. A strong proposal will certainly specify how the applicant plans to gauge its success. But there are no 'right' outcomes that an organization must cite (although the measures must, of course, relate to a foundation's interest in a given area). It is more important that an organization have a well-reasoned rationale for why it has chosen its particular metrics. Once these measures are chosen, however, the foundation will pay attention to them—so choose wisely!"

—*Matthew Klein, Executive Director, Blue Ridge Foundation New York*

Notes:
The complete proposal included the following attachment: staff biographies.
Proposal written by Eden Werring, Executive Director, Summer Search New York City; Jay Jacobs, Chief Executive Officer, Summer Search National; Linda Mornell, Founder, Summer Search National; and Rachelle McManus, Grants Manager, Summer Search National.

December 20, 2003

Mr. Matthew Klein, Executive Director
Blue Ridge Foundation
150 Court Street
Brooklyn, NY 11201

Dear Matt,

It felt like synchronicity last week, meeting you again after all these years. Thank you so much for your interest in exploring a relationship with Summer Search. A partnership with Blue Ridge is a thrilling prospect that could simultaneously anchor and then catapult us forward in exciting and tangible ways.

I understand that most of the organizations in your portfolio are less developed in terms of their model and their progress in New York. However, I hope you will see that Summer Search is still at a fragile point of inflection where the extensive and catalytic support—both financial and in terms of office space, back office assistance, technology, strategic planning, and fundraising—of the Blue Ridge Foundation could be transformative. With Blue Ridge's backing, we could refocus our time on shoring up our infrastructure by hiring and training new staff members and cultivating a stable and ongoing base of donors. I could also put more energy into our current, active board members who, although committed to the health and longevity of Summer Search in New York City, need attention as a new group.

There is, of course, a great need overall. As you can see from our budget and prospective funders for 2004, assuming that all of our 2003 contributors give again, we are still $205,000 short of our budget for next year. That, combined with what has been almost explosive growth in the last year, makes us vulnerable. Also, within five years, our goal is to serve 200 young New Yorkers annually, while remaining responsible to a growing alumni base. We have demonstrated the ability to fundraise effectively, but we are also very young and still in the heart of a start-up phase. The extensive support and validation from Blue Ridge would empower us to create a situation where—fueled by an entrepreneurial sprit and the desire to not only expand, but elevate, the model of Summer Search—we could plan wisely and strategically. The bottom line is that both the critical need and the seeds of sustainability are there, and it would be an honor and a privilege to partner with you and Blue Ridge in launching this program.

Finally, it would be amazing to contribute Summer Search's unique core competencies of highly dynamic, long-term mentoring and access to life-changing summer programs to the organizations in your portfolio. As we discussed, Summer Search is designed for collaboration. I am excited to talk with the staff at Groundwork, partly because of their close association with LEAP and Heads Up, which as I told you I have long admired. Regardless of funding opportunities, I am also eager to discuss referral partnerships with iMentor and Legal Outreach. I am sure there are also creative ways to collaborate with Taproot, Women's Law, and Digital Cartography; I am very intrigued by the way you bring these diverse resources together. Overall, I'm excited by the prospect of being part of such a vibrant community and working with the other programs in Blue Ridge's portfolio.

I have enclosed the letter you requested, in addition to some supporting materials. Again, I am extremely grateful to you and John for the chance to begin this dialogue about what could be a transformative opportunity for Summer Search in New York. I look forward to our next step. Thank you.

With best wishes for a warm holiday,

Eden Werring, Executive Director
Summer Search New York City
www.summersearch.org

Summer Search New York City

"The sky is no longer my limit, just another place to reach"
-- Jenise, Summer Search NYC Student

OVERVIEW

Mission

Summer Search NYC is a leadership development organization that invests for the long-term in low-income high school students from New York City. The mission of Summer Search is to nurture resiliency, altruism, and performance in young people who are at risk of failing to fulfill their potential in order to prepare these students to break the cycle of poverty for themselves and to lead in their communities.

Summer Search accomplishes this mission through a combination of full scholarships to summer experiential education programs, intensive long-term mentoring, and access to private resources normally unavailable to low-income students, including college counseling and professional development. Throughout this unique intervention, Summer Search students engage with other young people from diverse communities, find a forum to develop their authentic voices, and integrate their past and present experiences into expanded visions for their futures. The long-term goal of Summer Search is that individual students will not only transform their own lives, but that they will develop the skills and the values to become a new generation of leaders, transforming the schools and communities in which they live.

Major Activities

It is a specific objective of Summer Search to target a highly vulnerable but often overlooked population of young people: those neither at the top nor the bottom of the class, but those in the middle for whom Summer Search's program can provide the critical experience that alters their personal development and life choices. Students are nominated on the basis of three character (rather than academic) attributes: resiliency, altruism, and performance ("RAP"). Once in the program, students participate in a unique combination of services including:

1. Year-round mentoring: Students benefit from a mandatory long-term mentoring program that involves weekly contact with a highly trained Summer Search mentor. This mentoring begins when students are interviewed in their sophomore year and continues throughout high school and college. Mentoring emphasizes self-reflection and accountability and provides a consistent and sustained relationship with a caring adult who can help students develop relational, leadership and resiliency skills.

2. Summer experiential education programs: Students are provided with eye-opening summer opportunities on challenging programs normally only accessible to affluent kids, such as wilderness leadership expeditions (like Outward Bound), academic enrichment programs (like Cornell University), and community service and home-stays overseas (like AFS). Students participate on summer programs for two summers, after sophomore and junior years.

3. College Preparatory Services: College preparation, admissions and financial aid planning services are provided to help students navigate the college process successfully.

4. Alumni Support Services: Summer Search provides significant ongoing support for graduates of the high school program through internship opportunities and professional development, emergency counseling and financial support, and networking opportunities among friends and alumni of Summer Search.

Summer Search, Page 1 of 10

Results of the Model

The clearest indication that our model does, in fact, help students break the cycle of poverty comes from the significant college completion rate and increased earning potential of our alumni. **Ninety-five percent of Summer Search students come from families with no history of college attendance**, and outcomes for these students- who are not selected for high grades or academic achievement - have been extraordinary:

- **98**% successfully complete their summer programs
- **96**% stay in Summer Search throughout high school
- **100**% of students in the program graduate from high school
- **93**% of those go on to college
- **89**% of those in college graduate or are on track to do so

PROGRAM DESCRIPTION

Problem to be Addressed

According to the Annie E. Casey Foundation's KIDS COUNT study, 18% of New York City children live in "severely distressed" neighborhoods; that is, areas with high poverty, a high incidence of single-female-headed households, high teen dropout rates, and a high percentage of unemployed males. Young people living in these communities are surrounded by risk factors such as domestic and community violence, drugs, and teenage pregnancy, and often lack the kind of role models and community supports that could help them avoid such traps. In these communities, young people often also lack access to the people, knowledge, and resources that can help them achieve, and are left profoundly isolated and deeply at risk of failing to fulfill their potential. These are the students Summer Search targets.

These New York City students also face distressing educational trends. Studies show that increasing hopelessness can influence low-income students to "dis-identify" with school and unconsciously pull away from taking advantage of the opportunities that are, in fact, available to them. This is evidenced by the high school dropout rate for low-income high school students in many of the largest urban school districts, which is now over 50%. Among those young people who persist in high school, studies have shown declining percentages of college aspiration among first-generation students. Even a motivated first-generation student who graduates from high school faces significant challenges in the college planning process.

Low-income schools do not have the resources to provide adequate college and financial aid counseling, and the process is often convoluted and mystifying. Research shows that low-income, first-generation, immigrant and/or minority families tend to be "uninformed and fearful" about the college and financial aid process, and usually overestimate the tuition costs and underestimate the availability of financial aid. As a result of these barriers and misperceptions, 200,000 qualified low-income high school graduates did not attend college last year. While 71% of middle-income children participate in college, only 33% of low-income children do. Of that 33%, 50% will drop out without graduating, the vast majority in the first year.

Yet census research shows that when low-income students do complete college, they break the cycle of poverty for their entire family line, earn $1 million more over their lifetime, and send their own children to college at twice the rate of those without university degrees. However, when this fails to happen again and again, low expectations are reinforced and the cycle of poverty repeats. In fact, 50% of young people are born into poverty in New York City, and statistically more than half of these same children will become low-income adults.

Summer Search, Page 2 of 10

Goals and Objectives: *Why Do Some Kids Succeed?*

Research indicates that children who display and develop characteristics of resilience are those that overcome risk factors and mold positive futures. A resilient child can resist adversity, cope with uncertainty and recover more successfully from traumatic events or obstacles.[1] Unfortunately, resiliency is developed through exposure to stressors and some of these stressors may not be pleasant or socially acceptable.

Difficult early experiences, to be sure, do not determine a young person's future trajectory. But research shows that an important factor in overcoming early challenges is the presence of compensatory interventions in later life that trigger resilient responses. In large proportion, children who face stressors and succeed are those that displayed some resiliency which was then strengthened by beneficial external forces. Research also suggests that negative effects can be reduced by altering young people's exposure to risks or by changing their perceptions of risks and helping them develop coping strategies (Smith and Carlson 1997).

Young people who are best equipped to overcome adversities will have or be helped to have:
- Strong social support networks,
- The presence of at least one unconditionally supportive parent / parent substitute,
- A committed mentor,
- Positive school experiences,
- A sense of mastery and a belief that one's own efforts can make a difference,
- A range of extra-curricular activities that promote the learning of competencies and emotional maturity,
- The ability or opportunity to make a difference by, for example, helping others through volunteering, or under-taking part time work,
- Exposure to challenging situations which provide opportunities to develop both problem-solving abilities and emotional coping skills.[2]

Summer Search's innovative youth development program gives students all of these skills and opportunities to break the cycle of poverty and to bridge the social and cultural gaps they encounter on the way to personal success. In turn, the tangible success and leadership of these students has a ripple effect on those around them, and they become role models as well as voices for their communities.

Why Does Summer Search Work?

Summer Search fulfills characteristics of "authoritative communities," which according to the Commission on Children at Risk are the type of social institutions best positioned to address the lack of connectedness and community that is the main cause of the deteriorating emotional and behavioral health among American youth. Specifically, an authoritative community 1) is a social institution that includes children and youth, 2) treats children as ends in themselves, 3) is warm and nurturing, 4) establishes clear limits and expectations, 5) largely made up of non-specialists, 6) is multi-generational, 7) has a long-term focus, 8) reflects and transmits a shared understanding of what it means to be a good person, and 9) is philosophically oriented to the equal dignity of all persons and to the principle of love of neighbor.[3]

---

[1] Tony Newman, Children and Resilience, pg. 1

[2] Ibid, pg. 2.

[3] *Hardwired to connect: the new scientific case for authoritative communities,* The Commission on Children at Risk

Summer Search, Page 3 of 10

Leadership Model and Program Structure

Summer Search identifies and nurtures three enduring and interconnected qualities in young people: **resiliency**, **altruism**, and **performance,** or RAP.

Resiliency is defined by *Flexibility* (adaptability and capability to withstand hardship), *Self-expression & Insight* (ability to understand one's emotions and motivations and communicate them directly and openly), and *Accountability* (responsibility for one's actions and behavior).

Altruism is defined by *Empathy* (ability to identify with and understand the feelings and thoughts of others), *Conscience* (sense of duty, awareness of right and wrong, understanding of how one's actions affect others), and *Gratitude* (appreciation for others and desire to "give back" what's been given).

Performance is defined by *Individuality & Autonomy* (independence of voice and action, ability to make decisions and see one's behavior and identity as unique) and *Initiative* (persistence, the power to begin and follow through on a track)

By learning to be more **resilient**, young people make an investment in strengthening *themselves*. By learning to be more **altruistic**, Summer Search students develop the desire to help *others*. By learning to actualize their **performance**, students develop the skills to take *action* on behalf of themselves and others, thus becoming well-integrated everyday leaders.

The Summer Search program also encourages and teaches important leadership skills that are increasingly in demand in the workforce and greater society, including:

- **Communication**: authentic and focused one-on-one conversation, confident and articulate public speaking, and personal essay writing skills
- **Personal Development**: problem-solving, self-awareness, goal-setting/planning, interpersonal relations
- **Professional Development:** college preparation, networking, project management

To accomplish these goals of leadership development, Summer Search employs a comprehensive program model. Summer Search uses a unique selection process to identify kids with leadership potential and supports them through the long term to achieve their full potential. The program combines full scholarships to summer experiential education programs with intensive long-term mentoring and access to practical leadership resources, including private college counseling and professional development normally unavailable to low-income kids.

The extended mentoring relationship is a highly personal one in which mentors demand a high level of responsibility from students, challenging them to examine their mistakes and correct the potentially self-defeating behaviors and attitudes behind them. The summer program allows students to focus on themselves away from the pressures of home and school, to re-imagine their identities within a new, positive context, and to experience a focused period of healthy adolescent growth. Finally, access to private resources like college counseling, SAT tutoring and internships allows students to capitalize on the talents and skills they have worked so hard to develop. The result is a sustained intervention over high school and through college that promotes profound, lasting change in young people.

Summer Search, Page 4 of 10

Elements of the Summer Search Model

(1) Targeted Selection

Students are referred to Summer Search as sophomores by a network of teachers or counselors in schools, and staff from other youth-serving nonprofits. These individuals are encouraged to look not solely for academic achievement but for kids with a "special spark" or qualities of character, specifically "RAP" potential. Most often, these students are struggling in ways that leave them "invisible" to traditional interventions. Some students may deal with instability at home by playing a caretaker role, and will perform well in school overtly while struggling emotionally internally. On the other hand, some students may not be achieving in school, but on further scrutiny have subtle but significant strengths in other areas that can be developed.

Both of these subsets of at-risk adolescents are often overlooked, as resources are targeted towards the very highest or lowest achieving kids. Summer Search conducts a personal interview with each student at their school, where students are offered the unique opportunity to tell their life story (often for the first time) to an empathetic adult. Those students who show RAP potential, as well as the strength to open up and the imagination to envision stepping away from home alone, are accepted into the program. The interview becomes the foundation for a long-term, supportive relationship between each student and his or her mentor.

In 2004, Summer Search New York City will send 55 students on summer programs, including 38 new students. The New York City program draws students from every borough of New York City: 34% from the Bronx, 32% Manhattan, 20% Brooklyn, 13% Queens, and 2% Staten Island. Seventy-five percent attend public school and 15% attend parochial school on scholarship. Eighty-two percent of students in the program qualify for free or reduced lunch under federal standards, and 96% will be the first in their families to go to college. The ethnic/racial breakdown for Summer Search's NYC students is: 51% Latino, 40% African and African Diaspora, 7% Asian, and 2% Caucasian. The gender breakdown is 44% male and 56% female.

(2) Intensive and Long-term Mentoring

When Linda Mornell started Summer Search, the initial goal was to provide summer scholarships to underprivileged kids. She found though, that without a supportive adult relationship and a structured program to assist kids with understanding their experience and determining how to relate it to their own realities, kids were worse off having had the "eye-opening experience" than they were before it. An aggressive mentoring program altered this dynamic helping kids "re-enter" their community and make positive connections to how they could improve their own future. Over the years, Summer Search has refined and codified their mentoring approach. Training new mentors is a very deliberate and intensive process at Summer Search. Training is an ongoing priority for all Summer Search employees.

Pre-Program Preparation & Transition Home

Summer Search assigns a team of two staff mentors to each accepted student, most often the team that interviewed the student. Students are expected to make a commitment to the program and to managing their personal growth through regular weekly "check-ins" by phone and through actively preparing for their own summer trip. Most students follow through with energy; however, a few fall back and realize the program is not right for them. While mentors encourage all students to stay in the program, we allow this "self-selection" process to play out organically in order to protect students who are not emotionally and psychologically prepared for this big step out. After this post-interview phase, 95% of our students end up continuing in the program throughout their last three years of high school.

Mentors help students prepare for their upcoming summer programs by coaching them on practical skills like leaving clear voicemails, sending in summer program applications and making airline reservations. In addition, students prepare physically and emotionally for their strenuous wilderness trip. Mentors encourage exercise, provide a forum for students to express their fears, and help them develop strategies for handling the challenges they will encounter. While the mentoring is ostensibly targeted towards preparation for the summer, in a larger sense it helps students envision future goals while learning to delay gratification. Most importantly, these students are building a trusting and enduring relationship with an adult, some for the first time in their lives.

Students return from their summer programs with confidence and a new vision of themselves and their opportunities in life. However, the homecoming can also be trying as students return to the same challenges and limitations in their families, schools, and communities. Mentors are there to help them navigate this difficult transition, celebrate their successes, and integrate the experience into their lives for the long-term.

Year-round Mentoring & Community Events

In addition to the preparation for the summer program and the transition back home, mentoring continues throughout the year with consistent contact between students and staff. Through weekly telephone calls and occasional office visits, students have the opportunity to be actively listened to by an adult who is deeply empathetic, but who nevertheless exhibits high expectations and holds the students accountable for their actions. The mentoring focuses on helping students engage in honest self-examination: the ability to look inward to understand the motivations behind their behavior. Mentors help students develop insight into patterns that could hold them back from achieving their potential. Students learn to take ownership of their actions and of their future instead of focusing on external factors that they cannot control. In this way, students cultivate the skills and perspective to more actively resist repeating negative cycles of behavior.

Every year, Summer Search holds two events at local high schools that participating students attend before they leave for the summer and when they return. At these events, the entire Summer Search community, including all students, their families, referral sources, guests and donors, comes together to celebrate and honor the success and courage of the participants. Students lead the program by giving compelling speeches that speak to the depth and breadth of their growth. These events are a chance for students to celebrate their successes with their families and in the context of a new and positive community.

(3) Summer Experiential Education

Summer Search works with over 75 independent, privately-run summer experiential education programs. These programs generally fall into four categories: (1) wilderness leadership expeditions, (2) academic enrichment programs on college or boarding school campuses, (3) international community service and home-stay programs, and (4) special interest programs that emphasize and develop certain strengths, like visual arts, creative writing, math or science.

In general, these transformative programs recruit mostly at private schools and draw their participants from a very narrow economic group of privileged students whose families can pay the tuition. Unfortunately, many of these programs are plagued by high drop-out rates and less than satisfactory experiences with scholarship students. These summer programs use Summer Search to identify an important subset of low-income and minority students who, with preparation, might participate more successfully in these programs. In fact, Summer Search is the leader in the field in terms of identifying and preparing participants from low-income communities and nationally we are the largest single source of students to multi-national programs like Outward Bound and AFS. All of these summer programs consistently provide Summer Search over $800,000 annually in scholarships and Summer Search matches the remainder of the tuition and pays for airfare and equipment, creating a full scholarship for students.

Summer Search, Page 6 of 10

Summer Search's method of exposing low-income kids to the transformative power of leadership development programs outside of their communities while simultaneously creating more diversity in those programs benefits all participants. Most summer program directors are interested in increasing diversity but do not have the means to identify appropriate candidates. Summer Search provides a pool of pre-screened participants, who in many cases are more successful on their summer trips than the program's private applicants who come from more socio-economically privileged backgrounds. For this reason, 100% of the 75 summer programs we work with offer partial or full scholarships year after year. Because of this significant contribution from the summer programs, our cost per student is much lower than the actual cost of the full experience, and in-kind contributions exceed our administrative operating costs.

Summer Search usually assigns students to a month-long wilderness leadership program in their first summer after sophomore year. These programs enable students to push themselves beyond what they thought was possible, both physically and emotionally. As they begin to realize that their capabilities are equal to those of their more privileged peers, their self-confidence grows. This knowledge greatly enhances Summer Search students' later attitudes toward their own potential, as well as toward the attainability of long-term goals such as college.

In their second summer students participate in another summer program that focuses on their specific strengths or needs. For example, students with extraordinary academic potential may spend the summer on a prep school or college campus. Students who have not had a strong family presence in their lives may do a family home-stay overseas, and students with a particular talent in the arts may attend an advanced arts program to develop that strength. In many respects, the second summer is more specific in its focus and more oriented toward positioning students to be successful in the next phase of their lives.

The socio-economic program diversity has incredible effects on students. Summer Search students get a chance to interact and live alongside American peers from more privileged backgrounds, and as a result class and economic barriers that may have seemed insurmountable become manageable. Summer Search students are often leaders and facilitators in their groups, thus educating their peers and inspiring them to feel more of a stake in issues that impact low-income communities.

Their summer experience plays a substantial role in helping children strengthen their social and intellectual skills. Adolescents who have not experienced success in school need to experience challenge and success elsewhere to develop resiliency and the belief that they can overcome significant difficulties. Out-of-school programs provide opportunities for development and enrichment in alternative settings where children can excel. Their enthusiasm often transfers to the more formal environment of school.[4]

Summer experiential learning programs like the ones that Summer Search collaborates with provide multiple benefits:
- They are both physically and mentally challenging.
- They present underprivileged "city" kids with a completely different experience than any other they have undertaken.
- Summer Search students share this experience with kids of completely different socioeconomic and cultural backgrounds and perspectives.
- All kids in the group are put on the same footing – everyone is facing grueling challenges. Teamwork is essential to completing the program successfully.
- Kids complete the program with a sense of accomplishment and pride – they see themselves differently than before. Students report a greater sense of their own capabilities.

---

[4] *"Schools Alone Are Not Enough"* Mass 2020; Mass Insight Education, May 2002, pg. 2.

- Students gain valuable experience as they handle all logistics of their summer program including filling out admissions applications and financial aid forms, making travel arrangements and dealing directly with summer program directors.
- Students come away with a very different perception of the world and a vivid sense of other possibilities for themselves.

(4) College Preparatory Services and Alumni Development

Summer Search is committed to making sure that students successfully integrate their high school experience as a springboard for lasting future success. Summer Search students often come from lower-performing schools with overburdened counseling departments that cannot meet their needs. Most Summer Search students are the first in their families to envision attending college, and family members may not have the knowledge to guide them through the application process. Therefore, having access to a private college and financial aid counselor is essential for Summer Search students to be on par with students from schools and families with more support and resources. Many hidden costs are also associated with the college application process and can be deterrents for low-income students. Summer Search helps defray these costs, including college application and standardized testing fees. Through a partnership with Kaplan, which offers Summer Search 75% tuition discounts, Summer Search provides students who plan on applying to college with full scholarships to SAT preparation courses. Summer Search also provides support to students considering paths other than college. The goal with every student is that he or she successfully makes the transition out of high school and into the next phase of life.

After graduating from high school, alumni stay closely connected through the Alumni Association, which provides continued mentoring, a "safety net" of financial support for emergencies and enrichment opportunities, and access to paid summer internships and other professional opportunities. The continued relationship and consistency of support with Summer Search and alumni provides an opportunity for young adults to navigate the extremely vulnerable transition of their college years and to emerge into successful young adulthood.

With a primary objective being to help disadvantaged youth aspire and work towards a different future -- one which includes college -- Summer Search has secured college preparatory support for its' students from the College Access Center of New Settlement Apartments, a Bronx-based provider of preparatory services for low income students. At this point, our plan is to hire an in-house College Counselor and Alumni Director this spring who will oversee and provide this valuable resource to our students.

(5) Alumni Services

Summer Search alumni include recent high school graduates, post-baccalaureates and those already in their careers. To support alumni, the program has three components:
1) Professional development opportunities – internships and other support for college students
2) Scholarships and ongoing financial assistance (as needed limited assistance which does not replace financial aid)
3) Networking opportunities

We currently have only five alumni in New York, but the alumni network will be expanding rapidly in the next five years. A big priority will be to develop the full range of alumni services for NYC students, including summer internships to help position students for jobs upon college graduation. Although colleges should surface these opportunities for their less advantaged students, in large measure, they do not. Many of the internships Summer Search provides are generated by board members and donors. Others will be secured by working with third party national internship programs like INROADS and Sponsors for Educational Opportunity.

Summer Search, Page 8 of 10

SUMMER SEARCH NYC STAFF

In January 2003, Eden Werring, who had previously worked with Summer Search for seven years and served as Executive Director of the Napa-Sonoma office, and Stacey Fields, a Summer Search alumna from San Francisco, initiated a Summer Search office in New York City.

In an effort to build infrastructure and sustainability, we anticipate hiring program who will begin training to learn the Summer Search mentoring methods and a Development and Operations Coordinator who will oversee and manage office operations. In addition, Summer Search cultivates a network of volunteers, including a talented Board of Directors, a Young Leadership Committee dedicated to gaining visibility for Summer Search in the city, and the referral sources who identify potential candidates for the program. Summer Search relies on collaborations with schools and other non-profits that serve youth. In NYC, Summer Search will particularly focus on partnering with other youth development organizations as referral sources and gaining access to complementary services.

Nationally, Summer Search encompasses a national hub office and five local offices operating in San Francisco, Boston, Napa-Sonoma, New York City, and Seattle serve over 600 students and a growing alumni base of over 1,500 annually.

OUTCOMES AND EVALUATION STRATEGY

We plan to measure our progress in New York by utilizing a system of metrics that the other Summer Search offices have used and also by developing and employing new measurements. In other cities, we have tracked our progress to date with two key sets of information on leadership development: (1) traditional measures of achievement as compared to similar student populations throughout the United States and (2) qualitative evaluations of individual student progress against key indicators for resiliency, altruism and performance (with input from the student, the staff mentor, the referring teacher and the summer experiential education program).

Traditional Measures:

To date, in the other offices, we have tracked several factors to measure student success. As a benchmark, Summer Search's national success to date has been:

- Summer Search Retention Rate: 96%
- Summer Program Completion Rate: 98%
- Essay Completion Rate: 100%
- College Matriculation: 93%
- College Retention: 89%

Up to this point, we have tracked data from relevant populations, in particular, for college achievement and outcomes. Ninety-five percent of Summer Search students will be first generation college students. Nationwide, four-year college matriculation for first generation students is 30%. Four-year college matriculation rates for first generation Summer Search students are 88% (an additional 5% go to two-year colleges). College persistence rates for low-income students are 59%. In this regard, although not selected for academic achievement, Summer Search students are far exceeding the outcomes of their peers.

Qualitative Measures:

Long-term, we are currently instituting a plan to develop specific methods of measuring leadership growth as expressed by the key factors of resiliency, altruism and performance. This will enable to us to conduct even more specific evaluations of Summer Search student outcomes. However, for the short term Summer Search New York City will use several methods to collect specific data about the performance of the program, including the following: Student Essays, Ongoing Student/Staff Contact, Response from Referring Sources, Response from Summer Program Directors, and Alumni Involvement.

In addition to the results with individual kids, there is also an exponential "ripple effect" that is compelling and, over time, begins to affect schools and communities. The Summer Search process is not a "band-aid" solution, but a lengthy and sustained intervention that promotes change in young people that is both profound and lasting. Summer Search students are demonstrating that this investment in individual students is worthwhile as they go on to use their growth and talents to break cycles and become role models and leaders in their families and communities.

Summer Search NYC
2004 Budget

	2004 Budget
INCOME	
Unrestricted Donations (not committed yet)	570,000
Restricted Donations (committed)	30,000
Investment Income	-
Other Income	-
TOTAL OPERATING INCOME	**600,000**
EXPENSE	
High School Program Expense	
Summer Program Expense	137,500
Mentoring Expense	8,000
Student Materials	3,000
Events	6,000
Ongoing Support	1,500
High School Program Staff Expense	178,170
College Access Expense	
College Prep Assistance	8,000
Kaplan	4,500
College Access Staff Expense	-
Alumni Expense	
Alumni Events	-
Other Scholarships	-
Ongoing Support	-
Alumni Program Staff Expense	-
SUBTOTAL PROGRAM EXPENSES	*346,670*
Staff Development	
Training	4,000
Staff Recruiting	250
Organizational Development	
Planning	500
Board Development	1,000
Development	
General Development	5,000
Fundraising Events	3,000
Development Staff Expense	56,085
SUBTOTAL DEVELOPMENT EXPENSES	*69,835*
Management & Administrative	
Business Insurance, Dues and Admin. Fees	1,000
Bookkeeping, Professional and Legal Fees	2,500
Occupancy Expense	45,000
Office Maintanence and Supplies	10,000
Technology	15,000
Management & Administrative Staff Expense	56,085
SUBTOTAL MANAGEMENT & ADMIN. EXPENSES	*129,585*
TOTAL OPERATING EXPENSES	**546,090**
Excess of Income over Expense OR Deficit	*53,910*

Chapter 9

Other

In this chapter we've included proposals that do not fall naturally under the categories covered by other chapters of this guide. These proposals serve as examples of the different kinds of proposals that ultimately achieve success, and they are of interest because they demonstrate how grantseekers can design their requests to respond to critical needs, while still adhering to the basic format of a grant proposal. Here we include two unusual proposals: one to purchase media time for a prestigious cultural institution and one from a consortium active in other parts of the country seeking to establish itself in New York, while raising funds that it intends to regrant to other nonprofit organizations.

The first proposal included here is a request for $20,000 from the Baltimore Opera Company to the Baltimore Community Foundation for funding to pay for television advertising time. The ultimate goal of the grant request is to increase awareness of its programming among the opera company's potential audience. The bulk of this proposal is in the form of a letter that goes well beyond the standard cover letter. It is personally addressed to the foundation's program officer and is signed by the senior director of marketing and communications. After some negotiation with the funder, the terms of the actual funding awarded by the community foundation required the opera company to match the $10,000 grant and to find a media partner that would partially subsidize extra airtime.

The other proposal in this chapter is a request to the Edwin Gould Foundation for Children, of New York, New York, in the amount of $50,000 over two years submitted by Hispanics in Philanthropy to implement a Funders' Collaborative for Strong Latino Communities (at its New York location). Innovative in its approach, this consortium strengthens Latino-led nonprofit organizations by pooling funds from foundations and other funders and then re-granting these funds in the form of capacity building grants to the smaller organizations. The proposal provides a cogent overview of the Latino nonprofit sector and its acute need for building capacity to serve constituents.

A Proposal From
Baltimore Opera Company
Baltimore, Maryland

To
Baltimore Community Foundation
Baltimore, Maryland

Requested amount: $20,000; **Amount received:** $10,000

Funder's comments:

"While we accept a common application form at the Baltimore Community Foundation, we actually prefer to receive a straightforward narrative description of the background, the need, and the actual request. In this case the Baltimore Opera Company's marketing/communications director called to discuss a range of needs by phone, and this request is what we ultimately settled on. In the end what the Opera Company submitted functioned basically as a combined cover letter and executive summary.

"The arguments they made were very persuasive. I found it especially compelling, since a recent local arts marketing study that the Community Foundation funded corroborated the argument made here, namely, that Baltimoreans are not attending cultural events because they do not know that they are happening. The need to change marketing strategies was rock solid; and given the small experiment with *La Fanciulla del West*, *The Marriage of Figaro* presented the opportune time to test the effectiveness of television promotion. Further, the Opera Company's stated goal of increasing single-ticket sales could be readily measured. By the way, the suggestion that the media partner would match the media buy was critical to the success of this proposal.

"The strongest features of this proposal in my opinion were the need for a midseason change in advertising strategy to a more visual medium and the leveraging possibilities this presented. The proposal did not address long-term revenue projections but focused on turning single-ticket sales around, one production at a time, creating the opportunity to rebuild participation and, ultimately, donor loyalty over time.

"The proposal was easy to read. I found the presentation to be clear, the formatting not distracting and the arguments concise. Because we receive many proposals, I do not want to have to wade through a lot of extraneous information. As part of the attachments they included a summary of the Opera Company's mission, programming, and cost-cutting activities as well as a draft statement of its financial position, all of which were helpful. We did have to call to request audited financials.

"One thing that would have made the proposal even stronger would have been if it had acknowledged that reaching a new, more diverse audience might increase short-term earned income but that the longer-range approach added significant value, since it might include signing some single-ticket buyers up for subscriptions and providing opportunities to engage them in volunteer activities and encouraging them to become donors. I would also have liked a framework to better understand if increased earned income and contributions will be able to make up for static public funding and reduced foundation and corporate gifts. Such projections might ultimately prove to be wrong, but are a necessary theoretical construct."

—*Melissa Warlow, Program Officer, Baltimore Community Foundation*

[Editor's note: Baltimore Opera Company was awarded a $10,000 matching grant, the payment of which was contingent upon their raising another $10,000 for the project and signing a $20,000 contract to purchase air-time valued at $40,000 with a television media partner.]

Notes:

The complete proposal included the following attachments: list of board of trustees and IRS tax-exempt letter.

Proposal written by Deborah Goetz, Senior Director of Marketing and Communications, and Rosemary Eck, Director, Individual Gifts and Grants.

BALTIMORE OPERA COMPANY

The Lyric Opera House • 110 West Mt. Royal Avenue • Suite 306 • Baltimore, MD 21201
☎ 410-625-1600 • Fax 410-625-6474 • Tickets 410-727-6000 • www.baltimoreopera.com

BALTIMORE OPERA
COMPANY

MICHAEL HARRISON
General Director

October 29, 2004

Ms. Melissa Warlow, Program Officer
The Baltimore Community Foundation
Two Read Street
Baltimore, MD 21202-2470

Dear Melissa,
If only more people knew . . .Opera reflects life itself!
The main difference between life and opera is music with power, majesty and grand emotional
sweep. Every word is understandable because Italian, German, Russian and the other languages of
opera are translated into English and projected on a screen above the stage.

Audience members smile and weep and cheer and leap to their feet, wildly applauding the stars and
the casts. If only more people knew . . .

During the 2002-03 season, the Baltimore Opera Company presented five operas [*Lakme*, *Rigoletto*,
Die Fledermaus, *Lady Macbeth of Mtsensk* and *Madama Butterfly*] with five or six performances each. A
total of 58,754 individuals were in the audience during that season and we finished the fiscal year in
the black. Unfortunately the market forces after September 11 continue to plague all segments of
our economy, but cultural arts organizations here and around the country have felt a severe impact.

The 2003-04 season was cut back to four operas [*Il Trovatore*, *Don Pasquale*, *Salome* and *Carmen*] with
four performances each. *Carmen* was the exception with five performances and two additional lead
artists for one of them. A total of 40,917 individuals were in the audience.

No one blames our donors for their caution but, I have to tell you, it is cause for <u>serious</u> worry.

The Baltimore Opera administration has cut the budget in every way possible: four operas instead of
five are presented each season; the number of performances has been cut so a second set of lead
singers is not necessary; rehearsal time has been shaved to the bare minimum; and, when a staff
member leaves, work is divided among remaining colleagues.

We are doing our very best to maintain the production quality our audiences are trained to expect, but opera is not cheap. Musicians, singers, sets, costumes, wigs, props and all the details that spell excellence cannot and should not be curtailed.

Our fund raising efforts have increased in intensity and range. Marketing has become more imaginative and assertive. A major drive toward audience development has been undertaken in order to stabilize the audience and provide a platform for future growth.

Background

Over the past few seasons the Baltimore Opera Company has seen declines in both Subscription and Single Ticket sales. As audience members become increasingly reluctant to make long term commitments of time or money, more patrons opt to allow subscriptions to lapse and instead purchase tickets on an "opera by opera" basis.

Without the attendance commitment inherent in subscriptions, patrons are more likely to skip operas that, while worthwhile, may not be as compelling as *Carmen, Madama Butterfly* or *La Bohème*. Subsequently, as the education and commitment levels of future opera audiences wane, these patrons become less likely to be influenced by marketing efforts aimed at them. In order to generate sufficient ticket revenues and maintain an ongoing relationship with as broad an array of patrons as possible, the BOC must adjust its marketing strategy to rely *less* on subscription sales and more on Single Ticket sales.

While the company strives to maintain the quality of its productions on stage, every effort has been made to shave or maintain administrative costs at all levels including marketing (while executing the most efficient and cost-effective campaign possible).

Historically, the backbone of the Single Ticket media campaign has been radio but over the past few seasons top radio stations in Baltimore have increased their rates 50-100%. The BOC budget for working media spending has been flat during that time, resulting in a far lower share of voice and a less effective radio campaign for the same amount of dollars expended three years ago.

BOC Single Ticket working media totals (radio and newspaper)

		Media $	Total ST Sales	% of ad $ to sales	Avg. sales per opera
FY02	(5 operas)	$216,483	$1,061,894	20%	$212,378
FY03	(5 operas)	$239,896	$1,130,915	21%	$226,183
FY04	(4 operas)	$205,795	$ 730,362	28%	$182,590
FY05	(4 -- budgeted)	$208,401	$ 786,000	27%	$176,500

While the average working media expenditure per opera has increased from $48,000 in FY03 to $52,000 (9%) in FY05, the average single ticket sales per production have dropped by 25%.

Baltimore Opera
Page three
October 29, 2004

As a vast majority of societal, attitudinal and artistic factors contribute to slumping ticket sales, the BOC recently implemented both consumer research and media testing to determine if a different deployment of media dollars could significantly increase ticket sales.

Recent Consumer Research:

WB&A Research in Annapolis conducted telephone interviews among 100 individuals who attended *Rigoletto, Madame Butterfly, Lakme,* or *Die Fledermaus.* The research suggests that, in general, satisfaction with Baltimore Opera performances is very high among attendees. When these patrons were asked about whether they plan to attend in the future or why they have not returned to the opera, it became apparent that there was a lack of knowledge about BOC offerings. Given this lack of knowledge about the variety of performances being staged, the research suggests that the Baltimore Opera could increase attendance by simply making people more aware of the performances being offered. When asked what the BOC could do to entice them to purchase single tickets again, a common response was "advertise more".

Television Effectiveness Testing:

In mid-September an advertising schedule began, announcing the first opera of the season – Puccini's *La Fanciulla del West (The Girl of the Golden West).* During the first two weeks of the campaign, radio levels comparable to those employed during the FY04, but box office velocity was down almost 30% vs. comparable periods. Recognizing that a significant shortfall in single ticket sales would have a dramatic impact on our ability to execute other plans for the current season, it was determined that dramatic and aggressive marketing action was necessary to preserve the projected cash flow.

Using an existing television spot that positions Baltimore as a place where world renowned opera singers like to come to perform (and to enjoy the city's other attractions), the BOC implemented a two week television campaign. The company shifted $20,000 in funds from print and radio to determine if TV media would generate immediate sales. Box Office activity started to increase almost immediately. Ultimately the *Fanciulla* goal was not met, post analysis revealed that the shortfall would have been far more severe had we not implemented the Television plan.

All callers were asked by Box Office Sales Representatives how they knew about the opera. Advertising source tracking revealed that **23%** of total sales were attributed to TV. Website activity increased as TV drove viewers to the site who subsequently ordered through the website or phoned the box office. The website as an advertising source for sales jumped from 14% (last year's total average) to **44%.** Of those who purchased single tickets *La Fanciulla del West,* **43% were first-time BOC attendees** indicating that this medium can attract a significant number of new opera patrons.

The results indicate that while Television is a more expensive medium than radio, it delivers a vast audience, generates widespread awareness of a production quickly and provides both the audio and visual elements necessary to sell opera and differentiate it from other forms of vocal or classical

Baltimore Opera
Page four
October 29, 2004

music performances. The increased cost of advertising on television was more than justified in the sales results and inquiries generated.

Request For Funding

In order to insure that Single Ticket goal ($255,000) for *The Marriage of Figaro* (March 12 –20) is met, the BOC plans to implement a revised media plan that consists of:

- A 3 week Television flight
- NPR radio station schedules (no commercial stations)
- Baltimore Sun and Washington Post display Newspaper advertising
- Postcard mailings to approximately 30,000 households from the BOC database.

Implementation of this schedule will require approximately $20,000 more than is currently budgeted to support this opera. Because it has the highest potential tickets sales of any opera scheduled this season, we feel it is imperative that we implement the revised media schedule.

Achieving this ticket goal in March will contribute toward a balanced year end budget and will buy the company time to plan and implement a more aggressive marketing and media campaign for the FY 06 season.

Please consider a grant in the amount of $20,000 to fund the additional Television time which is not afforded by the current budget. In order to insure the effectiveness of the schedule we will work with a high profile media partner who will match that amount in no-charge commercial time - effectively doubling the media impact of the money.

Measurement

- Syndicated consumer research will be conducted to test for any increase in awareness of Baltimore Opera Company advertising and it's content.
- All phone calls to the BOC box office will be questioned about the source of their knowledge of the production and their response (advertising source) will be documented.

This is a succinct summary to save you precious time. The enclosed proposal will add depth to this summary and will help explain our case for a $20,000 gift. I will be pleased to provide any other details you may require for an even deeper understanding of our role in the cultural community we all love.

Thank you again for your thoughtful consideration.

Sincerely,

Deborah Goetz
Sr. Director of Marketing and Communications

A proposal
for
funding support
from the

Baltimore Community Foundation

October 29, 2004

Executive Summary

For over 50 years, the Baltimore Opera Company has been an integral part of Maryland's cultural arts fabric. As one of the five leading arts organizations in the state, and the only major professional opera company in Maryland, we are a necessary and important cultural institution for the state and surrounding region.

The 2003-04 season was successful in many ways. Our educational outreach programs reached 6,500 students in 34 schools for "Opera to Go." Performances of "Legacy of Hope" [the story of Marian Anderson], "Who's Afraid of Opera," and "The Three Little Pigs" were performed in ten Title I elementary and middle schools. We have recently secured a grant to take "Opera to Go" into the Baltimore Juvenile Justice Center. Dress rehearsal passes were distributed and used by 2,187 students in 79 area schools, including three Title I schools.

Community outreach programs involved two opera-centered lectures prior to every performance within the Lyric Opera House. Available to ticket holders without fee, 5,025 adults and young people attended to learn about the plot and music they were about to enjoy. Senior Box Office received over 500 passes. "Too Many Sopranos" at Artscape was enjoyed by over 1,400 attendees.

It is critical to note the economic importance of the arts. A thriving business community depends on the cultural opportunities a given region has to offer. A lack of funding for the arts is as detrimental to the economic development of a region as high crime or bad schools.

Ironically, the arts can provide a solution to education and social challenges as well. Music and arts in the classroom raise test scores, improve academic performance and bolster self-esteem. After school arts programs, for example, can have a dramatic effect on juvenile crime – which in turn affects economic development.

I'm sure you are aware of the economic climate in Baltimore and throughout the nation – for all non-profits, but the cultural arts organizations are really taking it on the chin. No one blames our donors for their caution, but I have to tell you, it causes serious worry.

The Baltimore Opera administration has cut the budget in every way possible: four operas instead of five are now presented each season; the number of performances has been cut so a second set of lead singers is not necessary [no one can be expected to sing the principal role in any opera six times within ten days]; rehearsal time has been shaved to the bare minimum; and, when a staff member leaves, his or her work is often divided among colleagues in the department.

We are doing our very best to maintain the quality our audiences are trained to expect, but opera is not cheap. Musicians, singers, sets, costumes, wigs, props and all the details that spell excellence cannot and should not be curtailed.

Please consider a gift of $20,000 to help Opera Company realize increased ticket sales by intensifying our presence on regional television stations.

*"What's good for the arts
is good for the economy.*

*The mayors of cities
with strong economies
tell us that the arts have helped
their communities thrive.*

*Federal support for our nation's
cultural organizations is sound public policy."*

Representative Louise M. Slaughter,
U. S. Congress

The Baltimore Opera Presents . . .

Economic Prosperity

If one can possibly ignore the sweeping, emotional majesty of the music, the extraordinary voices that float and soar through the Lyric Opera House, the magical transformation scenery provides, and the dramatic celebration of human history, there are other reasons why the Baltimore Opera Company invites your financial support.

The arts do much more than provide a pleasant form of relaxation and entertainment at the end of a long day. They drive economic development. Study after study by Chambers of Commerce, city and state governments and leading universities tell the same story.

To attract and retain business, and to lure the top talent needed to make businesses successful, it is critically important that a region come fully equipped with a dynamic cultural environment.

A healthy cultural environment is every bit as important to the quality of life, and thus the economic vitality, of a region as parks, schools and transportation. Supporting the arts is more than giving back to the community: it's critically important to our financial future.

Please, dear friends at the Baltimore Community Foundation, consider a $20,000 gift to invest in television advertising aimed at increasing our audiences to result in the financial stability of the Opera Company *and* the future of the City of Baltimore.

2002-03

With productions of *Lakme, Rigoletto, Die Fledermaus, Lady Macbeth of Mtsensk*, and *Madama Butterfly*, the Baltimore Opera Company featured the debut performances of Antonia Cifrone, José Luis Duval, Vladimir Glushchak, Marc Heller, Karen Huffstodt, Heather Lockard, and David Malis. Our appreciative audience welcomed return singers Nicole Biondo, Mark Delavan, Jeffrey Kneebone, Fernando de la Mora, Theodora Hanslowe, Susan Patterson, Youngok Shin, Kathleen Stapleton, Tomas Tomasson, Patrick Toomey, Vladimir Vaneev, Gran Wilson, and Liping Zhang.

At the end of the season, over 60,000 audience members enjoyed grand opera in Baltimore performed by 3,380 individual artists, including principals, orchestra and chorus members.

2003-04

The season opened in October with the energy and magnificent music of Giuseppe Verdi's *Il Trovatore*, starring Dimitra Theodossiou as Leonora, Frank Porretta as Manrico, Marianne Cornetti as Azucena, and Giovanni Meoni as Count di Luna. Andrea Licata conducted and Stefano Vizioli directed.

The comic bel canto opera *Don Pasquale*, composed by Gaetano Donizetti followed in November, starring Simone Alaimo as Don Pasquale, Armando Ariostini as Dr. Malatesta, Cristina Barbieri as Norina, and Harold Gray Meers as Ernesto. Claudio Desderi conducted and Stefano Vizioli was stage director.

Richard Strauss' *Salome* opened in March. Nina Warren sang and danced the role of Salome, Chris Merritt brought his world acclaimed role of Herod, Jeffrey Kneebone portrayed John the Baptist and Jim Cornelison sang Narraboth. Christian Badea conducted.

Carmen by Georges Bizet enjoyed an opening night on May 1. Milena Kitic sang the lead, José Luis Duval was Don José, Carla Maria Izzo portrayed Micaëla and Randall Jakobsch was Escamillo. Alberto Veronesi conducted.

At the end of the season, with one less opera than the season before, 2,491 artists had engaged and enthralled nearly 41,000 members of the audience. Critical reviews were favorable too.

2004-05

The Opera's season opens on October 9 with our first-ever production of *The Girl of the Golden West* by Giacomo Puccini, staring Giovanna Casolla as Minnie, Frank Porretta as Dick Johnson and Ned Barth as Jack Rance. Andrea Licata, a master of the Puccini repertoire, returns to the Lyric podium to conduct.

November 13 is opening night of *The Puritans* by Vincenzo Bellini, another Baltimore Opera premiere, starring Elizabeth Furtral as Elvira, Gregory Kunde as Lord Arturo Talbo and Giovanni Meoni as Sir Riccardo Forto.

Wolfgang Amadeus Mozart's *The Marriage of Figaro* opens March 12 with a stunning cast, including Robert Gierlach as Figaro, Susan Patterson as the Countess, Sebastian Catana [a former studio artists, now performing at the Metropolitan Opera House] as the Count, Nicole Biondo as Cherubino and Madeleine Gray as Marcellina.

Christian Badea returns in April to conduct the final production, Jacques Offenbach's *The Tales of Hoffmann*, with Roberto Aronica as Hoffmann, Valeria Esposito as Olympia, Renata Lamanda as Giulietta, Antonia Cifrone as Antonia, and Jeffrey Kneebone as the various villians.

Every opera performance features English surtitles projected directly above the stage, so the audience can follow the dialogue, arias and ensemble music.

A Proposal From
Hispanics in Philanthropy
San Francisco, California

To
Edwin Gould Foundation for Children
New York, New York

Requested amount: $50,000; **Amount received:** $75,000 over three years

Funder's comments:

"The Edwin Gould Foundation typically requires a letter of intent and then a full blown proposal from those seeking grant support. Regarding the Funders' Collaborative for Strong Latino Communities, I first attended an informational meeting held for potential funders in the New York City area co-hosted by New York Regional Association of Grantmakers, Rockefeller Foundation, and the Hispanic Federation. Subsequently, several face-to-face and telephone conversations took place. And later on as part of our decision-making process, I did speak with Hispanics in Philanthropy (HIP) leadership on several occasions to assist me in understanding the various responsibilities of the different groups involved in the Collaborative and how it all operated on the ground. This particular model of collaboration requires several layers of responsibility. Early on we had conversations with other funders already involved in the Collaborative, as well as with HIP board members and supporters of HIP. It was necessary to initiate a strong relationship between HIP and our foundation in order to move forward. The proposal was virtually the last step of the application process in this case.

"With this proposal as with others, the executive summary is always helpful because it serves as a one-page synopsis of the entire project. It helps to put things into perspective before delving into the full details of the proposal. The HIP proposal's needs assessment was especially strong. The need statement should be the most compelling part of any proposal along with how the grantee plans to deliver solutions for the identified needs. The need for Latino-led nonprofit organizations across the country to build their capacity—through strategic planning, fund and board development, and technological and accounting infrastructure to better serve the growing Hispanic populations—was a strong reason to consider this proposal. In addition I found this proposal particularly convincing because it incorporated evidence-based information and data- guided programming design. It also included a description of expectations and challenges and delineated the project's theory of change.

"The writing style was clear. Even though the project is complicated, the presentation of the information in an outcome-based and linear fashion provided me with a straightforward way to analyze the data provided. The budget was also clearly presented, which is important. It was absolutely imperative that the financial materials be in order and that they support the proposal narrative in telling the story of how HIP could make the Funders' Collaborative for Strong Latino Communities happen.

"In my opinion, the strongest feature of this proposal is the description of the immediate community need, and the ability of HIP to deliver what is promised, in terms of coordinating, regranting, and building a funding community that could take a proactive approach. Also important was the collaboration between national and local foundations in bundling their grants in such a way as to be most effective. The different nuances that exist in each community whether in New York, North Carolina, or Argentina, could only be addressed through local grantmakers coming together for the decision-making process.

"Finally, I want to emphasize that the application process often includes so much more than just the proposal. Proposals are very important in communicating a need, an idea, and a potential solution, but the most critical information is not always generated on paper. The reputation and strength of the leadership and staff, the ability to rally together a network of people, and the learning/field building that will take place are all equally important in the case of the HIP proposal."

—*Helen Alessi, Senior Program Officer, Edwin Gould Foundation for Children*

Notes:
Proposal written by Sarah Charukesnant.

July 1, 2004

Ms. Helen Dorado Alessi
Program Officer
The Edwin Gould Foundation for Children
23 Gramercy Park South
New York, NY 10003

Dear Ms. Dorado Alessi,

Hispanics in Philanthropy would like to request a two-year grant of $50,000 for the New York site of the Funders' Collaborative for Strong Latino Communities, an initiative to strengthen Latino nonprofit organizations.

This Funders' Collaborative should interest the Gould Foundation for many reasons. First, an important goal of the Collaborative is to educate funders about issues in the Latino Community, a community that is growing in New York as well as nationally. Collaborative funders, which represent private, community, corporate and international foundations, will learn about issues in the Latino communities at the local and national levels within the US and Latin America.

Second, the Collaborative is structured to leverage the impact of local funders. As a local funder (with grants geographically limited), Gould's contribution would be matched one-for-one with national funds that the Collaborative has raised, thereby doubling your investment in local Latino nonprofit organizations.

Most important, the Collaborative offers funders an opportunity to have a greater impact on Latino nonprofit organizations that any foundation could do on its own. In addition to giving capacity building grants to worthy Latino nonprofits, we will convene grantees across sites and provide in-depth culturally specific training. Through a combination of direct grants, peer training, convening and networking of grantees, the end result will be stronger Latino nonprofit organizations that can better serve and advocate on behalf of the Latino community.

To date, the Collaborative has raised more than $17 million from more than 100 donors in 15 sites across the U.S. and Latin America. Grants have been made to more than 250 Latino-led nonprofits.

Hispanics in Philanthropy is currently designing the next phase of the Collaborative, which will extend and deepen the impact of this initiative. The preliminary fundraising goal is $50 million over the next five years. The Gould Foundation would be instrumental in helping HIP achieve this goal.

Enclosed is a proposal that sets forth how the Collaborative works. Please let me know if you have any questions regarding the proposal or the Collaborative. We at HIP deeply value our long partnership with The Edward Gould Foundation for Children, and look forward to fostering that relationship as we strive to strengthen Latino communities.

Warm regards,

Diana Campoamor
President

HISPANICS IN PHILANTHROPY
200 Pine Street, Suite 700
San Francisco, CA 94104
(415) 837-0427 – tel
(415) 837-1074 – fax

Proposal to

THE EDWIN GOULD FOUNDATION FOR CHILDREN

For

The Funders' Collaborative for Strong Latino Communities

New York Site

July 2004

EXECUTIVE SUMMARY

HIP requests $50,000 over two years for the Funders' Collaborative for Strong Latino Communities (Funders' Collaborative), an initiative to strengthen Latino nonprofit organizations through capacity-building grants, grantee convenings and in-depth, technical assistance training. The Collaborative has four principal objectives:

- to strengthen the organizational capacity of small- to medium-sized Latino nonprofits;
- to increase philanthropy's understanding of Latino nonprofits, the communities they serve, and the role they play in civil society;
- to foster leadership among Latino nonprofits that incorporates a vision of inclusiveness and collaboration; and
- to increase the net amount of philanthropic dollars flowing to Latino nonprofits.

The Funders' Collaborative works much like other collaboratives – it pools together funds from different foundations and other funders, matches it dollar-for-dollar with national funds, and the combined pool is then available for local regranting. This Collaborative specifically targets Latino-led organizations and is specifically for capacity building. A local site committee, comprised of representatives from each of the contributing foundations, is responsible for decisions at the local level. These committees will define site parameters, tailor guidelines, adapt Request for Letters of Intent (LOI), review LOIs, review proposals, make site visits, and make final grant determinations.

One of the added values of this particular Collaborative is that it is not only local, but also national and transnational. Local New York based organizations that receive funding become part of the larger project – which includes an intensive Leadership Training Institute for grantees across all sites and an evaluation component. The national and transnational components also apply to the funders of the project, who participate in an Assembly of all funders that meets once a year. The aim is to expose funders and grantees to each other at these various levels and to build ownership locally as well as overall.

The Collaborative serves HIP's mission of increasing philanthropic resources to Latino communities and increasing Latino participation in philanthropy, and also builds on HIP's assets – particularly its strong membership of institutional and individual members within philanthropy. HIP brings to the Collaborative a strong network of individuals with experience in collaboratives and within Latino communities. The Collaborative will build on HIP's experience, and that of other Latino nonprofits. Because HIP is not a grantmaker and also not a nonprofit that would directly benefit from a grant of the Collaborative, HIP is one of the few Latino organizations that can serve as an intermediary that brings funders and nonprofit organizations together.

1

PROPOSAL NARRATIVE

I. Introduction/Context

Who makes up the community? What assets currently exist in the community? What challenges currently face the community?

Of the approximately 35 million Latinos in the U.S., almost 3 million are in New York City alone, comprising 27 percent of the population. Almost half (48 percent) of the entire population in the Bronx is Hispanic/Latino, with Manhattan and Queens averaging a quarter (27 and 24 percent respectively of the population). Although already high numbers as U.S. Census figures, they are likely to be below the true number.

New York's Latino population includes recently immigrated communities, such as Dominicans, Colombians and Mexicans, and more established communities, such as Puerto Ricans. The Latino nonprofits tend to reflect this immigration growth – with larger numbers of nonprofits established by the Puerto Rican community and more recent nonprofits catering to newer communities.

Given this growth in the Latino community, the role of the Latino nonprofit sector has become that much more important. Latino organizations have long played a critical role advocating on behalf of the Latino community and today they are often Latinos' only source of assistance and advocacy. Historically, the Latino community-based organizations have worked to address the economic and social shortfalls in Latino communities by providing a range of services to recent immigrants as well as to their second and third generation counterparts.

Prior to beginning this project in 1999, Hispanics in Philanthropy surveyed Latino organizations nationally, to better understand their capacity building needs and to guide the work of the Collaborative. This research revealed that most Latino nonprofits were under-capitalized, lacked infrastructure, and needed technical assistance – even among the larger nonprofits that had the staff and the time to respond to the survey (there were 131 nonprofit respondents in the NYC area).[1] Included in the findings from the research, were the following observations:

---

[1] The study was conducted in 1999 by three organizations in different parts of the US. For the East Coast, the Institute for Puerto Rican Policy of the Puerto Rican Legal Defense and Education Fund (PRDLEF); for California, the Tomás Rivera Policy Institute; and for the Midwest and Southwest, the National Economic Development Law Center (NEDLC).

2

- The average Latino nonprofit executive director in New York City was 50 years old and had been in his/her current position for approximately 10 years, signaling the possible graying of Latino leadership and the need to cultivate the next generation of Latino leaders;

- Although the survey had an over-representation of larger nonprofits, 49% of those surveyed (66 organizations) had not received any type of technical assistance. Of the 67 organizations that had received technical assistance, the two most common types of assistance were in fundraising and computer and technology, received by 15 agencies each.

In follow up focus groups, Latino nonprofit executives were candid about their organizations' weaknesses and what kind of remedies are needed to help carry them into the twenty-first century. Their top rated difficulties when surveyed included: the ability to pay adequate salaries to attract qualified personnel, being too dependent on government funding, inactive boards, and the problem of securing enough core funds to operate adequately. It is likely that if these same organizations were surveyed now, they would probably state greater challenges, with the post 9/11 economy in New York, budgetary crisis and the continuing growth of the Latino population.

The Funders' Collaborative in New York

The New York site has not yet launched a grantmaking cycle, but will do so in 2004. Current funders include: The Edwin Gould Foundation for Children, the Westchester Community Foundation, and the Hispanic Federation, Rockefeller Foundation, JP Morgan Chase Foundation, and the Open Society Institute.

The leadership efforts for the Collaborative in New York have come from two current HIP board members: Helen Dorado Alessi at the Gould Foundation and Ligia Cravo at the Hearst Foundations. Both of them have met with local funders, have encouraged follow up with HIP staff, have assisted in the establishment of the NY HIP office (based out of the Gould Foundation) and have been strong advocates for HIP in the region.

3

Once a grantmaking cycle is launched in New York, the biggest challenge will be to be responsive to the demand without setting expectations that cannot be met. New York has many Latino nonprofits that will be eligible for funding, yet there will not be nearly enough resources to meet the demand. Depending on the amount of funds raised, the site will most likely make between 10 and 15 multi-year grants.

II. The Initiative

What are you going to do? Describe your major strategies, the specific activities you will undertake, and the timeline you will follow:

What the Collaborative seeks to accomplish is a stronger Latino nonprofit sector that can better serve the Latino community. HIP's theory of change is based on the assumption that the nonprofit sector plays a critical role as a vehicle for participation and engagement of the Latino community and that it needs sustained support. HIP seeks to assist in the strengthening of this sector through capacity building grants, culturally specific training and networking. The work of the Collaborative will promote change for disenfranchised communities (of which a large portion of the Latino community is comprised) not through direct services to individuals, but indirectly, by strengthening the institutions which provide services, as well as serve as vehicles for participation of these disenfranchised communities.

The overall policy and direction of the Collaborative is managed at the national level, through the guidance of an Assembly of all local and national funders. The Collaborative's grantmaking is implemented through local "sites," which can encompass a part of a state, region, or any other geographically defined area. The requirements for a "site" are that it have at least $250,000 committed in local funds and that there be at least two local funders involved. Funders in the New York site will determine the geographic parameters for the site once they have raised the requisite funds and are ready to begin the grantmaking process.

Once the grantmaking cycle is launched, representatives from each of the local funders will form a site committee, which does the following: define site parameters (geographic restrictions), tailor guidelines, adapt Request for Letters of Intent (LOIs), review LOIs and proposals, make site visits, and make final grant determinations. All decision-making that is related to the particular site is done by the committee of local funders. The grantmaking phase of the project usually takes between 8 and 10 months.

4

In addition to grantmaking activites, other Collaborative activities include coaching and training twice a year for all current grantees across the different sites. There are two grantee convenings held every year at each local site, and a transnational convening of all the grantees from the U.S. and Latin American sites called the Leadership Training Institute. (The first Leadership Training Institute took place in July 2003.) In addition to local site work, funders are also invited to participate in the project-level Assembly of funders (annually) and on various committees – evaluation, capacity building, steering, transnational.

What avenues for participation exist in the initiative for those served or affected?

The Collaborative encourages the participation of its constituencies through many avenues. As mentioned earlier, prior to launching the project, HIP commissioned a research study of Latino nonprofit organizations nationally to guide the work of the project. HIP also seeks input from its grantees prior to the local and transnational grantee convenings, to ensure that these convenings are reflective of the local community's strengths and needs. One of the goals of these grantee convenings is to foster networking and collaboration amongst Latino nonprofits, at the local and national level. Grantees have also participated in HIP's capacity building committee, which developed the concept for the Leadership Training Institute and the Institute's grantee advisory committee, which planned the program.

Throughout this process, the Collaborative seeks input from Latino nonprofit agencies, even those that may not be selected as grantees. In outreach sessions and application sessions, HIP asks prospective Latino agency applicants to share their ideas for implementation of capacity building and their assessment of the sector's needs.

How does your initiative differ from, complement, or otherwise relate to similar efforts in the community?

HIP's work, particularly that of the Collaborative, represents a unique accomplishment unparalleled by local and national agencies alike. This Collaborative is funder-driven and greater in scope than any other national and international project. Because of its strong membership, HIP is uniquely qualified to manage the Funders' Collaborative. HIP brings to the Collaborative a strong network of individuals with experience in collaboratives and within Latino communities. The Collaborative builds on HIP's experience, and that of other Latino

5

nonprofits. Because HIP is not a grantmaker and also not a nonprofit that would directly benefit from a grant of the Collaborative, HIP is one of the few Latino organizations that can serve as an intermediary that brings funders and nonprofits together.

III. Outcomes

What are your goals and objectives? How will you effectively measure these?

The goal of the Funders' Collaborative is to enhance the capacity of Latino nonprofits in the U.S. and in Latin America, so that they may help Latinos become more active and engaged in the economic and policy arenas in the U.S. The Collaborative seeks to encourage greater philanthropic investments, better understanding, and more effective, more coordinated grantmaking in Hispanic communities. The Collaborative has four principal objectives:

1) To strengthen the organizational capacity of small- to medium-sized Latino nonprofits;
2) To increase philanthropy's understanding of Latino nonprofits, the communities they serve, and the role they play in civil society;
3) To foster leadership among Latino nonprofits that incorporates a vision of inclusiveness and collaboration;
4) To increase the net amount of philanthropic dollars flowing to Latino nonprofits.

For the Collaborative as a whole, the measurable objectives are: to raise $50 million over the next five years; to develop and implement a system of distributing the funds to local communities and regions throughout the U.S. and Latin America; and to increase the knowledge of Latino issues for the funders that are part of the project. For individual grantees, the measurable expectations will be an increase in skills and management capacity. Our hope and expectations are that, as a result of the Collaborative's work, we will find stronger Latino nonprofit organizations that are better able to serve the Latino community and that will have stronger networks and relationships among themselves and with the philanthropic sector.

Is this a new initiative, an expansion of an existing one, or a model from another place? How will you sustain it in the future?

6

Within the U.S., thirteen Collaborative sites have been established and are in the grantmaking process: Northern California and the Central Valley, the Upper Midwest, Colorado, Delaware Valley (Philadelphia area), Connecticut, New Mexico, Chicago, North Carolina, Southern California, Massachusetts/ Rhode Island and Southeast Wisconsin, New York, and South Florida. There are also two Latin American sites that have gone through the grantmaking cycle – Argentina and the Dominican Republic.

Please substantiate the need for this initiative.

The Funders' Collaborative seeks to strengthen Latino nonprofit organizations because of the timely opportunity to impact the Latino community, given the growing demographic changes and the growing changes in the nonprofit sector at both the national and local level. This initiative will address the key issues of sustainability, growth and long-term development faced by Latino nonprofit organizations, as well as the need to enhance the knowledge and experience of funders regarding Latino issues. The aim is to strengthen and bring additional resources to Latino nonprofit organizations, particularly those that are small, isolated and under-funded and yet have the potential to confront and challenge the larger policy issues affecting Latino communities. The Collaborative will build on the existing role that these Latino agencies serve within Latino communities not only as providers of service, but also as laboratories of leadership development, for articulating public policy, and as a means of organizing Latino communities around issues of common concern.

If this initiative is unable to obtain ongoing funding at the end of the Foundation grant, what will remain in the community in built capacity?

At the end of five years, the Collaborative expects that Latino nonprofit grantees will have a stronger organizational infrastructure – with better boards & staff, more financially sound systems, and strategies for public policy in place. These grantees will also have greater networks locally and nationally among their peers, as well as greater exposure to funders. For the funders that comprise the Collaborative, the expectation is that they will be better informed about issues in the Latino community, have more experience with local and national Latino nonprofits, and that they will continue these relationships beyond the Collaborative.

7

The broader aim of the Collaborative is to provide a vehicle for increased civic participation by Latinos and to provide Latino nonprofits the tools they need to have a greater impact on the issues that affect the community. Through the Collaborative, Latino nonprofit organizations will be better able to articulate the Latino community's needs and to play a more visible role in the greater community. As stronger, more financially stable and organizationally sound organizations, Latino nonprofits will be able to play the role for which the independent nonprofit sector in the U.S. was developed – as another voice in addition to the public and private sectors. This will benefit not only the Latino community, but also the greater community.

IV. Collaboration/Other Support

To what extent does this initiative depend on the collaboration with others? How will the collaboration work? What are the roles, if any, of each of the collaborators?

The structure and design of the Funders' Collaborative is dependent upon the collaboration of as many foundations as possible. As a collaborative, it relies upon constant and ongoing feedback from the members that comprise it. As was described above, the Collaborative is governed nationally by all its members; at the local level, a site committee is comprised of funders as well as advisory members from nonprofits and other community groups, if the site so chooses. For the other sites, foundations that are members of the site committees have appointed one or two individuals to represent that foundation within the Collaborative's decision-making. As was explained previously, the committee of funders generally meets on a monthly basis during the fundraising and grantmaking period, and is responsible for all local decision-making. However, the level of involvement is entirely up to each individual funder. They can choose not to review the LOIs or proposals and consequently not be on the decision-making committee. In that case, they would forfeit their vote and be informed of the decisions made.

8

Hispanics In Philanthropy
Funders Collaborative for Strong Latino Communities
New York - New Jersey Site

Committed Funders:	Local Site Funds	management fee	Management Fee	Comments
Edwin Gould Foundation	50,000	6,250	10%	
			mixed due to time of	
Westchester Community Foundation	92,500	10,500	commitment	25,000 at 15% and 67,500 at 10%
Hispanic Federation	50,000	5,000	10%	
Washington Mutual	35,000	5,250	15%	
Rockefeller Foundation	100,000	15,000	15%	
Total Confirmed: $	**327,500**			
Regional Match (JP Morgan Chase)	100,000	15,000	15%	
National Match	227,500	34,125	15%	
Total Site Budget:	655,000			
Program Management Fee		91,125		
Total Grantmaking Budget $	**563,875**			

Chapter 10

Letter of Inquiry

Many foundations ask for a letter first, to determine if there is a potential match, before an organization submits a full proposal. Usually this letter of inquiry, also called a letter of "intent," marks the beginning of a multiphase application process, sometimes involving subsequent conversations, submission of a full proposal, or other forms of follow-up, and perhaps a face-to-face meeting or meetings with the funder. Occasionally the letter of inquiry will be strong enough to convince the funder to go ahead and award the grant without requiring additional information. And, while this practice is relatively rare, a few grantmakers, such as the Lifebridge Foundation, which submitted a proposal for inclusion here, may make funding decisions based solely on the letter of inquiry.

The letter of inquiry in many ways functions as a mini-version of the full proposal, since all the details of the project—such as anticipated expenses, time frame, and other aspects—must be included in the letter, albeit in abbreviated form. All of these elements, therefore, need to have been fully thought through before the grantseeker sits down to write. The letter of inquiry responds to the same "who, what, where, when, why, and how much" questions that a full proposal does, but with much greater brevity.

A standard letter of inquiry is up to three pages in length. Like any other business letter, it begins with a salutation addressed to an individual at the foundation and ends with the signature of the grantseeking organization's CEO and/or board chair. For ease of review by the grants decision maker, these letters may include subheadings to highlight various sections. Some have brief budgets attached, although this practice is optional.

There are two letters of inquiry included in this chapter. While quite different in content, they both adhere to the basic formula described above.

First is a letter of inquiry to the Lifebridge Foundation of New York City, from Grupo Osanimi (Osa Foundation) of El Cerrito, California, requesting $5,000 for its Secoya Ethnobotanical Garden Project, the aim of which is to protect the rainforest lands of the

Secoyan people in Ecuador. While this short letter is signed by Grupo Osanimi's volunteer grant coordinator, it does not address the letter's recipient by name. Rather, it begins with "Dear Program Officer." This lack of personalization is not recommended, since it may be taken as an indication that the grantseeker has not done her/his homework. In this instance, Grupo Osanimi invites the funder to contact the organization to discuss the project in more detail. This invitation is key, since the ultimate objective of a letter of inquiry is to achieve one of three outcomes: to provoke enough interest in the funder to request a full proposal; to instigate further conversation; or to get the funder to say "yes" based on the letter itself. In the case of the Lifebridge Foundation, this letter was all it took for the grants decision maker to arrive at a positive decision.

The second letter of inquiry included here is an initial step required by this particular funder as part of its proposal submission process. After the letter of inquiry is reviewed, applicants may be invited to apply. This letter is from the Z Space Studio to the Walter and Elise Haas Fund, both of San Francisco, California. The $43,000 in grant funds requested would be used to help finance archival exhibits and group discussions during the run of a play related to the 25th anniversary of the Peoples Temple Jonestown tragedy. As noted by the grants decision maker, this letter's use of compelling language and dramatic phrasing grabs the reader's attention immediately. Selective use of bolding and bullets also makes this a particularly effective letter of inquiry.

A Proposal From
Grupo Osanimi (Osa Foundation)
El Cerrito, California

To
The Lifebridge Foundation, Inc.
New York, New York

Requested amount: $5,000; **Amount received:** $3,000

Funder's comments:
"The Lifebridge Foundation offers small start-up grants and seed funding to groups and individuals who find it difficult to receive funding from traditional sources. Lifebridge accepts only introductory letters of no more than three pages and from these, a decision is made as to whether to invite the organization or individual to submit a full proposal. In general, projects are looked at carefully with an eye to how much the organization can accomplish with minimal funds and the extent of their reach in terms of how many people will benefit.

"While the wording of this proposal is not dramatic in any way, the writing is simple, clear, and concise, providing all the information needed in an introductory letter. Its tone is respectful and open. With consummate skill the writer weaves together some rather complex elements in a way that is informative, so that the prospective funder can understand the context, circumstances and unique problems and challenges faced by the organization.

"One element of this proposal that we found compelling was the global/local perspective. In other words, Grupo Osanimi is clear about the relationship among the issues facing a particular and specific group and how these issues are relevant to the larger whole. The group's involvement of traditional elders, youth, and a governmental organization shows that they understand that 'we're all in this together' and demonstrates their understanding that the Lifebridge Foundation is looking for inclusive and replicable models.

"The paragraph headings distill into a few words the information to follow, which is very helpful for a small foundation with limited staff and many letters to read. Grupo Osanimi is not asking for very much by way of grant money at all, and they show that they are able and willing to look elsewhere to support the rest of their funding needs.

"As a postscript: Since Lifebridge Foundation awarded this grant, a few colleagues have 'coincidentally' visited this Ethnobotanical Project and tell us that they found it to be a beautiful, informative, and moving experience. Clearly, this tiny grant has had the impact we hoped for."

—Barbara Valocore, President, The Lifebridge Foundation, Inc.

Notes:

Proposal written by Jonathon Miller Weisberger and John Bela. Contributions to the proposal made by Ladna Miller Weisberger, Vice President.

Grupo Osanimi
P.O. Box 1004
El Cerrito, CA 94530
www.osanimi.org

May 25, 2000

Program Officer
Lifebridge Foundation Inc.
P.O. Box 793 Times Square Station
New York, NY 10108

Dear Program Officer,

On behalf of Grupo Osanimi it is my pleasure to submit to you and the Lifebridge Foundation Inc. this letter of inquiry. Pending your approval, we would like to submit a full proposal requesting a $5,000.00 grant to support the Secoya Ethnobotanical Garden Project. Please feel free to call me after reading this letter. If your schedule allows, I would appreciate the opportunity to discuss this project with you in more detail.

Grupo Osanimi
Grupo Osanimi is a rainforest and cultural heritage conservation composed of volunteers, activists, scientists, and indigenous people working at ground level in Ecuador, Mexico and in the USA. Since 1990, Grupo Osanimi has worked to preserve traditional knowledge, to protect tropical rainforests, and to support indigenous communities in their struggle for territorial and cultural autonomy. We are a project of the Tides Center, a non-profit 501(c)(3) organization based in San Francisco, CA, and we work in Ecuador with political and logistical support form UTEPA (The Ecuadorian Ministry of Foreign Affairs for the Ecological Development of the Amazon and Awá Regions). At the moment, I would like to draw your attention to an important project with the Secoya People in Amazonian Ecuador.

Executive Summary
The Secoyas live in a remote region of the northeastern Ecuadorian Amazon, one of the worlds few remaining "hot spots" which sustain nearly half of the world's plant and animal species. While the Secoyas are fortunate to have obtained legal ownership of a substantial portion of their traditional homelands, petroleum extraction, logging, cattle ranching and colonization have drastically reduced their population. Numbering fewer than 350 people in Ecuador, the Secoya culture and their rainforest homeland are in peril.

Traditional land use and forest management strategies practiced by the Secoya people are essential for maintaining the ecological integrity of their homelands and for preserving their unique culture. Unfortunately, traditional knowledge is disappearing at an alarming rate, as the last generations of traditional elders come of age. Unable to withstand the onslaught of globalization, many Amazonian cultures vanish and their traditional homelands succumb to unsustainable management promoting short-term gain.

Don Cesareo Piaguaje, a 77-year-old Secoya elder and healer, initiated the idea for a healing arts center and an ethnobotanical garden to practice traditional medicine, to produce traditional medicinal products, to propagate rare medicinal plants for reintroduction to the forest and to teach the younger generations Secoya traditional knowledge. The idea was discussed and approved at the 8th. Annual Secoya Congress. Grupo Osanimi funded and coordinated the construction of the first Secoya Cultural Center and organized the first Secoya Cultural Heritage Revival, a successful workshop involving 200 people spanning four generations of Secoya families.

The Secoya community is in need of international support to avoid cultural dissolution and to protect their incredibly biodiverse homeland. Grupo Osanimi, working in partnership with the Secoya community and UTEPA is seeking to expand its program to address the unmet needs in this underserved community.

The Secoya Ethnobotanical Garden Project

Ethnobotanical Garden, Plant Nursery and Propagation Center
Traditional elders will oversee the collection of plants from other elders who live throughout the forest, and they will receive them in the traditional way. A seedbed will be established and plants will be propagated in traditional swidden agricultural systems.

Monthly Habitat Restoration Work
Workers will plant thousands of medicinal plants in the understory forest and will reintroduce trees and medicinal plants into old cleared garden sites and cattle ranches. Traditional elders will oversee the propagation of and reintroduction of plants into the forest.

Traditional Medicine Health Care Clinic and Plant Medicine Production Facility
Secoya elders will staff traditional healing clinics at the community centers. They will provide their healing services to the Secoya community using plants propagated in the gardens. Secoya youth will serve as apprentices and assistant to the elders and will assist the elders in harvesting and preparing medicines.

Traditional Lodge – *Tui'que'wu-e*
Project staff will coordinate the construction of a Tui'que'wu-e (a traditional lodge). Currently there are no standing Tui'que'wu-e left in Secoya territory; the last one collapsed in a storm two years ago. These lodges are beautiful round long houses with a dirt floor and a palm roof.

Cultural Heritage Validation Workshops
Project staff and traditional elders will coordinate workshops for the entire Secoya community at the Tui'que'wu-e. Activites will include recounting myths and tribal legends, and teaching traditional medicine, plant cultivation, and arts and crafts.

Funding
The total budget for the Secoya Ethnobotanical Garden Project for the next year is approximately $18,000. To date we have raised $3,000 from the Rainforest Alliance for the construction of a traditional lodge, and we're projected to raise $3,500 from individual donors earmarked for this project. We would like to request a $5,000 grant from the Lifebridge Foundation Inc., which would fulfill more than half of this project's unmet funding requirements.

Conclusion
Thank you for the opportunity to submit this letter of inquiry. This is a crucial time for an ancient people on the threshold, who are testing the ability of their culture to survive in a rapidly changing world. Grupo Osanimi has established a strong social and political framework to do estimable work with the Secoya people. Endorsed and supported by UTEPA and building on years of experience working within Secoya communities, this project presents a remarkable funding opportunity. Please get in touch with me if you would like more details about this project or about our work.

Best wishes,

John Bela
Volunteer Grant Coordinator, Grupo Osanimi
jb@osanimi.org

A Proposal From

The Z Space Studio

San Francisco, California

To

Walter and Elise Haas Fund

San Francisco, California

Requested amount: $43,000; **Amount received:** $40,000

Funder's comments:

"I was already quite familiar with this project's artistic development when the Z Space's artistic director called to ask my advice—as a program officer who was familiar with their efforts—about how to approach another foundation. After we talked, I told him that I saw a possible connection between an aspect of the project and the Walter and Elise Haas Fund's arts guidelines, which emphasize the potential of the arts to build social capital, and I encouraged him to submit a request.

"The Walter and Elise Haas Fund uses a process of reviewing letters of inquiry (which applicants may submit through the Fund's Web site or on paper) and later reviewing full proposals submitted by invited applicants. The Z Space Studio opted to submit their letter on paper rather than through the Web. Before reading this proposal, of course, I was well aware that the story behind the play was painful and compelling, but the proposal letter quickly set up the 'other story'—the way in which the play's development and presentation were 'an enormous community project' that brought together people who had been stigmatized by their association with Jonestown. The second paragraph of the letter really brought home the significance of the project and its connection to our foundation's guidelines; that was my moment of making an initial positive assessment.

"This proposal's particular strength was in telling the story of Jonestown and at the same time presenting many details about the effort that went into creating the play, in a clear, measured, well-outlined form. I was caught up in the story behind the proposal, but the proposal did not ramble on. It made its points directly using vivid, but spare language. The writing style is gripping and dramatic without being melodramatic or flowery. It is like a well-paced short story.

"The need statement is presented at several levels. One need is implied in the gripping, sad story behind the play. The letter convinces me both because of its content and the quotes it uses to remind me of theater's particular power in tackling difficult subject matter. In illustrating what the project already has accomplished, I am further convinced of its timeliness and significance.

"Late in the letter the theater introduces its financial requirements for completing the project. Without hitting the reader over the head with the idea, it introduces the role this particular production has played in expanding the Z Space Studio's production capacity and the potential long-term significance of the partnerships that have been built around it. Therefore, the second level of need more or less embedded in this project is for expanded organizational capacity. Having already laid the groundwork for a strong need for the play itself, strengthening an organization and its partnerships is the icing on the cake.

"The Walter and Elise Haas Fund provides grant applicants with a budget template to use, and the Z Space Studio made good use of the form. I did have some questions about the budget and the financials, which were fully answered upon request, and I needed to better understand the relationship between the play's development and production phases (described in this proposal) and how the four organizations were sharing both revenues and fundraising responsibilities. I saw evidence of a clear detailed plan.

"This proposal's strongest feature in my view is its readability. It's gripping to read and avoids jargon. It also makes very good use of subheadings and bullet points. When I was writing my analysis for our board docket, it was easy to find the information I needed. The grant applicant provided all required attachments. Because the proposal was submitted in December, and its financial statements were from the previous calendar year, I requested and received a year-to-date statement in a follow-up query. Finally, I'd just like to say that I wish I received more proposals that resembled this one in terms of clarity."

—*Frances Phillips, Arts Program Officer, Walter and Elise Haas Fund*

[Editor's note: While the original letter of inquiry requested a grant of $43,00, when the full proposal was ultimately submitted the amount requested was $40,000.]

Notes:
Proposal written by David Dower, Artistic Director and Founder.

Developing Bay Area Theater Since 1993

Dec. 3, 2004

Frances Phillips
Walter and Elise Haas Fund
1 Lombard, Suite 305
San Francisco, CA 94111

Dear Frances:

I write in search of the help of the Walter and Elise Haas Foundation for a major community cultural event scheduled to take place in April of 2005 after four years of development here at the Z Space.

As you are very well aware, in the summer of 2000, we commissioned the writers of *The Laramie Project* to create a play based on the individual voices of Peoples Temple, which imploded at Jonestown on November 18, 1978. **We had no idea what we were tapping into.** The project was originally conceived as a play based on interviews with survivors and family members of the lost. It has grown into an enormous community project, bringing together five leading local institutions, hundreds of individual area residents, and philanthropies from around the country. We are looking for help in completing the funding needed to help this important project reach its full potential.

The Project

The Peoples Temple Project now includes:

- **The Play**: commissioned and developed at **Z Space,** written by *Laramie Project* lead writer Leigh Fondakowski and featuring an ensemble of Bay Area artists and *Laramie* veterans, the powerful piece is set to open in a co-production with Z and **Berkeley Repertory Theater** on April 15, 2005. Far from the lurid, tabloid nature of so much of the writing on Peoples Temple, the play reveals and elevates the human heart of the community which perished that day.
- **The Archive**: housed at the **California Historical Society**, the Peoples Temple archive contains over 150,000 documents and more than 10,000 photos which until now have never been processed. Through the course of the four years of work on the play, Z's researcher/dramaturg Denice Stephenson has organized the collection to the point that scholars, family members, and artists are now able to conduct research among the files. CHS will keep the collection open to the public on weekends during the run of the play and create exhibits from the archive for their gallery and the theater's lobby.
- **The Book**: based on the documents of the archive and published by **Heyday Press**, the book will serve as a companion reader to the play itself. It contains documents only recently unearthed in the CHS collection that change the scholarship around the events leading to the Jonestown tragedy.
- **The Education Project**: based at Berkeley Rep, the program brings the stories of Peoples Temple survivors into East Bay high schools, where students will work with the new interviews both as source material for important regional history and as the starting point for understanding the techniques of verbatim theater.
- **The Documentary**: produced by Amy Miller and Pam Rorke Levy for **KQED**, this hour-long film and a half-hour episode of *SPARK** will document the process of creating this multi-faceted community project.

Why the Peoples Temple?

In November, 1978 a San Francisco Congressman was assassinated on a Guyanese airstrip and within hours there were over 900 dead bodies lying face down in the nearby jungle. The media reports of the Guyana tragedy are

131 Tenth Street, 3ʳᵈ Floor, San Francisco, CA 94103; 415/626-0453; www.zspace.org

almost exclusively sensational—the gripping tale of a charismatic lunatic who led his brainwashed minions over a cliff. The truth, as always, is much more nuanced and complex but little evidence of that has crept into our public memory of it. Then the story is abruptly crowded to the back pages, as nine days after Jonestown San Francisco Supervisor Dan White assassinated Mayor George Moscone and Supervisor Harvey Milk. This chain of events, though unrelated one to the other, are indelibly etched on the hearts and minds of people who lived here in those times. Tony Kushner, in *Homebody/Kabul,* writes that the present is always a horrible place to be when horrible things happen.

> " And it remains awful to us, the scene of our crime, the place of our shame, for a several-decades regnum of imperceptible but mercifully implacable recedency we shudder to recall the times through which we have lived, the Recent Past, about which no one wants to think; and then, have you noticed? **Even the most notorious decade three or four decades later is illumined from within.** Some light is switched on. The scenery becomes translucent, beautifully lit; features of the landscape glow; the shadows are full of agreeable color. Cynics will attribute this transformation to senescence and nostalgia; I, who am optimistic, have you noticed? attribute this inner illumination to understanding. It is wisdom's hand which switches on the light within. Ah, now I see what that was all about. Ah, now, now I see why we suffered so back then, now I see what we went through. I understand."

This project was begun here at Z Space in recognition of the approaching 25th Anniversary of the deaths at Jonestown. We started with the goal of one play, based on the combined sources of new interviews with survivors and the CHS archive. We imagined that, like all Z projects, the play would be accompanied by post-play discussions and community forums to "illumine these events from within". Our vision was simply to give faces and voices to the pile of face-down bodies in that unforgettable photograph. We were very quickly aware that we had struck a nerve in the Bay Area that, in some terribly prescient way, anticipated the direction that our nation's mood was swinging. It soon was clear that this project not only was an attempt to understand the past and reclaim the voices of the lost, but also a way of understanding the gathering forces of fear and religious fanaticism in our present. During this timeframe we've seen 9/11, escalating violence from Muslim, Christian, and Jewish fanatics, and now our most recent election season. And all along the way, people who have come into contact with the material, whether through public readings of the play in progress, or through visits to CHS or the exhibit we did at the Main Library to commemorate the 25th (which passed on November 18, 2003) have found themselves overwhelmed by the need to talk, the need to know more, the need to connect this past to our present in a way to grieve the loss and understand their fear. And so it has grown from a simple new-play commission to the community-wide project it is today.

Some quick highlights from the Temple stories:
- More than 80 people survived the tragedy in Guyana. Thousands more survived in the United States. The stories they tell of why they joined, why they stayed, how they survived, and what they understand about the world we're living in today are powerful, timely, and compelling.
- The Peoples Temple was over 80% African American and was one of the first integrated congregations in the country—begun in the mid-1950's in Indiana. The CHS collection contains passport photos for over 4,000 Temple members, each now identified, many from the Bay Area. Flip through the pages of these albums at the archive and you feel the power of this integrated ideal and the enormity of the tragedy that was its demise.
- There is *still* no comprehensive list of the names of the people who died in Guyana. We are working on it and are very close at this point. 450 bodies were buried in a single mass grave in Oakland, unidentified and unclaimed. To this day family members are wondering if their children, parents, or grandparents were among them. At least four of those buried here were children of Guyanese, in Jonestown to go to school.
- It was a socialist community which was in large part responsible for the election of George Moscone, met with President Carter and Walter Mondale, and had plans in the works to relocate to the Soviet Union. Religious evangelism and revolutionary politics remains a volatile cocktail to this day.
- Jonestown began life as an Agricultural Mission of the Temple, and was never intended to support more than a few hundred missionaries. Its population swelled during a hasty and poorly planned exodus from the mounting criticism in San Francisco. Suddenly there were over 1000 Peoples Temple members in Guyana, many of them children and frail elderly.

- African American leaders in contemporary SF frequently cite the deaths at Jonestown as the root cause of the loss of influence and leadership in the black community which they say continues to this day—Jonestown "ripped out the progressive heart of the Fillmore" is how Rev. Townsend describes its impact.

These are just some of the highlights around which the dialogue is swirling as we go forward. Over 400 people attended the last round of readings—where three hours of script were read and discussions lasted another several hours more. The former head of the Council of Churches, Donneter Lane, says of this project "We have finally begun the dialogue that can lead our community to healing." She's correct in her assessment—many of those interviewed have never spoken publicly of their involvement, living through this "regnum of decades" enveloped in guilt and shame over the way their dreams and loved ones died. Today the archive is the site of frequent visits from survivors and family members sifting through photos and documents for mementos of their loved ones—a long-deferred project of fully identifying the faces in the photos is coming to completion. Besides the thousands of pages of interview transcripts generated by the process of creating the play, whole new collections have surfaced during this project. Collections from private investigators, from family diaries, from psychologists who dealt with survivors in the immediate aftermath, and oral histories taken in Jonestown of the residents there—histories that have been hidden in a closet since the deaths out of fear, guilt, and shame will all ultimately find their way to CHS permanently. These only came to light in the middle of an interview with the writers of the play and present a unique view of life in Jonestown and its residents.

The Need

We are facing a combined funding shortfall of $350,000 to bring the full potential of the project to fruition. Much of it results from the extraordinary costs of mounting the play itself—over a dozen actors in a world premiere production drawn from the more than 3,000 pages of source material. We are pleased to announce the decision of the Hewlett Foundation to make a year-end gift to Z Space of $100,000 toward the production itself. We anticipate other supporters to be forthcoming on behalf of the play. My primary goal in approaching the Haas Foundation is to ensure that the potential of the project to spark and foster community dialogue is fully leveraged. I write to request $43,000 to support the expenses related to the archival exhibits at CHS and the Berkeley Repertory Theater, extended public hours at CHS during the run of the play, and the public forums at the theater and other public venues throughout the spring. The four-year creative process for the play was fully funded through the efforts of the Z Space. The education piece is fully funded at this point by Berkeley Rep supporters. The documentary is being funded through sources at PBS, local supporters of KQED, and additional fundraising by the producing team.

As you know, this is a project that involves important and challenging Bay Area history, leading Bay Area institutions, and a diverse set of outcomes aimed at sparking a dialogue among a large and diverse community of participants. It is also one of great artistic integrity in all aspects, from the ensemble creating the play to the publishers of the book and the creators of the film the artists involved here are nationally renowned. Over the four years of work on it, Z has earned the enthusiastic support of the Creative Work Fund, the Irvine Foundation, the Rockefeller Foundation, the Fleishhacker Foundation, and the Flintridge Foundation among others. We feel confident that any philanthropic supporter will feel equally enthusiastic about their support of this final phase of the work.

Z Space has taken the lead role in fundraising for the project while others turn their attention to the requirements of producing these outcomes. I would love to talk with you about the project in further detail, show you where we are now, and where we are trying to go. I am also prepared to simply go through a more traditional proposal process for if that is more appropriate.

I look forward to speaking with you at your earliest convenience.

Sincerely,

David Dower
Artistic Director
The Z Space Studio

Chapter 11

Cover Letter

When it comes to proposal writing, the cover letter is a key element that makes a positive first impression. Since first impressions are important in fundraising as in other endeavors, it is vital that the cover letter portrays the organization, the project and those who will benefit from it, and the people who will run it in the best possible light.

The cover letter follows the format of a standard business letter, and its contents do not vary a great deal. It lays out the basics of the appeal: the amount requested, a highly abbreviated description of the project, brief background about the organization and its staff expertise, an explanation of why this particular foundation is being approached, and reference to any prior contact between the grantseeker and the funder. Usually it offers to answer questions and/or to meet with the funder's representative in person.

Since the cover letter is typically only one page in length, using succinct and clear language is essential. The amount of the request should be prominently stated. You'll notice that many of the cover letters included here and those accompanying proposals throughout this guide mention the amount requested in the very first paragraph. The cover letter is almost always signed by the nonprofit's chief executive officer and/or chairman of the board. This indicates the highest level of organizational support for the request.

In this chapter we have included cover letters only, without their accompanying full proposals. As with the proposals in the rest of the guide, all relate to projects that were ultimately funded by the foundations to which they were addressed.

The first cover letter included here is from California Youth Connection's proposal to the Pottruck Family Foundation of San Francisco, California. It requests $39,978 in support over two years. In this case the "ask" is actually put off until the end of the letter. Instead, the letter first focuses on the goals of the organization and a brief description of its programs.

The next cover letter accompanied a proposal from the Washington, DC-based Higher Achievement Program and is addressed to the Lois and Richard England Family Foundation, also of Washington, DC. Although this cover letter is quite short, it includes a personal handwritten note from the executive director of this youth-focused organization inviting questions from the foundation representative.

The third cover letter in this chapter accompanied a proposal from the Hospice of the Western Reserve, located in Cleveland, Ohio, to the Saint Luke's Foundation of Cleveland, and is a request for $55,000 to support a program for end of life care. The cover letter indicates that this was an invited submission, and it is signed both by the organization's chief executive officer and the board president.

The fourth cover letter was submitted by The Student Conservation Association of Arlington, Virginia to the Meadows Foundation of Dallas, Texas, as part of a three-year grant request for $225,000 for funds to support development and implementation of an environmental awareness program for Texas youth. This cover letter uses enthusiastic and compelling language to very good effect.

The final cover letter in this chapter is from a proposal submitted by Youth Communication: Metro Atlanta to The Community Foundation for Greater Atlanta, requesting $25,000 to support a peer-education and youth development program. All of the basic elements of a cover letter are present, and the amount requested is mentioned right up front.

A Cover Letter From
California Youth Connection

To
Pottruck Family Foundation

CALIFORNIA YOUTH CONNECTION

FOSTER YOUTH BUILDING A
FOUNDATION FOR THE FUTURE

604 Mission Street
Ninth Floor
San Francisco, CA 94105

415.442.5060
800.397.8236
FAX: 415.442.0720

www.calyouthconn.org

May 13, 2004

Ms. Nancy Wiltsek, Executive Director
The Pottruck Family Foundation
1016 Lincoln Blvd., Suite 221
San Francisco, CA 94129

Dear Nancy:

Founded on the principle of youth empowerment, California Youth Connection (CYC), is a non-profit advocacy organization composed of current and former foster youth that strives to improve the foster care system by making it possible for these youth to have a say in child welfare services. With 23 county-based chapters, including four in the Bay Area, and over 450 members statewide, CYC works at the state and local levels to educate legislators and policy makers about how policies and programs affect foster youth. Members sit on and participate in committees, monitor and testify on legislation, and give presentations throughout the state on their experiences in foster care and their recommendations for change. One of the primary goals of the organization is to improve social work practice and policy by empowering youth to articulate how things can be done differently.

CYC builds the leadership capacity in foster youth to act as strong advocates for preserving or improving the resources foster youth need to succeed. By offering youth extensive training and technical assistance, youth increase their confidence and self-esteem, knowledge of how policy is shaped, and become spokespeople for all youth in care in California. In the spring of 2004, CYC evaluated the effectiveness of our model and results demonstrated an increase in the leadership skill level of our members. While we have always observed their personal empowerment through their work within the organization, we also believe that participation leads to greater success in the adult world. In this regard, CYC plans to develop an additional evaluation tool to examine this relationship.

Our goal is to continue to build leadership capacity in San Francisco and Alameda foster youth, which will result in both individual and policy-related benefits. We also intend to evaluate the relationship between CYC participation and successful adulthood. Because of the length of time it will take us to collect meaningful data about the relationship, CYC is requesting $39,978 over two years from The Pottruck Family Foundation. Funds will be devoted to core support of our ongoing programming of training youth in leadership and advocacy, as well as for evaluating the efficacy of our model in terms of positive, longer term outcomes for youth exiting the foster care system.

Attached please find our proposal, most recent annual report, financial statements, organizational and proposal budgets, and other requested documents. Should you require additional information, please contact me either at (415) 442-5060 ext. 15 or jknipe@calyouthconn.org. Thank you for your consideration of our request.

Sincerely,

Janet Knipe
Executive Director

A Cover Letter From
Higher Achievement Program

To
Lois and Richard England Family Foundation

**HIGHER
ACHIEVEMENT
PROGRAM**

19 I Street, NW
Washington, DC 20001-1425
www.higherachievement.org
202.842.5116
202.842.5123

February 14, 2005

Margie Siegel
Lois & Richard England Family Foundation
PO Box 11582
Washington, DC 20008

Ms. Margie,

Attached, you will find Higher Achievement's letter inquiring about support from the Richard and
Lois England Family Foundation. We are requesting your continued investment in the talent and
drive of Higher Achievement scholars; middle school children from under-resourced inner city
communities in the District of Columbia. Your investment will support the high quality operation
of four year-round Achievement Centers in the District of Columbia.

Please contact me with any questions or ideas that develop from this inquiry. We hope you will consider
this request.

My best,

Maureen Holla
Executive Director

Enclosures

Margie,
Call me with any ideas/
questions inspired by the
attached. GH

A Cover Letter From
Hospice of the Western Reserve

To
Saint Luke's Foundation of Cleveland

HOSPICE HOUSE & HEADQUARTERS

300 East 185th Street
Cleveland, Ohio 44119-1330
216 383-2222
216 383-3750 fax

September 30, 2004

Ms. Peg Butler
Grants Manager
Saint Luke's Foundation
4208 Prospect Avenue
Cleveland, OH 44103

Dear Ms. Butler:

On behalf of Hospice of the Western Reserve (HWR), thank you for your invitation to submit the enclosed proposal to the Saint Luke's Foundation requesting a **$55,000** grant to assist in the development of a *Program in Enhanced Dementia Care at End of Life*. The program will be one of several established by HWR to assist patients and their families in coping with the complex and debilitating conditions associated with a terminal illness. A grant from the foundation would provide partial funding to establish and implement the program for the first year.

The development of the Program in Enhanced Dementia Care at End of Life was the natural outgrowth of HWR's mission to relieve suffering, promote quality of life, provide caregiver support and support effective grieving. Recognizing the multi-dimensional aspects of care that dementia presents to patients and their families, HWR conducted extensive research in the field of dementia and examined current patient care practices at HWR to determine if more could be done. The findings indicated that additional services specific to patients diagnosed with dementia would be most beneficial. An HWR dementia committee (organized in 2003) designed a program that offered comprehensive staff education, improved patient care and caregiver support, and increased community awareness about dementia and care options at end of life. Hospice of the Western Reserve will continue to invest in this initiative and seeks the assistance of the Saint Luke's Foundation to establish this program.

We welcome the opportunity to discuss this proposal with you. Please contact us at (216) 383-3773 if you have questions or need additional information.

Sincerely,

David A. Simpson
Chief Executive Officer

Laura K. Navin
Board President

En: Proposal

A Cover Letter From
The Student Conservation Association

To
The Meadows Foundation

The Student Conservation Association

changing lives through service to nature

Since 1957

September 8, 2004

Mr. Bruce Esterline, Vice President for Grants
The Meadows Foundation
Wilson Historic District
3003 Swiss Avenue
Dallas, TX 75204-6049

Dear Mr. Esterline:

SCA is very grateful to the Meadows Foundation for its support and guidance over the past three years. The Foundation challenged SCA to increase both the number of students fielded in Texas and the number of young Texans serving in SCA programs nationally. SCA has met that challenge with great success! The number of students in SCA programs in and from Texas and the number of colleges and high schools visited by SCA has increased by 100%.

SCA is now prepared to further invest in Texas youth and take steps to further expand its Community Programs by establishing offices in Houston and Dallas to reach more youth across the state of Texas, especially in urban areas. Given the Foundations' initial investment, SCA seeks continued support from the Meadows Foundation to proceed to the next level of programming.

SCA invites the Meadows Foundation to initiate the Dallas component of SCA's Texas expansion with a three year grant of $225,000 ($75,000 for three years). This grant enables SCA to offer the life-changing benefits of its programs to an expanded group of young people throughout the Region. The centers in Texas will serve as a catalyst for SCA programs in the region as SCA increases youth opportunities across the State.

With Meadows Foundation support, SCA has increased the number and diversity of young Texans participating in SCA's Conservation Crews and Conservation Internships in Texas and across the country. Building on the Foundation's investment three years ago, SCA and the Meadows Foundation can increase conservation opportunities for Dallas youth through the Texas Initiative. I have enclosed a proposal and budget for Texas programming. Please let me know if you need any additional information.

Sincerely,

R. Flip Hagood

R. Flip Hagood, Vice President

SCA Mid-Atlantic/Southeast 1800 North Kent Street, Suite 102, Arlington, VA 22209 • 703-524-2441 • (Fax) 703-524-2451 • www.theSCA.org
National Office: Charlestown, NH • Boise, ID New Paltz, NY Oakland, CA Pittsburgh, PA Seattle, WA

SCA is an equal opportunity/affirmative action employer committed to workforce diversity

A Cover Letter From
Youth Communication: Metro Atlanta

To
The Community Foundation for Greater Atlanta

YOUTH
communication

METRO ATLANTA

ORGANIZERS OF VOX
TEEN NEWSPAPER

145 Nassau Street
Suite A
Atlanta GA 30303
PH: 404-614-0040
FAX: 404-614-0045

dear_vox@bellsouth.net
www.voxrox.org

Board of Directors
Jay Bernath
C&S Wholesalers

Nicole Carter
DeKalb County Schools

Kristin Davenport
CheckFree Corp.

Janet Frankston
Atlanta Journal-Constitution

Laurie Goldberg
Cartoon Network

Wendy Heaps
CDC

Liza Hogan
CNN.com

Mary Kaplan
Wachovia Bank, N.A.

Maria Khordorkovsky
Centennial High School

Mindy Larcom
FOX 5 News

Ray McNair
Turner Broadcasting Systems

Keosha Morgan
Mays High School

Paul Nozick
Alston & Bird, LLP

Anna Richards
Junior Achievement

Debbie Segal
Kilpatrick Stockton

James Sullivan
Alston & Bird, LLP

Lars Thrasher
DeKalb School of the Arts

Ashley Watson
BellSouth Corp.

Carolyn Wingfield
Georgia Power, Co.

Executive Director
Rachel A. Wallack, MSW

Ms. Lesley Grady
and assigned Program Officers and CPI Committee
Community Foundation for Greater Atlanta
50 Hurt Plaza, Ste. 449
Atlanta, GA 30303

July 14, 2004

Dear Lesley, Community Foundation Program Officers, and Community Programs and Initiatives Committee members,

It is my pleasure to authorize the enclosed grant request for $25,000 to support VOX, a unique peer-education and youth development program. As you may know from previous involvement with Youth Communication's initiatives, the VOX program brings together diverse groups of teenagers from more than 40 different neighborhoods and schools in an educational and community-building program that engages teenagers in hands-on leadership, communications, and technology training that links their experiences to community and family life.

Working together to create and circulate our community's only teen-run media, youth involved with YC learn many valuable skills. Moreover, by supporting teens as active leaders in our organization's governance and programming, YC supports youth development in many areas – most significantly, personal growth and community engagement.

During the last two years, the YC Board of Directors has worked with donors, teens, and staff to craft a comprehensive strategic plan, which includes four main goals: strengthening our infrastructure, expanding the diverse groups of teens engaged in our programs, focusing deliberately on teens' skill building and impact evaluation, and determining how to leverage our core competencies.

The teens of VOX turn to us as a Board to support their work through the initiatives of this dynamic plan, taking 11 years of effective youth development work to the next level. With support, we will be able to strengthen our infrastructure, putting systems and volunteers in place to enhance our staff, facilities and volunteer capacity to serve more teens and engage them even better.

I know our Executive Director, Rachel Alterman Wallack, will welcome any questions you have. Thank you for considering the enclosed proposal.

Sincerely,

Ashley Watson
Chair, YC Board of Directors

Chapter 12

Budget

If a grantmaker first turned to the budget section of your grant proposal, would he or she be able to understand the project? The budget is such a critical component of the overall request that many grantmakers refer to it *before* delving into the narrative of the grant proposal, usually right after reading the executive summary. The budget is important because it presents the financial picture of what the organization intends to do during the grant period, specifically outlining what resources will be required. Without a complete understanding of the project and all of its likely expenses, a proposal writer cannot prepare a good budget.

Though no single budget format will fit every project, there are standard elements that grantmakers expect to find in proposal budgets. The budgets included in this chapter look very different from one another, but they share several common characteristics. They all cover a set time frame. All include detailed lists of expenses, with several clearly separating personnel and non-personnel costs. Some include projections of support to be received or revenue to be earned. Complex budgets, like the one from Hospice of the Western Reserve included here, are often enhanced by accompanying budget narratives. This helps explain any large or unusual items and also serves to respond in advance to potential questions a grants decision maker may have.

Keeping the budget clear and self-explanatory for the proposal reviewer should be a primary objective of any budget design. Some funders have specific forms or formats to follow, and in that case, it is important to adhere to those specifications. Additional or explanatory information, if needed, can be added in the form of footnotes or in brief narrative text at the end of the budget.

The five budgets in this chapter are presented without their accompanying proposals, but as with the cover letters in the previous chapter, each was part of a proposal that was eventually funded. They are for grant requests ranging from $2,000 to $55,000. While representative of a variety of budget formats, none of the budgets in this chapter is "perfect." Several could be made even clearer by such means as better use of headers, consistent underlining, and displaying fewer figures and dollar signs on an already crowded page.

Readers of this guide will find other excellent examples of grant proposal budgets throughout the book. As examples we call your attention to the three-year budget included in the proposal from Chinatown Community Development Center in Chapter 2 and the special project budget in Rome Area History Museum's proposal in Chapter 1.

The budget from the Athens-Clarke County Library in Athens, Georgia, included in this chapter accompanied a request for $2,000 to the Georgia Humanities Council to support a simple, straightforward project to enhance a touring exhibition on Frankenstein hosted by the library. The budget clearly details exactly how the funds requested from the Georgia Humanities Council will be used. It also delineates the responsibilities of each participating member of the library's administrative personnel—even though the funds to pay for those staff members will come from in-kind support or other funding sources.

The second budget presented here is from a one-year request for $55,000 submitted to the Saint Luke's Foundation of Cleveland by the Hospice of the Western Reserve for its Program in Enhanced Dementia Care at End of Life. This budget uses forms provided by the foundation. There is a significant amount of detail required in the budget form (including the agency's own contribution to the project and the contributions expected from other funders) and a complete explanation of all direct and indirect costs required in the budget narrative. Using this form entails a rigorous analysis of the grant project, so that, while the budget is relatively lengthy, no item or expense is included without clear justification.

The third budget in this chapter is from a request for $35,823 in kayaking equipment submitted to the Richard and Susan Smith Family Foundation of Chestnut Hill, Massachusetts, by Outdoor Explorations of Medford, Massachusetts, for its youth project. The budget provides details on the specific items and necessary quantities of equipment to be purchased with grant funds.

Next is a budget from a request for $7,500 for the Pediatric Palliative Care Program of the Elizabeth Seton Pediatric Center (formerly the Pediatric Center of the New York Foundling Hospital) submitted to the Adolph & Ruth Schnurmacher Foundation, of New York, New York. This budget breaks expenses into traditional personnel and other-than-personnel costs and is easy to read. It also gives an estimate of how much the hospital itself will contribute to the project. Some indication of the specific amount of the grant request to be covered by funds from the foundation would enhance this budget still further.

The final budget is for a small project: a request for $2,000 to the Agape Foundation from United Genders of the Universe! for a year-long Gender Education and Advocacy and Speaker's Bureau project. This budget is clear in its essentials, giving itemized amounts for the project's expenses as well as a list of the expected sources of funding.

A Budget From
Athens-Clarke County Library

To
Georgia Humanities Council
For a Grant Period of Six Weeks

Detailed Budget and Budget Explanation

	Grant Funding	In-Kind/Other Funding
Personnel – Speakers/Scholars' Honoraria		
Roxanne Eberle	$100	
Sidney Perkowitz	$200	
Virginia Blum	$500	
Steve Stice	$100	
*Travel		
Virginia Blum – round trip airfare from Lexington, Kentucky to Atlanta/Athens, plus lodging and meals	$400	
Personnel – Administrative		
Project Director – planning, promotional activities and program execution: 50 hrs @ XXXXX		XXXXX
Business Manager – grant accounting, check processing: 5 hrs @ XXXXX		XXXXX
Public Relation Specialist – press releases, PSA announcements, exhibition brochure design, flyer and design and distribution, feature story work: 25 hrs @ XXXXX		XXXXX
Web Designer – web pages for the exhibition, programs, and related links: 4 hrs @ XXXXX		XXXXX
Materials		
2 videos –		
Terror of Frankenstein (with shipping) $15		
The Real Frankenstein (with shipping) $25	$40	
Printing		
500 color flyers – 8 ½ by 14 double sided	$140	
Exhibition Shipping (ALA cost estimate)		$1,500
Space Rental		
Library Auditorium:		
4 speaker/discussion programs by scholars @ $50/use		$200
2 film showings (Frankenstein film and documentary) @$50/use		$100
Opening Reception (Required by ALA/NLM)		
Friends of the Library		$125
Advertising		
2 ads in the *Athens-Banner Herald* newspaper 5.75"wide x 6.5" tall ($260/ad)	$520	
Totals	**$2,000**	**$4,545**

*Travel
Dr. Blum will make her own travel arrangements, flying into Atlanta or Athens. Best price air fare from Lexington to Atlanta is approximately $250, and shuttle cost to Athens is $60 roundtrip. $90 is budgeted for lodging and food. Regardless of actual cost, she has agreed to $400 for travel.

A Budget From
Hospice of the Western Reserve

To
Saint Luke's Foundation of Cleveland
For a Grant Period of One Year

SAINT LUKE'S FOUNDATION OF CLEVELAND, OHIO
PROPOSAL PROJECT BUDGET FORM
(To be submitted with proposal and electronically - include budget narrative)
Name of organization: **Hospice of the Western Reserve**
Project title: **Program in Enhanced Dementia Care at End of Life**
Amount requested from Saint Luke's Foundation: **$55,000**   Year **1**   (i.e. 1,2,3)
Person completing budget (name, phone, e-mail): Lin T. Williams (216) 383-3716 lwilliams@hospicewr.org

For multi-year projects, separate budgets must be submitted for each year (indicate year 1, 2, etc.)				
Budget Expense Item	Saint Luke's Request	Agency Contribution	Contributions From Other Funders¨	Total Project Budget
Personnel:				
Salary and wages (list each position)				
Dir. of Clincal Programs (Project Director)	XXXXX	XXXXX	XXXXX	XXXXX
Quality Management Coordinator	XXXXX	XXXXX	XXXXX	XXXXX
Clinical Team Leader	XXXXX	XXXXX	XXXXX	XXXXX
Community Facility Coordinator	XXXXX	XXXXX	XXXXX	XXXXX
Social Worker	XXXXX	XXXXX	XXXXX	XXXXX
Community Relations Coordinator	XXXXX	XXXXX	XXXXX	XXXXX
Alternative Home Team Leader	XXXXX	XXXXX	XXXXX	XXXXX
Director of Professional Relations	XXXXX	XXXXX	XXXXX	XXXXX
Team Leader - Counseling	XXXXX	XXXXX	XXXXX	XXXXX
Hospice Nursing Asstistant	XXXXX	XXXXX	XXXXX	XXXXX
Spiritual Care Coordinator	XXXXX	XXXXX	XXXXX	XXXXX
Home Care Nurse	XXXXX	XXXXX	XXXXX	XXXXX
Registered Nurse	XXXXX	XXXXX	XXXXX	XXXXX
Coordinator of Volunteers	XXXXX	XXXXX	XXXXX	XXXXX
Director of Planning and Evaluation	XXXXX	XXXXX	XXXXX	XXXXX
Pharmacist	XXXXX	XXXXX	XXXXX	XXXXX
Director of Bereavement Center	XXXXX	XXXXX	XXXXX	XXXXX
Clinical Resource and Education	XXXXX	XXXXX	XXXXX	XXXXX
Medical Director	XXXXX	XXXXX	XXXXX	XXXXX
Total Fringe (@25%)	XXXXX	XXXXX	XXXXX	XXXXX
SUBTOTAL PERSONNEL	$38,858.71	$44,950.04	$39,522.50	$123,331.25
Nonpersonnel Expenses: (list)				
HWR Staff Education:				
Printing/Copying	$0.00	$4,000.00	$0.00	$4,000.00
Publishing	$0.00	$1,000.00	$0.00	$1,000.00
Materials & Supplies	$0.00	$1,000.00	$0.00	$1,000.00
Books & Journals	$0.00	$4,840.00	$0.00	$4,840.00
Continuing Education:				
Travel, Lodging & Meals	$0.00	$3,500.00	$0.00	$3,500.00
Materials for Outside Conference Presentations	$0.00	$500.00	$0.00	$500.00
Patient Care Resources:				
Cognitive Assessment Tools	$3,500.00	$0.00	$0.00	$3,500.00
Expressive Therapy Screening Tools	$500.00	$0.00	$0.00	$500.00
Training Materials for Respite Care Volunteers	$200.00	$0.00	$0.00	$200.00
Environmental Safety Upgrades	$0.00	$0.00	$35,000.00	$35,000.00
Caregiver Education & Support:				
Caregiver Resources	$6,000.00	$0.00	$0.00	$6,000.00
Caregiver Survey	$500.00	$0.00	$0.00	$500.00
Community Education & Awareness:				
Public Education & Information	$400.00	$500.00	$0.00	$900.00
Anticipatory Grief & Support Materials	$500.00	$0.00	$0.00	$500.00
Community Needs Assessment	$0.00	$0.00	$18,000.00	$18,000.00
SUBTOTAL NONPERSONNEL	$11,600.00	$15,340.00	$53,000.00	$79,940.00
Indirect @ 9%	$4,541.29			$4,541.29
TOTAL	$55,000.00	$60,290.04	$92,522.50	$207,812.54

*CONTRIBUTIONS FROM OTHER FUNDERS FOR THIS PROJECT (in the narrative, list funder, dollar amount, and indicate if proposal is pending or awarded/received)
SALARY AND WAGES (In narrative, list each position to be funded by Saint Luke's including percentage of effort.)

SAINT LUKE'S FOUNDATION OF CLEVELAND, OHIO
PROPOSAL BUDGET NARRATIVE
(submit with proposal and electronically)

AGENCY NAME: Hospice of the Western Reserve

PROJECT TITLE: Program in Enhanced Dementia Care at End of Life.

The budget and budget narrative should clearly outline all expenses the applicant agency will incur to successfully implement the proposed project.

DIRECT COSTS

Itemize all personnel costs by providing the title and amount requested from Saint Luke's in the first column. In the second column, list percent of effort and primary responsibilities and tasks for all key project personnel. **If Executive Director is directly involved in the project, a percentage of effort may be allocated. Otherwise, Executive Director's effort should be allocated to Indirect Cost category as executive oversight.**

Itemize all office space, utilities, office operations (printing, postage, etc.), equipment, supplies, travel, training, and professional services needed to directly support the implementation of the project.

INDIRECT COSTS

This includes overhead costs required for the applicant's operation, but not directly associated with a specific project; and can also include executive oversight, accounting, and facility maintenance. Up to **9%** of the project's total personnel and direct costs may be requested for overhead expenses.

DIRECT COST BUDGET ITEM   EXPLANATION

PERSONNEL:**	
Director of Clinical Programs (Project Director) XXXXX	**@ 13.9% effort.** Oversight of all aspects of project.
Quality Management Coordinator - XXXXX	**@ 1.3% effort.** Design of project evaluation tools, collection and analysis of data.
Clinical Team Leader - XXXXX	**@ 2.5% effort.** Development of professional education and training, curriculum, resources and materials.
Community Facility Coordinator - XXXXX	**@ 2.5% effort.** Development of resources and materials for public information and education including grief support materials. Also providing hired consultant with organizational information to conduct a community needs assessment.
Social Worker - XXXXX	**@ 2.5% effort.** Development of professional education and training curriculum, resources and materials.
Community Relations Coordinator - XXXXX	**@ 2.5% effort.** Development of resources and materials for public information and education including grief support materials. Also providing hired consultant with organizational information to conduct a community needs assessment.
Alt Home Team Leader - XXXXX	**@ 3.8% effort.** Development of professional education and training, curriculum and materials. Also development of caregiver resources and caregiver survey.
Director of Professional Relations - XXXXX	**@ 1.3% effort.** Development of patient care resources including assessment and screening tools and reviewing with Hospice House staff, environmental safety upgrades to accommodate patients with dementia.
Team Leader - Counseling - XXXXX	**@ 3.8% effort.** Development of professional education and training, curriculum, resources and materials. Development of caregiver resources and caregiver survey.
Hospice Nursing Assistant - XXXXX	**@1.3% effort.** Development of patient care resources including assessment and screening tools and reviewing with Hospice House staff,

	environmental safety upgrades to accommodate patients with dementia.
Spiritual Care Coordinator - XXXXX	**@ 3.8% effort.** Development of professional education and training, curriculum, resources and materials. Development of caregiver resources and caregiver survey.
Home Care Nurse - XXXXX	**@ 3.8% effort.** Development of professional education and training, curriculum, resources and materials. Development of caregiver resources and caregiver survey.
Registered Nurse - XXXXX	**@ 2.5% effort.** Development of professional education and training, curriculum, resources and materials.
Coordinator of Volunteers - XXXXX	**@ 1.3% effort.** Development of patient care resources including training materials for respite care volunteers and reviewing with Hospice House staff, environmental safety upgrades to accommodate patients with dementia.
Director of Planning and Evaluation - XXXXX	**@ 1.3% effort.** Oversight of project evaluation.
Pharmacist - XXXXX	**@ 1.3% effort.** Advising in development of patient care resources.
Director of Bereavement Center - XXXXX	**@ 1.3% effort.** Development of patient care resources particularly pertaining to bereavement information and anticipatory grief support materials.
Clinical Resource and Education - XXXXX	**@ 2.5% effort.** Development of professional education and training, curriculum, resources and materials.
Medical Director - XXXXX	**@ 1.3% effort.** Oversight of the development and application of patient care resources.
NONPERSONNEL:	
Patient Care Resources:	
Cognitive Assessment Tools	Costs include (1) printing and reproducing 300 symptom cards for HWR clinical staff, (2) developing dementia-specific CAM (Confusion Assessment Method) tools to be incorporated into HWR's computerized charting system and (3) designing and formatting computerized forms to summarize clinical information on patients with dementia.
Expressive Therapy Screening Tools	Costs include printing and reproducing 30 guides for accurately identifying persons with dementia.
Training Materials for Respite Care Volunteers	Costs include printing and reproducing a training guide and training materials for volunteers.
Caregiver Education & Support:	
Caregiver Resources	Costs include (1) printing and reproducing a guide for caregivers to assist them with understanding and managing persons with dementia, (2) printing and reproducing memory books for caregivers to record memories, histories and experiences of persons with dementia and (3) printing, packaging and reproducing materials to aid caregivers in the creation of documents that express their values and legacies.
Caregiver Survey	Costs include development, printing and reproduction of a caregiver survey to assess the needs of caregivers.
Community Education & Awareness:	
Public Education & Information	Costs include (1) printing and reproducing a dementia fact sheet for general distribution, (2) designing, printing and reproducing bookmarks with basic facts about dementia and HWR contact

	information and (3) designing a dementia information section of HWR's web site. Updating of the web page will be the responsibility of designated program staff and HWR Communications and Public Relations staff.
Anticipatory Grief & Support Materials	Costs of printing and reproducing anticipatory grief educational materials and information for general distribution.

* Other potential funders include: The Eva L. and Joseph M. Bruening Foundation, Mt. Sinai Healthcare Foundation, The A.M. McGregor Home and HCR Manor Care Foundation. The Bruening and HCR Manor Care Foundations were contacted by telephone for an initial inquiry; proposals have not yet been sent.

** All personnel will be involved in the development of patient care resources, requiring 1.3% effort (already included in the percent effort displayed for each position). Some personnel will also be involved in other areas of the project (including professional (staff) education, patient care resources, caregiver education and support, and community awareness and education).

OUTDOOR EXPLORATIONS
inclusive disability adventures

Youth Kayaking Proposal Budget
Smith Family Foundation Small Capital Grants Program

Capital Item	Unit Cost	Quantity	Total Cost	Timeline
3 Adult Double Kayaks (for program leaders)	$1,000.00	3	$3,000	
6 Single Youth-Size Kayaks	$800.00	6	$4,800	
12 Double Youth Size Kayaks	$800.00	12	$9,600	
Kayak Trailer	$3,000.00	1	$3,000	
Ball Hitch to hook trailer to van (hitch + installation cost)	$120 for hitch platform/hitch, and $280 for installation	1	$400	
Storage shed for storing the new kayaks on OE's property (estimated cost)	$5,000.00	1	$5,000	All items will be purchased within 6 months of the grant award.
Sprayskirts for kayaks	$55.00	21	$1,155	
Storage Covers for kayaks	$40.00	21	$840	
Two-piece Paddles for kayaks	$99.99	36	$3,600	
Dry bags for kayaks	$29.99	21	$630	
Tow ropes for kayaks	$14.99	16	$240	
Extrasport Personal Flotation Devices (Life Jackets) for Youth	$45.00	30	$1,350	
Pull-on neoprene kayak booties	$35.00	36	$1,260	
"Bilgemaster" Pumps for kayaks	$27.00	10	$270	
Adaptive material - Minicell Foam	$17.00	10	$170	
Adaptive material - Kayak seat backing	$16.00	10	$160	
Adaptive material - Adjustable back band	$66.00	3	$198	
Adaptive material - Self-inflating back rest	$24.00	3	$72	
Adaptive material - Self-inflating kayak seat	$26.00	3	$78	

Total Capital Expense Budget for OE Kayaking Program | $35,823

www.outdoorexplorations.org
CHALLENGING PERCEPTIONS, CHANGING LIVES

A Budget From
Elizabeth Seton Pediatric Center
(formerly the New York Foundling Hospital Center for Pediatric, Medical, and Rehabilitative Care)

To
Adolph & Ruth Schnurmacher Foundation, Inc.
For a Grant Period of One Year

The Pediatric Center of the New York Foundling
(New York Foundling Hospital Ctr. for Pediatric, Medical, and Rehabilitative Care, Inc.)
Palliative Care Enhancement Budget
July 1, 2004 - June 30, 2005

EXPENSES

Personnel Expenses

XXXXX	XXXXX
XXXXX	XXXXX
XXXXX	XXXXX
XXXXX	XXXXX
XXXXX	XXXXX
XXXXX	XXXXX
XXXXX	XXXXX

Other Than Personnel Expenses

Pediatric Palliative Care Fellowship	$20,000

Conferences & Professional Development

Reiki Master: 3 courses of 2 sessions apiece	$3,000
Printed Materials and Other Training Supplies	$3,000
Speakers' Fees @ $200 per speaker	$800
Conference attendance: registration and travel	$2,000
Palliative Care Quality Improvement Collaborative (PC-QuIC) Membership	$15,000
Membership, National Hospice & Palliative Care Organization (NHPCO)	$250
Membership, Children's Hospice International	$350
Refreshments for Grand Rounds	$250

Palliative Care Resource Library

Informational Materials	$1,000

Memorial Services

Flowers	$500
Refreshments	$100
Printed materials (programs, invitations, flyers)	$50
Decorations and gifts	$50

Memorial Garden

Planters and Garden Gear	$300
Plants, potting soil, mulch, etc.	$200

Other

Funeral expenses	$3,600
Care packages	$300

Total Other Than Personnel Services	**$50,750**
TOTAL EXPENSES:	**$114,051**

INCOME

Agency Contribution: Personnel Expenses	$63,301
REMAINING NEED:	$50,750

A Budget From
United Genders of the Universe!

To
Agape Foundation
For a Grant Period of One Year

Project Budget Information:

United Genders of the Universe!

Gender Education and Advocacy Speaker's Bureau Project

Budget for the period: August 1, 2004 – July 31, 2005

EXPENSES:		REVENUE:	
Item	**Amount**	**Source**	**Amount**
Stipends for 10 Speaker's Bureau volunteers ($50) and coordinator ($200)	$ 1,200.00	Agape Foundation Grant	$ 2,000.00
Travel costs	$ 120.00	Individual Donations	$ 400.00
Advertising/Promotion and Outreach	$ 450.00		
Producing educational materials	$ 150.00		
Fiscal Sponsor Fiduciary	$ 240.00		
Speaker Trainings	$ 200.00		
Supplies	$ 40.00		
TOTAL EXPENSES:	$2,400.00	**TOTAL REVENUE:**	$ 2,400.00

Appendix A

Glossary of Terms Related to Proposal Writing

Attachments: Documents appended to the proposal narrative that complete the proposal package. Most grantmakers will expect to find the IRS tax-exempt letter of determination, list of board members, brief staff profiles, current operating budget, and audited financial statements among the attachments.

Beneficiary: Recipient of a grant or service.

Budget narrative: An optional section of a proposal's project budget used to explain any unusual line items in the budget or to provide more detail.

Capacity building: The strengthening of a nonprofit so that it can better achieve its mission.

Capital campaign: An intensive, time-limited fundraising endeavor to meet a specific financial goal in order to fund a special project such as the construction of a facility or the acquisition of equipment.

Challenge grant: A grant that is paid only if the recipient organization is able to raise additional funds from other sources. Challenge grants are often used to stimulate giving from other donors.

Common grant application form: A format adopted by groups of grantmakers to allow applicants to produce a single proposal for a specific community of funders, thereby ensuring consistency and thoroughness and saving time.

Community foundation: An organization that makes grants for charitable purposes in a specific community or region. The funds available to a community foundation are usually derived from many donors and held in an endowment that is independently administered; income earned by the endowment is then used to make grants, some at the explicit instruction of the donor (alive or deceased) and some at the discretion of the community foundation's board. Most community foundations are 501(c)(3) public charities and are thus eligible for maximum tax-deductible contributions from the general public.

Company-sponsored foundation (also referred to as a corporate foundation): A private foundation whose assets are derived primarily from the contributions of a for-profit business. While a company-sponsored foundation may maintain close ties with its parent company, it is an independent organization, often with its own endowment, and as such is subject to the same rules and regulations as other private foundations.

Conclusion: The final section of a proposal narrative, summarizing the main points. Usually no more than two paragraphs in length, the conclusion offers the grantseeker a final opportunity to make the case for support, and to portray the benefits and beneficiaries of the project.

Construction grant: Funds to build, renovate, remodel, expand, or rehabilitate real property.

Corporate giving program: A grantmaking program established and administered within a for-profit corporation. Because corporate giving programs do not have separate endowments, their annual grant totals generally are directly related to company profits. Corporate giving programs are not subject to the same reporting requirements as corporate foundations.

Cover letter: The first page in a proposal package. The letter is usually one page in length and contains the funding request, reason for approaching the funder, reference to any previous contact, description of the application contents, a brief project description, and an offer to provide additional information. The letter is usually signed by the organization's chief operating officer.

Donee: The recipient of a grant. Also known as the grantee or the beneficiary.

Donor: An individual or organization that makes a grant or contribution to a (usually nonprofit) donee. Also known as the grantor.

Endowment: Funds intended to be invested in perpetuity to provide income for continued support of a nonprofit organization.

Evaluation grant: Funding to enable a nonprofit to assess the overall success of its strategies and methods and to determine to what degree the organization is fulfilling its mission in the most effective and efficient manner.

Evaluation plan: A proposal component that describes how the grant project's impact will be measured to determine how well its objectives have been achieved. This can be done by informal monitoring reports or by a formal plan to measure the product or analyze the process, depending on the nature of the project.

Executive summary: A proposal component that provides the abstract of a grantseeker's case for a project or organization and a summary of the key information in the proposal that follows.

Family foundation: An independent private foundation whose funds are derived from a member or members of a single family. Family members often serve as officers or board members of family foundations and have a significant role in grantmaking decisions.

Fiscal sponsorship: An individual or new organizational grantseeker's affiliation with an existing 501(c)(3) nonprofit organization for the purpose of seeking, receiving, and administering grants. The fiscal sponsor may charge a small fee for this service.

501(c)(3): The section of the U.S. tax code that defines nonprofit, charitable, tax-exempt organizations; 501(c)(3) organizations are further defined as public charities, private operating foundations, and private nonoperating foundations.

Form 990: The information return that public charities file annually with the Internal Revenue Service.

Form 990-PF: The public record information return that all private foundations are required by law to submit annually to the Internal Revenue Service, and that are part of the public record.

General operating support: A grant for the day-to-day operating costs of an existing program or organization. Also called an unrestricted grant or basic support.

Grantee: Recipient of foundation funding.

Grantmaker: A foundation, corporate giving program, or public charity that awards grants to nonprofit organizations and in some instances to individual grantseekers. Also known as a funder.

Grantseeker: A nonprofit organization or individual seeking to obtain foundation, governmental, or other grant support for projects or programs.

Guidelines: Procedures set forth by a funder that grantseekers should follow when approaching that grantmaker for funding.

In-kind contribution: A contribution of equipment, supplies, or other tangible resources, as distinguished from a monetary grant. Some corporate contributors may also donate the use of space or staff time as an in-kind contribution.

Independent foundation: A grantmaking organization usually classified by the IRS as a private foundation. Independent foundations may also be called family foundations, or private nonoperating foundations. *See also* Private foundation.

Letter of inquiry/Letter of intent: A brief letter outlining an organization's activities and its request for funding that is sent to a prospective donor in order to determine whether it would be appropriate to submit a full grant proposal. Sometimes referred to as LOI.

Matching grant: A grant that is made to match funds provided by a donor.

Mission statement: A concise statement in which a nonprofit organization describes its identity, purpose, and the beneficiaries of its work.

Multiyear grant: Funding awarded to a project that spans more than one year.

Need statement: A proposal component that explains why the grantseeker's project is necessary by succinctly and persuasively describing the problem that exists. The need statement often includes relevant supporting data and statistics. Also called the statement of need.

Operating foundation: A 501(c)(3) organization classified by the IRS as a private foundation whose primary purpose is to conduct research, social welfare, or other programs determined by its governing body or establishment charter. An operating foundation may make grants, but the amount of grants awarded generally is small relative to the funds used for the foundation's own programs.

Operating support: *See* General operating support.

Organization information: The section of a proposal that describes the mission, history, and governing structure of the nonprofit grantseeker, its primary activities, audiences, and services.

Overhead: A proportion of ongoing expenses such as rent, utilities, certain administrative salaries, and other costs that some funders will support as part of a project budget.

Private foundation: A nongovernmental, nonprofit organization with funds (usually from a single source, such as an individual, family, or corporation) and program managed by its own trustees or directors. Private foundations are established to maintain or aid social, educational, religious, or other charitable activities serving the common welfare, primarily through the making of grants.

Program development: Funding to support, improve, or enhance specific programs within an organization as opposed to general support of that organization.

Program officer: A staff member of a foundation who reviews grant proposals and processes applications for the board of trustees. Only a small percentage of foundations have program officers, or indeed any staff at all.

Project budget: The document created for a grant proposal that outlines the anticipated costs of personnel, non-personnel, and overhead expenses, as well as revenue.

Project description: The component of a proposal that provides details about the goals, objectives, and methods related to a proposed project. Typically this section also includes details about staffing and administration, a timeline, and a description of project evaluation and sustainability.

Proposal: A written application, often accompanied by supporting documents, submitted to a foundation, corporate giving program, or government agency in requesting a grant. Some foundations and corporations do not use printed application forms but instead require written proposals, others prefer preliminary letters of inquiry prior to a formal proposal, and a few have online application forms at their Web sites. Grantseekers should consult published guidelines before proceeding.

Regranting: The process whereby a nonprofit organization receives grant funds for the purpose of donating those funds to other nonprofits.

Renewal grant: The process of asking a donor to give another gift to renew their support of an organization, for one or more years.

Seed money: A grant or contribution used to start a new project or organization. Seed grants may cover salaries and other operating expenses. Also referred to as start-up funds.

Tax-exempt: Refers to organizations that are not required to pay taxes, such as federal or state corporate tax or state sales tax. Individuals who make donations to such organizations may be able to deduct these contributions from their income tax.

Timeline/Timetable: A graphic representation of the sequence of steps needed to complete a project, often included in the project description section of a grant proposal.

Trustee: A foundation board member or officer who helps make decisions about how grant monies are spent. Depending on whether the foundation has paid staff, trustees may take a more or less active role in running its affairs.

Appendix B

Selected Resources on Proposal Development

Compiled by Sarah Collins,
Manager of Bibliographic Services, The Foundation Center

Anderson, Cynthia. *Write Grants, Get Money*. Worthington, OH: Linworth
Publishing, 2001.

> This is a proposal-writing guidebook for school media specialists and other
> K-12 librarians who wish to improve library programs and facilities.
> Written for novice as well as veteran proposal writers, the book covers all
> stages of the proposal writing process. Appendix includes samples and a
> glossary.

Barbato, Joseph and Danielle S. Furlich. *Writing for a Good Cause: The Complete Guide
to Crafting Proposals and Other Persuasive Pieces for Nonprofits*. New York, NY: Simon &
Schuster, 2000.

> The authors share practical instructions about the art and craft of writing
> related to fundraising proposals, as well as case statements, newsletters,
> and other communications devices used by a typical development office.
> Includes glossary.

Barber, Daniel M. *Finding Funding: The Comprehensive Guide to Grant Writing*. 2nd ed.
Long Beach, CA: Bond Street Publishers, 2002.

> This handbook provides advice for writers of proposals to government
> agencies, foundations, and corporations. The book includes a section on
> responding to a request for proposals and instructions for creating a letter
> proposal. Includes glossary.

Brewer, Ernest W., Charles M. Achilles, Jay R. Fuhriman, and Connie Hollingsworth. *Finding Funding: Grantwriting from Start to Finish, Including Project Management and Internet Use.* 4th ed. Thousand Oaks, CA: Corwin Press, 2001.

> The book is targeted to those in the field of education and specifically to those submitting proposals to agencies of the federal government. Part 1 explores the research process and how to use the *Catalog of Federal Domestic Assistance* and other resources. Part 2 covers the elements of a standard proposal to a government agency or foundation, a sample proposal (funded by the U.S. Department of Education), and a discussion of how proposals are handled once received by funders. Part 3 relates to project management, explaining how to execute a project once it is funded.

Burke, Jim and Carol Ann Prater. *I'll Grant You That: A Step-by-Step Guide to Finding Funds, Designing Winning Projects, and Writing Powerful Grant Proposals.* Portsmouth, NH: Heinemann, 2000.

> The main part of the book is organized according to the sections of a proposal and covers project planning as well as proposal development. The book also explains how to write a letter of inquiry. Each chapter concludes with a checklist. The appendices contain a glossary and sample proposals.

Carlson, Mim. *Winning Grants Step by Step: The Complete Workbook for Planning, Developing and Writing Successful Proposals.* 2nd ed. San Francisco, CA: Jossey-Bass Publishers, 2002.

> This workbook contains instructions and exercises designed to help with proposal planning and writing and to meet the requirements of both government agencies and private funders. Provides a special resource section that includes how to research funders, how to evaluate a proposal through the funder's eyes, and a bibliography.

Chapin, Paul G. *Research Projects and Research Proposals: A Guide for Scientists Seeking Funding.* New York, NY: Cambridge University Press, 2004.

> Directed to scientists who wish to design and write proposals to funding agencies. Includes project planning, information about specific government funders (as well as more general recommendations about researching private foundations), and grants management. With glossary and index.

Clarke, Cheryl A. *Storytelling for Grantseekers: The Guide to Creative Nonprofit Fundraising.* San Francisco, CA: Jossey-Bass Publishers, 2001.

> Clarke puts forward the notion that proposals share much with great stories: characters, setting, and plot. She shows proposal writers how to craft documents that include elements of drama. The book also covers the research process and cultivation. Includes a sample letter of inquiry and sample budgets, as well as information on packaging the proposal.

Collins, Sarah, ed. *The Foundation Center's Guide to Winning Proposals*. New York, NY: The Foundation Center, 2003.

> The guide reprints in their original form 20 proposals and four letters of inquiry that succeeded in securing foundation support. Each proposal is accompanied by commentary by the funder who awarded the grant and proposal writing advice. Includes glossary and bibliographical references.

Geever, Jane C. *The Foundation Center's Guide to Proposal Writing*. 4th ed. New York, NY: The Foundation Center, 2004.

> Geever guides the proposal writer from pre-proposal planning to post-grant follow up. The book incorporates excerpts from actual grant proposals and interviews with foundation and corporate grantmakers about what they look for in a proposal. It includes chapters on researching, contacting, and cultivating potential funders, as well as a sample proposal and a selected bibliography on proposal development.

Geever, Jane C., Liliana Castro Trujillo (trans.), and Marco A. Mojica (trans.). *Guía para escribir propuestas*. New York, NY: The Foundation Center, 2003.

> Prior third edition of this guide in Spanish. Includes new appendix of technical assistance providers who will assist Hispanic nonprofits.

The Gill Foundation

> (http://www.gillfoundation.org/tata_materials/tata_materials_show.htm?doc_id=90214) has a 2001 proposal submitted by Nashville CARES available in PDF format at its Web site. The sample grant is punctuated throughout with useful comments by a representative of the Gill Foundation, pointing out effective aspects of this "clear, concise, and simple" proposal.

Hall, Mary Stewart and Susan Howlett. *Getting Funded: The Complete Guide to Writing Grant Proposals*. 4th ed. Portland, OR: Portland State University, 2003.

> Hall explains the components of a standard proposal, with advice about project development and researching funders. This edition includes a recommended syllabus for those who teach proposal writing.

The Idea Bank

> (http://theideabank.com/onlinecourse/samplegrant.html) has at its Web site a number of proposals available online for fire and safety organizations, including an indication of which ones have been successfully funded.

Kosztolanyi, Istvan. *Proposal Writing*. Baltimore, MD: Johns Hopkins University Institute for Policy Studies, 1997.

> This short book outlines the standard elements of a grantseeking proposal and includes a handy checklist. The pamphlet was specifically developed

for nonprofit managers in Central and Eastern Europe and is available in Bulgarian, Czech, English, Hungarian, Polish, Russian, Slovak, and Slovene languages.

Miner, Jeremy T. and Lynn E. Miner. *Models of Proposals Planning & Writing*. Westport, CT: Praeger, 2005.

> Provides a step-by-step strategy for creating proposals and other documents for applying to both private funders and government agencies. The models that are reprinted include a letter of intent, and a complete proposal (for the Robert Wood Johnson Foundation and the Emory T. Clark Family Charitable Foundation), as well as a preliminary and final application to the U. S. Department of Education. The book also explains how grantseekers can assess a request for proposals. Indexed.

Miner, Lynn E. and Jeremy T. Miner. *Proposal Planning & Writing*. 3rd ed. Westport, CT: Greenwood Press, 2003.

> This book focuses primarily on researching and securing government grants, but also contains many elements that are appropriate for proposals to private funders. Includes bibliographical references.

New, Cheryl Carter and James Aaron Quick. *How to Write a Grant Proposal*. Hoboken, NJ: John Wiley & Sons, 2003.

> The authors cover the key elements of standard proposal formats, including the executive summary, need statement, project description, evaluation, and budget. Each chapter contains examples and checklists.

Nonprofit Guides

> (http://npguides.org) has at its Web site sample proposals, a proposal cover letter, cover sheet, letter of inquiry, and budget, among other useful items.

Orlich, Donald C. *Designing Successful Grant Proposals*. Alexandria, VA: Association for Supervision and Curriculum Development, 1996.

> The author presents the standard elements of proposal writing, with checklists at the end of each section. Includes a copy of a funded proposal and a reading list.

Quick, James Aaron and Cheryl Carter New. *Grant Seeker's Budget Toolkit*. Hoboken, NJ: John Wiley & Sons, 2001.

> In this guidebook on project budgets, the authors explain the calculation of direct costs, with chapters specifically describing personnel and travel costs. The book also discusses the estimation of overhead and indirect costs and elaborates on the entire budgeting process, including writing the budget narrative. Sample budget worksheets are included.

Robinson, Andy. *Grassroots Grants: An Activist's Guide to Proposal Writing*. 2nd ed. San Francisco, CA: Jossey-Bass Publishers, 2004.

> The writer provides step-by-step guidance on how to create successful proposals, design projects, and manage grants. Several sample proposals are included.

School Grants

> (http://www.k12grants.org/samples) This Web site offers a number of education-focused and successful sample proposals. Most are directed to corporate or government funding sources. Downloadable in PDF format.

SERA

> (http://www.sera.com/index.php?section=funding&option=funding&page =funding_templates) includes brief instructions and templates for a proposal, letter of inquiry, proposal cover letter, and budget at its Web site. These templates are available in HTML or MS Word format.

Wason, Sara Deming. *Webster's New World Grant Writing Handbook*. Hoboken, NJ: John Wiley & Sons, 2004.

> This handbook covers project planning, funding research, proposal development, and writing. A sample proposal is included. With glossary and index.

Wells, Michael K. *Proven Strategies Professionals Use to Make Their Proposals Work*. (Grantwriting Beyond the Basics Series). Portland, OR: Portland State University, 2005.

> This book provides a treatment of specialized concerns related to the proposal, such as evaluation methods, project development, researching the need section, and effective use of attachments. Includes one sample proposal, bibliographical references, and index.

INDEX

*Some proposals have multiple subjects and/or types of support.

Population Group*

Disabled 292
Families 74, 177, 206, 245
Homeless 191
Immigrants/refugees 93, 102, 149
Military personnel 323
Minorities 117, 177, 298, 360
Nonprofit organizations 5, 292
Prisoners 217, 317
Sex workers 93
Women 93, 191, 298
Youth 13, 21, 33, 46, 133, 177, 245, 259, 269, 287, 333

Grant Recipient Location

CA 46, 74, 149, 317, 323, 360, 377, 381
DC 292
GA 83, 206, 245, 259
MD 349
MA 227, 287
NE 102, 191
NJ 117
NY 62, 93, 165, 177, 217, 298, 333
OH 5, 13, 21, 269, 307
TX 33
WI 133

Grantmaker Location

CA 46, 74, 149, 323, 381
GA 83, 206, 245, 259
MD 349
MA 227, 287
NE 102, 191
NY 62, 93, 117, 133, 165, 177, 217, 298, 317, 333, 360, 377
OH 5, 13, 21, 269, 307
TX 33
VA 292

Grant Size

$2,000–$4,999 292, 323, 377
$5,000–$9,999 13, 83, 191
$10,000–$19,999 102, 177, 206, 349
$20,000–$49,999 21, 33, 46, 62, 74, 93, 217, 245, 269, 287, 307, 381
$50,000–$99,999 5, 165, 317, 360
$100,000–$249,999 133, 259, 333
$250,000–$499,999 117, 149, 298
$500,000–$1,000,000 227

---

*Since many grant projects benefit society at large or the populations of certain cities or regions, not every proposal is directed at a specific population group.